ITALY: The Places In Between

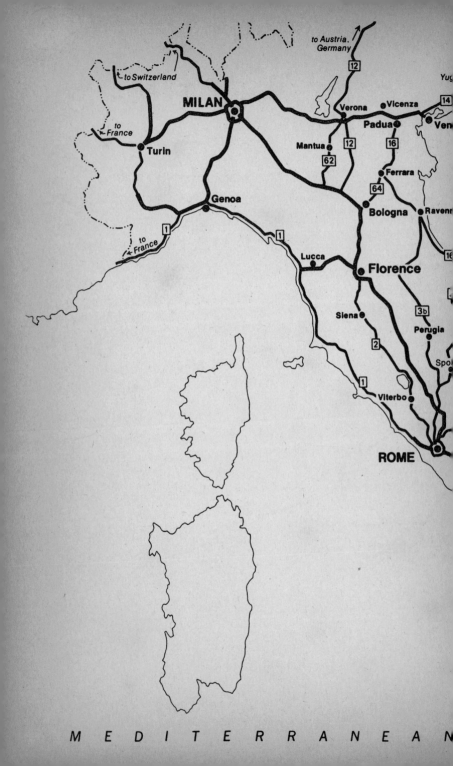

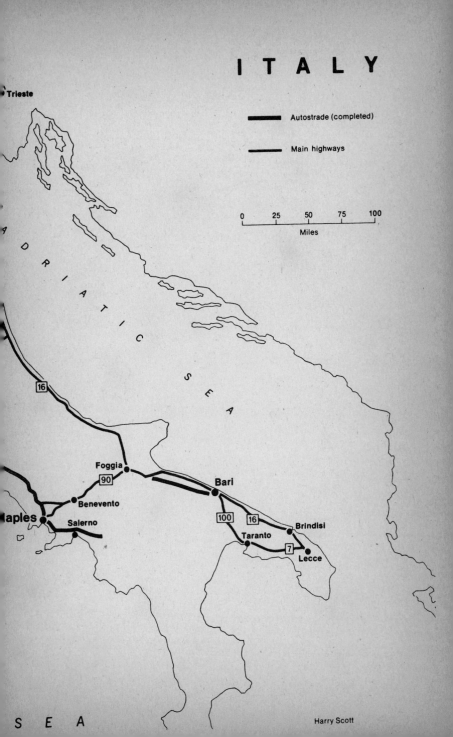

Other books by Kate Simon

New York: Places & Pleasures
Mexico: Places & Pleasures
New York (with Andreas Feininger)
Kate Simon's Paris
Kate Simon's London
Bronx Primitive: Portraits in a Childhood

ITALY: The Places In Between

REVISED AND EXPANDED EDITION

Kate Simon

PERENNIAL LIBRARY

Harper & Row, Publishers, New York
Grand Rapids, Philadelphia, St. Louis, San Francisco
London, Singapore, Sydney, Tokyo, Toronto

Library of Congress Cataloging in Publication Data

Simon, Kate.
  Italy: the places in between.

  Includes index.
  1. Italy—Description and travel—1975–   —Guide
books. I. Title.
DG416.S47 1984   914.5′0492   83–48940
ISBN 0–06–015310–5
ISBN 0–06–091131–X (pbk.)

90   10 9 8 7 6

FOR
Louis
Nora
Amelia

Contents

Introduction

THE WRITER of any personal guide-travel book should, in justice, display right off his tastes and prejudices, to give the reader an opportunity to say, "I think so too," or, "Not my sort of thing at all." Thus, we might disagree about the quality of the baroque outside of Rome or find limited—or limitless—the appeal of Romanesque into Gothic. We may or may not agree that beautiful is not necessarily pretty, that "gray" and "silent" are not always synonyms for dullness, that they can describe moving places. We may or may not agree that an omnivorous taste for seventeenth-and eighteenth-century church art, the sort that rolls its eyes to heaven and is painted with melting lollipops, is a peculiar gluttony.

We undoubtedly agree that Italians are vigorous, engaging, histrionic and courteous, that Italian food is wreathed in an aura of high pleasure, that the wine is inexpensive and quite good and that Italy is a Circe dressed in silken landscapes, which sometimes conceal behind cadenced billows many treasures, treasures too often overlooked by the visitor. The regal streets of Montepulciano, the embrace of Siena's Campo, the sublime Giottos in Padua, the raffish port villages of Puglia, the dancers on Etruscan tombs in Tarquinia, the mesmeric cathedral of Orvieto, to make a spotty selection from an interminable list, are frequently lost in the exhausting effulgence of the great centers. That which follows is a sampler, an absolutely nondefinitive book, of some of these places, easily found on or near the routes between the major cities; what, for instance, you might miss if you go directly from Rome to Florence, from Milan to Venice, from Rome or Naples to catch a boat at Brindisi, nonstop.

The voyages and walks that follow can be shortened, lengthened, recombined. For example, any map of Italy will show you that Orvieto and Viterbo combine easily, that you can visit Montepulciano and Pienza via a short detour off the Rome-Florence highway, that you can round back to Rome from Puglia by way of the Amalfi coast, and so on. As for the walks, none of the towns treated here are very large, all of them old, many of them hilly; some shaped like snails, others like webs, circling the Duomo piazza or that of the Palazzo Comunale or Popolo. (Apropos hill towns—there are those few who say one hill town is like another, somewhat like saying if you've seen one Botticelli you've seen them all.) Antique paths are usually wayward and direction matters little; therefore, "turn left" or "follow the stairs" are only suggestions, possibly lures. A few attractions of a town, past and present, are placed before you to do with as you choose, in any manner you choose; they are not stations on forced marches but rather the rewards of meandering that may enhance you, and Italy for you.

The present, revised edition, for instance, opens the possibility of entering Italy by way of Milan, which makes stops at Bergamo and Brescia logical, if not imperative, on the journey toward Ferrara, Mantua, Padua, et al., reaching for Venice. An earlier attempt at exploring the fabled Villa Maser of Palladio was foiled by a car breakdown, or repairs in the villa and the public shut out, or one of the many bedevilments that haunt travel writers. The sun shone, the car ran, the villa was open *this* time. Ergo, you have a description of Maser. The delightful Adriatic towns with the Italian Gilbert-and-Sullivan names—Molfetta, Barletta, Bitonto, Bitetto and their neighbors—were earlier pictured as a colorful string that connected Rome and Naples with the ports that took one across the Adriatic to Greece. Why not introduce the traveler to a few pearls of the north encountered on a trip to or from Austria, to or from Jugoslavia? That give us, and you, the region known as the Fruili, the zippy city of Treviso and the Roman and medieval rarities in the area and their attractive sites.

Older friends were explored for changes in mood and quality, and those exist. Siena, once a retiring beauty visited by scholars and Germans with heavy tomes that described every brick in the medieval and Renaissance buildings, has come out of her shyness and sports new hotels, new restaurants and many less-learned visitors—which has in no way diminished her charms. Vicenza is not quite so heavy and odd as it once was, though still deeply marked by, and with, Palladio. An increased number of visitors seems to have given it a lightness, and then of course, there is the sun that shines out of the beautiful villas in the nearby countryside.

The dance of the lire and dollar was something to be absorbed by in the most recent studies of Italy. There is no advice to give on the subject except to watch the foreign exchange columns in the newspapers and guard against the shock of thinking that 20,000 lire is a colossal sum. It winds down to less than $15, and the object for which you want to pay that $15 will be priced as it might be in the States; few bargains, few outrages, except if you choose to go to the outrageous shops with the initials that make you royalty. But all of that is not within the purview of this travel writer, whose closing pleasure is to wish you good Italian weather, good Italian eating and good Italian company.

1

ROME TO TUSCANY AND FLORENCE

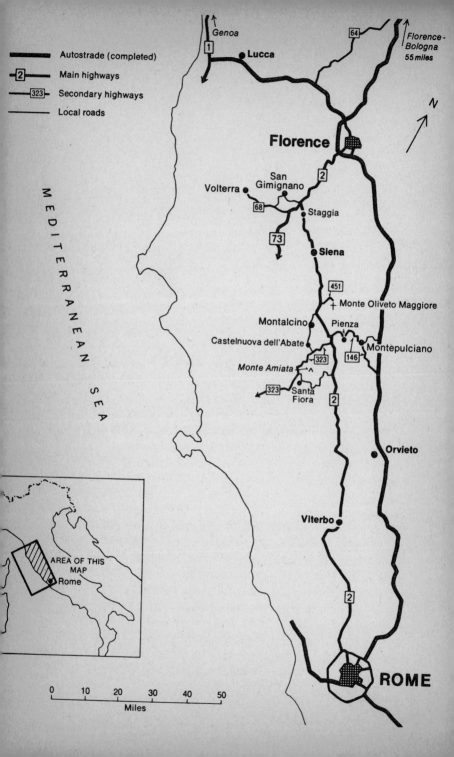

Siena

WERE IT THE BEST of all possible worlds and time capable of being poured and stopped as by a faucet, the approach to Siena should be threefold, once by car or bus, once by train, once by a magical ceiling-dissolving balloon, each approach landing in an appealing symptom of the Siena syndrome. One of the western gates to the city welcomes cars with a Latin inscription that translates roughly as "Wider than her gates does Siena open her heart" and Siena *is* courteous and hospitable—except in tobacconists' shops, where, understandably, selling one envelope and one sheet of paper, one stamp, one pack of ten cigarettes, one box of matches, through long hours, makes a soured life.

The heart narrows in the *tristezza* of mid-September to spring, when Siena folds her arms and broods through the gray, damp days. It broadens when the hotels rehire last summer's help, the restaurants sharpen their décor and the Palio costumes are taken out of the *contrada* closets for resplendoring. Though there are only two Palios run regularly and, occasionally, an extra third for a foreign dignitary or a pope, the Palio season is stretched to its greatest possible length, beginning in the spring, when the elaborations of the *contrada* churches are regilded, the chords on last

3

year's drums replaced, the house of the horse freshly white-washed and last year's pinups covered by a fresh photo of Pope John Paul II, to continue in a spiral of frenzy that splutters and dies in the last glass of wine drunk at the last *contrada* dinner in October.

If you come by train, your seat companion might be a gentleman reading *Orlando Furioso,* the equivalent of *The Canterbury Tales,* perfectly reasonable however for the intellectualism of Siena. Out of the train and into a taxi and another confrontation with the Sienese sense of being unique, apart. The driver almost sideswipes another car, a norm of Italian driving. He says, "Did you notice that license? One guess. A Florentine, of course. Dreadful people, pretentious, verbose, show-offs. Romans are almost as bad. The Milanese? Not too bad, but they're vulgar, materialistic. The local people, from Grosseto, Piombino and the Tuscan towns and villages, are good, fine people, but toward the south, and worse continuing southward, they are monsters."

"But," one counters, "Florence is not exactly in the south."

"True," he says, "they are the cancer of the north."

Many centuries ago, Siena rivaled Florence and continues to think so, after old defeats in battle and consequent losses of territory and lives and in spite of the Medici shields on many walls. Although Florence is in Tuscany, the cradle of Italian literary speech, the Florentines have hideous, grunting accents, say the Sienese, while theirs is pure, exquisite. This sentiment is often spoken in something like Arabic-Italian; all "c" sounds are lacking or slightly aspirated, so that *casa* becomes *hasa,* a *coppa* of *gelato* brightens to *hoppa,* although cultivated Sienese speech is as musical as they say it is. You will probably hear that Giotto copied from Duccio, that Florentine painting is a decayed imitation of the Sienese, and so on. Don't argue; it is impolite and useless to fight one of the endearing faults of a delightful people.

The third mode of travel, the magic balloon, might take you first into a room of the university where a class in Italian for foreigners is in session. No one is ever called upon to recite, only volunteers answer; a rule to preserve the face of those unprepared for a public display of linguistic fumbling. Siena *sensibilità* at its most sensitive. The balloon drops you next through the upper floors of the Palazzo Pubblico before the murals of Ambrogio Lorenzetti, which depict early-fourteenth-century Good Government, the dream, the illusion of Siena, an ideal (it includes a few rough spots, usually overlooked) that exists firmly as reality in the minds of some of the elderly courtier-intellectuals; it is a significant symbol to them that the Bad Government panels are practically extinguished while the Good remain clear, lovely and almost entire, a mystical stamp of verity.

The light must have its dark and the honey its blood; Siena inflicted injuries and the oppression of conquest on surrounding towns. She was a mighty power, as ruthless as she could afford to be, the home of warriors and bankers to the papacy, of medieval wheelers and dealers who could turn loyalties on and off with lightning speed, and yet she was an extraordinarily long-lived free commune. The essence of the belligerence, the intense rivalry, the fanfares and battle colors, the marching, the drums and war chariots, the splendors of Renaissance costumes, the unseen but never quite secret deals and counterdeals and the commune spirit remain in the Palios and the passions they trigger.

The Palio is actually a long silk banner, currently a painting of the Assumption of the Virgin (for the August 16 race) in a timid late-cubist manner. To possess this, to hang it in a *contrada* church or museum, a short, brutal and crooked race is run. To be in Siena only on a Palio day is to see it in orgasm and consequently at least a bit deceptive. See it before, see it after, although between the hithering and thithering mounting like a dancing madness, the spiraling hysteria of a Children's Crusade (medieval allusions come easily in Siena), it is possible, with enough resolution, to explore the city.

It may not clarify the frenzy altogether, but it should help to follow the Good Government mural with a visit to the house-museum of the *contrada* Torre, on the via Salicotto behind the Palazzo Pubblico. As you might know, a *contrada* is, sociologically and emotionally, an expanded family with all that means in a culture whose only meaningful unit is the family. The members of a *contrada* may not all be crazy about each other, but making the best of proximity, interdependence, joint traditions and the financial responsibility and team effort required by the

Palio produces an abstract affection that works better, in the long run, than love. They have no wish to escape each other and often take vacations together, and when one Sienese introduces himself to another he will designate his *contrada* as if it were part of his name. During the waxing, exploding and reluctantly waning time of the Palio the *contrada,* traditionally an almost autonomous townlet within the city, is controlled by a *capo,* who is in complete charge of all Palio activities, including judgment of turbulent disputes concerning who is to be taxed how much to make up the millions of lire spent and for what purpose.

The Palio race is a development of ancient games harking back to the Romans—some say to the Etruscans—through changes that echoed courtly games, such as bucolic imitations of jousting, the goading of buffaloes, which suggests early bullfighting, and long hazardous races through the city.

Torre, one of the prosperous *contrade,* has a varied and largish museum, attractively arranged to keep great memories vivid: its first win in 1599; the summer, two hundred years ago, when it won both Palios; the great silver platters won as awards for the skill, beauty and fine comportment of its group. In the section set apart for matters of horse and jockey, the silver-studded trappings and the evolutions of the jockey's costume and equipment: the spiked iron maces they once used (the knives sometimes used later are not in evidence) and the hard helmet since replaced by a less conspicuous protective cap. Surrounded by the flourish of banners—about one hundred and fifty of them—the shine of metal on fifty carefully preserved drums, the coats of armor and the velvets and furs, two local boys, quite young, are brought in by the keeper of the house to demonstrate the use of the drums and flags. Their work is profoundly serious, adept, unhurried, priestly. These boys practice every night—drummers beginning as early as six, the flag boys at ten or eleven—in total, obsessed dedication, as Spanish and Mexican boys practice veronicas with a rag cape.

The *contrada* church has its own specialized characteristics. The sixteenth and seventeenth centuries saw the first changes in neighborhood churches, which led to the present Palio-adapted structures. There are no stairs, or very few, and no side aisles; the

organ is placed high in the back, the altar is shallow and there are
no choir stalls; in short, a box with churchly trappings, arranged
to allow maximum space and no impediments to horse, jockey
and *contrada* crowd. The priest is of the church but primarily of
the *contrada*, and it is he who appears in Siena's newspapers at
the side of the horse, under the heading, "Ritorna Vincitor."
Except for baptisms, also frequently performed at the *contrada*
fountain, the church is rarely used at other times of the year; it
belongs to the Palio.

At 10:30 A.M. on August 13 the Piazza del Campo explodes
with colors of balloons, pinwheels, scarves and banners, a dazzling flash of sunlight on stained glass, as one passes the low
arches along the via di Città. The dispossessed pigeons wheel
nervously, the boys wear their *contrada* shirts and cockades, the
girls have draped their *contrada* scarves on their hips, Carmen
fashion, babies wave their neighborhood flags, below the windows of the Palazzo Pubblico hang the banners of all the *contrade*. Big cameras for television and newspaper and little cameras that will return to Osaka, Dijon and Paterson are trained on
the crowd gathered to watch one of the several pre-race tryouts.
The police in pristine white begin their slow, inexorable march
to clear the track of walkers and arguers.

Drums roll, and precisely at 11:00 a shot is fired and the
horses are led out of the palazzo by two white-gloved policemen.
As they walk to the starting line, one notices that numbers are
painted on the horses' rumps, since the jockeys, like conductors
of orchestras, do not wear their silks for rehearsals. They look
rather like waiters of rural trattorie, in their white jackets bound
in black braid and black-buttoned, as they lead their horses
around the ring, bowing and waving in response to the applause,
after they have run the casual-to-listless race that determines
which ten Palio horses will be chosen of a field of eighteen. It is
an easy beginning; only the young bother to shout *"Dai, dai,"*
urging the unheeding jockeys and especially themselves to ex-
citement and the sore throats and husky voices they will carry
about for a week as a badge of passion and fidelity. A half hour
later, these boys will follow the jockey and horse to the *contrada*

stable to walk the horse under its totem of porcupine or rhinoceros or panther, the boldest offering expert advice. "He's thirsty, give him some water." "No, not yet. Let him cool off first." Neither horse nor handlers pay much attention, but the boys have stepped into the awesome terrain of know-how and inside information to be unfolded and elaborated at the dinner table.

That afternoon, sometimes between lunch and the late afternoon tryout, new signs appear: a hand-lettered poster at the side of a *contrada* seat advertises a dinner on the night before the Palio, a moderate price for adults, half for children, tickets available at Luigi's bar, Mario's tobacco shop, and Guido's grocery store. One of the local newspapers advertises its enormous colored Palio supplement, an exhaustive iconography of jockeys and horses. Only a Sienese could wade through all of it, and always with intense interest and high emotion, carried along streams of self-deception, although he knows—but this is no time to admit it—that the races are fixed. (He insists that there are always possibilities of accident, his out in discussions with uninspired, non-Sienese minds.) On the Piazze Gramsci and Matteotti, other elements of Sienese life try to make themselves felt, if only as faint reminders. The Communist newspaper, *Unità,* chooses this week for its *festa:* games for children, many eatings stands, a popular entertainer, dancing and a soccer match between Yugoslav and Italian lady athletes, a busy program that manages not to interfere with Palio schedules. The church advertises special masses and their meaning in the Palio, reminding all that the Palio *is* a religious banner and it *does* celebrate Assumption Day. The city administration feebly hopes that someone will apply for the jobs it advertises. Nothing but cafés function normally; everyone is out, wandering, arguing, in a group symbiosis of mutual excitation.

The Duomo is as overwhelmingly full of too much to see as other great cathedrals, and like many of them (except the unrivaled peak, Saint Peter's in Rome), dedicated equally to the greater glory of the Virgin Mary and rivalry with some other cathedral. Pisa has Nicola and Giovanni Pisano? We hire them for Siena. Rome has Bernini? Let's bring him to work here. Donatello? Michelangelo? Get them out of Florence. Nothing but the best and, if possible, better and bigger. Not the most altruistic way to build and fill a church, this competitive drive has produced magnificent collections of church art, however.

The Duomo complex is best seen from the side of the church of San Domenico, where its compact gray and white presence appears large and calm, a Lorenzetti Virtue who expresses the non-Palio mood and conduct of the city. This indirect approach continues through the tortuous streets devoted to Saint Catherine and the Goose (page 16), into the via di Città, then the via del Castoro. Above, the extravagant height of the double-arched Facciatone (big façade), a blind giant that was meant to be the façade of a cathedral grand enough to rival that of Florence. The Black Plague of 1348, financial reverses and the perilous weakness of the disproportionately slender columns—among other reasons—called a halt to the building and left a unique, evocative piazza.

The prehistory of the church probably followed the usual pattern: a temple on a height, very likely Etruscan; later, Roman, replaced by a small Christian church. The site might thus be considered the core, the oldest part, of Siena, the oldest houses those that slope away from the ecclesiastical prominence. The ecclesiastical center was to have been linked, as a symbol of accord between church and civic powers, with the Campo by a long, regal stairway continuing from the steps that now drop to the baptistry, another fantasy of grandeur that faded with other city planning. The only present evidence of balanced lay and church influence is the fact that the Mangia tower of the government and the campanile of the Cathedral are carefully of the same height.

Other than by sheer size and pride framed in winged space, and its accretion of mosaics and detail in the style of Orvieto (page 130), the Duomo façade attracts as a combination of Gothic imposed on Romanesque; a peaceable low, wide movement pulling against the surging vertical, and since this is Italy, the spiritual soaring quickly arrested. The lower Romanesque section of rounded arches, in recessed, carved bands topped by the animal symbols of the Evangelists, is reminiscent of churches in Puglia (page 341) and for good reason. It was the work of Giovanni Pisano, whose father, Nicola, was originally "di Puglia" and may easily have been among the numerous artists in the Pugliese courts of that extraordinary, pre-Renaissance "Renaissance" prince, Frederick II. From that long distance, via Pisa, come the Oriental abstractions and the practice of enlivening monochrome stone with bands of contrast. The French Gothic was introduced by restless artists and craftsmen, the bees who carried the pollen of innovation from one region to another; here, particularly, a group of Cistercian monks who directed the building of the later (fourteenth-century) sections of the Duomo. Although the façade seems perfectly balanced at first glance, a slower look reveals two pink blocks, probably from the first church, on the left side, not repeated on the right, and one end pier narrower than the other, testimony of various ideas, hands and patchings that affected the church in its long time of building, beginning in the late twelfth century.

The conflict between Gothic flight and flat, squared space is noticeable again in the interior as numerous iron bars, probably meant for a ceiling or a broad rail to contain the foreign-inspired urge toward uncomfortable height. There was a change of mind or taste, obviously, and the clusters of pillars, tall and fiercely rigid in their alternations of black and white, stretch up and up, into distant starry vaults. The famous incised and inlaid marble floor is also a product of centuries (from the fourteenth into the sixteenth). The choicest sections are kept covered except for the period between August 15 and September 15 (roughly) but there is always visible an ample stretch to exemplify the early and straightforward, the later concentrations on virtuosity, the still later whirlwinds of distortion in the excessive lights and darks of mannerism.

Above the biblical figures and pagan sibyls and the shields of Siena are riches of other masterworks: the incredible pulpit created by the Pisanos, father and son, and Arnolfo di Cambio; the handsome Piccolomini altar with a figure, in a niche, believed to be the work of the young Michelangelo, and several figures by Bernini; a tomb figure and a wonderfully shaggy John the Baptist by Donatello; the inlaid woodwork in the choir stalls, finely worked even under the seats, the ultimate of art for art's sake; the Piccolomini library and its sleek, infinitely charming frescoes of Pinturicchio bound in bravura perspectives and bands of Pompeian ornament.

The splendors of the church reach their climax in the Museo dell'Opera at the side of the Facciatone, where there is a room devoted to the Duccio Maestà and the smaller panels that surrounded it and were attached to its reverse side. It was originally hung in a central area of the Duomo, before the altar, but the expansion of the Duomo made its position impractical and it was retired for a period to be rehung as two panels, back and front. A later expansion caused the paintings to be removed and discarded—cut up, sold, stolen. A few of the panels seem irrevocably gone; a few remain in England and the United States. After a stubborn, difficult task of searching out, authenticating, buying back and restoring, the almost complete set—some forty-odd of sixty—hangs in the hushed, mellow illumination of an air-controlled room. If you have seen the Giotto frescoes in the Scrovegni chapel in Padua (page 318), these will seem a repetition in miniature of the life of Jesus and Mary, and there are superficial resemblances. Siena's pride as womb of language and art—the pride that causes marble quotations from Dante to speak from many streets in the city, sometimes a bit out of context, sometimes implying a love for the city that Dante did not always feel—insists that Duccio was Giotto's predecessor, an indisputable fact. But the Scrovegni frescoes were painted a few years before the Maestà, and furthermore there is hardly any way of claiming a "predecessor" between two men so close in age who both drew from a varied, rich world of church art; who both made brilliant, arresting places in a long line of continuity, Duccio to bring the traditional Byzantine-Gothic to its richest, warmest culmination, Giotto to deflect it to paths that ran toward the Renaissance.

In spite of his conservatism, irresistible waves of art development and his own genius urged Duccio away from the frozen accustomed. Although his figures are often in the spellbinding, remote and unfleshly mode of his time, there is more often a weight and amplitude of body beneath the drapery, a sense of portraiture, a canny, subtle relationship of line, color and gesture that lie far beyond the borders of that time. The traditional elements, the steady and expected, act as nice foils for departures. As it does in much early church painting, a development of action may appear in one painting like penny-machine movies, ground out of a series of strips: a figure is shown asleep (a masterly passage), then awakened and then departing, all in one panel. The customary lines of gold that marked unearthly drapery shining of heaven still appear, for instance, on the robes of the Christ figure after the Resurrection. The Crucifixion maintains the conventional golden background of the Byzantine, or "Greek," style, but the weight of the hanging bodies, the distortion in the shoulder of the thief on the left, almost pulled out of its socket by the abnormal stretch from the waist, the plumb-line drop of the sagging head, the spiny, angled group of men, the long lamenting line of sorrowing women are painting outside of periods and strictures of styles.

The only non-Duccio painting that shares the velvet atmosphere is a different sort of enchantment, a Nativity of Mary by the occasionally more interesting older brother of Ambrogio, Pietro Lorenzetti. It is a work of 1342, thirty years after the Maestà, and a telling example of the strides taken by Sienese painting in the first half of the fourteenth century, the advances in perspective, the readiness for naturalism. In spite of halos on the main personages, and the majestic size of St. Anne, the painting is a solid accouchement scene blending and contrasting a wealth of decorative detail in a manner that oddly suggests Vuillard, some five to six centuries later.

Below the Duccio and Lorenzetti wonders and above, there are a number of objects worth a respectful look: in the sculpture gallery, a few of the monumental and expressive figures of Giovanni Pisano, executed at the end of the thirteenth century to stand on the ledges of the cathedral, then taken out of the weather that was consuming them and replaced by copies. (Notice the tensed turn of the head and the controlled anxiety in the face of a figure referred to as "Maria, daughter of Moses.") Up the stairs, past various church ornaments and a splendid, alert head, into a room of ceremonial objects—needlework in gold thread, an example of the golden rose that was the gift of popes to kings, a sinuous polychrome angel, a silver arm designed as a reliquary for the arm of San Giovanni, and a large gold and crystal casket adorned with many exquisite crystal and gold pears, apples, leaves, acorns and flowers coquettishly arranged around a skull and bones.

On the floor above the necrophile daintiness, the plainer Madonna of the Big Eyes, she who had the place of honor before Duccio's Maestà was hung in the Duomo, and several rooms beyond there is a sign in several languages that leads out to the Facciatone. The view gives on the massive churches of Santa Maria dei Servi and San Francesco and, closer by, the enmeshed patterns of overlapping tiles, little green lizards crawling over and under the brown, red, tan and gray ceramic wavelets. On a neighboring roof a woman loads a clothesline behind the ornaments of a fourteenth-century palazzo, and directly below is the car-strewn piazza born of miscalculation and misfortune.

Going back toward the via di Città, turn left into the via del Poggio and wind with it, greeting the old lady who always fills one window and the brown hound who guards a balcony. This obscure path leads to a magnificent archway near the Baptistry, a disappointment in spite of the fact that its font is the work of many gifted hands, including Donatello's.

Head for the via Diacceto, which acts as a high arched bridge over lower streets that rush down, along with daredevil motorcyclists, to the neighborhood of Saint Catherine and the Fonte Branda under the cliff that is the church of San Domenico. Continue on toward the Piazza Indipendenza and into the arches, single, double, photogenically medieval, of the via della Galluzza. At its left the steep vicolo del Costaccino makes *its* run for the many-fingered hand of the Fonte Branda–San Domenico complex. This meshwork of narrow streets inhabited by carpenters, basketmakers and laundries doesn't seem to be too poor, although the presence of a busy street fountain indicates very modest housing. As the street climbs, however, to change its name to Costa Sant'Antonio, it takes on the hostile glower of poverty, spent at its meeting with via della Sapienza. Here one can turn right for the Etruscan Museum at Number 3 or, at

Number 5, the Biblioteca Comunale, which occasionally arranges exhibitions of its treasures—Dante illustrated by Botticelli, some of the prolix and argumentative correspondence of Saint Catherine, ancient books illustrated by Sienese painters.

With each successive tryout—two a day—the mobs in the Campo become louder and thicker, the prices of tight seats more expensive, more luxurious banners of red and old rose trimmed with gold adorn the piazza. The riders have changed to their white clownlike costumes and stiff jockey caps. The screaming is louder with each trial race and one doesn't know why. A couple of jockeys and their horses seem to try, the rest pull back almost immediately in the short run of two laps, rather than the three of the actual race. Nevertheless, the boys and their girls march behind their horses singing, as they will continue to sing for a week, becoming less folkloric, less Gregorian chant, less interesting and tuneful while the visitor's eye turns in its sandpapered socket searching, yearning, for a few quiet night hours.

The three- and four-year-old boys who learned, according to the Sienese boast, to speak the name of the *contrada* before they said "mamma" are bought their flags and scarves with ceremonious solemnity, as if they were the First Communion suit. Even here, in these lives of scant years, blooms the multicolored passion flower of self-intoxicated joy and sorrow, of intense rivalries and the yearning to be as beautiful as the young men dressed by Sodoma and Gozzoli who followed the great bullock-drawn war chariot when it was laden with a glory not yet spent. One little boy, draped to the ankles in a scarf of orange and white with a green oak tree and his *contrada* rhinoceros, transfigured with stunned joy, carries two plastic horses before him, a shaman bearing sacred emblems. Light drumbeats sound from around the corner; the drummer follows, another little boy of about the same age. Fury, envy, frustration tear the smooth little face apart; a howl bounds up the walls, the plastic horses are thrown on the flagstones, insulting, loathsome. True, little boys are desperately spoiled in Italy (which accounts for some male conduct), but the boiling up of Palio feelings allows additionally for excessive responses, a useful safety valve for people burdened with the self-imposed chore of exemplifying Tuscan refinement.

It is a rough guess but there seem to be ten thousand Etruscan sarcophagi of repetitious design, many of them markedly unbeautiful, throughout Italy, and Siena's archaeological museum has its share. However, it doesn't exaggerate, and among the rubber stamps, a few are worth a pause. Look for the lively meeting of Paris and his goddess friends; another still shows its terracotta paint and, below its warriors, swords and shields, the teasing Etruscan inscription, scratched in crudely and backward as if by a child learning its letters. One multicolored stone box seems to have emerged from a chromo factory yesterday; another appears to have been the work of an Indian artist to judge from the plump drapery and shape of a lady whose jewelry sets off her naked breasts in the Indian fashion.

Some is cooky-cutter art, some of it highly refined, the sort of thing called "decadent" by purists, and certainly not all of it is worth prayerful concentration. The museum is well arranged, not discouragingly crowded, not heaped, and it might interest you to look at a few of the unusual pieces. For one, an Arianna with a few rosebuds in her hair, slightly tousled, her mouth a bit crooked, a touch that brings her completely to life and lends a knowing, flirtatious slyness to her almond-shaped eyes; a girl born two thousand years ago and as sturdily real as the shoes on your tired feet. One of her companions is a beguilingly arrogant little Aphrodite, and another wears a far-fetched Mayan headdress. It can't be, this linkage of cultures, you think, until you see, as you leave, a photo of a stone snake found in Etruscan country and easily mistaken for a Mexican snake god.

Return to the Campo, observe the duet of light and shade on the piazza, the shadow of the tower turning with the sun. At about 11:00 A.M., the shadow is a long, diagonal stripe that cuts the shell, and in the dark ray people shelter and talk, the pigeons bobbing near their feet; the small children dart, stray and gather like fish in a narrow stream. At the fruit stalls the local housewives and the international young are buying their luncheon grapes, the cafés are filling with tourists and summer students. As the shadow tower diminishes, the indefatigable talkers—and how much there is to say out of the wisdoms of a provincial town in the course of frequent daily encounters!—meet at the round edge of the piazza fan, and the old ladies whose domain is the sides of the fountain talk and talk while one of them, never dropping a word, turns to shave a piece of stale bread for the spoiled, demanding pigeons.

More than in most Italian cities, to turn a corner in Siena is to be presented with a gift. You might climb up the via della Sapienza to the Banchi di Sopra to see again the mighty palaces of two rival banking firms, the Palazzo Tolomei of the early thirteenth century and the Palazzo Salimbeni of the fourteenth century, and their Gothic and Renaissance neighbors. Or, return to the Costa Sant'Antonio, facing the great strange red and white chunk in the sky above the angles of roofs: once more, the Facciatone that haunts Siena as the Mangia tower sings to it. A complex of loggie and arcades above the vicolo del Tiratoio introduces the enclave devoted to Saint Catherine, a confusing mixture of old house and numerous chapels heavily laden with scenes of her life and works. One chapel sells, another begs; one is luminous with Pompeian design, another is a dank room of closets and a samovar that acts as a fountain. The most interesting unit in the prodigious hagiography is that painted by Sodoma, and shared, at least equally, by the *contrada* goose who stands in all its proud foolishness of yellow bill and yellow feet in an inlaid marble shield set in the center of the floor of the church. The light fixtures are conspicuously attached to golden geese; below the stern saint (and one yields her the right to be disapproving of this forced coupling with a goose), at either side of the main altar, two large geese preen and expand their wings, their curvaceous bodies immortalized in white marble set off by black. Each wears a crown. Saint Catherine, who sacrificed, fasted and flagellated herself, who took perilous journeys on behalf of the church, who castigated noble sinners without fear, who was wounded and blessed with Christ's stigmata and exchanged her heart with that of Christ, wears a white cowl and sometimes a halo, never a crown.

If one symbol had to suffice (and it speaks for many Italians) for the not at all disconcerting light fidelity to religion combined with contempt, the love for the traditional manipulated to serve present purposes, the Saint Catherine–Goose complex might serve. To spice up the minestra of total skepticism that doesn't quite accept or discard anything ("Why take a chance? There may be something in religion, who knows?"), this hard-working neighborhood turns in a substantial Communist vote, as does most of the province. "Contradictions? No. Why? You must know that although we are officially Catholic we have been passionately anti-clerical for centuries and still are. Communists? Naturally. It is only recently in our history that we emerged from the serf-lord class system; some of us may even be the descendants of slaves brought from the East to serve Tuscan princes in that glorious enlightenment, the Renaissance. It is about time we began to respect our own labor and control our own lives. Tradition? Religion? Why throw them out? We can manage it all."

At the lower end of Saint Catherine's street, Dante speaks again, this time from the Fonte Branda. It was not only the Sienese sense of design and taste for contained grandeur but also the respect for water, which always ran short, that may have made singular works of Siena's fountains. They are not splashing, dappled affairs but rather decorative small houses that open from sections of a complicated underground water system. The Fonte Branda, an expansion and later restoration of an eleventh-century original, is a set of three double arches that bears the heads of four old marble lions and the inescapable handsome black and white shield of Siena. The water under the deep arches is limpid and gives off a strange, muted light, water and light clear enough to show the newspapers and boxes that boys must float in any available pool.

San Domenico is a domineering, stern Old Testament prophet of a church, built, unmade, rebuilt, restored, ripped apart and patched up over a number of centuries. Its immense size produces a sense of threatening emptiness, of space floating off, unused and uncontrolled. The paintings and the stained glass and the horizontal bars of the ceiling help peg the church to earth, but not quite firmly enough. Because it is uncomfortably large, worshipers gather in small chapels, leaving the rest of the space a desert of transit between memorials to and remembrances of

Saint Catherine, who prayed here. Surrounded by yet another set of Sodoma paintings lie her brown leathery thumb, a whip she used for punishing her rebellious flesh and her shrunken tanned head in a white cloth. One can make an imposing psychological structure of this Italian passion for shrunken heads and fingers and chins (as well as Saint Catherine's fondness for blood), but this is not the place for it and you are free to do your own conjecturing. To balance the repellent bits, San Domenico offers a portrait painted by a contemporary of the saint and possibly a disciple, Andrea Vanni. It stresses the long white line of the saint's headcloth, the pallor of the exhausted face, the long white fingers holding white lilies; thin, tragic, a moving figure painted with awe and love.

The streets fling out more and more window banners and the magnificent flags of the *contrade* bloom from the walls of the Palazzo Pubblico, the drums become an incessant thrumming, a quality of the air. Siena's other summer sounds fade—the twittering of swallows, the grumbling of pigeons, the voices and violins and pianos practicing for the concerts of master classes in the Palazzo Chigi. Most of the young musicians and other foreign students are out with the peripatetic Palio young, buttering their Japanese, Hungarian, English and Dutch with jazzy Italian phrases, wearing *contrada* scarves and determinedly immersing themselves in the Palio ferment. From the Fonte Gaia café on the Campo, the salon of journalists, poets and music students, the fervent arguments have turned from yes and no about Stockhausen and Boulez to vituperation and praise for the various *contrade*. The *contrada* Torre? The tower has to be held up by the stupidest of animals, the elephant. What is so intelligent about a rhinoceros (who stands for Selva) or, for God's sake, a goose? No, mine is the panther, sleek, swift, beautiful, sly and clever; we'll win, I know.

At full noon on the Campo, the sheltering shadow of the tower disappears and slowly, very slowly, begins to reappear on the other side of the piazza, brushing the palazzi, leaving a streak of light near the crest of the tower, a tall bloom that holds and dominates the sun as it holds the rest of Siena; too graceful to loom, it simply makes itself always felt as pride and heard as the music of distant horns and trumpets.

Assuming that you are on the Banchi di Sopra (since Siena's geography is a major pinwheel of main streets containing small pinwheels, any point returns easily to almost any other) you will find it changing its name to Montanini, still Montanini on one side of the street at the vicolo dello Sportello, while the other changes its name to lower-middle-class Camollia. It soon becomes Camollia altogether, not the most fascinating or appealing street but a stimulating walk through unself-conscious middle-classness and white-collar respectability. Garibaldi slept or paused in a house that seems to mark a transition: the shops become smaller, more local, unaware of tourist tastes or money. A box of space that is a greengrocer's impales a bunch of celery and a bag of walnuts on the red-brick wall; on the other side of the narrow entrance, a basket flowing with bunches of green, purple and yellow grapes. One shop sells in units of one-half banana, and the local Chigi palace is a semicollapsed derelict adorned by a dry brown garland and a sign which informs us that Arrigo Boito, the composer of *Mefistofele* and librettist for Verdi, came here as a guest of Count Chigi Saracini to revive his tormented genius and his anguished heart, a warming cliché that appears in other cities about other members of that pitiful tribe, musicians. Next door to Boito's shelter is the Sede of the Istrice, the Porcupine *contrada* hall at the top of one of the numerous Sienese crafts villages of upholsterers and polishers (half of Siena seems to earn its living in tourism and the other half in carpentry and furniture making or reviving), housed in palaces turned tenement. One of these is the house of the Renaissance architect and painter Baldassare Peruzzi, whose tablet portrait shows him to have had a clever profile and a languid eye.

Between a modern market and a café emblazoned with a porcupine shield, the Porta Camollia comes into view. The name is said to derive from a medieval combination of *casa* and *muliebre,* and that means, depending on the playfulness of your informant, a brothel or a nunnery in the vicinity. Along with its welcoming legend it shows the world a great row of studs and shields and volutes, an enormous rusted crown and the Medici crest held between a pair of warriors. Dante speaks again and the city tumbles again, down the steep via di Vallerozzi. Try to hug the walls, since cars and motorbikes use the street as if it were a ski run, though the walls are not huggable. They stagger around an elementary wineshop, waves of light stench, a sick house with remains of frantic classic frieze; a discouraged street that no longer bothers, if it ever did, with being aristocratically Sienese. That the neighborhood is not tradition-tethered is witnessed again in the yard of the church at via Fontenuova and via del Pian d'Ovile. Instead of the recurrent gentle she-wolf suckling two babes—Siena's close link with Rome by way of two nephews who fled the wrath of uncle Romulus to found the city—this neighborhood has a modern, lean, howling wolf. One of the little men is feeding, the other is a strident creature who prefers to beat his foster mother.

A red brick square like a truncated tower with Gothic arches over a sturdy complex of vaults soon appears. One pool under the arches is heavy with darkened detergent foam, the other carries pigeon feathers, a can, a bone, a drowned newspaper, but the water is glistening clear. This is the Fonte Nuova, and anyone who has been for a while in Italy knows that an entity called "new" is apt to be very old; the new fountain was built in the fourteenth century to supplant an even older one at the end of the path called, reasonably, the vicolo del Lavatorio, the place for washing. The downward curve of the via del Pian d'Ovile heads through a no-man's land of cars and warehouses to another city gate, the Porta Ovile, where a Madonna in a recent imitation of antique painting and a toothless San Bernardino (like Voltaire, he seems never to have had teeth at all) are adorned with plastic loops and paper lanterns, fresh and wax flowers arranged by busy, happy ladies preparing for one of the innumerable saints' days imminently near. Outside the arch, on a broad street named for Simone Martini, a poor little café, with a few silent customers as rusty as the metal chairs they sit on. It might be Sicily if it weren't for the bulk of the church of San

Francesco rising over a cityscape of roofs and gardens, a patch of
vine arbor, one bush of outrageously large pink rose, a toylike
open steeple that yokes two bells.

The Piazza San Francesco is large and an important neighborhood meeting place for the women who sew and knit and gossip
on the semicircle of benches under trees, their fleet eyes fixed for
a moment on the sewing, on a listener's face, and flashing always
toward their young on tricycles. One or two of the younger mothers neither sew nor knit, but like daring lilies of the field and
consequently separate, smoke cigarettes and read books. Out of
the sun, now, into the via Rossi and the via Giglio delle Vergini,
the latter street almost perennially in a poor enthusiastic *festa*
under loops of paper ornaments and homemade paper flowers.
The street is medieval Siena in its darker phases. To have lived
the princely life in a fourteenth-century palace, among warmly
colored paintings, under bright-patterned wooden ceilings, the
cold blocked by tapestries bought from Flemish merchants, servants to feed the broad fireplaces, was one thing; to live in a
medieval warren—one that still may wear faded beauty spots of
shields and traces of handsome old doorways and windows on
its weary face—is a dark and damp life, particularly when drinking and washing water have to be carried up an icy hill on a
winter's morning.

The gray alleys open to the irregular spaces of a violated piazza, the site of the church of Santa Maria de Provenzano, the
miraculous Virgin honored in the July 2 Palio. The façade is
laden with huge, dour saints and the ubiquitous putti heads with
wings and swells and unswells of fruit very much like their
cheeks, one enormous putto so closely pressed between two giant
volutes that he appears to be bursting and cross-eyed in the effort
to free himself. The red of Siena brick turning black or falling
away from the innards of stone, the swaying, uncertain dark
dance of the via Sallustio Bandini, leads to the church of San
Virgilio on the short street of that name. This pretty Chiesa Uni-
versitaria, which adjoins an upper floor and entrance to the university, is baroque, with attractive inlaid stonework, a charming
angel and cuddly putti, a skillfully painted ceiling and a few well-

made tomb portraits. Nothing unusual in the combination, except that the church is not overdressed nor as shrill as baroque churches can be.

Across the street from the church there is the vicolo del Castellare, where you might have seen the horse of the *contrada* Civetta taking his food and ease. What is a *castellare?* Much that now appears picturesque, sweet, mellow and glistening in a dew of "medieval charm" was designed for mistrust, aggression and greed; at best for a life of armed truce. A *castellare* was an organization based on these motives and the practical means of expressing them: a compound of warriors and businessmen who kept their families, servants and soldiers alert and ready to close off all approaches to the outer world, to create a self-sustaining instant fortress. The old *castellare* has lost its teeth and is now an enchanting small court so carefully kept that on the day after a *festa* only one broken bottle and a few discarded paper flowers lie in an obscure corner, a place of surprisingly deep angles and arches, handsome doors and people quietly talking on shallow, narrow steps. An ironwork flower lights the legend, seven hundred years after the event, of Giovanni di Ugurgieri, who, accompanied by his cohorts, left the *castellare* to do battle at Monteaperti, where Siena won an unforgettable battle against Florence.

The street of Cecco Angiolieri trots down to the Piazza Tolomei, along with its pleasant small shops and a hotel in one antique tower, toward an equally antique doorway that seems tightly shut forever. According to the tourist literature it is a chapel which encloses the tomb of the poet for whom the street was named. He was the clever, talented, dissolute son of a wealthy Sienese family who kept him short of cash, probably because he would spend it on a tough working-class babe with whom he was besotted; not so besotted that he couldn't look at and write of himself and his love with merciless derision at times. While most of his poet contemporaries (the latter half of the thirteenth century) were writing exalted religious verses or gracious lyrics derived from the courts of love, Cecco was hurling knives of insult at life, parents, mistress, fate, as strident as contemporary protest verse.

Return to the Campo. It may be about 12:30. Little boys in pants to their knees and little girls dressed to mid-calf feed the pigeons and scream a confusion of thrill and terror as the bold, sullen birds come to peck at their outstretched hands, quivering and spilling the feed bought from the old lady and her talking companion in the center of the piazza. In the far corner of the Campo boys of five or six play Palio; one drums while the other waves a small banner. The drumbeats are muddled, the twisted banner will not fly as it should, but they keep doggedly at it. Out of one of the tunneled streets that lead to the Campo comes a delegate accredited to Unesco by France. He has changed into sagging shorts, a wrinkled shirt and an old fishing hat in which to greet one of the most beautiful of piazze and the noblest of towers. The city will respond by displaying for him the blazing pageant of the Palio.

The race trials continue, twice a day, as incomprehensible and haphazard as before. The crowd grows thicker, augmented by new freshets of tourists, mainly French and English professors, lank and pale in their unfortunate, flapping shorts, their rubber-sandaled young and their sincere, plain wives. The patient waiters drag out the tables and chairs and drag them in again, along with the café umbrellas and their stone bases, twice a day. The drumming tightens to steady, clear rhythms and the boys discard their scarves and *contrada* shirts to put on their velvets and brocades. The ceaseless *passeggiata* becomes ceremony. The costumed young men, some in their blond Palio wigs, gather in front of the Palazzo Pubblico to receive their banners. In concert they wave—it isn't waving, rather a slow floating, a caressing of the air, light soft breezes made visible—the banners, all in one set of elegant, controlled cadences, all the vivid designs unfolding, spilling and rolling their colors into the great, victorious shout of the mob in the piazza.

City elders dressed like characters in *Simon Boccanegra* march majestically behind a group of trumpeters and the war chariot that holds an enormous candle, soon followed by soldiers in chain mail and tabards. And the young of each *contrada* shape their march, too, accompanied by mothers, black-clad grandmothers and priests. It has rained, and the mud on the dirt and stones causes a dainty lifting of priestly skirts. The German photographer lady who seems to have walked with her large pack and bulbous dirty feet from Tibet, who eats grapes fallen from carts and paper sacks, gets in the way of the priest and children she photographs. The bells of the Mangia tower ring in surprisingly hollow and hoarse elderly voices. The procession paces slowly, drums beating, banners waving, through the streets of Renaissance and Gothic palaces in front of which all Siena seems to be gathered, even the skeptic who remarks, on seeing the white bullocks of the war cart, "Like India, we too have our sacred cows." As the cortege approaches the Duomo, the bell tower gives out its sounds. The candle is lifted out of the carriage and brought into the church to the roll of drums and the shouting of the young. Each flag bearer dips his banner to its duplicate already hanging in the church. More fanfare and the elders march in, the chain-mailed warriors lower their spears and the whole glittering display gathers at a side chapel along with a large number of black-gowned ladies. Still another flourish of trumpets ushers in a group of scarlet and white church dignitaries and dark-suited stony-faced members of church societies. The sound of drums and trumpets and young shouting bangs against the vaults of the ancient cathedral, too old in time and Palios to be surprised or shocked at the pagan noises.

The big candle is attached to a cluster of the black and white pillars, then lit; over the loudspeaker of the immense church comes a prayer and a blessing and the explanation, once again, that this Palio *really* belongs to the Virgin. In spite of the reassurance, a few visiting nuns look bewildered and frightened at this excess of noise and brilliance and vanity. It doesn't disturb the Sienese grandmothers who genuflect lustily and lustily sing the hymns. The Palio is hung near the main altar, all the banners dip to touch it in obeisance and for good luck. Then everyone trots back to the Campo to await another afternoon pre-race. (Whatever the Palio is—a vacation for the spirit, a re-enactment of memories and dreams, it is indisputably good exercise.)

The race is as peculiar as the others, today attributed to the fact that rain has made the track muddy. The dispersing crowd argues as it pushes out of the narrow exits, and continues to argue in the *rosticceria,* where mama is buying the supper she had no time to cook, and at home, particularly if a husband and wife were born in different *contrade.* The explosions can be fierce, a release of suppressed resentments, and neither talks to the other or his relatives for weeks.

A few paces from the street of Cecco, among the state archives kept in the Palazzo Piccolomini (notice the chaste grandeur of this Renaissance palace and its beautiful ironwork, and remember that it is open only in the morning and never on Sunday), there is a concrete testimonial to the habits of the poet who boasted that his loves were three—women, drink and gambling. In a section of the archives devoted to personages and events mentioned in Dante's *Purgatory,* there is a legal notice, dated 1282, that records fines paid by Cecco and a friend for wandering in the night, probably drunk and belligerent, without permission.

While you are here spend some slow time on the collection of documents, astonishing as living antiquity and as minor art works that show the joy of making a lovely thing, if only a page of lettering. Frederick II sent missives that resemble Persian miniatures; Siena made a payment in 1186 to an astrologer for services to the commune and recorded the fact as a masterpiece of calligraphy. The essence of this matter, however, is not the fine Italian hand, but the politics, battles, power conflicts, accomplishments and defeats, pleasures and terrors of the province and its people. Fringed with rows and dangles of seals, there are papal bulls, treaties, the imperial documents of Charles VI, of Maria Theresa of Austria, of Ferdinand and Isabella presenting their ambassadors to the republic of Siena. In 1544, Cosimo de' Medici asks the governor of Siena, the Spaniard Diego de Mendoza, to arrest two homicides. The Sforza ladies and the Farneses and the Medicis write to their husbands in battle about how things are going at home.

Concerning the arts, many, many documents: in 1266 Nicola Pisano signs a contract for work on the Duomo and with it, sends an invoice for making the pulpit; Jacopo della Quercia, like most artists incapable of meeting a deadline, writes an apology for a delayed return to work in Siena. A badly damaged fourteenth-century manuscript of the *Divine Comedy* appears near a consideration by Boccaccio of Dante's treatise on the Italian language. In a case of its own, like a miniature chapel, one finds the pale, trembling letters of the will of Boccaccio, dated August 28, 1374. Bread and circuses, the trusty Roman pacifiers, stayed with the Italians, and the dukes and princes saw to it that public entertainments were frequent and elaborate. To the pair, Siena added culture; an agent was paid, and the payment recorded, to seduce scholars away from the University of Bologna for her own newly established school. In 1396 a Maestro Giovanni di Buccio of Spoleto agreed to come to Siena for public readings of the *Divine Comedy*.

The archives of every Italian city-state hold thick wads of treaties with popes and emperors; those of Siena bear the signatures of Pope Sisto IV, Ferdinand of Aragon and Naples, the Duke of Milan, the Duke of Este, the leaders of the communes of Florence, Siena, Venice. (They were rarely binding and usually arranged with the understanding that pacts were breathers between battles, face-saving gentlemen's agreements during periods of hiring new troops, re-arming and looking for wealthy new allies.) A document as neatly and precisely written as a piece of typing carries the information that Gian Galeazzo Visconti, the powerful Milanese warrior, agrees to "take the *signoria*," to be head of government of Siena, for a term beginning 1399. (It was an intelligent and suspicious habit of the communes to take their *podestà*, captains or heads of the Signoria, as they were variously called, from among the gifted war lords of other republics.) Laid out neatly in their cases and tersely labeled, a series of sixteenth-century papers: 1552, the order for driving out the Spaniards and destroying their fortress; 1554, bits of paper that are permits for receiving bread; 1555, a list of who had what quantities of wheat; later in 1555, a list of the *bocche inutile,* useless mouths; 1559, a document of the Sienese government-in-exile at Montalcino. These laconic slips allude to one of the most dreadful episodes in Siena's history, the siege which forced hundreds of "useless mouths" out of the city gates to their death.

A considerable number of the documents deal with money, a

reflection of Siena's mercantile and banking prominence, and that brings us to the prime reason for being here, the *tavolette* of the offices of taxation and control of commerce; the business administration, in short, of the city. Sometime during the thirteenth century, one administrative head decided that the bindings of books of records should be painted by the city's artists, and it became yet another Sienese distinction to have the loveliest, most invaluable ledgers. In time the volumes and their *tavolette* (tablets) grew too large and the book covers became paintings that hung in offices, but for centuries they covered costs for masonry, how much money was collected for the hospital, how much was spent for orphans' bread, the wages of carpenters, the exits and entrances to the city. There are about a hundred or more *tavolette* in the archives, the spacing and lettering of the titles often as satisfying as the painting. The busy Ambrogio Lorenzetti took time off from his frescoes to work a few covers; Taddeo di Bartolo is represented in a jolly painting of monks over a legend of superb lettering and also a beguiling *Lady in a Cloak Embroidered with Gold* who might appropriately have covered the 1387 records of the guild of needleworkers. Of the prolific Sano di Pietro, a group of merchants in ample cloaks and little black shoes like bats surrounded by a looping, dancing frame of illumination that embraces Siena's wolf and her human young, the black and white seal of the city, her lion, and more specifically to the point, a bale of cloth and a small, bright scale for weighing gold.

Everyone in late medieval and early Renaissance Siena was classy, to judge from the voluminous cloaks of the older men and the young aristocrats in parti-colored stockings and pleated velvet jackets in *Le Finanze del Comune in Pace e in Guerra*. A mason at work looks well fed and well groomed; so do the craftsmen being paid in shining golden disks, while one satisfied worker-gentleman jauntily trots out with a small sack, apparently laden with gold coins, suspended from a stick. Everyone was prosperous and contented; the persistent illusion, once again, of the Good Government, and it might have been—at least for a while. The *tavolette* record not only how Siena dressed and conducted her business and government; there are battle paintings that depict precisely the city and her neighbors; incidents in the lives of her saints; romantic sketches (late seventeenth-century) that linger on one pale corner of a street.

The documentation is wide-ranging and fascinating, embracing offers of indulgences, early advertising, music, science, literature, religion, art, death and taxes and case after case on the *contrade*—edicts concerning the conduct of the race, lists of horses to be raced and their owners, poetry written in honor of a Palio victory and prints of the Campo in various festive guises. The visit, and it may easily be extended to a number of visits, ends with signing the visitors' book of handmade paper in an antique cover, and a close view of the Mangia tower that seems to pull one along in its flight.

With the approach of the big day, more and more tourists crowd the Campo, and the middle-aged male population of Siena take its dogs for frequent walks, stopping enthralled before rosy new territories opened by English and German short shorts. The little boys are thoroughly maddened, drumming on the fountain, the bulges of palace stone, on street cobbles, on fences, on each other. Now that the tourist crowd has reached its fullest blossoming, a fat, itinerant tenor with a high, sobbing Neopolitan voice sings to the café sitters. (He isn't too bad, worse has happened in unlucky years of the prestigious Maggio Musicale of Florence.)

At about five or six in the afternoon of the 15th, the horses are taken to their churches for blessing. We might follow one group which slips into the vicolo Girolamo, across from the Duomo, one of those steep, arched-over Siena alleys—typically possessed of an open pissoir—which slopes to the Piazza della Selva and the church of San Sebastiano. It might be time for Vespers, but the usual sprinkling of old women is now a breathless, expectant crowd waiting for jockey and horse. The festive Palio lamps, garlands of white and orange and oak leaves, have been taken out of the house of the Society of the Rhinoceros next door to illuminate the church portal as well as the rest of the neighborhood. Across from the church, the *contrada* symbol, a bronze baby rhinoceros, stands on its fountain in a minute forest of fresh branches and oak leaves. The horse and jockey blessed, everyone returns to the Duomo, where the last parade before the Palio gathers again and there is a show of flags crossing, weaving, flying, rippling, in steady vigorous movements, for a church dignitary seated at a window at the side of the Duomo. The flags now seem to have a life of their own, brightly colored fish lolling and turning on the surface of a lazy sea. The *contrade* again meet at the same chapel; this time each gesture, each blessing, each snatch of song is followed by a bellicose war shout. Deafened by the drumming and fanfares and disturbed by the belligerent songs and shouting, one realizes that this is a farewell service for Crusaders, the blessings and vigorous hymns are war songs and primitive battle cries.

Back to the Campo in the later afternoon. Human shapes and colors and a Babel of languages flow as a free-form endless happening. Five little girls push one young baby in a slight carriage, shaking its dainty lace umbrella to a storm-tossed drunkenness, impeding the kimono-tight steps of a brocaded Japanese lady. The three-year-olds chase and flurry the pigeons and vice versa. Shoppers with flaccid baskets and swollen baskets cross and recross the piazza. Two Indian ladies in queenly saris drain the color from the cotton miniskirts of book-laden Italian-language students. For the third or fifth or twelfth time, one notices the German "professor" who is fluent in bad Italian, French and English and a fount of all wisdoms spoken in full voice: which brands of cigarettes to smoke, the revelations of graphology, what one should think about China, the United States, Russia and Siena. He has, obviously, a great need for young audiences and finds them particularly docile and deferential, attractive and male in the Campo. On another curve of the fan a café is shrilling with young English voices reading and discussing several sections of an old issue of London's Sunday *Times,* deploring what they missed on the telly, adoring what a rock star said in or about Canada.

You have already been welcomed, in theory, by Ambrogio Lorenzetti. It might be the time for an exploration of his contemporaries and neighbors in the Palazzo Pubblico and the palazzo itself: very probably—no, certainly—the most pleasing town hall in the world. Think of some you've seen, of the heavy domes and Victorian fat, of stone cannelloni, rusted heads and soot-covered garlands and awkward stairs, and then sit down at a café across the piazza and between bouts of fighting off the bees, as numerous and harmless as the pigeons, look again at the felicitous, welcoming curve of the façade, the pavan of windows and arches that paces its surface, the lilt of the small, white chapel near the entrance and the strong, slender tower, an aristocrat of towers named for the coarse first bell ringer, Mangiaguadagni (one who eats his earnings), a spendthrift glutton whose name was simplified to Mangia, "he eats."

Give the *cortile* some time before you mount the stairs to look at Simone Martini's Maestà, whose present enameled serenity belies a less tranquil history. It was originally painted in 1315 on the wall which, at that time, shared its lower section with a salt warehouse, part of the market still flourishing behind the palazzo. The salt damp ate into the wall and painting and Simone Martini was forced to repaint much of the center of the fresco. After his death other painters took a hand (and still do) at restoring fading sections and that may account for interesting deviations. The baldachin under which the Virgin and her host sit became the roof of a Gothic tourney tent and other portions, as well, of the reworked area turned more "Gothic" than "Byzantine" Sienese, more lyric and fluid, terrible awe replaced by ease and grace. The legend-prayer at the bottom of the painting is civic rather than religious: Simone asks for no cures or miracles or fame, only that the Virgin not listen to those who create malevolence and harm in the community.

On the other side of the room rides the *condottiere,* the mercenary captain Guido Riccio la Fogliano, on his way to win a battle for Siena. Painted by Simone Martini in 1330, it is a revolutionary painting, reputed to be the first secular portrait in Italy, that depicts horse and rider united as an unconquerable centaur cloaked in brocades of diamonds and vines.

The irresistible Good and Bad Government in an adjoining *sala* is, like the Simone rider, a significant breakthrough in Italian painting, a political document devoted to Utopian ideals expressed in medieval symbols and superb portraiture of the city and the Tuscan countryside. Take it slowly and with the assistance of the indispensable opera glasses; it is a cornucopia that spills an abundance of charms haloed with genius. The warm allure of the large Virtues, the ladies dancing in the streets of the medieval city mesmerize, and one must give them due time before the release to examine details: a bird in a cage at a window, the gestures of a mason building a tower, a group of schoolboys and their teacher. As you move toward the ideal rural life: a blind beggar crouching against a wall near the horse of the elegant lady riding out to hunt, and two passersby talking, one literally popeyed in the vehemence of argument. Continuing on from city to country, one also traverses a continent in painting style; the perspective, the details of the landscape, turn Chinese and one is again astonished at the sprawling meshworks of influence in a world that was difficult and even dangerous to travel. Observe the placing and detail of minute birds, the sharp hunting dogs, the swinging rhythm of a man sowing and one solitary saddened figure. And should you have decided that Ambrogio Lorenzetti was an early Rubens who painted large, soft women like silken counterpanes and took a little time off for landscapes, having a look at what is left of Bad Government—at the gaunt, tormented fallen friar, the disturbingly beautiful Justice holding a broken scale and hellish fragments blazing darkly out of decay and death.

The loggia of the palazzo shelters the old, original Fonte Gaia of Jacopo della Quercia, demolished by too much Palio, pageants, generations of little boys drumming on its edges and pigeon droppings, these shards brought here for safety and a copy placed in the Campo. The rooms beyond the loggia display a set of city documents, not strictly of the "archives" type: portraits of town worthies of various times, drawings and sketches of pages and flags of the contrade and schemes for illumination. The carts used in Palio processions were, once upon a time, stupendous structures that represented Parnassus and its full complement of gods and goddesses or the Olympic Games or an elaborate charade of Public Faith. In 1804 someone suggested the Palio costumes be modernized to range a broader world. The result was an engaging amalgam of classic Greek, bucolic and American Indian, which obviously never took; Renaissance splendor brooks no competition.

The final *prova* (rehearsal race) is at 7:00. The crowd packed inside the Campo and the stands is a shade more jumpy and irritable. The day has been hot and, for the first time, the white, smooth tide of policemen finds it difficult to clear the track. Standing in this patient, crushed mob, wondering again about Italian feet and their extraordinary durability, is a puzzling experience. Except for those pressed against the openings in the outer barriers of the shell, no one can see unless he is of supernatural (or supernational) height, and then he might not see because half of the adult shoulders are seats for children. The other children cling to skirts and trouser legs in a damp dark forest of buttocks and thighs. (Their only consolation is the miraculous advent of a bulbous-nosed man who cleaves his way through the impenetrable crowd to sell bubble gum called Brooklyn.) One knows by the drums, the shot, the stiffening and turning of heads and the shouting that the race is on. The Sienese swear that they can tell by a flash of color or the fleeting shape of a rump who is ahead, who fell at the perilous corner. You have seen nothing in the thickets of heads and shoulders.

That night, all the *contrada* lamps are out on the walls, banners hang from the humblest windows, long staffs bearing small lights are mounted in the iron torch holders of several palazzi, the arguments grow more heated in the cafés which stay open late to administer cooling, calming *gelato*. Far into the night drums beat, the young men shout and fight; from several corners, derisive choruses of cocks crowing, created by a string-and-rosin affair sold on the streets. No one sleeps.

The Pinacoteca suffers of a common local failing: what is Sienese, and particularly painting, is good. Not so; not all of it is worth scrupulous examining except by experts or certain tourists who like to check off title and painter in catalogues without necessarily looking at the paintings. Its repetitions are difficult to handle, particularly by the conscientious traveler who feels guilty if he doesn't see everything in a museum. The paintings *are* repetitious, depicting the same personages in the same acts, and there is no reason why you shouldn't dash through the Pinacoteca or skip it altogether if the Museo dell'Opera and the Palazzo Pubblico were enough.

On the other hand, moving slowly and looking closely, if one has the time, temperament and interest for it, reveal significant differences: the repetition becomes less insistent and begins to fade, the small masterpiece in a hidden corner reveals itself. Certain details crop up interestingly: the black-and-white-edged towels used by Pietro Lorenzetti in his accouchement scene, for one example, appear again and again to make lively passages for other painters. The same saint, in the same attitude, will be an austere grayish-green abstraction in one painting and a naturalistic, well-fleshed man in another; one sorrowing Virgin is a graceful curve, another is a lacerated shard; one period sees the afterlife in tones of heavenly music, a later period is possessed by hell-fire.

The chronological progress of paintings is downward, the second floor for the early works and below for the paintings of fatty decay. The collection begins with the rigidities of the twelfth and early thirteenth centuries, whose stiffness relaxes here and there—as in an accomplished thirteenth-century San Giovanni Battista—to run back to the safeties of the traditional "Byzantine." Among these paintings of considerable naïve appeal (notice a Saint Peter with his ears stuck well out and a beguiling Birth in the Manger) there is a strange and moving Crucifixion of 1319 by Ugolino di Nerio, the body attenuated, hanging heavy and bloodless, accompanied by a distraught Saint Francis. The same name appears on the label of a fine group of saints around a foolish Madonna, as if the painter were bored with Madonnas (usually exactly ordered by church fathers: so large, with such an expression, in just such a robe) and enjoyed the freedoms allowed him in painting lesser figures. Ugolino makes amends, however, in a deeply felt, awesome *Madonna of the Sorrows*. Of the school of Duccio, the loveliest, attributed to the master himself, is a small *Madonna dei Francescani* on a patterned blue background, the Virgin in dark blue bordered with a strong golden line, the child a subtle contrast in lavender and behind them both, a red cushion; above, a choir of angels and below, tiny, lively portraits of a group of Franciscan monks—a work very like a number of the Maestà panels.

In a room that has moved on in the fourteenth century, you will find the paintings of Bartolo di Fredi, which include an *Adoration of the Magi* set against soft, lovable hills immediately outside Siena's gates, in easy view of the Duomo. Oriental, exotically garbed courtiers, bejeweled, brocaded and silken, have parked their camels and blooded hunting dogs—the dogs of Flemish tapestries—near the gate while the kings in their splendid robes and crowns, surrounded by splendid gentlemen and fat-rumped horses in rich bridles, gaze on the child. The fourteenth-century love of luxury, of the worldly and the sensual, appears again and again in Bartolo's paintings, especially those of fair, Persian-cat ladies who enact saints and a *Coronation of the Virgin* in which Christ and the Virgin are dressed fashionably and tastefully, as calm and aristocratic as figures in a British historical film. It was obviously not devout painting, but Bartolo di Fredi could do that when he wished, as in a massive Virgin so straightforward and convincing that it might have come from the hand of Masaccio.

The parade of Lorenzetti and his followers continues: female saints and angels who seem to be members of the same family, the get of a multiple vegetable birth like a great tree of yellow roses, candidly plump and luxuriant, the cover girls of their time in Siena; almost, one begins to think, the only inhabitants of fourteenth-century Sienese art. Then, a balding Saint Paul whose slant of forehead to nose continued as a long sharp beard makes a dry, strong portrait; or a scratchy, faded Crucifixion witnessed by a Saint Francis dragging sorrow and anguish. After you have seen enough of Pietro Lorenzetti's creamy blondes, beautifully coiffed and dressed in court gowns, search out a small painting of San Tommaso and San Jacobo and a horrifying Bosch-like allegory of a cruel, mad world of desolation and death surrounding a wooded cloud that separates the crucified Christ and the Virgin Mary from the stinking rot.

The work of people often referred to as "minor"—Taddeo di Bartolo, Andrea di Bartolo, among others—hangs in Room 11. Look at the Crucifixion of Taddeo, observe one weeping figure, the mouth and nose covered by a sleeve, only the suffering eyes and hair visible, then turn to the triptychs of Bernardo Daddi to judge the justice of the label. It cannot possibly refer to the masterly portraits of Old Testament prophets by Sassetta and his equally monumental *Doctors of the Church,* although it might apply to the frail Botticellian gowns and faces painted by the Maestro dell'Osservanza.

Giovanni di Paolo either never slept or else masterminded a large atelier that worked long days, and you may find your mind and eye recoiling from his abundance. Don't, nevertheless, pass by a Judgment or a gem of a Madonna and Child, golden and swanlike, wrapped in soft folds of dark robe, seated in a mille-fleur garden against a background of Tuscan checkerboard fields.

Sano di Pietro was as prolific as Giovanni di Paolo and as busily involved with well-dressed and confidently painted saints. But he obviously enjoyed more painting his imaginative predelle: one group of yeomen use two crucified figures for target practice; two friars operate on the leg of a Negro lying in a shallow pit; the same two are either undressing or stealing money from a sleeping man. All this fun and games next to a docile, large-eyed Saint Catherine and the hieratic, serene volumes of a *Coronation of a Virgin.*

If you've held out this far, explore a few more predelle to find a huge dog carrying in his teeth an animal as offering to a nun or saint; scenes of flagellation, choruses of musical angels, saints having their flesh scraped by nailed boards, flocks of birds listening to Saint Francis and a gold-paneled *Virgin and Child with Saint Catherine* straight out of "Snow White and the Seven Dwarfs."

In a side room there are two small paintings, believed to have been details of larger works or meant to adorn a household object. One is a darkened, somewhat scratched landscape of a boat, a small castle, a farmhouse and a stretch of obscure land in the background. The other is the *Città sul Mare,* an extraordinary mingling of perspectives in turrets and crenelations painted in faded grayish pinks, greens and touches of white to create a dreaming, surrealistic walled town. These are generally attributed to Ambrogio Lorenzetti; whatever the name, both are masterpieces and prophetic, among the earliest European landscape painting; no civic lessons, no saints, no damnation, simply the sheer pleasure of painting.

Painting turns soft on the lower floor, the colors timid and chalky, the spicy portraiture turned sticky, the impact of narrative vitiated in shows of skill; in short, the opening of the long path that leads to the chromos that paper Catholic communities throughout the world. Notice, for one, the famous Sodoma Christ in Room 32. He is plump because, one has the feeling, Sodoma wanted to show off his deft modeling and fat is better than thin for the purpose. There is clever painting in the pull of rope on flesh, the thorns are painfully sharp and the trickles of blood convincingly bloody, the eyes swim in splendidly painted tears and not a breath, not a tremor of emotion in the well-padded victim or the spectator.

Canvases grow busier and less meaningful as they move into the seventeenth century, concentrated on El Greco-ish figures and stormy, soupy allegories that lean heavily on earlier masters. One Assumption owes its attractions to Botticelli, another to extravagance: prancing horses, gilded chariots, mythological figures, the Virgin Mary surrounded by elders ready for the hunt. Somewhere in the crowd there is room for death's-heads, smartly dressed ladies, pink unicorns pulling cartfuls of virgins, a few dead people, a few dying, the whole crazy pageant played out against distant castles and chalk mountains scored by black snakes of road. For relief from too many vapory Beccafumis, look for a keen self-portrait by Francesco Vanni and, in Room 35, a painting by Dürer of a saint with small, sad eyes and a drooping nose; a bald, intelligent, suffering old man. Back to the Italians again, with a Zuccari painting of England's Queen Elizabeth, pale, thin, hook-nosed and bejeweled, her background a group of ornamental gentlemen performing a pavan or bourrée or whatever. With several portraits by Montagna and Lotto, you are free of your obligations to ART in Siena.

The Campo. 7:30, when the fading sunlight kindles the glass of piazza windows, is the hour of the dogs. The big poodles and the small, the ugly and adored, the blooded and the oddities, the long-nosed and the snuffling short, are all out to take the evening air. One harried puppy is pulled, snapped back and almost strangled between its impulses and those of a sharp little girl crazed with her mastery, especially as it affects five male contemporaries who run in frenzied paths after, before and around the miniature Diana and her bewildered puppy. (The dog-walking of 10:30 P.M. takes over the Banchi di Sopra, often perked up by a handsome team of distinguished gentlemen and their sinuous young fox.)

By the way of the via San Pietro, one comes to Quattro Cantoni, a meeting of roads, marked, as every major section of the city is, by the wet-nurse wolf, and if it isn't too long before or after Palio time, there will be a large painted panther to introduce his *contrada*. The via San Quirico stops at an elaborate gate and a balcony hung with curly ironwork lamps and a portrait of the Panther in monochrome mosaic. The *contrada* house-museum is alive with swords, armor, velvet and fur, brocades and banners, some of it quite old and carefully preserved, the church a glistening, gold-brushed structure with a painted ceiling and an ornate chapel. At the side of the balcony, if the gate is open, one looks down into the fabric of Siena and the elements that make its bounding roof rhythm: deep narrow houses like tall boxes set at different levels; flowered balconies below outdoor kitchens; high up, an outdoor workshop; five feet below, a sudden burst of garden, and fans and fans of roof tiles.

The via dei Stalloreggi is medieval Siena with no primping, Siena red shading to dusty charred on several fine palaces that mourn their fall from glory. At the corner with via Castelvecchio there is a votive fresco by Sodoma, a Pietà enclosed in dusty glass and a fine stone frame. The attached sign calls this the Madonna del Corvo, to commemorate a legend that at this spot a dying raven fell, the first victim and harbinger of the mid-fourteenth century Black Death that devastated the city. At the bottom of the street, the house of Duccio, "in his time a wonder, today a splendid monument of Sienese painting," according to the tablet on the wall. The gate near Duccio's house opens to the Pian dei Mantellini, which curves toward the domes and steeples of Santa Maria del Carmine and a court that houses both cars and classic statuary in an alternation of heads and full bodies. The bodies are caged in chicken wire to discourage a neighborhood artist who managed, nonetheless, to tear open a section of wire in order to pencil pubic hair on a young discus thrower.

The street called Diana has *its* quotation by Dante, an air of improving itself with paint and new doors, and at the meeting with the via San Marco, a playful baroque church whose sign says that it is the "Casa del Cavallo" (the house of the horse) and above that, a crowned shield bearing a snail rampant, as rampant as a snail can be. The snail shield appears on a number of walls, alternating with small bird cages hanging from pegs, as the pleasant street turns toward its Porta San Marco, which resembles the Facciatone, a brick sweep that begs to be finished. The massive wooden doors open to a view of distant hills, especially lovely during a misting summer rain when the fields turn from gray-green to gray to pale yellow under rain clouds that float toward them, rest and pass.

To the right out of the via San Marco the street dips under an archway surmounted by a loggia of flowerpots and one white sheet. On one side of the arch, a holy image and its showcase of silver hearts; on the other side, a rusty green pissoir painted with a faded red snail and the number 48½, possibly the number of races won by the *contrada*. And the half? Anything can happen in a Palio race.

A tight area expands its lungs and breaths as it enters the Prato Sant'Agostino from the Porta all'Arco. In back of the playground and parklet is the golden classic church of Sant'Agostino and to the right of that, the slope of via Mattioli and its open, flat bell yokes over a scramble of roof tiles. At the edge of the playground, one faces across green valleys to distant new housing and the dignity of Santa Maria dei Servi. Immediately below, a leap from the thirteenth century to the twentieth is represented by girls in shorts whirling on roller skates. At the left, the façade of San Giuseppe near an old protective gateway, and swinging around (still leftward), a liveliness of carpenter shops filing, planing, polishing and arguing; a red lion sitting like an ugly tabby on the terrace otherwise adorned with colored clothespins. Above the clothespins, a court with remains of Bacchic frescoes next to an attractive sloven of a house, ocher laced with green shutters, a jungle of fuchsias at one window, an ambitious balcony dangerously laden with potted plants. Its neighbor is a faintly frescoed palace whose puffy rustication doesn't awe banners of newly washed sheets. Certainly not the most aesthetic or perfect parts of Siena, it is the pleasing mixture of the old and the new, the defeated and the hopeful, the exuberant and the decayed, that makes it appealingly comfortable.

Bypassing a mess of cars, marked walls and announcements (the portico of the church is shared by a secondary school) one comes into the light, high and wide presence of the basilica of Sant'Agostino. The treasures of the church are secluded mainly in the Piccolomini Chapel (find the sacristan): luscious enamels poured out smoothly by Sodoma; a triptych concerning Sant'-Agostino by Simone Martini and as idyllic, elegant and Sienese as you would expect it to be; a Massacre of the Innocents by Matteo di Giovanni (late fifteenth century) in which the irresistible urge to paint brilliant costumes distracts from the dreadful import of the events, as do the calm, poised faces that look away indifferently from the slaughter to gaze at the spectator. Outside the chapel there is a Crucifixion by Perugino in which, with great artfulness, nothing at all really happens; a handsome tall marble altar complex and, if you are there at the right time, a talented musician practicing on the rich-voiced church organ.

Returning to the piazza you may encounter a funeral society gathered behind a long black banner and two torches. They wear their ancient black hooded cloaks, a dour, threatening costume unbearable to one member of the troop who has put on bright orange pants to flash among the sooty legs. They continue down the hill of Pier Angelo Mattioli to the cemetery while you make your way toward the roundels and volutes of San Giuseppe (Saint Joseph and, appropriately, the church of the Carpenters' Guild) and through his arch, which frames the Mangia tower, into paths of uncertain walls, of houses aged beyond repair, usable only as supports of raised gardens. Out of the via Sant'Agata and into the Casato di Sopra and its twist downward as the Casato di Sotto, then plunge down—and plunge is the precise word for these precipitate alleys—into the vicolo del Sambuco. Body sloping well back, wondering how these hills are negotiated on icy days, go past the street toilet and under a plank holding flowerpots, past boys lolling and playing cards as if the fall of cobbles were a large divan, past old doors framed by thick cobwebs, under lines and flags of wash and pale-yellow street lamps, past a cobbler's shop whose wall is a frieze of wooden feet, under a spill of branches from a fig tree overhead, past a truck delivering old clothes and ladies knitting and babies crawling, past people staring out of windows stunned by your presence in their isolated street, past the canaries peeping from cages hung on the street walls. The vicolo della Fonte repeats the composition as it leads to a tall stand of wall jutting down from Casato di Sotto, part of a dry fountain that shows vestiges of lordly capitals on its cracked pilasters and, at its depths, dirt that combines poorly with the romantic legend that this height was the spot chosen by betrayed and abandoned lady suicides.

As you go up the stairs to Casato di Sotto, look at the attractive stone window surrounds of the house you face and up at a heavy angle of gray Renaissance stones and above that, a dance of tiles, curves, slips and slices of sky, eaves, tiny arches, vines, laundry and tips of greenery. Nearby, attached to a wall, is a modern medieval lady whose bronze dress enfolds the significant buildings of Siena and its valleys and next to her, an eagle and an explanation for the attractive bronze relief: "to the noble contrada of the eagle, as a symbol of an old friendship," given by the Ente Provincale per il Turismo to the *City* of the Eagle— another manifestation of the near-autonomous quality of the *contrada,* a miniature city within the city. (According to the Sienese these "cities" were the only places in Italy that held democratic elections during Mussolini's time.)

The superb parade, the honeyed motion of flags alternating with great flights as the boys twirl and thrust them into the air, never losing the steady rhythm called by the insistent drums, the

garlands, the blond wigs, the luxurious cut velvets and furs and
the absurd race are over. The jockey of the Porcupine is weeping
and all the beautiful Porcupine pages have torn off their wigs and
silken caps and are weeping, too. The winners, the Goose,
scream and embrace, one hysterical page kisses and kisses his
contrada banner. The men in the stands shout at each other, the
women weep or are sullen or indulgently amused. A half hour
later everyone marches after the winning *contrada* and the Palio
banner, the winners now weeping in an excess of joy or because
this exultant time will soon be gone for too many months. Flags
and drums continue, now wielded by skillful amateurs; people
gather on the main piazze to cheer the winners and to roar expla-
nations at each other. Everyone knows exactly what happened
and insists on giving his full, vivid version of the event. The
victorious young go on through the night, howling, cursing, fighting, growing hoarse and more hoarse, joined by the flags and the
howlers of a closely friendly *contrada.* (Here it must be explained
that the defeat of an enemy is as important as winning. Thus, in
the combinations and deals, two friendly *contrade* may join to
buy off the jockey of an enemy one year, and the next year one
may recombine with the former enemy against the former friend;
a common historical pattern.)

You are on your way back to the Palazzo Chigi on the via di
Città, ready to enjoy its warm stone and brick of various periods,
including original fourteenth-century sections. The tower isn't
quite where it should be; that doesn't seem to matter, nor impair
the ripples of Gothic, Sienese-arched windows, whose trilling
ends in a burst of green song from a rebel tree that breaks
through the formal line of palaces. The courtyard is, like many,
hung with shields and plaques, and in the vaults are fancies and
contortions of the Renaissance. If the master classes of the Chi-
giana Music Academy are not in session, one may ask permission to see some of the rooms of the palace, wondering what it
might mean for students to work under the eye of a Botticelli
painting or a Sassetta. (Toward the end of the summer the students offer concerts that are free and interesting both for the
programs and the possibility of hearing a young Japanese or

Hungarian or Dutch demigod perform in a hall of rococo sugar and whipped cream, gold ribbons and roses and, in the dignified anteroom, a Donatello Virgin and Child.)

A tunnel in the upper section of the palazzo takes one to the via dei Percennesi, a street still very much its thirteenth-century self: arches into arches, cut by irregularly slanted arches as bridges or minuscule terraces and all of them mutual supports for sets of tall ancient houses. By way of the via San Pietro, go to the via del Castelvecchio, its silent medieval houses (a few in the area decorate their walls with pieces of Roman stone) and another *castellare*. Look for a low sloping tunnel that leads to a court whose houses show vestiges of arches, medieval outer stairs, wooden-beamed eaves and a hidden garden. One must imagine the entrance tunnel heavily gated, armed outside and in, and the maze of fortress—which may have included all the houses in the immediate neighborhood—dependent on the enclosed garden and cistern or fountain, should supplies be cut off by attack.

The Campo. 9:00 P.M. Daylight hangs on with a few ragged rays. In the shell a young man, a skillful soccer player, is kicking a large white ball to a tiny boy, not more than five years old, who runs like a wound-up toy, ceaseless, rapid, taking deft sideswipes at the ball, now and then picking it up for a short, fast bounce. The father must have caught the boy as he emerged from the womb, set him on his feet and said, "Let's play ball," and they have been playing since, to judge from the child's expertise.

As full night lowers and lines of audience and musicians trail across the piazza for a concert at the Palazzo Pubblico, father and son run in and out among the dim figures. The father's gray shirt fades, the black hair and navy pants of the little boy disappear, only the bobble of white shirt darting after the bobble of white ball remains.

The piazza dark is illuminated solely by muted yellow lamps in dragon-tongued iron cages and the pale-green water light that glows in the fountain and the *cappella* of the palazzo.

By this time you have found that the shape of the Campo consists of nearly a dozen blades deftly set together, leaving narrow, obscure street openings. One of them, the via Salicotto, must have enjoyed a gaudier and more flavorful life than it seems to now. For one thing, it was the early ghetto, and, for another, the market was much larger, extending into the site of the Palazzo Pubblico, and probably included the alley named Pescheria, fish market. Where there were big markets, there were travelers with money and time for whores, troublesome enough for Prince Mattias, of the Medicis who controlled Siena in the sixteenth and seventeenth centuries, to have engraved on the wall at the top of Salicotto a sign that prohibits *meretrici* (prostitutes) from living on this street on pain of arrest and trial. The vai del Perrone borders the local spindle-shaped cluster of streets, the Salicotto quarter, with a number of restaurants and shops, and as it becomes the via San Martino, a row of carpentry shops. These were once the coffinmakers of Siena; only one such shop is visibly left, the others may be hiding in the dark, winding courts like that which trails from Number 69. (Snoop in courts, always. Italy is not a secretive country in spite of the defensiveness of its old cities, and Italian politeness will protect you if welcome doesn't.)

Near the Campo end of the street of Salicotto and into the via delle Scotte one finds a plaque, common to many Italian towns: from this place the Germans took a number of Jews aged thirteen to seventy-one. Sharp turns and zigzags in and out of the via degli Archi, the vicolo della Fortuna, the vicolo delle Scotte and their neighbors reveal ancient houses looking on the new, which are designed to accord with their elderly relations, and pointed street arches that sometimes hold a regal lamp or lead to close tall angles of houses meeting in dim corners. The vicolo della Manna is its own private garden village hiding in a tip of street behind a wall that spews green fronds. In and out again, up and down, under arches faced with brick and others supported by timber, through the vicolo della Coda to that of Vannello, up and down the vicolo dell'Oro for a set of substantially buttressed buildings, bulging at the top and narrow at the bottom, a second warning for *meretrici* to stay out.

The church of Santa Maria dei Servi (at the top of the street of that name) is somewhat diminished by a foolish fresco on the right side of its façade, rescued by its superb bell tower and humanized by the visitors who take the sun on its steps and try to gather into their camera lens a view of Siena's roofs and towers. Through considerable restoration and obvious changes Santa Maria dei Servi retained its Romanesque proportions. The interior is a little of this and that linked by "Gothic" trompe l'oeil. Among the paintings of several degrees of excellence there are two remarkable pieces by Pietro Lorenzetti. One of them is the banquet of Herod at that point in the proceedings when the head of John the Baptist is handed out the door and the other, a shocking Slaughter of the Innocents, truly a massacre, an event of anguish and horror, interesting to compare with the same scene as it appears in another chapel, painted by Matteo di Giovanni, about a hundred and fifty years later. Ubiquitous, unfortunate clichés mar this church as they do many others in Italy: a life-sized Virgin Addòlorata in a classic mantle, her chest bristling with innumerable knives and a large, sweet Christ apparently made of marzipan. One wonders and wonders and wonders, again and again, going from church to church in Siena, how a people who covered their account books with gems of miniature painting, a people who sang as they accompanied Duccio and his Maestà to the Duomo, who produced a painted world of Saxon queens and felicitous landscapes, who control jealously the harmonies of shape and color in their city, can submit their churches to repetitions of sadistic chromos in the round.

At the side of the church, in an oasis of intense quiet, one goes by the house, inevitable in every Italian city, where Garibaldi slept or spent an hour or two and a turn of stairs that gives on the via Val Di Montone (the ram, a *contrada* name), which takes one to the gardens and wide views that surround the psychiatric hospital and to the splendidly battlemented Porta Romana. From the entrance to the first arch, the steady hammering and clanging of a metalworks shop built inside the arch itself; on its dusty white wall, an attractive arrangement of black iron arabesques as flowers and birds to form lamps and hinges and store signs. If one erases the electric light and welding torch the scene might accurately be that of a similar atelier six hundred years ago. The space toward the outer arch is a large square court furnished with a stone ledge, pleasant for sitting and reading, if auto traffic permits, and among the iron rings for horse reins, the crenelations of their embroidery of shallow archlets and a monumental Medici shield, there is a shelter that never sheltered enough the remains of a fresco which shows a scrap of sky, glittering LSD stars and a few angelic faces attributed to Sassetta.

The via del Sole is a narrow walled alley that supports high gardens on its upper side and spills petals into the street. Below it, a cultivated valley; ahead, the changing contours of the city as you move toward its dense clusters of streets. Closer and closer come the red and gray curves and turning, bending slits of street. At one side, a great complex of stairs runs to and from a high bright platform and new housing; you will notice that the modern buildings, like the old, keep their balconies on inner courts, that Siena's smoothness of contour derives from the absence of front balconies. Through a break in the long street go up to the elephant and tower of the Torre *contrada,* in an opening off Salicotto just below the airy, freshly made vicolo dei Contradini. Halfway along the via dei Malcontenti (named for the fact that it was a path to the the the via di Porta Giustizia, which, in turn, led to the gallows or executioner's ax) take a longer, more distant glance at the market, the heir to a site that was, 2,500 years ago, an Etruscan temple-arena-market enclave, later Roman and continuously market thereafter. The round central market building, faithfully Sienese in its earth-red color, is actually of the eighteenth century and a useful compositional hub for the big piazza which might, without it, sprawl shapelessly, losing the attractive composition of rhythms and angles provided by the crenelations and loggia pillars of the Palazzo Pubblico counterpoised against the slopes and roof levels of lower, ancient houses.

The evening of the 17th is the beginning of the end. The town band, now back in their guise of tired old gentlemen in shining navy suits, lead a shapeless group of the Goose young, again in their costumes except for the wigs, with babies' nipples in their mouths, carrying signs that boast of their victory, the emphasis on scornful scatological references to the enemy, Torre. When they turn the corner of the Palazzo Pubblico, where the land of

Torre ends, they shout derision into the dark, silent street and begin their fraying assault on the tired town. It is a silly, unsightly conclusion to a stirring spectacle and this oafish denouement makes a dull, spitting thud. But one has realized, some time before, that this is a boys' festival, basically; lengthy, frenetic rites of passage ceremonies, an interminable bar mitzvah.

Stupid with sleeplessness, one can gather enough sense together to realize that for the adults too, Palio time is a remarkable purge. Seething dissensions can be expressed as *contrada* conflicts. Anyone who chooses to has the right to be irrational for a while, the intelligent can relax and be happily, primitively doltish, the shrewd can be tricky, the gambler can play, the plain boy can become a Renaissance heirling; the field is open for titillations of uncertainty, for superstition, prayers, songs, tears and noise. The priests earn extra attention and the old ladies extra prayer sessions, the girls new ornaments, the babies new toys; something for everyone, in short. Why don't we institute Palios in the United States? They might take care of those dreaded long, hot summers. Neighborhood pride would flourish and a sense of local responsibility would develop. Everyone would be kept busy, the women refurbishing, letting out, taking in, cleaning, polishing; the men arranging for horses and jockeys, whitewashing the Casa del Cavallo. One group would see that the banners are fresh and their staffs smooth; another would check the boots and have new ones made; someone would see to hats, another to wigs. The older girls could help plan the dinner menus and arrange for the transport and placing of tables and chairs. The boys, who otherwise might be looking for trouble, would be busy drumming and practicing flag throwing. Best though, is the great exhausting repository for emotions the Palio provides. We haven't the medieval palaces nor the Duomo, nor anything like the perfect Campo, but with movie know-how and a minute fraction of what riots cost, we could build appropriate sets. The United States needs Palios; most of the world could use a few.

The Campo. 11:30 P.M. The lost depth of the shell and the furry dimness of its rim make the few stragglers returning from the concert seem extremely small and distant. The road in front of the Palazzo appears to be a river at whose edge rides the palace itself, a strange and wonderful ship in a fogbound harbor, a ghost ship out of ancient legends. Should it be raining, the frail, mist-stained light that touches the tower will catch in the fine wires of TV sets and ignite them thinly, the last threads of spent fireworks, slender shadows of furled banners.

Notes

PENSIONI. Other than the largish conventional hotel, the Excelsior, Siena's pensioni (sometimes breakfast and one meal) and *alberghi* are mainly unpretentious, if occasionally eccentric. A marked exception is chic, resort-like—revived antiquity set in a park!: the Park Hotel on the via di Marciano, a fair distance out of the center of town and expensive. Fine for resting but who wants to sit passively in Siena?

The Canon d'Oro on the via Montanini spreads from its sampler desk and sitting room to a maze of up and down and left and right, which must be memorized if you are ever to find your way back to bed. The service is solicitous, at times downright merry. You may be able to pick up an ancient copy of the *Partisan Review* and the second-violin section of a Bartók quartet left by former clients on one of the tables scattered around the halls, and for all this the cost with bath is moderate. Bathing in one of the generously distributed hall bathrooms will bring the cost down.

A medieval bunching of central streets enfolds two inexpensive small hotels: La Toscana, which lives nicely in a tower, and the more basic Tre Donzelle.

At the other end of the scale is the Palazzo Ravizza (pensione) at 34 Pian dei Mantellini, run by inheritors of the palace. Some of the rooms are authentically palatial, but you must reserve well in advance—months, a year. You may have a little difficulty with the staff. They are old, and one is reluctant to ask a forgetful, transparent old man for anything for fear that he might turn to a heap of fine, white dust in a corridor. The rates will be higher than elsewhere, but the atmosphere and furnishings more rarefied.

The easy, unpretentious Chiusarelli on the viale Curtatone presents no problems at all; well-located, moderately priced and decent, if quite basic meals.

Al Marsili, on via del Castro, is elegant, highish, with a view of the Cathedral.

Or you might try the Mariotti Da Mugalone, 8 via dei Pelle. High moderate.

Villa Scacciapensieri (translatable as *sans souci*) is on a bus line, and a few minutes away from the center of town. Gardens, well-kept rooms, careful meals served outdoors and a belvedere from which to look down on the city. High moderate.

RESTAURANTS.   The Duomo and Pinacoteca area and that of San Domenico (via San Pietro, Sapienza, etc.) are dotted with restaurants that serve basic, identical meals from tourist menus at about 12,000 lire and less. Or, at the same prices, the Tre Donzelle (try the trout) and the Pesche d'Oro on via Porrione.

For a bit more, outdoor tables wherever there is a strip of space to put them, and sprawling into the street at Palio time, try the Severino, below the Duomo, and Il Biondo (a favorite), off the via Montanini.

Two or three thousand additional lire will buy you deviations from the staples and a certain elegance of décor and service at: Turiddu, off the Piazza Indipendenza; Guido, off the Banchi di Sopra, sought out by visiting Italian gourmets and gourmands for their veal dishes confected with thin-sliced raw white truffles and rich cakes; Nello, on the via Porrione, and have an apéritif at the zinc bar of the dignified old bar-groceries shop across the street, run by a very old man and his middle-aged son, aware of the fact that they own something of a museum piece and are pleased to show it.

Roberto, at the top of the via di Calzoleria, is an all-purpose dispenser of pizza, sandwiches, meats, cheese, chicken and salads to be taken out, eaten on foot or in upstairs rooms or, when the neighboring hardware shop is closed, on the street. Inexpensive.

Daintier sandwiches, cakes, ice cream and coffee can be had at the branches of Nannini; *zuccotto,* a local sweet of frozen mousse and spongecake, and *panforte,* a flat nuts-and-dried-fruit combination, are available to inescapable. Not inexpensive.

The most décor crowded into any one unit of Siena exists in the Medio Evo restaurant, on the via dei Rossi. In its box of medieval tower it has crowded two she-wolves, a fountain, something that looks like a prison cage, coats of arms, "classic" busts and columns, a slab of sarcophagus, to mention only a few samples. If you can concentrate on eating, order the chicken in lemon sauce.

Zeno is a trattoria near the Cine Esmeralda on the via Romana, not worth a long struggle to find (Italy is full of them), but if you happen to be in the neighborhood, and can find seats at a table to share with a few regulars, it will be a steamy, noisy, filling experience. Mama, papa and all the kids work like grinning, happy slaves clearing, clattering, serving, conversing, and above their noise, the shouted conversations of clients. The menu is limited household style, earthy and full-flavored; let the patron-waiter bring you what he thinks you should have (all you have to spend of your limited Italian is *buon giorno* and *mangiare*). The full spread from pasta to fruit and country-style bread floated on honest, proletarian wine, plus a dessert wine as you roll out, should cost about $4. (One warning: there is a regular with a professorial manner and squint eyes who lies in wait for the stray foreigner to ask if he knows Dante. Say no, always, unless you are equipped in time and Italian to recite with him long stretches of the *Divine Comedy*.)

More Notes

For visiting the hamlets described below and some of the larger towns, local buses may do (from the piazza in front of San Domenico), but trips out of Siena are not frequent and the service between small towns sparse, causing an expenditure of considerable time. If you have neither a car nor endless time, ask your hotel desk to make arrangements with a taxi driver or, better still, a university student to whom the family car is usually available for a day's work or two. About $25 a hearty midday meal and the cost of gas, shockingly high, should buy you a full, interesting day.

One of the greatest bargains in Italy is the summer university (Scuola per Stranieri) in Siena. The fee is very low (about $100 for the summer), and the student card gives one Italian classes; lectures in art, music, history, literature, etc.; free admission to museums; inexpensive guided tours of the area; reduced-cost meals in some restaurants and two cafeterias restricted to students. You will have a club where you may read and talk over inexpensive drinks and, should you need it, the university will suggest an inexpensive pensione or a family that provides room and/or board. It is living and learning among a great diversity of ages and nationalities, cosseted in the most permissive of schools amid a citizenry that treats one as an honored guest of the city.

Siena—Environs

"ENVIRONS" must be defined by the amount of time one has and is willing to spend—an hour or two, a half day, a day or two. There are small wonders a few kilometers from the city's gates, which require a short stroll, and greater ones, an hour or two distant, that ask slower exploration.

A few possibilities among the many:

By way of a few miles of Tuscan landscape and an unusual number of pigs one reaches a hamlet called Torri and its abbey, whose formal name is the Abbazia Vallombrosiana di Santa Mustiola. At the end of an imposing austerity of Romanesque-Gothic church, unfortunately pressed into breathless space, one comes to the gleeful cloisters of the early eleventh century. Little black and white scallops bound along a stream of slender columns, some with white capitals and some black; the columns rounded, grooved, carved as wiggling snake tracks. Each capital is squared off in four different designs, and none, in any set or any column, is a repetition of another; they are imaginative, playful and sometimes masterly, as, in one corner of the court, a ribbon design deeply incised in the hard stone and, below, a lunging, fiery griffon-serpent. (The abbey cloister must be seen before 7:00 P.M., because the house that surrounds its triple tiers—the upper sections are later additions—may still belong to a couple of another, politer, well-dressed time, the man an especially appealing courtier of polished neatness; spare neat body, neat Vandyke beard; neatly designed face; neat, graceful gestures.)

For intense romantic decay, and a demonstration of how a poor populace settles into antique ruins, go on to Staggia (well-marked on the main highway, N2). The whole town must have been enclosed by the wall whose remains surround a ruined thirteenth-century castle. A round tower, pierced by Gothic windows, a grand fireplace flanked by ornamented pillars, a suggestion of window seats, are the recognizable remnants of the castle. The rest is chickens scratching in the earth, huts and pens of wood patched with tin and, past a stretch of medieval pavement, minimal dwellings lit by minute bird cages near the low windows. The local bread is apparently baked in an improvised oven in a fissure of the tower, and anyone who needs a stone for grinding or for barring an unlockable door helps himself to the inexhaustible bones and sinews of the tower and walls. The resident duke—and one wonders how much he paid and whether he still appears—greets visitors dressed in a greasy, sloping vest and pants stiffened by age. Out of his grizzled stubble, splashing through his assortment of stumps, comes a plaint about how he wants to tear all this old junk down and build something modern (with what money, if his teeth and vest are valid testimonials of his financial condition?), but the Belle Arti Committee, which protects ancient monuments, will not permit it. Once more the problem that crops up again and again: When is an ancient monument, too long neglected and too far in ruins for rebuilding, ready to be considered a wreck for relinquishing? The zealots will not let a stone be taken off perilous stone; yet the stones will fall of their own weight and age in any case, and effort might better be concentrated on finding money to light churches and museums and pay guards so that hundreds of masterpieces now imprisoned in dimness or behind locked museum doors may again be visible.

In 1313, Bernardo Tolomei, of the banking family whose avocation was maintaining murderous feuds with its neighbor bankers, the Salimbenis (you will have noticed the dangerous proximity—also a way to keep a close eye on each other—of their palaces in Siena), decided to remove himself from the giving and taking of death, and selecting a cracked piece of the creta (chalk) country that appears in many Sienese paintings, founded a Benedictine monastery. Monte Oliveto Maggiore is an impressive set of tall, broad red buildings screened, scored and framed by lines of cypresses. The moated entrance, restored, is about the only vestige left of the early abbey; the rest is largely of the fifteenth century, when the abbey was a Renaissance center of culture. Beyond the entrance, decorated with della Robbia works, are long stretches of walks and gardens, white monks striding purposefully, a bar, a restaurant and a general air of keeping up with the times; an amiable place for spending a relaxed hour. But Italy is a world of relaxed hours, the goal here is the cloister walls of Signorelli and Sodoma murals, which treat of the life of Saint Benedict. It is a stimulating experience to see similar subjects treated by two painters who worked contemporaneously (although Signorelli was considerably the older), both much sought after, both handling religious matter with little piety, the devotion dedicated to manner and techniques rather than to matter and emotion. The major number are by Sodoma, who took over after Signorelli left for a variety of possible reasons: the discouraging number of walls to cover limited to one subject, the constant supervision of the abbots, the inadequate pay, and above all, the better offer and greater freedom offered by the Duomo of Orvieto (page 136).

Vasari revered Signorelli, the work and the man, whom he describes as "of the highest character, sincere and loving with friends, of gentle and pleasing conversations with everyone, and, above all, courteous to all who need his skill, and a good master to his pupils." He loathed Sodoma, grudging in his praise where he was forced to praise and more colorful than he was usually apt to be, carried away by his fascination for this "bestial" man whom the monks called "il Mattaccio" (imbecile or madman), who was born Giovanni Antonio Bazzi da Vercelli and who called himself proudly the Sodomite. "His manner of life was licentious and dishonorable, and he always had boys and beardless youths about him of whom he was inordinately fond, this earned him the name of Sodoma; but instead of feeling shame he gloried in it, writing stanzas and verses on it, and singing them to the accompaniment of the lute. He loved to fill his house with all manner of curious animals; badgers, squirrels, apes, catamounts, dwarf asses, Barbary racehorses, Elba ponies, jackdaws, bantams, turtle-doves . . . so that his house resembled a veritable Noah's ark. . . . He thought of nothing but pleasure, worked when he pleased and only cared about dressing himself grandly, wearing brocaded doublets, cloaks embroidered with gold, rich cuffs, collars and such trifles, like a mountebank. . . ." It is a comment on his time and place that patron bankers and the "generals" of abbeys found him diverting and respected his talent more than did Vasari—except on such occasions when he painted naked harlots into a monastery scene. (They were subsequently dressed by the painter, after the head of the abbey threatened to have the murals destroyed.)

One comes first on the Sodoma murals—airy draperies and pale, fanciful, Japanesey landscapes, a virtuosity of arches within arches and slant glimpses of diminishing arches. The pallid and sweet-faced monks, almost lost in boxes of exuberant Pompeian grotesquerie, sometimes drop mounds of cloak, haphazard falls that are painted with more careful skill than is spent on the faces. The vague, done-with-a-talented-left-hand, lazy, facile painting changes when the laborers around him catch his eye and a robust, vivid human comes to life, or when he paints his magnificent self as a stylish coxcomb surrounded by two badgers, the raven whom he trained to imitate his voice and, at some distance, a large exotic bird.

Signorelli's work is big, fully colored and forceful. The famously beautiful women of an inn scene—particularly the gesture of one woman pouring wine—the solidity and postures of the monks, have been frequently commented on. Notice, also, a shadowy figure in the doorway: its stance, the sway of body and the weight on one leg palpably felt and, in other sections, the fullness of the bodies of horses, the brutal faces of warriors and, always, the sense of vigorous movement and ample space for each gesture.

The abbey church has little to show that is comparable except—remarkable accomplishments in their own medium—choir stalls imbedded with wooden intarsia work by a Fra Giovanni da Verona of the early sixteenth century. He carved, shaded (always in wood of different tones) and shaped lutes, viols, closet doors which open to reveal complex hoops within hoops and the intricate perspective of mingled star shapes, Siena's Mangia tower and a king of tortoise-shell cats sitting on a fine loggia. This sort of work, like too much delicate embroidery, can have a certain repellent quality, that of observing a man obsessed, but it was an extraordinary art and these are among the best specimens left us.

Southward, through turned-black earth now, and dark ashy furrows of burned soil, past blind castles on the highest hills begging for demolition or succor. (You may have one or a number of them at bargain prices; all it requires is channeling water and electricity, cementing the wind out of the cracked walls, shoveling out centuries of debris and creating Home, Sweet Home in a thirteenth- or fourteenth-century fortress.) Into woods and out again, up hills and slow turning descents toward expanding landscapes, through rough, weedy terrain, meticulous cultivation and clouds of umbrella pine, and on to the slope of Tuscany's highest peak, Monte Amiata. It is a winter sports resort that you might skip except that you will be skipping chestnut groves and fir forests and mercury fields. If you are on a bus, or traveling with a Tuscan driver, you will be told that this mountain shows the colors of the Italian flag—white of snow, green of fir trees and red (stretching it a bit) for chestnuts. Your informant will also probably tell you to look for a rock formation that shapes the profile of Dante. And why not, if it pleases him? Monte Amiata has a cable seat (*seggiovia*) for viewing the cold mists and is probably best when the snows shine crisply in the winter sun, but it does lead to Santa Fiora; shivering in the mists and drinking too much tepid coffee is a small price for the ride to, and an hour in, that town, a short distance to the south.

Santa Fiora hangs flirtatiously on the side of its hill, bedizened in red roofs, a new playing field and an exorbitance of roses. She turns to show her tower and then discloses a piazzetta that might have been designed for *l'Elisir d'Amore,* crowded on Sundays with Italian vacationers dashing in and out of shops and bars, hanging around the smiling stage set. Though fairly isolated, Santa Fiora hasn't dreamed away the centuries; one has a sense of enterprise: the playing field, a stand of new, modest houses, a place for near-stylish dancing. Older charms, neither depressed nor abandoned, include a quote from Dante which reports that Santa Fiora was secure from the feuds of medieval lords, not exactly lavish praise, but then not *every* village was mentioned by Dante. It is not a large town; spend a while tasting it, going in and out of its streets, which often lead to breath-taking views, and linger for a moment at the pool, whose trout flash through the clear waters of springs fed by the snows of Monte Amiata. The *pieve* (parish church) is unpretentiously attractive and full of the works of the della Robbias, especially Andrea. (One finds a good deal of painted or glazed terra-cotta in communities that would have preferred marble but couldn't afford it.) These are sometimes overburdened by colored fruits and leaves; the most chaste, an Assumption in blue and white with few traces of other colors, is also the most richly detailed and delicate, yet vigorously alive.

Returning northward to Castelnuovo dell'Abate, ascending, twisting, descending through vine and olive and fruit and via a short, rough spur of road out of that village, one comes to the Abbey of Sant'Antimo, standing in superb isolation among the olives. The narrow road is blocked by a parked car, and to everyone's irate pleasure—if one is traveling with Sienese—the license plate identifies it as Florentine. *"Senz'altro!"* (Of course!) The path is cleared by an embarrassed Englishman in a borrowed car and the abbey offers itself for closer perusal as a distinguished example of French Gothic on Romanesque and warmer, more appealing than one would expect of such ancient, solitary grandeur. There are reasons for the almost intimate charm: the columns that nest the altar, the enfolding gesture in the narrowing flow of uneven naves, the presence of two irregular small chapels that clasp the semicircular apse and, mainly, the pale travertine and alabaster decorations that radiate a subtle luminosity.

For a time the abbey was in high favor, granted much land and benefices by the Pope and powerful enough, in the thirteenth century, to engage Siena in battle. Fortune's wheel turned, papal faces frowned, the abbey decayed and was suppressed in the fifteenth century. There is nothing left of the treasures that must have blazed the church but a wooden crucifix, an equally ancient Madonna, a group of pale, retouched frescoes of Spinello Aretino and, near the altar, a stone inscription that dates the building to 1118. The rest is immense space under a very high ceiling, the wizardry of medieval sculpture in the alabaster capitals and a tiny crypt, part of a ninth-century structure. The full impact, however, of Sant'Antimo comes with walking around it, to watch the arrangements the tower makes with one tall cypress, to follow the ripples of chapel, to sense again the utter loneliness.

The campanile, its turrets, yellow-gray stone houses and their caps of faded tile turn and turn over the deep valley as one mounts to Montalcino and its fortress, as dour and ponderous as any, but an endearing place to the Sienese because Montalcino was the seat of the Sienese government-in-exile, starved out and beaten by a combination of Medici and Spanish forces in 1555. It is a telling experience to come with a group of Sienese who cast a polite look at the handsome court, let their eyes linger on the shield of Siena over the portal and move on to stand tearfully—even after a gay, bibulous lunch—before the banner that led the cortege of several hundred families who would not live under Spanish rule. It is a tattered, faded flag that depicts the Virgin and Child and a saint, possibly Joseph, to echo the story of homeless wanderers seeking shelter and bears a legend about Siena's indomitable struggle for liberty. Reading the legend in a choked voice, the spokesman of the Sienese adds dramatically that this banner, this torn flag which shouts "Libertas! Libertas!," is the last vestige, the last cry of the free commune in all of Italy and maybe in all the world.

The town, extraordinarily perched, offers the staggering views and the old churches of many Tuscan hill towns and, as well, two inviting small museums, the Civic Museum and the Museum of

Sacred Art (part of the ex-convent of Sant'Agostino), that share some beguiling works and a few superb ones, such as a set of panels by Bartolo di Fredi and a jewel of painting by Sano di Pietro. In the collection of illuminated manuscripts, there appears a Bible written and painted in the twelfth century, and in the display of local ceramics, well-designed pieces of several centuries. Since it is a courageous, confident village—its history includes routing the Spaniards—Montalcino has organized an Etruscan museum, too. Have a look—it is a pocket museum—but save whatever Montalcino time remains for walking around the village and following the disk of Tuscan countryside that opens from its streets.

Whether one chooses Pienza first or Montepulciano makes little difference in distance, but there is a chronological logic in starting at Pienza. (Count on the better part of a day for both towns and the curious beautiful-ugly countryside between them.) Centuries ago, the hamlet that is now Pienza was part of the domain of the Abbey of Monte Amiata and later the property of the potent Piccolomini family, whom you met several times in Siena. In 1405 the family produced in this rural holding a son named Aeneas Sylvius, who grew up to be a fair example of the Renaissance gentleman—clever, politically adroit, a connoisseur of the arts, a friend of poets and artists, a traveler who stopped to observe the courts of Germany and Austria. When he turned to the church for a career, he rose steadily—the Piccolomini name was no hindrance—to become Pope Pius II at the age of fifty-three. His escape from the dissensions, wars, power plays, mercurial alliances and general chicanery that invested his time was a dream of building a regal city, an annex to the papal court, in his old home town. He contracted with the architect Bernardo Rossellino to build a cathedral on a piazza surrounded by palaces, and by 1462 there was enough Renaissance splendor to merit a name, Pienza, the city of Pio II.

The square, as Renaissance urban planning would have it, is balanced, contained; pugnacious rustication is subdued here to frame without violent contrast the dignified white marble façade of the church, pared to a simple perfection of classic themes. At the side of the square is a matching fountain whose slender pillars are crutched by metal supports attached to a neighbor's wall. It is said that Pio II was so pleased with Rossellino's church—a serene temple outside, and inside a lightness and gaiety brought from German churches, brushed by the Gothic and adorned by contemporary Italians—that he cursed with denial of the comforts of the church whoever might cause its destruction. How does one excommunicate shifting earth? The church still stands and lures, but it must be shored up periodically at great expense and then threatens with a new, unexpected crack.

The sacristans, who maintain a fresh passion for the church through the many years they serve it, are especially proud of its sneaky scorn for masons. They insist that Pienza's church has a better list than that of the tower of Pisa and they position one here, there, at the side of the altar, in the center of the nave, to point out with considerable delight that a column is distinctly not parallel with the line of a hanging censer, the window out of plumb with a vertical of decoration. The sensation is that of being in a fun house or the queasiness caused by the light tremors of a minor earthquake. Entranced by the eccentric beauty, the sacristan points out Gothic, Romanesque and Saracenic (obscure or invisible) bits and the portrait of Pius II in the Assumption by Vecchieto, which he calls the *capolavoro* (masterpiece) of the church, although you might be better pleased by a Sano di Pietro. Stunned by golden flights of Sienese angels in peaked, carved frames and the turbulent pleasure of their guardian, one is apt to overlook another and possibly superior *capolavoro,* the marble altar in a side chapel by Rossellino. Don't neglect it, nor Rossellino's splendid font in the baptistry, where the sacristan may point out a fanciful progress of spheres of power in the faces of the putti: the first innocent and angelic, a second with the face of Mussolini, the third like the Chinese Mao, a fourth with a negroid profile.

The Museum of Sacred Art, still on the piazza, presents the insistent dilemma—had enough? want more? In any case, it is not large, its contents don't demand close attention except for an unbelievable cope of medieval English needlework: dozens and dozens of scenes of saints' lives, which must have absorbed countless hours and hands and eyes of devout women.

The surprisingly pristine condition of the Piccolomini Palace, to the right of the church façade, is the result of careful resuscitation by members of the family early in this century. It is not an enormous palace, and many of its fifteenth-century magnificences have gone elsewhere; there is still enough to please the eye and shape a reality of ducal living: massive, thronelike chairs; chests large and small, inlaid with delicate ivory and boldly carved; fine ceramics, signorial fireplaces, ornate ceilings of Spanish leather patterned like brocade and one that combines carved and painted wooden boxes in a manner that creates clever repetitions of square P's for the family name; red velvet, twisted columns and a Sybarite's bed for the Pope; a sedan chair; family portraits; books bound in parchment; a collection of armor; a group of musical instruments; priceless rugs; homely spinning wheels. The best, however, is a loggia at the back of the palace that gives on a hanging garden and an infinity of landscape that enfolds Montalcino and the peak of Monte Amiata.

Several palaces built by reluctant cardinals fill the rest of the piazza and its immediately adjoining areas and, across from the church, the indispensable café from which one watches and begins to judge the quality and mood of the present town. Young people are lacking, and Italian noise; the old men sit silently, the dark-clad women walk singly and resolutely to the bakery to deliver the cakes they have just taken out of ovens, to deliver the bundles of linen they have just finished ironing. It is obviously not a prosperous town, and after a quick visit to the façade of a thirteenth-century church (turn left at the fountain), its adjoining cloister busy as bar, club and kindergarten, and an expensive antiques shop, walk into the streets prettily called dell'Amore, della Fortuna, del Bacio, to taste the gray poverty that is too self-respecting to enjoy the ebullient garbaginess of a poor town in the south. The via della Volpe achieves liveliness by draping grapevines on its houses and laundry, then tightens to become the via Stretta, really narrow, a stony slit with a view. One finds a noble stone seal, a small garden terrace and surprisingly few flowerpots (for Italy)—and those are frequently tin cans. There is a citizen on the Largo della Chiocarella who maintains a plankful of flowerpots that curtain a window, and, below, another citizen planes wood in a troglodyte cave at the side of a strip of court that leads to narrow, faceless tunnels. And there is the via della Bucca, also clothed in vines, and the naked via Torta, which winds to the via Gozzante, a street that hides its gray bones with children and cats and that incredible view. It is all clean, very, and the walls are raw or patched, their bricks and stones gapped like fallen teeth; beautiful textures and tones for painting, hardly as satisfying for living since the cardinals stopped buying services, wines and girls and hurried back to Rome and their family palaces in more entertaining centers.

The 15 kilometers between Pienza and Montepulciano loop through late-summer fields of tawny, faded velvet, crumpled pale tans and golds, beards of russets and dark scars of burning; the wrinkled blurred hide, scraped to creta gray here and there, of an old lion. The houses of hay, preparing for winds, wear their tassels of rope and stone to hold the roofs down, the tall stacks gathered on a pole have been sliced down like great golden cheeses. Circling under hills, around minute villages of one tower and one steeple, past silos, cows, pigs, turkeys, chickens, one courses through the very veins of Tuscany to Montepulciano.

Those of Florence are of course Fiorentini, those of Lucca, Lucchesi, and the people of Siena call themselves Senese, logical identifications. The citizens of Montepulciano call themselves Poliziani, in honor of a brilliant young man—a humanist scholar and a native son—who collected manuscripts for the Medeci and wrote an early version of the opera *Orfeo,* and as a reminder that theirs is one of the perfect Renaissance enclaves. In the shared history of many Tuscan towns, Montepulciano was Sienese property, then Florentine, then changed about again, countless times, finally to remain Florentine. In 1511, Florence sent the architect Antonio da Sangallo the Elder to rebuild the fortifications of the city. He stayed to build churches and new palazzi, in such numbers and at such speed that he called for his son and Vignola to help. Although it may not have been as precisely planned as Pienza, Montepulciano profits from being a larger unit that consists of a greater variety of palazzi in more highly developed style (the time gap is more than half a century) and an atmosphere of a big city—in miniature—were it not for provincial art-nouveau swags on its shopfronts and its museum, a fascinating provincial clutter. (They may, at this printing, be gone; too bad.)

The small *cortile* of the museum, in a Sienese-Gothic palace at 11 via Ricci, near the crest of the town, is the usual prickly box of old odds and ends that leads to a nineteenth-century tutti of dog-eared postcards, a few pieces of fine furniture, a silver mask of the patron saint of the city, a stupendous clock, a della Robbia frame, at least one urn to keep the Etruscan franchise and, inevitably, some books of Poliziano. The gallery proper, which has arranged easels and wall supports to wrest good light from its limited windows, gives the same undiscriminating space to an excess of poor Tuscan painting (from insipid to ridiculously mannered), to daubed curios, to paintings that deserve respectful separation from the common herd of works. It is this grab-bag quality, the "what next," that makes it attractive. Here a fifteenth-century Babe on a golden tray, the rest of the manger and entourage so precisely painted as to appear Flemish or a tour de force by Dali. There, a dark almond-eyed androgynous Christ bathed in blood. The head of an old woman, possibly by Caravaggio, is so thoroughly immersed in mannerist chiaroscuro that there is little left to see but a wrinkled, sunken mouth, and perhaps that was the idea. A Coronation of the Virgin by Spinello Aretino is a fantasy of pattern and colors swirling in a courtly dance. Unleashed fantasy of a later time appears in a long panel of *The Triumph of Joseph the Hebrew;* risen from lowly estate, he now sits in a golden chariot, wearing a crown and ermines, preceded by a flurry of trumpets and followed by warriors in Roman armor. A seventeenth-century painter sees Cleopatra with flowers in her red hair, windy drapery and a storm-stained sky as background for her pearly breasts.

One of the charms of the museum is that its labels and booklet do not always agree. The booklet says that a bitter, intense portrait of the sixteenth century is attributed to Tintoretto; the label says no. A portrait described as the work of Rembrandt is labeled Ribera. (It affords a certain pleasant freedom, an open field for one's own expertise. And, incidentally, the booklet is worth having not only for its helpful map but also for the new color it gives to English: "A. Allori, said the Bronzino," "The altars were paid to Andrea della Robbia hundred bushels of wheat," "the devant of the altar dedicated to the Father God.") Whether called "scuola" or more directly and courageously labeled, the Dutch collection is impressive for a small museum. It includes a "youthful" Hals in which everything is uproariously gay, even the cat; two Sustermans, one of a shrewd man and the other a cannily observed stern, elderly woman; and from the hand of Vandyke, a robust, pink-cheeked, clear-eyed Peter the Great. The most memorable work, however, is a Saint Francis by Margaritone d'Arezzo of the late thirteenth century. The booklet describes it as a *stupenda tavola;* it is—thin, tall and hieratic, blocked out in restricted forms except for the dramatic curve of the saint's hood. From the cowl, under the straight Franciscan fringe, peers a worn, innocent face, looking out at the world with candid, worried eyes. It may or may not have been a portrait; yet one feels it to be *the* portrait, as definitive as Holbein's Henry VIII or Velázquez' dwarfs.

The major art of Montepulciano is primarily its palaces, Renaissance and earlier, which line the two long streets that struggle up the hill, changing their names as they pause for breath but generally referred to as the via Ricci and the via Roma. Across from the Museo Civico is the Palazzo Ricco, a fine work of either Sangallo or Peruzzi (intense building activity in a short period and lost records make specific attributions difficult at times); toward the top of the town is the Palazzo del Capitano in the Sienese style of the fourteenth century and, at the very top, the Piazza Grande, quite grand and a compendium of styles. The Palazzo Pubblico, of the end of the fourteenth century, sits on one side of the high, hushed square and on the other stands the Palazzo Tarugi, perhaps by Vignola, perhaps by one of the Sangallos; in any case a light, gracious house, serenely balanced and ornamented, accompanied by a Renaissance fountain occupied with lions, griffons and heraldry.

The Duomo came some time later to replace an older church whose tower remains. The bare scramble of bricks and stone on its unfinished façade is hardly inviting; the interior improves matters with distinctive ironwork, a famous "Lily" Altar of Andrea della Robbia and a richly colored triptych by Taddeo di Bartolo. The altar is guarded by two large Renaissance androgynes, Faith and Science, supposedly ladies and supposedly *capolavori* of their time; for us, now they serve as prophecies of the twenty-first-century unisex. Nothing to worry about nor be amazed by—except their beauty—in the two Annunciation figures carved in wood by a fourteenth-century Sienese, Francesco Valdambrino, and a glowing Madonna and Child of his compatriot, Sano di Pietro. The via Vanuzzi shows *its* palace, the Palazzo Contucci, whose honors teeter again between Peruzzi and a Sangallo, then slips down from the far side of the piazza to the house of Poliziano and a curious meshing of spaces, not quite stairs, nor slopes, not yet country nor still town; an arbitrary division, however, attempted by a loose flow of stairway that ends in a flourish of long, easy volute.

As relief from palazzi you might want to explore some of the lesser divertisements of the city, the improvisations on themes of grandeur, for example, neither rich enough nor talented enough to quite make it. On the via Ricci, at Numbers 8 and 10, there is a small brick easel for a Maltese cross over white classic bandings, and those over a stupendous window edged in a stone pasta of curves. The door is capped by a gorgeous broken pediment and accompanied by two plump bunches of fruit and leaves, which turn into volutes. It seems so overscrupulous a study of the neoclassic as to appear an eighteenth-century English confection, by Robert Adam perhaps. A neighbor at Number 2 leaves a more generous field of brick and white stone to surround its mustachioed, armored, long-curled cavalier, imbedded in a curvaceous niche under a ponderous stone crown.

At this point the via Ricci takes a jog, dips under an arch and gives way to the via del Paolino, the church of San Francesco on its vast, unused piazza and, below, the green banners of Tuscan fields changing in tone as sun and clouds chase each other across the sky; a red toy farmhouse, distant animals that move like bacilli on a slide, fringes of tree, and the compact shape of the church of San Biagio trailing a dark avenue of cypresses. Another sort of landscape, jocund and intimate, reveals itself in the twists and turns that lead to, and become, the via Parri: flowers dripping from balconies and roofs and walls, leaping at each other from opposite sides of narrow paths, bursting from minute triangles of piazza, crawling up paths and in and out of classic urns, hugging the balustrades that zigzag with the stairs that tie up the various levels of the town.

Ultimately the splash of flowers pours into the via Cavour. To the left is the Palazzo Cervini (by Sangallo the Elder for the future Pope Marcello II), designed as three sides of its own miniature piazza, discreetly shapely and the quintessence of that amorphous word "taste." A countrified version of the same quality floats through the tight streets off the via Cavour; the via dell'Oste, for one, a deluge of flowers on creamy walls, glittering cleanliness, the triumph of taste and civic pride over medieval cramped dark.

The agora of Montepulciano is the via Roma where, in skillfully hand-lettered manifestoes, each party accuses the others of the rise of terrorism, of complicity in the Soviet repression of Poland, of inciting student riots and of starving pensioners. At about number 12, there is a handsome palazzo in advanced decay (strange for this careful city), then a slit that opens another, less dainty medieval quarter called the dark (Buio) Borgo, which is followed by majestic doors and sturdy, gleaming knockers in another stretch of palazzi. Soon, an aged clock tower, its striker a black-masked Pulcinella in the traditional broad hat who combines with the irregular piazzetta below to compose ready-made operetta scenery. The street widens to the Piazza Manin and the church of Sant'Agostino in the frequent disconcerting mixture of beauties and beasts. Its façade is well-proportioned Gothic-Renaissance, encompassing stately wooden doors, finely carved floral ornaments and a handsomely wreathed rose window. The tall, light interior is worthy of better things than the mess it vaults. The stars of its show are a company of big, shining, newly painted plaster monks who serve as entourage for the knifeboard Madonna mourning over a ghastly Christ with a big hole in his side. Elsewhere, a frightening Christ weeps and bleeds superrealistically under his crown of thorns, and to make it all gay and inviting for the bambini, the church fathers have installed in a chapel of its own a Disneyland crèche: a little bright mill wheel splashing water, a comet and star that flash on and off, dozens of doll people and cute animals, a gaudy sentimental background and a music machine that pipes in an interminable stream of "Silent Night."

You can catch your breath and revive your taste for things Italian during the moments it takes to walk under the arches of the via della Cantine into a fan of tiled roofs splayed out over faraway fields and, back on via Roma, to see the kaleidoscope of colors made by hanks of wool jammed into bookcases on the street. The palace at Number 29, not contented with the Renaissance, wears studs of Etruscan and Roman stone, while its palatial neighbors prefer to share their march down via Roma with cafés, a few antique shops, an itinerant knife grinder and crisscrossed rainbows that spring from a stall of myriad plastic toys. The toys usually shine from the walk in front of Vignola's Palazzo Avignonesi, whose rusticated stones have been gentled and the usually belligerent grating on the lower windows bellied and pulled back, like the swoop of a kite, into a final, courtly curve; the grooved pilasters leave their cold channels to coil gracefully in a finishing flourish. At either side of the portals, there are weeping lions, vanquished relatives of the Marzocco, the ruling Florentine lion in the adjoining piazza.

San Biagio, a familiar patch in the diverse canvases of view from the town, is at the end of a short ride and not too long a walk on the Strada di San Biagio. The phrase "nobly classic" is the usual shorthand—and it is difficult to find a better phrase—for this church designed by Sangallo the Elder and finished in 1545. It is a Greek cross in pale-gold travertine, shaped of colossal columns and pilasters surrounding classic ornaments that move in large, calm cadences. The dome is a harmony of alternating niches and columns, its own *tempietto*. San Biagio is Roman, Greek, a light suggestion of the Egyptian. And Renaissance, as a re-creation of the artistic best of the antique world and as a symbol of man's new stature, grown to stand with God among rational harmonies in heavenly luminosities.

Note

Montepulciano's favorite restaurant was and probably is Dal Cittino, near the Palazzo Cervini. There is no décor, nothing one would call cuisine and, between one and two in the afternoon, frequently no seats on either of its levels. You will naturally order the much advertised Vino Nobile of Montepulciano and you will be disappointed; it is much like other red bottled wines and lacks the snap of less exalted, more authentic juice served in plain carafes elsewhere in the area. Your neighbors, however, will be more satisfying—the black-suited merchants and farmers who crowded the lower city gates earlier in the day to discuss crops, prices and local politics, and the local intellectual, addressed variously as *professore* and *commendatore,* a perpetual-motion talking device who can turn six companions into mutes, no mean accomplishment in talkative Italy.

San Gimignano of the towers, just enough left of its dozens to suggest the actuality of a thirteenth-century city, begins to play peekaboo soon out of Colle di Val d'Elsa, northwest of Siena; now a low and distant dream cloud, later more substantial as a dream skyscraper city floating above an incomparable stretch of Tuscan landscape. The landscape is a delight of patterns created by civilized fields, low, long gray-green clouds of olives, dark vines bounding through squares of golden corn, the dark and the light joining to slip softly down to a brook, rising to a crest of perfectly spaced trees. (It is quite conceivable that one might spend several happy hours riding back and forth between Poggibonsi and San Gimignano—becoming increasingly convinced that once upon a time a local sovereign ordered the perfect landscape painted and had his peasants lay out their fields in strict accordance with the canvas—with an occasional deviation into a lost hamlet that is not yet sufficiently impressed by the automobile to give up its age-old custom of spreading corn to dry on its main and only street.)

You will see, among the towers of San Gimignano, the commemorative tablet in the Palazzo Pubblico that marks Dante's visit here as unsuccessful peacemaker between warring factions; glance at Lippo Memmi's Maestà, a shallow copy of that by Simone Martini; look at the rest of the town's civic collection and the chic Gozzoli people who accompany Saint Augustine on the walls of his church, lead and supporting cast free of the slightest whiff of the moral torment that the saint suffered; eat too much of the local nut sweet (*panforte*). And then you may decide to stay. San Gimignano owns at least one good hotel, La Cisterna, whose sophisticated restaurant has talented cooks, a good cellar and windows that frame Tuscan views. Unless there is an opera performed in the piazza—a now-and-then summer thing—there will be nothing much to do in the evening but walk among the mossy old shadows, watch the late daylight glide down the towers and wait for the quiet illumination that lowers a mysterious, romantic veil on the town.

Volterra

As the floating towers of San Gimignano disappear, the mellow hum of Tuscan landscape becomes a snarl, soft greens turn harsh to rise in crests of raw anger, exsanguinated gray veins score the unyielding earth. The moors of the Maremma have begun to drag their uncharitable way to Volterra and on to the sea.

Before mounting to the heights of the city, continue on the lower road for about 2 kilometers, skirting the bitter valley and stands of Etruscan wall, into a scrappy trail of houses of alabaster workers dominated by an immense, taciturn church. The end of the road falls into an immeasurable hole still tearing at the earth. Near the surface, the yawning depth is lined in gold-yellow that descends to gray, crusted with scrubby bushes, and below, far below, a hell-maw of broad, matted jungle. Near the perilous edge, tomato-sauce cans, grape stems and apple cores, left by citizens who haven't the courage to move closer to their bottomless garbage dump.

Under the distant green mat of this earth flaw, called Le Balze, much of Volterra lies buried—its Etruscan necropolis, Etruscan temples, Roman temples and dwellings, chunks of ancient wall, medieval churches and palaces—and the fact that the edges of the city are even now eaten by the void may explain Volterra's mood, sharpened by its tall isolation in cold mists. It is not inviting or engaging, or flirtatious as many Italian towns are. It is aloof and poignant, a city of hard, gaunt beauty, clean of light charms. Decline from prominence as a potent principal of the Etruscan League and the crumbling of the ground at its feet have made of it a Lear whose hauteur and rages are now muted, austere resignation.

Landscape, yawning Balze, Etruscan wall and the astonishing Piazza dei Priori shape the quintessence of Volterra. The piazza is ringed with weighty buildings, one of them, the Palazzo dei Priori, finished by the mid-thirteenth century and, consequently, the oldest seat of government in all of Tuscany. Should you come on a Saturday, make it the afternoon, because there is a morning market that mars the severe perfection of the square and its palaces of lay and ecclesiastical powers.

As the eye slips down along the gray stones, the piazza takes on life and color from its big café, from the fruit stalls and the black-aproned ladies who attend them inside the piazza arcades and especially from the large shop of the alabaster cooperative, full of flying horses, huge green turtles and gigantic vases that hold full-blown carved roses, all in alabaster.

One of the fruit-filled alleys will lead into the double-arched vicolo and via delle Prigioni and on to an avenue of Renaissance palaces, whose low windows covered with grillwork permitted princelings to watch the street life of lower-class bambini. The via di Sotto shows a medieval complex recently freshened, the Casa-Torre Toscano, and at the end of the via Sarti, on the streets of Buonparenti and Ricciarelli, several other tower-houses among the Renaissance palaces. The church for the medieval buildings was probably San Michele, its outer tranquillity disturbed by décor which includes a Madonna and Child derived from the della Robbias and improved by violent color.

South of the Piazza dei Priori, by way of the via Turazza, sits the Duomo, an expansion of an earlier church to the Pisan-Romanesque (thirteenth century) one now sees. Local authorities like to think that it was the work of Nicola Pisano, to whom a number of similar structures are attributed. Pisan it is, though not of a master hand, displaying the customary light and dark alternations of stone, the winning blind *loggetta* balanced by geometrical designs in colored stone. The long side of the Duomo is the wall of a large chapel, almost a church in itself, that holds such attractions as a fresco by Benozzo Gozzoli and a skilled fifteenth-century manger scene in painted terra-cotta, and repels with its accusing Virgin stuck with an armory of knives. The Duomo proper (redone in the sixteenth century) is, at first glance, a savage wilderness of columns and arches and stripes. The walls are hung in gold-striped red brocade, the confessional boxes adorned with purple satin, the total effect barbaric, fauve. Many of the details are in the usual church-decor idiom, except for early woodwork in the apse, two sublime candleholder angels by Mina da Fiesole and an artfully real and just enough unreal Madonna and Child in polychrome wood attributed—and opposed by a number of knowing voices—to Jacopo della Quercia.

Past the Baptistry follow the via Flacco and its mazes of adjacent paths that rise from and slide back to the wall and the panorama of unhappy countryside. You will surely have noticed innumerable alabaster chess sets, ashtrays, vases, urns, animals, what have you, in various degrees of excess or control of design, in every shop; in bars, in bakeshops, in stationery shops; on a set of planks in a garage. Working in alabaster from nearby quarries, as is abundantly obvious, is the town's industry (not a particularly lucrative one), and it is in these streets, near the wall, that one finds a concentration of ateliers, small workshops that live in clouds of chalky white. The artisans are white-capped, white-aproned men with clown white faces, and women in whitened kerchiefs and housedresses streaked with white dust; white plaster heads, used as samples, seem to be frozen faces disappearing in snowdrifts. The process is interesting to watch, a craft that calls for sure control of a cutting wheel and fine judgment in the use of a variety of files. It is startling to see the speed with which a file eats into the side of a vase and satisfying to watch the artisan space the notches and score them, one precisely as deep as the other, in little time and confident, economical gestures. As you watch, make sure to stand at the side of the window, often the only source of light, and don't ask too many uninformed questions, or any at all if your Italian requires long pauses while you search for words; friendly foolishness may cost a worker some portion of his meager earnings. And don't try to go into the workshops; no selling is done there, and a number emphasize the fact with a sign, "Vietato," forbidden.

The street properly called Laberinti twists into scraps of court patched with ancient steps and fresh new stone and everywhere the white alabaster dust. The sudden sky, falling to vast emptiness, is framed by the Porta all'Arco, the wide high Etruscan tunnel on whose façade bulge three dark masses, once heads, whose present facelessness stares bewildered and displaced on the valley. The broad street of the gate rises toward the Piazza dei Priori, taking with it old houses, a piece or two of alabaster in every window and one novelty, a metalworks shop that also turns out objects in wood.

Up and up and up the stairs of the Palazzo dei Priori, confronted by escutcheons and wreaths in a diversity of media and styles, until one comes to the guardian's apartment. He unlocks the door to a curious, eclectic collection of paintings: an early Pietà of a disproportionately small, full-grown Christ lying in the lap of an enormous Madonna while static angels deplore; shapely Sienese figures imbedded in golden niches by Taddeo di Bartolo; a sharply etched, winning set of small panels of the life of Mary by the fifteenth-century Benvenuto di Giovanni; a mannerist Deposition, of distorted modeling and grotesque expression; a Domenico Ghirlandaio *Jesus in Glory with Saints,* slick and discreetly goldshot, rather like a good color photograph for advertising heaven. Equally sleek yet infinitely stronger is an Annunciation by Luca Signorelli, an enchantment of gossamer veilings, full curves, classical ornaments and impassioned perspective. Though the collection is mercifully small, there is more to see if you have the time for it and for the council room on a lower floor. The Sala del Consiglio Comunale is a resplendent room (refurbished in the sixteenth century) of painted vaults, lamp holders shaped like griffons, the walls covered with a bright design of linked shields and at one end of the chamber a blond Annunciation attributed to Jacopo Orcagna, the brother of the more gifted Andrea. The adjoining smaller council chamber is especially attractive, almost filled by an enormous fourteenth-century table surrounded by handsome tall leather chairs and on the walls, sections of rescued fresco, one believed to be a San Gerolamo of Luca Signorelli, and a respectable portrait by a member of that talented community, "Unknown" (*ignoto,* or *anonimo,* in Italian).

In spite of its pieces of color and design the stone palace is not a comfortable place; it seems, like the piazza itself, haunted, and one yearns for the street and people. The via Guarnacci, a busy shopping street of warm, low shops like crowded kitchen hearths, stops at vicoli with telling names—that of Sant'Angelo, of the oven (*forno*) and of the killing or butchering place (*ammazzatoio*)—and then continues on to the Porta Fiorentina in an antique portion of the city wall. Immediately left of the gate, and downward toward a greener, more hospitable stretch of landscape, one finds a nice juxtaposition of new playing fields and a Roman theater, a few of the columns still standing, stage and pit arrangements clearly discernible, and behind these, a large rectangular clearing that may have been part of the theater or the site of a neighboring temple. A street that hugs the wall, Mandorlo, strays into a number of vicoli that house ancient workrooms under equally ancient arches. In front of the shops is a common back-street sight, large rocks of alabaster, some rough, some smoothly rounded and minutely scored as if they were pieces of finished modern sculpture, and all around—on the walls, on the pavements, on the cobbles and in the hair of tumbling babies—the alabaster powder.

With Volterra's Etruscan Museo Guarnacci (called, as they all are, "Archeologica" to admit older, newer, other finds), one meets again the stumbling block of how much Etruscan is enough? Whatever the immediate answer, consider the fact that Volterra was a dominant center and its unfaithful earth an omnivorous hoarder, and that the white-veiled ghost has scraped up the money and energy to build an inviting showcase. The mixture is necessarily as before, after and elsewhere: a city of the dead in countless sarcophagi and cinerary urns; pottery black and terracotta, fumbling to deft Greek; bronze as pins, mirrors, containers, helmets and figurines; carvings in stone. Difference and rarity emerge, as always, in pieces that crawl out of the mass of clichés to stand alone and uniquely pleasing, and here they have the additional singularity of being worked in alabaster.

The injustice of prepackaged selection, particularly of such a carefully shown collection (except for the miscellaneous "let's dump everything else in these glass cases" on an upper floor), can be justified only by straitness of time and interest. If this holds for you, the contents of the package might include a prodigious headless figure holding a headless child, an Etruscan inscription pressed into one of the arms; an imaginative display of white architectural ornaments on walls of yellow-gray and green; among the stele a bearded, spread-legged, bold Assyrian figure; a serene head touched by an archaic smile; one of the many coarse-headed, small-bodied effigies slouched above a lively set of figures, the relief so high as to seem free-standing sculpture. The alabaster urns are often elaborate compositions of dead worthies with straight-out ears (a sign of Etruscan beauty? a tribal characteristic?), accompanied by dashing chariots and spirited horses. Among the many repetitions of mournful farewells, a troop of warriors equipped with horses and spears and accompanied by musicians saying a moving goodbye to one of their company. Somewhere in the assemblage you will come on a number of boxes whose pagoda tops are decorated with rams, griffons and dolphins, and a Roman husband and wife sarcophagus, she staring hard into his inattentive face, insisting, "Look me straight in the eye and tell me where you were last night." A breather in the formal garden of the museum now, and then up the stairs to an alcove that holds a useful lesson in accommodation—an old and present Italian strength—an Etruscan urn equipped with a medieval lock to safeguard the remains of San Clemente. Beyond a richly designed piece of mosaic are the inexhaustibly engaging Tanagra-like figurines; fine small masks and animals, a tiny voluptuous lady, a remarkable hand and the attenuated Giacometti-like people in bronze. In the muddle of heaped cases, delicately worked ivory objects and glass, frail alabaster vases and a superb bowl, and in the collection of refined jewelry, a pair of earrings which consist of a tiny black face capped in filigreed gold, as worldly as a Cellini ornament.

Reminders of the dead turn heavy and morbid in the church of Sant'Agostino and continue along the streets that surround it as shopwindows filled with glass cases marked "Pax" and "Requiem" for household shows of *mementi mori*. Forget it and continue southeastward to the formidable *fortezza,* similar to many that punctuate Italian walls. The complex was originally built in the fourteenth century, remade and enlarged in the fifteenth by Lorenzo, the magnificent Medici. It was a dungeon in Renaissance times when the city was dominated by Florence and for the last hundred and fifty years again a prison. Not much of it can be seen, nor would one necessarily want to visit the ponderous grimness. It might be of some small interest, though, to know that the older semielliptical tower is referred to as "Femmina," and part of the Medici contribution is a round tower called "Maschio."

The innumerable churches wait, breathing slowly and heavily, and the inevitable Museum of Sacred Art, which, if you insist on being thorough, is to be found on the via Roma as part of the Episcopal Palace. It is the streets, however, and their tangents, the chalky dwarfed workshops, the fiercely uncompromising central piazza, the Balze and the walls that mourn the desolation they look on that make Volterra unforgettable.

Notes

Although Volterra is worth slogging across the moors for, on foot if necessary, it may not be worth a night's stay. However, the Albergo Nazionale, on the via dei Marchesi, quite central, will afford you a modest room. As for eating, the restaurants are countrified-decent and crowded at lunchtime on market day. The town has unalloyed rural tastes; the hare that appears on menus during the hunting season is enthusiastically spiced and the local wine undiluted and heady. A notch above the others in worldliness is the Etruria (on the Piazza dei Priori), which has outdoor tables. Il Porcellino, named for the animal mounted on the tower of the Palazzo Pretorio, sets its tables on the narrow sidewalk of the via delle Prigioni. On the same street is Da Beppino, a favorite with some of the market people. In the general melding of conversation, there is often one hoarse, loud voice, that of an indefatigable tiny old man from the country who can ingest wads and runnels of spaghetti without stopping for one second his calliope discourse. To oppose his hyperactivity, for a while fascinating, for a longer while a nuisance, there is the ample calm of the proprietress-waitress, a smooth-faced Etruscan Ceres.

Lucca

LUCCA MIGHT BEGIN in the tourist office of Pisa, where the mood of gay oddities is set by the fact that information on Lucca is sometimes available only in Dutch. (The office in Lucca is, however, better supplied.) Then, in only twenty minutes by bus or car, through orchards and vines, along canals and yawning quarries, under crushed fortresses and above spunky small industrial plants, past tunnels and bright new gas stations, one reaches the talkative world of Lucca, its ebullience enhanced by contrast with subdued—one almost writes "submerged"—Pisa.

Behind the Pinacoteca off the grand Piazza Napoleone there is a small street, that of the spinners (dei Filatori), which leads to the treed walk on the city walls, both echoes of the apex of Lucca's history, the twelfth and thirteenth centuries, when her power was as great as that of Florence and Pisa, when Lucchese silk and banking found their way throughout Europe. So famous was Lucca and its wonders that a sacred oath, used by William II of England, it is said, was "per sanctum Vultum de Luca," referring to an image in the ancient Duomo. The mood of Lucca is no longer of ancient might, though relics of rich piety remain to enhance the town; the wall, a specter of sieges and famine, burn-

77

ing and blood-letting elsewhere, has been pleasingly fleshed out as a broad esplanade. It is the longest of its kind in Europe, the city's park for taking the air and views, built through the sixteenth into the mid-seventeenth century, when the struggles for supremacy over other Tuscan cities were long over and the silk industry still prosperous.

The aura of lightness may be attributable to the fact that the city was under the control of women at various times, first the Longobard Matilda, early in the twelfth century, and much later, two ladies seriously concerned with uplift, public works and the cultivation of the arts: the sister of Napoleon, Maria Anna Elisa Bacciocchi, and shortly after, Maria Luisa the Bourbon. Add to that the innumerable minute piazze and engaging vicoli, each with its bar or trattoria—three tables on the street and groups of men playing cards, reading newspapers, arguing mildly.

And Lucca offers the people-watching pleasures of an almost interminable *passeggiata* on its shopping streets. The boys stroll together, as do the girls, except for an engaged or extremely enlightened pair. Fluffy baby carriages act as prow for a family cutting its way through the crowd. A girl in a smock, carrying a pile of shoe boxes, a boy with a tray of cakes, still in his white work coat, press purposefully through this leisured world of which they are not yet part. Small gangs of adolescents wander through the crowd like desperate lost sheep and always, enlacing and releasing groups of strollers, little boys who push and pommel each other. The city is for outside, for the mélange of its periods, for the wild joy of decoration on its churches, for the extravagances of ironwork in street lamps and the painted ceilings in shops. A few of the churches are justly famous, and there is an impressive museum that absorbs the treasures of those decayed and abandoned, but with Florence nearby and Pisa around the corner and Siena not too far away, these don't call for studious attention, and that can be a great relief and Lucca's greatest asset.

Wherever one turns there is an invitation: to the vivid piazza that hums around the splendors of Saint Michael's church, to the distinguished museum, to medieval towers and Renaissance palaces. It might be reasonable to start at one of Lucca's earliest monuments and one of the city's prime delights. Carrying the map supplied by the tourist office on Piazza Guidiccioni, cast a dazzled eye on San Michele (the time for concentration will come later) and go behind it to the via Buia. Pondering the mystery of why this is called the "dark" street in a townful of narrow medieval paths, looking into shopwindows, examining one brilliant display of door handles in a diversity of materials and contortions, you should come to the Piazza dei Mercanti, an outdoor living room filled with tables and umbrellas, flower boxes, potted trees and well-dressed, well-padded people. The toy square opens to the shopping street of Fillungo, which curves and turns easily, almost voluptuously, in its free-of-traffic hours. It shows an impressive number of jewelry shops, one of which is dignified by two sets of triple windows in carved dark wood, like sections of choir stall from a baroque church; perhaps they are. A modern shop of glass and cool order faces a beribboned, ladylike old sweetshop; glass eaves and silvery art nouveau in the well-fed, optimistic late-nineteenth-century French style shine out of a tangential alley.

The widening of the street as Piazza Scarpellini presents a proletarian face of inexpensive clothing, baskets, bird cages, bellows, plastic auto seats and an arch that says "Anfiteatro Romano Sec. II" and "Mercato." Roman amphitheaters and markets are hardly rarities in Italy, but there are few, if any, like this combination of Roman oval circled by medieval houses of fairly uniform height, interrupted by small arches and four tall portals that must have been the entrances to the theater. Although the soft yellow brick wears an occasional balcony dripping varicolored blankets and sports the ubiquitous lines of sheets, the effect is of a smooth-surfaced antique ring—unlike many pieces of antiquity, devoid of sadness, even when the lusty wholesale market is finished. That is, actually, the best time to go, undistracted by the market noise and color, accompanied only by a few parked cars, a pile of crates, six mashed peaches and tomatoes, a few spirals of orange peel and lettuce leaves that eluded the garbage sacks, and one lone, stubborn vendor who insists on sitting with his remaining watermelons and tomatoes.

Vestiges of the theater also cling to the outer circle of streets and houses, but vestiges of Rome are inescapable and better seen elsewhere. Return, instead, to the via Fillungo, which ends at the Virgin and Child over the arch of the Portone dei Borghi, a doorway to the large Piazza Santa Maria, crowded with souvenir stalls among its bars and trees. Having shopped or rejected, turn back toward the arch to find the via dei Carozzieri and then left, to a sight of Ghibelline swallow-tailed turret cheek by jowl with an ignoble red-brick building of international "Victorian" style, past a lost street which contents itself with auto-repair caves, to the apse end of the church of San Frediano. The balustrade of the wall-esplanade launches two lions and eagles of stone who stare down on the superb tower of the church, and below, following the columns on the apse, flows a shining stream of copper ewers, kettles, lamps, andirons, braziers, candlesticks and bells that comes to rest at the patient flank of the church. On a wall above the brass and copper, a piece of unabashed Italian prose in stone: "Here Niccolo Paganini was a guest in 1809 of the family Bucchianeri. Love and poetry tormented the genius but the musical city gave his magical violin the wings of glory." It could have been a less florid strophe, but it wouldn't have been Italian.

The majesty of the twelfth-century Basilica of San Frediano draws from its isolation on this edge of the town, fairly quiet as the rest of Lucca is not, and the plain façade, which cedes all attention to the large thirteenth-century mosaic that rises at the top. It depicts Christ's Ascension with two large angels at either side and, below, the twelve apostles, six and six, arranged on either side of a glistening lancet window. The columns that divide the three dignified naves bear, as one has come to expect in very old churches, interestingly varied capitals. The reconstructed twelfth-century baptismal font, whose templelike upper section is crammed with biblical scenes, is a good example of mixtures of influences from the north, from the southeast and, strongly, from the Roman sarcophagus. The most rewarding objects, however, are several sure, vigorous works of the Sienese sculptor, Jacopo della Quercia.

The via Anguillara has nothing to offer but a short walk through a bit of Luccan charm; simple houses, a piece of thirteenth-century overhang, a strip of sixteenth-century grating and one tree, a green balloon soaring out of a yard. The via Fontana is laden with Renaissance window cages; the via degli Angeli and the via Battisti bulge handsomely with palazzi, mainly of the seventeenth and eighteenth centuries, breeders of great doors and huge knockers, ornate ironwork balconies hung with graceful lanterns and strong stone frames around the windows. One doorway finds room for masks, urns, trumpets, shields and fruits and a baby riding a sea monster on a recessed plaque, rather like a baby's tub floating in a sea of late-Renaissance stylishness. Although a number of these palazzi are their own climax in style, the superclimax is the Palazzo Pfanner of the late seventeenth century, on the via degli Asili, quite large and fronted by a vestibule that leads to an extraordinary complexity of arches and colonnades surrounding diverse sweeps of stairs in a confusion of perspectives that only the Baroque could create or sort out. At the corner of the via degli Asili and the via San Giorgio stands the house where the composer Catalani was born, and off San Giorgio (near the via Moro) is the mighty Palazzo Santini, now the Municipal Building, originally of the fifteenth century.

From the windows of houses and the Teatro Comunale del Giglio and from record shops, you will have heard, wherever the banshee cars and motorbikes permitted, strains of good music, worthy of the place that sheltered Paganini and gave birth to Boccherini, Catalani and, above all, Puccini. You can pay your respects to him by sauntering through the bowed shapes of wood and glass usually called "Dickensian" and bolder Empire ornaments on the via Calderia to its meeting with the via di Poggio (Number 28-30), where a swan and lyre enwreathed in laurel speak the city's homage. According to the tourist-office map, the house of Boccherini should be on the via Roma, but whether they are mistaken or the plaque was taken down, at least one visitor couldn't find it.

Lucca's second major piece of sorcery is the façade of San Michele, too tall for its church, which was meant, centuries ago, to be enlarged and heightened. The thirteenth-century ornamentation of the façade was added and added to, until now it is an overlarge, irrepressible giggling thing, and enchanting. It has no caution or restraint or modesty but, like a child dressing up out of a trunkful of clothing and costume jewelry, puts on everything. The base is fairly sober, a matter of tall blind arches in which are imbedded the commonly seen recessed stone diamonds. Then, the soaring of four orders of slender columns, each determinedly different from its neighbors; some writhe, a few are knotted, some swirl, a few limit themselves to geometric patterns in zigzags or diagonals, others take on zoosful of animals in singles, doubles and heaps, and when there seems to be no room left for the thinnest breeze to enter, a few columns shed forms like bark dripping from trees. Saint Michael and two angels stand at the summit to call a stern halt to the dervish dance of decoration.

In the middle of the endless Piazza Napoleone there looms a heroic, effulgently sentimental goddess, crowned and appropriately draped, holding a scroll and a flower-tipped staff, casting her large maternal shadow on an adoring young Apollo. The monument erected in MDCCCXXXXIII (a pedant has penciled in a correction, substituting XL for the four X's) was an act of gratitude to Maria Luisa, who brought *acqua salubre* to Lucca, water which is still salubrious but doesn't taste particularly good. The goddess faces a long stretch of yellow palace, which grew and grew from its beginnings as a fortress designed by Giotto, some fifty years later demolished by the local citizens because it was occupied by enemy Pisans. In the early fifteenth century it was the site of the fortress-palace of the powerful family of Guinigi (of whom we shall hear again), battered down by an explosion when lightning ignited the gunpowder storage. The present building, the Prefettura (police matters), is of more recent themes on a late-sixteenth-century plan. Its interest to the general public, not specifically involved with the police, or the society for the prevention of TB, which shares some of the abundant space, is the general lordliness and the Pinacoteca, reached by way of an arcaded court and a stairway crammed with nineteenth-century coffering, griffons and wreathes and Lillian Russell angels in peplums threatened by Corinthian jungles on the pilasters. Having come this far, one might as well see the collection, which includes a few attractive "unknowns," several extraordinary portraits by Bronzino and Sustermans, the work of

Beccafumi, Andrea del Sarto, Pontormo, Tintoretto and Titian, but by no means in profusion. This collection of the art treasures of Maria Luisa was once much richer, depleted for selling by her Apollo, her son.

The Pinacoteca is open from 9:30 to 4:00, closed Mondays and open only until 1:00 on Sundays, but you might prefer to spend limited museum time in the recently reorganized Museo Civico, off the Piazza San Francesco, on the via della Quarquonia as it meets the street "of the bastard." The restored fifteenth-century villa was that of the governor–war lord–dictator Paolo Guinigi and is now being filled, skillfully and intelligently, with examples of antique arts and decorations, spiced up by the presence of passionate, neoclassic ladies who grace the garden at the side of a graceful arcade. Sarcophagi? Of course, and Etruscan jewelry and Greek vases and bronze figurines, most effectively spaced, and a Roman mosaic that shows a poised lady who had the presence of mind to bring along her umbrella before being happily carried off by a sea monster. The range stretches over several centuries, to include the early, naïve pieces of church ornament often too high to see properly on their native walls: curly lions and docile bulls surrounded by circlets of stone braid, birds and trees on a Celtic cross, stone inlays carrying little monsters, lissome lady saints and rigid apostles. (And notice, as you go, the considerate structures that support the art and the details and design of the villa itself.) Of the fifteenth century there is a fresco, marked "Tuscan," that shows a style close to that of Filippo Lippi, and of the seventeenth, a particularly winsome tapestry angel. A Civitali Annunciation in high relief is so skillfully made that a magically carved vase takes the eye from the greater event and its personages. In quite another style are the quick, small figures by another native son, Urbano Lecchesi, who lived and worked in the nineteenth century.

An interesting section—and one must keep insisting on the taste and appeal of the arrangements—deals with vats and measuring cups of copper and wood and yardsticks (one measures the *braccia lucchese* used for the famous silks), and on an upper floor, luxurious house furnishings and ecclesiastical garments, and yet more church art. It is here, as in other Italian museums, that the incurably repetitious sets in, conducive to an open-eyed blindness that sends one speedily through and out, having seen nothing. Try to stop for a few exceptions; for example, a Christ by one of the Civitali, a tender and earthy fifteenth-century Madonna whose Child embraces the large, high breast like an eager young Oedipus. Another work, steeped in the mannerisms of the late sixteenth century and completely diverting, shows David sitting on a white horse, wearing a plumed hat and bearing on his standard the head of Goliath; around him a bevy of garlanded maidens in flowing Renaissance-classic gowns dance and tootle on recorders, more nymph than nice Jewish girls.

Along the green string of canal and its miniature bridge on via del Fosso to the esplanade and a stroll among the trees, or southwestward, now, to the via Guinigi, engaged in the difficult job of maintaining its historic elements while offering hospitality to baby carriages, window boxes and kitchen curtains draped around chatting neighbors. The family palazzi absorbed not only this strip but most of the surrounding neighborhood in the thirteenth and fourteenth centuries, not necessarily out of love; mutual protection was the primary purpose of medieval clannishness. The red-brick structures, which might be dour were they not pierced by rows of trilobed gothic windows for a lighthearted Venetian effect, must have supplanted clumps of medieval tower. Now there is only one conspicuous tower left, older than the house it leans on, a jaunty old knight with great plumes of trees waving from his scalloped cap. (The best view of the tower can be had from the via Mordini at its meeting with the via delle Chiavi d'Oro—street of the golden keys—which must have been a reference to the rich family.) At the corner of the via Sant'Andrea, across from the tower, you might identify the shape of a medieval loggia, where members of the family gathered to witness marriage processions and funerals, and near the top of the street of the Guinigi, the small church of Santi Simone e Giuda, stripped and almost derelict, which needn't hold you except for its unusual saint in polychrome wood.

There may still be on the via Mordini a gayer memorial to Puccini, a café called the "Fanciulla del West" in opulent golden

letters fitting for her time and the composer's. A neighboring
barbershop is fringed with gorgeous chenille ropes; other, earlier,
gorgeousnesses are the door knockers of the via Fillungo where it
takes an angle for a run southward. Along with its shops the
street carries tangents into clusters of Lucchese specialities: on
and near the parallel street of the Moro, well-preserved medieval
houses and the church of San Salvatore; around the corner from
the roaring pizza establishment on the via Buia (you are back on
Fillungo), the thirteenth-century Torre del Ore, which stopped
striking the hours five hundred years ago; the ponderous medieval palace once inhabited by a Barletti family and, at its side,
the Chiasso Barletti. It is a gaudy alley swelled with inexpensive,
basic shops that favor lengths of pink plastic tubing, small restaurants and cafés, noisy card players and comfortably padded
ladies billowing over kitchen chairs set among eel-like swarms of
children.

Out of the Chiasso (one of whose definitions is "noise") one
continues southward to the house of Lucca's sculptor, Matteo
Civitali, whose praises, sung from the wall, include the statement
that he was the first to portray the male nude in the full round
after the resurgence of art. This makes sure that detested Florence doesn't claim the honors with Michelangelo, born thirty
years after Civitali. The enthusiast apparently forgot about Donatello, born fifty years earlier. Another tower or two, one of them
attached to a neatly restored house of the 1200's, brings a confrontation with the church of San Cristoforo, which asks nothing
but a long, admiring look, deserved for its good proportions and
rose window, the easy flow of the gray and white banding and the
carving in the restrained decorations. The effect is more Pugliese
than exuberant Lucchese, except for the presence of two metal
bars that determined the standard measure for silk in 1296, when
San Cristoforo was the church of the silk merchants' guild. Under the modest wooden ceiling, a Madonna remaining of a pillar
fresco, a few candles on an unadorned altar, a stone that represents the tomb of Matteo Civitali (although his actual remains
are in an unknown place), his artist sons remembered on one of
the pilasters, and the names of Lucchese war dead, to whom the

church is now dedicated. The rest is nothing but solemn emptiness enclosed in a calm, sure drawing of arches, pillars and
ceiling.

Near the house of Catalani, on the via Roma, find the Corte
dell'Angelo, which leads into a neighborhood that is so artfully
picturesque as to seem to have been arranged for the nineteenth-
century sketches that poured out of Italy by the thousands—a
collage of mattresses airing and sheets on lines, cats and pigeons
stepping around each other, wooden balconies spilling flowers, a
newly painted door, an old door swinging from one hinge and a
glass-covered shrine painting. By way of a meager alley one
emerges to a piazza shaped by a café, a house that bears the
tracery of older shapes and the side of the church of San Giusto,
of the twelfth century and lavishly carved at its main portal. At
the end of the piazza, the well-designed dark-yellow Renaissance
palace, attributed to Civitali, which now houses the Cassa di
Risparmio.

The church of San Martino, the Duomo, was designed in the
thirteenth century. The tower, rising as increasing numbers and
slenderness of openings, crested with battlements, is in the Gallic-
Lombard style, as is the façade, much like that of San Michele
though it lacks the ambitious height. That which San Martino
lacks in height, it makes up in density. (The naïve, show-off joy
of both façades brings to mind the story of the juggler whose best
form of worship was to juggle the balls for the Virgin's amusement.) Lions nip at something or other on the bundles of columns of the lower arcade, and the columns above, again different from each other, sprout fruits, leaves and animal figures that
prophesy Le Douanier Rousseau. A few columns make do with
diamonds and linear abstractions, and one seems to be a misplaced souvenir of the leaning tower of Pisa. Heads meet at the
joining of arches, so do roses and pomegranates, and all connec-
tive tissue is engraved, stamped and embroidered in every imag-
inable way while it maintains the predominating contrast of
green and white.

Inside the portico there is more unique matter, less gaudy and
more imposing as significant places in art history. Among the
brilliantly colored griffons and snakes, there are sculpted panels

of the life of Saint Martin and a group of allegories of the months that escape the dry stiffness of the early thirteenth century to become sculpture with a fullness of volume and freedom of movement that indicates high talent and singular advance, particularly marked in the decapitation of Saint Regulus which appears over the portal. Above another door there is a Deposition that at first glance seems to follow the crowded compositions of Roman sarcophagi, but the urgent gestures and emotion that force their way through dust and wear, the sagging deadness of Christ and the fluidity of draperies make important departures from the classical model.

A drop from the near-sublime is to notice that one corner of a wall is protected by spiked arcs of iron, an ornament in corners of many churches. They may have had a particular, other purpose in older times; now they serve to keep the corrosion of urine from seeping through exhausted walls. Turn back to the façade, to Saint Martin dividing his cloak with a beggar, a copy of the original inside the cathedral and, like the portico panels (though not necessarily by the same artist), a breakthrough to Gothic naturalism, the nature of man and horse restudied from life rather than Roman and Byzantine art alone. The tall, serene interior space encloses a light Gothic matron's gallery and a *tempietto* designed by Matteo Civitali to house the famous Volto Santo, rarely brought to public view. There are innumerable picture postcards to show you the large Crucifix of wood in Byzantine style, laden with armorlike chunks of worked gold, the image a Romanesque copy of a ninth-century original. At one side of the large reliquary is a Civitali Saint Sebastian, easy in his arrow-pierced flesh as the Renaissance liked him to be, and elsewhere, several works of the Civitali family—font, pulpit and tombs, one of them accompanied by angels as fresh and free as Bernini's, almost two centuries younger.

The dome is too high and foggy to show anything of its painting except that it swirls cloudily, nor are several paintings by masters easily visible, particularly those buried in thick marble frames. The masterpieces inside the church are two works of Jacopo della Quercia, created within the first ten years of the fifteenth century. One is an austere, spare translation into stone of Saint John the Evangelist and the other a tomb for the young Ilaria, the wife of Paolo Guinigi. As other sculptors have wrested from the marble religious awe and the might of princes, Jacopo has drawn tenderness, which breathes from the folds of Ilaria's gown and the little dog of fidelity at her feet; it perfumes the chaplet on her head, makes silk of her stone cushion and hushes the wings of the cherubim that guard her.

Walking to the right from the apse of the Duomo, past antique shops and clutters of old things, looking back on the campanile and sides of the church, one comes soon to a magnificent yew tree on the via Della Rosa and near it, the tiny church of Santa Maria della Rosa in Pisan-Gothic style (look at the detail along the sides), built by the Merchant's Guild at the beginning of the fourteenth century. Continuing on the retiring street, the Pisan-Gothic enthusiast will find, to the north, the church of Santa Maria Forisportam (thus called because it was outside the city walls in the thirteenth century, when it was built), which shields the familiar lion chewing on a lizard and a Virgin and Child of the twelfth century. The avoider of churches, scorning their age and spinsterly charms, can take the via dell'Arcivescovado, a street of antiques and religious articles, of a large shrine with an ugly Crucifixion and several old street lamps. Or, find the gayer street of the Battistero, which leads to a small introductory piazza that announces the amiable Piazza dei Servi and its Santa Maria church. (There is no avoiding ecclesiastical bulk for long.) That Piazza narrows, then opens to the battered face of the church of San Bernardini and a long ocher house of steady, remorseless horizontality, the apogee of Renaissance fortress. It is a sulky building, but get close enough to examine the door knockers, a design of cross-barred Saracenic circlet under the head of a Moor in a mantle of leaves.

The via dell'Olivo, off Santa Croce, wanders inviting curves of paths, where one meets the church of San Quirico serving as a movie house, stable doors, horses' heads as rosettes on a band of stone, small cafés, balconies, shrubs, flowers, always laundry, arches with green beards, cats and orange peel and a fountain that forgot its purpose centuries ago. And this can go on all day and into the night and more days and more nights, if extra feet were part of the imperfectly planned equipment of the human body and if time would allow itself to be held. You might start back via the city's later adornments, mainly commercial and busily concerned with cute babies. (A *profumeria* on the via Roma once draped ten lively ceramic children along its façade. Near the back of San Michele, a high-class emporium of imported groceries fancied itself in elegant pillars, and over its doorway, babes gamboling among leaves. A shop that sold cloth, an electrical-supplies neighbor and a pharmacy were each host to a pair of ceramic children, all white and plump and nude, under flowers or sitting on wine kegs or involved with grapes; one precocious Lolita wore a small shawl, a hat and an umbrella, nothing more; some of it may last into your Lucca time.) Negozio d'Ombrelle lives in aristocratic sweeps of gold lettering. And everywhere there are plaques. Possibly more than any other city, with the exception of London, Lucca praises its famous men, indigenous or merely passing through, with wall ornaments. They stay even when the legends have been erased by years and the elements, as has happened to two handsome, romantically mustachioed and coiffed gentlemen, apparently brothers, who turn their stormy, artistic glares down on the Piazza dei Mercanti where you have returned for a final mound of *granita di cafè* and another last gaping at the *passeggiata*.

Notes

The leading hotel is the Napoleon, followed by the Moderno on the via Vincenzo Civitali and the Universo on the Piazza Napoleone, both fairly moderate, and a scattering of small *alberghi* attached to restaurants and card players. Consult the Ente Provinciale about these.

The class restaurant is the Buca di Sant-Antonio, on the via della Cervia. If the Universo is functioning, it should offer a satisfactory meal. Should a wedding or First Communion party have taken over, try the Giglio next door.

The city also has innumerable trattorie. You might try one near Puccini's house, part of the Albergo di Poggio, or an *alber-*

goristorante called La Pace near the church of San Michele, or another on the Corte Portici, to indicate random examples. For a collection of snacks in the nice old cultural center, try the Antico Caffè Casselli.

The best, because the largest, place to park is the Piazza Napoleon. Lucca's is reputedly the best olive oil in Italy, of the first pressing and greenish in color. Not too cheap in Italy, but prodigiously expensive on your home turf. Whether you try to lug a bottle or two home depends on your passion for olive oil and bargains.

It is not easy to find, but many consider it worth the small trouble; a restaurant called La Mea, on the lovely old road that runs from Lucca to Camaiore. Two-thirds the way to Camaiore, you'll notice the name splashed on a slab of wood. The rest looks like a long-abandoned farmhouse. Venture in among the loosely related buildings to find one high-ceilinged room covered with a startling variety of pictures, the sort that are often gifts of artistic friends. Wine is served in big bottles and the food is as generously brought forth: wonderful pasta, veal cooked delicately, like gigot, a small chicken smashed flat and spiced with nectar. This may be one of the last of the country *locandas* in the area—a family enterprise as many of the old ones were—and a place to respect and cherish for its integrity, longevity and merciful prices.

The Subject Is Eating

IN THE PORTFOLIO of misconceptions carried on a first voyage is often a vision of Italian food that is a simplified reduction to pasta and veal drowned in tomato sauce which would taste of iron filings if it weren't heavily laced with garlic. Garlic in tomato sauce is, however, not the national elixir; north of Naples you will find it in comparatively few dishes or unobtrusively wafted through a more complex sauce. Unlike the bread you are served at Luigi's or Joe's around the corner, Italian bread—from a crusty, huge country loaf through half-empty rolls, to wheels and deformed little planes that have the brittle consistency of pretzels—frequently lacks salt. It is taken for granted that the drippings one wipes up will supply the missing flavor.

An Italian's concept of hot and cold differs considerably from yours; his palate abhors intense heat and cold. If you want your soup hot, ask for it *caldo, caldo,* and if you want your coffee cold (*caffè freddo,* black and sweet), have the barman give you a piece of *ghiaccio,* ice. Outside the major cities, it is a struggle without rewards; near-warm and near-cold are the best you will be able to achieve. Accommodating as he would like to be, it is difficult for an Italian to understand the masochism of searing or freezing one's tongue and taste buds, or exchanging temperature for flavor. Thus fruit, bred for intensification of flavor, not looks, is allowed to perfume your table at room temperature. It may, in the country, still be wrapped in spiderwebs, still inhabited by a patron spider (all taken care of by a bowl of water served with the fruit), but it never arrives as pretty little corpses done in by white chill.

An Italian bar, in our sense of alcoholic succor, is not. Although it often adorns itself with salable bottles of whisky and liqueurs, its purpose is to nourish sagging spirits bored with the day's work, aching to know the latest soccer news, incapable of lasting the long hours before the midday meal. The bar is first-aid station for these and other ills, dispatching visiting nurses in the guise of solemn, long-aproned boys with trays to those mired in one of life's unspeakable tricks, like jobs and weather. The black, condensed coffee it serves is taken in the twinkling of an eye, the speed of an injection. For slower ingestion—but always fast—the barmen steam out of their glistening machines the white-foamed cappuccino (named for the garb of Capuchin monks) and caffe-latte, coffee and nonagitated milk. Bars heap, depending on location and degree of style, open sandwiches, thin sandwiches on white bread, pizza dough and rolls in fetching, unusual combinations—cold fried egg and tomato, flattened artichoke hearts and bits of chicken, most of it bordered in baroque curlicues of mayonnaise. Less sturdy early-morning tastes are fed sweet rolls closely related to the French classics, brioche and croissant. The method of paying for these goodies may seem complex but in actuality makes for speed and efficiency. In large bars on main streets, price markers appear with each category of sandwich or cake. You make your tentative choice, tell the cashier the price and how much with coffee? She gives you a slip, after payment is made, to be presented to the men at the counters. In smaller places, habitués pick up their selections with tongs, place them daintily in small paper napkins (it is very crude to eat out of the naked hand) and then approach the cashier.

The late-afternoon transfusion for men is an apéritif, usually bitter, herbal and undoubtedly salubrious. The ladies content themselves with coffee and cakes in the wintertime, awaiting patiently the bounty of warmer seasons: *frullato di frutta,* a nectar derived of fruits mingled and mashed in a blender; *granita di limone,* lemon ice; *granita di caffè,* coarse coffee ice heaped with whipped cream unless one is quick to say, *"senza panna."* Or *la signora* may decide to refresh herself with ice cream *(gelato),* never more than a few feet away and portable in a cone with no loss of dignity.

The *tavola calda* (hot table, literally) is an amorphous institution of variations on the cafeteria theme. One selects from a repertoire of basics, then takes the dish to a counter and stool and eats it quickly; a *tavola calda* is designed for inexpensive, fast turnover rather than conviviality. Solitaries often eat in *tavole calde* because of their impersonality and the speed of order, ingestion and departure that takes the sting off eating alone, a sad thing anywhere and tragic in Italy. A *tavola calda* can be its own entity or part of a large café that sets aside one corner for the chairs and table, to which waiters bring one's selection, or they can be attached to delicatessens. These latter provide a wide range of cold meats, stuffed tomatoes and peppers, a few fried items for reheating and, always, pasta out of a ceaselessly boiling caldron. It would be unjust to expect too much of these places; a split personality rarely functions well. However, there is often the pleasant surprise and, always, the undemanding price.

For cheap, voracious feeding look out for signs on rural roads that hail a *sagra*—a country food fair of nuts, fruits, pork, pasta, sausage, bread; anything in season and abundance. The supply will necessarily be monotonous but ringed with country jollity and, besides, you may find regional specialties that rarely appear on menus.

The best and most expensive train eating is provided in the restaurant car, a boon on a long trip since it spreads a full meal over a fair stretch of time and fuzzes the remaining hours with stuffed somnolence. (Reserve for either of two sittings with the waiter who comes through the train.) Lower in cost is the airplane tray meal served at your seat. In theory you can choose from the menu left at your place. It doesn't seem to work out that way immutably, and if the meal you have doesn't match the meal you wanted, there isn't much to do about it; the boy who dropped the tray in your lap is gone quickly and forever. Unless you pack your own lunch, the best inexpensive bet is a *cestino*— a lunch bag—sold at many stations. The cost hovers at about $2 or a bit more, depending on how much food you think you will need, and usually includes cold chicken, cheese, fruit, rolls and wine. All stations, except those of remote lost hollows, sell sandwiches, ice cream, packets of lasagna and drinks, and if you weren't fast enough for the fleet vendors, there is succor from boys who ply the trains with drinks, coffee and sandwiches.

Should you begin to feel immoral and hear your seams groaning, it will be comforting to know that most pasta can be ordered in half portions (*una mezza porzione di . . .*). You can substitute for soup or pasta a delicacy called *bruschetta,* thick-sliced country bread toasted on an open fire, rubbed with garlic and doused with oil. Other possibilities are *porcini,* enormous, rich mushrooms that appear in late summer and fall or, in the spring and early summer, an artichoke omelet.

And on the subject of pizza, there is too much of it in Italy as in our own country. The ease of making dough platters to hold scattered bits of this and that has driven out the family that made its own pasta, invented variations on its own fine sauces and served only the freshest fruits and vegetables—and all of it at not much more than the price of pizza. The family gave up or, in many cases, joined the profitable pizza trade. Some day there should be a great Requiem Mass—as noble and dramatic as Verdi's—to honor the many Mammas and Babbos, waitress daughters and waiter sons and spinster aunt dishwashers who succumbed to the scourge from Naples.

Many of the lovely words that purl out of Italian mouths, you will notice, deal with eating: *"Ha mangiato bene?" "Si mangia bene." "Che mangiamo oggi?" "Dove mangiamo?"* All are invitations to long, animated discussions. Should you be on an Italian excursion bus that takes off at, let us say, 8:00 A.M., the exchange of greetings and autobiography will last until about 9:00, to be followed—first from one quarter, then another and soon burbling through the bus—by requests for a coffee stop, which will include a nibble of cake or a small sandwich. At 10:30 paper parcels will unfold and chunks of bread, slices of prosciutto and medicine bottles full of wine come into action. From that time on, until the lunch stop at 1:30, lascivious fantasies are exchanged about delicious possibilities: pasta, chicken or veal, salad, fruit and wine, always familiar, always a promise of pleasure.

The lack of interest in diversity, in new dishes (except in some tourist restaurants, with regrettable results), the deep content-ment with the accustomed, bespeaks an attitude toward a meal that makes of it a daily *festa*—like other *feste,* eagerly anticipated and tradition bound—whose opening ceremony is placing the slithering heap of gleaming pasta on the altar-table. Italian *joie* and conversation, the gurgle of wine out of carafes, the waiters who swoop, dance and murmur under their offerings are seduc-tive ornaments that deny monotony, as paper hoops and gar-lands of electric bulbs deny the poverty of a *festa* street. As soon as a restaurant menu becomes "international," no matter how good, the ebullient life seeps away, a hush settles. Unpretentious, friendly wines are discussed too lengthily, the ingredients of a dish described too respectfully, the waiters are no longer brothers or fathers; one is dining in an imitation of the French manner, cut off from the ruddy, noisy zest of eating in Italian.

The pace of an authentically Italian meal is distinctly musical. The first movement, the pasta or soup, is a *presto agitato,* fast and eager. The meat is cut, lifted and chewed in a calmer *allegro,* while the fruit introduces a stately *adagio* of slow, careful selec-tion, aristocratic discarding, exquisite peeling with knife and fork, the deliberate, slow jaws returned to serenity. We have now reached the interminable *lento.* Although your bread, wine and first course were brought with the speed that accompanies emer-gencies—a hungry man is a man in serious trouble—the waiter, having fed you, turns to more urgent matters, rather like the physician who no longer finds you interesting after the acute ailment disappears. It may be that, like other Schweitzers, he scorns thanks and money. Whatever, getting your check will take time and more time. And no one but your wife and the Americans at the next table will understand your impatience. Why should you be annoyed when you've been so quickly and fully fed while others, *poveretti,* are tearing their bread in agony?

One learns, in time, to sit out the waiter's evaluation of the state of his patients and begins to realize that the passion for Italian food is less a need for veal in six styles or chicken in three than a yearning for Italianness. So, even if your diet forbids you *penne, agnellotti,* fettuccine and spaghetti with a hundred names, you will eat pasta because you see it eaten with a total joy, a concentration of pleasure, as if it were a rare Lucullan dish rather than the habitual staple served at least once a day. You will plunge and wallow in the manipulating, slurping, moistly shining, sexy happiness, not so much to eat as to share the buoyant Italian greed for experiencing deeply, everything, from roaring in a winner at the races to the wash of peach juice in the mouth.

2

A LONG, LONG WEEKEND NORTH OF ROME

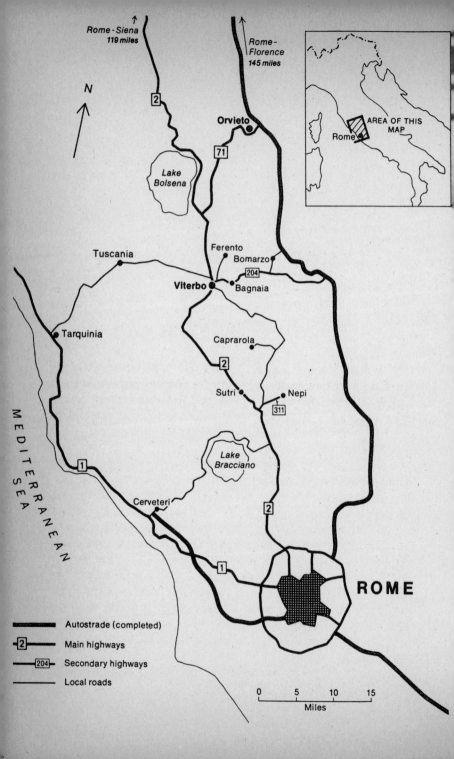

Cerveteri, Tarquinia, Tuscania, Caprarola, Sutri and Nepi

THE VIA CASSIA (SS2) is as old as the time when the Etruscans were having dealings with the growing provincial community of Rome. It ran through several Etruscan centers toward the outskirts of Pisa, where, centuries later, French pilgrims gathered to take this road, which they called the via Francesca, down to holy Rome.

Proceeding on the famous road, now leading away from Rome, for about forty minutes or so, depending on the traffic, then turning westward on the Bracciano road and southward toward the sea (not too long a ride over pleasant country roads), one comes to Cerveteri, or rather the necropolis of the capital Etruscan city of Caere, a formidable maritime power in the seventh century B.C. The city contended successfully, in partnership with Carthage, against Greek marauders for a time, but in the fourth century B.C. its largest port was plundered by Greek forces from Syracuse. In the general Etruscan decline, Caere soon became a Roman holding and continued to decline, a city defeated by crescent powers and the malaria that infected the coastal plains.

In spite of its unfortunate history and the fact that its present

interest is entirely—and over an enormous stretch of land—funerary, Cerveteri is a frank and airy place, a cheerful place for a
picnic and simple heathfulness: sun on the paths and shade in
the tombs, the mild exercise of climbing up and down into the
tumuli, of walking easily through alleys scored by ancient wagon
wheels and bumps of tufa (porous, volcanic rock) polished by the
sides of Etruscan funeral carts. And maybe the peaceful atmosphere derives somewhat from the soft, mammary roundness of
the countless tumuli.

You will see none of the burial treasures of art and gems sys-
tematically plundered in the nineteenth century and now held in
private collections and the museums of Europe. The finds of the
twentieth century, supervised by the government, are in the
Etruscan Museum of the Vatican and the Villa Giulia. One sees
only the overwhelming numbers of tombs and grassy tomb
mounds in burial modes of several centuries, a pitting and pim-
pling of tufa that must look like a moonscape from above. Between one rise and another, one passes a trench covered by flat
rocks or a round stone dug out to make a pit for an urn, or a
stone box for a child's body. These were the most primitive
tombs, probably of the eighth century B.C., which gradually gave
way to larger and larger mounds that held the remains of several
generations of one family, the rooms arranged rather as in
houses. If that is so, and experts believe it to be, the tombs are
the only remaining records of domestic building and decorating
styles used by the Etruscans. They often have beamed ceilings,
primitive false arches, connecting doors that slant outward in a
distinctly Egyptian manner, painted supporting pillars, stone
seats and chairs possibly modeled on the wooden furniture in
actual use and plain beds for men, peaked headboards for wom-
en. One of the community graves seems to be an annex of the
poorhouse, full of shadowy, open boxes, efficiently crowded into
no décor whatsoever; in death as in life the city ran the full
economic gamut from hives to palaces.

For some reason—lack of space, imitation of foreign styles?—
later burial places, as late as the second century B.C., were at the
end of long tunnels slanted into the ground. Skepticism might
have set in, or a fear of tomb robbers; one famous underground
room of the third century B.C. was not filled with real objects at

all. Its domestic utensils and weapons, lengths of rope, knives, bowls, helmets, pillows and pets were represented in painted plaster to become precise and attractive documents of Etruscan life.

The town proper holds on to its walls and towers of the Middle Ages and has set in one portion of its medievalism an unusually clever, engaging museum under an antique wooden ceiling, hugged by an appealing curve of medieval wall. The imaginative arrangements consist of fairly common Etruscan objects (if any object so old can be called common). The rarities have gone elsewhere, but, as always, there are one or two uncommon objects; here a pair of large, stupendously ornamented terra-cotta vases modeled on bronze originals. The major work, however, is the museum itself, which has deftly combined uncluttered medieval with uncluttered modern and achieved a model for small, provincial museums.

If it is time for lunch and if you haven't picnicked among the sunlit Etruscan dead, there are pizzeria and trattorie, near the main square and behind the museum, that spread generous areas behind their unprepossessing entrances. One neighbor of the museum had a large straw-covered platform below the walls, nice waiters and a very decent cook.

Tarquinia should begin with a visit to the Louvre, to several museums in Germany and to a number of important Etruscan museums in Italy, especially the Villa Giulia in Rome. But that is an expert's sort of vacation, and a little background of knowledge might suffice. It has had to, even for experts. The powerful Etruscan confederation of city-states—an indigenous government style still, at least psychologically, in evidence—mined iron for export in exchange for precious metals and jewels and art from the East, prowled the seas, from which it wrung impressive loot, spread and infused its agglomeration of cultures into a major portion of Italy over five centuries and produced people skillful enough to make astonishingly modern bridges of false teeth. But it has left no buildings, few documents, no literature, no as yet decipherable language.

Although the Etruscan language was obviously spoken by a

great number of people for a great number of years, although names and words appear on tomb paintings and sarcophagi, scholars have been able to identify little more than one hundred words and those mainly concerned with burials. The Etruscans must have left documents of their mining, their importing and exporting, the marauding and the conquests and defeats: how much it cost to build a tomb, who were the most talented jewelers and painters and how much they were paid; what slaves were captured where and taken where, to perform what work. Who designed the civil codes for the large, prosperous communities? Who of the leading families married whom? What were the bridal gifts and the ceremonies? Nothing, nothing is surely known. Greek and Roman accounts wander among legends, envy and fear. The only reliable witnesses are the boundless quantity of artifacts and art as sculpture and, particularly, tomb paintings— hieratic, lithe, Grandma Moses or worldly, sometimes touched, sometimes deeply affected, by archaic Greek, Hellenistic Greek, Indian, Egyptian; in short, ancient Mediterranean arts gathered and mixed to create the uniquely Etruscan.

The towers and turrets, the yellow-gray walls, the unreal, slightly demented Don Quixote presence—like that of a hundred Italian towns—that totters above the highway are Tarquinia according to the map, but not historically. This specter is the medieval town of Corneto, its name changed about thirty years ago to keep green the memory of Tarquinii, a major Etruscan town, whose actual site was a long flat rise a short distance away from the later town and clearly visible from the enormous necropolis. Following the upward turn toward the towers and turrets and the giant flowers of café umbrellas, one meets a small, distinguished museum housed in the attractive Palazzo Vitelleschi. The Gothic courtyard is lovely, and so is the loggia, with its fragile arches and well-designed wooden ceilings and a view that brings together all the golds of wheat and hay bordered by patchwork of red-tiled roof.

There are still, at this writing, a few unfinished dark corners in the museum, but many fine pieces already stand in well-designed modern glass cases brushed with a light that enhances their antique mystery. One room is devoted solely to a masterpiece of Etruscan art, a pair of not-quite-life-size winged horses, traces of terra-cotta color on their tensed coats now almost entirely dusky blond, the relief set off by a matte gray-brown wall. In another room, one finds pieces of exquisite jewelry and a few small bronze female heads, probably late and possibly once used as ornaments, to judge from the chains attached to their disdainful elegance. The pottery develops from simple terra-cotta cinerary urns, through distinctive black vases and urns with playfully busy handles and supports, to vases whose fine drawings of prancing satyrs and zesty nymphs and heroic, muscular conflict between gods is distinctly Greek in inspiration and craftsmanship. A small vase, signed by a master, is a buoyantly designed and decorated head of a woman who speaks of the same *joie de vivre* one finds in many of the tomb paintings.

For some years an upper hall was not quite ready for the public, but a request and a tip opened a long room of tentlike structures built around tombs whose decay was imminent. Some have been rescued almost too late, but there is enough to see in three or four tombs of a late period, a time when modeling in color and careful delineations of musculature had progressed but the earlier pagan awe and gaiety had quite gone. Many of the sarcophagi in the lower halls are much livelier, detailed with vivid carvings of animals consuming each other and topped by coarse, naturalistic heads and chests and foreshortened bodies that trail off like those of mermen. On looking closer, though, one finds the foot of a bent leg poking out of the shroud folds, again and again and in the same way, as if one craftsman's solution to a technical problem was quickly picked up by all the others.

The tomb trip, in one's own car or a taxi (unless you are on a bus tour), leaves from the entrance to the museum more or less on the hour, except those hours dedicated to lunch. With luck your guide might be a museum official, a knowing man whose Italian is slow and clear, his French fair, his English timid, although he understands more than he will betray. Whoever guides and whatever few of the many tombs are open to visitors, the visit will be indelible. Through poppy-studded wheat and tall haystacks, between the glide of long fields to the sea and the rise of dark blue hills inland, over paths bordered by red, white, pink and purple wildflowers, one comes on a strange landscape of low brick roofs that cover explored tombs and the round hills of dozens, maybe hundreds, not yet explored. Those explored long ago and looted were carefully covered again and shifting soil and grass restored the mound shapes.

A pause in front of the first tomb, while the guide chooses the right key from a big ring, for a bit more of once-over-lightly Etruscology. Tarquinia was the local capital in the confederation of twelve city-states. Bologna, of the deep, learned arcades and proud cuisine, was a northern capital. Alluring and forbidding Volterra, a keening, Hecuba city, was one of the confederacy. Perugia commemorates its Etruscan prominence with a massive arch. Orvieto was a capital city and so was Arezzo, as were a number of long-retired towns. The beginnings of this energetic, enterprising people is a misty scrim of several theories. From time to time, each theory stumbles on rocks of fallibility and contradiction: the wrong artifact dug out of the wrong place or an unsuitable vestige that shatters a neat timetable. One savant holds out for an indigenous western Italic people who blossomed and withered between the eighth and fourth centuries B.C. Another theory favors a migration of peoples from the east, primarily Greece, to these shores and their infiltration northward and eastward as far as the Adriatic coast. A compromise theory links an indigenous people, encapsulated as "Villanovan," with the seafaring invaders from the east; from this fusion of bloods emerged the Etruscan.

Whatever the origins, or the facts closed in the stubbornly taciturn language, the tombs still have a good deal to tell about the Etruscans, though there should, in time, be much more to learn when other tombs are opened. Local authorities say the tomb raiding began with the Romans who carried off jewelry, vases, works of art and the beautifully incised bronze containers that held favorite objects to accompany the dead, as they accompanied the Egyptian dead. The next concerted marauding was the work of the Renaissance, when the learned and art-loving, fired by the beauties of antiquity, looted several tombs. During the eighteenth century and the nineteenth groups of foreign scholars, sometimes under the aegis of Italian proprietor-princes, came to excavate and carry away. Late in the nineteenth century the tombs became government property. Through the many centuries there was always a peasant who fell into, or stumbled on, an aperture in the earth, collected a few shining things, covered the aperture and remained silent.

The tombs have names, not Etruscan, not important, simply designations derived from the name of the scholar who opened a particular tomb or from some conspicuous element in the design of the tomb. The keys are turned in the lock, the rough door is pushed open, and one enters a long, stepped descent through the mossy, metallic smell of damp age to astonishment—no matter how often one has seen how many reproductions of Etruscan tomb paintings, there is always breath-taking astonishment—at the slant-roofed little houses, usually one-chambered, covered with thoughts of death and celebrations of life. The oldest are priestly and stiffly Egyptian in their somber rhythms and the flat frontality of the figures with turned heads. They are exceedingly regal, though brought forward from their remoteness by obvious remnants of the painter's uncertainty. Redrawings and enlargements are frequently visible as, for instance, in the head of a horse that carries the young Troilus to an encounter with the truculent Achilles. The subject is conventional Greek; much less conventional is the crouching bull (for which the tomb is named) with a long tail, an elongated body, wide horns, a blue chest and staring, shocked blue eyes, possibly because he doesn't like the erotic goings-on nearby.

Some late tombs favor grotesque, frightening demons and repetitions of checkerboard designs on the slopes of the ceiling, vines and grapes clambering over each other along the imitation center beam. Under these slapdash designs, however, there are enchantments: suave, ardent dancers, lithe players of flutes and lyres and singularly Etruscan vignettes that urge a few basic pleasures. One triangular section, for instance, compresses a good deal of high living into its limited space. The narrow ends enclose a wineshop, a maker of wreaths, a dancer, an atelier of musical instruments. The center section is given to a large, plump gentleman, some of his avoirdupois obliterated by the censorship of time and decay; enough left, however, to show that he is wearing a rich necklace. One of his surprisingly slim legs embraces the back of an elaborately dressed lady, all bracelets and jewels and a tall sloping headdress over a flat forehead and slant eyes that relate her startlingly to Mayan ladies of another place and time. (Perhaps another thread of transoceanic influences to add to the confusion?) And even in the midst of sexual grappling she touches him lightly, delicately: the Etruscan touch that, beyond any other single element in this air, evokes the sound, the smell and feel of Etruscans.

Feasting couples—men bronzed, women pale, homosexuals a color in between—loll at tables covered in what appears to be Scotch-plaid tablecloths, the woman often in a beautifully draped and folded skirt, the drapes painted with the dash of Japanese prints. The man, in a simple, loose toga, speaks affectionately, animatedly with her, though she might be his wife. They may be watching a pair of dancers, he a young god whose arms and legs are long, slender vessels of contained vigor, she supple and womanly in a short minidress veiled by a long, voluptuously curved transparent skirt. (We still can learn from the Etruscans, if only about real sexiness.)

One tomb (about 510 B.C.) shouts joy. Young men fish, dolphins leap, a boy dives from a rock into the abundant sea while another boy scrambles up the rock to take his turn. The air is birds and birds, red, yellow, blue, who float and skim and turn in sunny rhythms under a string of bright garlands. The subtly varicolored sea undulates among striated rocks that spew bushes and flowers; fishermen gesture and smile in full glee. One boy, preparing to shoot a bird with a slingshot, is partially obliterated by the vigorous drawing of a tensed arm and the swelling strain of leg muscles that sings of youth and pleasure. There is no stiffness here, no "archaic" grimaces; this is a fullness of living observed by a keen, happy eye and an awesomely talented hand, recording pleasure cherished by the dead and, as it turns out, a rampant, noisy pleasure for the living.

It may not have been so for slaves, but the leisured Etruscan of 500 B.C. obviously led a robust life, robustly phallic and earthy. The tombs of men were often topped with phalli now partly hidden in obscure corners of museums. Even the later, solemn paintings that deal more overtly with death breathe fleshliness. A panel that depicts an old man being led—probably—to the land of the dead also shows an energetic terra-cotta body tearing off in another direction, toward life, leaving as testimony to his fear a spray of flatulence and a splatter of feces.

As a client now goes to the studio of a designer and decorator to look at swatches and sketches, so the prosperous Etruscan went to the ateliers of painters to choose motifs for his tomb. The choice and execution were frequently and naturally conventional though the convention included a wide range of influences. As in all times and arts, there were the innovators—the artist who painted the "Baron's tomb," for one. Somewhat later than the hunting and fishing exuberance, the tomb moves into a quiet of smooth, aristocratic elongations and the spareness of abstraction. A stately row of long-maned red and black horses, the red moving from right to left which is the direction of life, the black moving toward death (this is the guide's interpretation, as valid as anyone's in this ignorant time), sets off simply modeled and softly colored figures and plants contained in gray shadows. The effect is of a total stillness, a misty remoteness of serene death long ago and far away.

Among the regal and the playfully masked, the flights of drapery, the precise little trees, the twist of an arm and foot that echoes Indian dancing, the whirling skirts, the white women and sun-darkened men, the athletic nudity of slaves, the carefree eroticism, notice an antique symptom of an immortal Italian preoccupation: smart shoes in the usual Italian diversity of styles. And again and again, watch the hands that are in themselves dance movements and the touch of those hands, light and tactful, tentatively affectionate, never holding. It was the Etruscan hand and its gesture that moved D. H. Lawrence most deeply, and from its meanings for him he made a comforting, if rueful, portrait of the Etruscan as a direct, fleshly man not yet divided from himself nor severed from the roots and essences of living. Judging from the tomb paintings in Tarquinia, he may easily have been right.

This might be the time to explore Viterbo (page 113), and then round back toward Rome via Caprarola, a wine and fruit town that can be expected to reveal appealing fountained corners and crumbs of antiquity as other local towns do. Caprarola, however, uses its main street, ribbed with alleys that drop to broad views and dressed in flowered balconies, mainly as introductory passage to the overwhelming Palazzo Farnese, one of many Italian enclaves of talented, useless show, an immense box of tricks of unbridled imagination and unabashed luxury that was bought with High Renaissance money in homage to its own invincible radiance.

The pentagonal palace that stands behind two extensive esplanades and a moat was originally a fortress designed by the younger Sangallo and turned into a palace by Vignola at the behest of Cardinal Alessandro Farnese in the late sixteenth century. Although it is used as a government summer palace, the place has gone to seed—who can keep these monuments to vanity alive?—and it has lost a good deal of its finery. The Roman busts that stood in the niches of the *cortile* have been moved to the Farnese Palace in Rome. The splendiferous furniture that supported, fed and bedded royalty is also gone, and the once-nude putti that peek out of stone carvings now wear cobweb nightgowns. Led by a young guide, polite and indifferent, who lets one wait at the enormous portal until a group large enough to deserve his efforts has gathered (the hours vary, but 9 to 12 and 3 to 5 are usually safe), one mounts coil on coil of steps held by paired columns decorated in "grotesque" designs to reach the loggia of the *cortile* and then proceeds from room to staggering room, only a few of the many, but enough for most tastes.

Apocalyptic allegories tear across the ceilings above landscape paintings that are reviews of the palaces, fortresses and holdings of the Farneses in other parts of Italy, a series of self-portraits, in a way. From the windows there is the same commanding view, the breadth and depth of "king of all I survey" that marks the landscapes. The chapel makes its nod to religion with frescoes of the apostles and then relaxes with pagan flights and doodles in plaster work. Farnese pomp and glory reappear in frescoes of royal marriages, glittering offspring and mighty deeds in war and peace. And more and more huge, explosive rooms, frescoed and delicately adorned with plaster, and a stop in the "whispering gallery" to see if it really works and to look at the Archangel Michael, Daniel's angel and Lucifer plummeting from heaven along with his rebellious cohorts. The last room one visits is the "sala del Mappa-mondo," painted with evocative maps, probably correct in their time although one suspects an occasional aesthetic distortion; "Giudea" is a vast area, and Pacific regions then unknown are consequently unacknowledged. After a fleeting glimpse of the forbidden formal gardens that are part of the summer palace, one descends to the esplanades, which have evolved as parking lots, and to a ledge on the main street at the side of the palace. A gap in the street frames the church of Santa Teresa, dressed in smart beige and gray picked up with subtle contrasts of volutes and pilasters, quite like a small aristocratic palazzo that looks from cool, lowered lids at the blazing extravagance of its neighbor.

And on, still toward Rome, to Sutri. If one could manipulate time as it manipulates us, it should be noon on Sunday. Everyone is out in the Piazza del Comune, clustered around the dolphin fountain waiting for the all-day *passeggiata* (with time off for lunch, and a nap) to begin. The girls meet, kiss, admire each other's neat, homemade dresses and take off on their slow march through the town in twos and threes with arms linked. The young blades shake hands, clap each other's shoulders and then retire to sprawl like emperors in the seats of the café for leisured examination, plus sound track, of the sunny, ambling girls. Church is soon out and that which is Caesar's will be rendered unto Caesar later in the afternoon, according to a number of posters, in the form of a Communist Party meeting. (You may have noticed that this is not an overchurchly area and even lacks the usual coveys of elderly female church mice who wipe the dust off the angels; which doesn't at all mean that Italians find Communism and Catholicism incompatible.)

The Duomo has resisted improvements of its uncomplicated antique form and holds on to pieces of thirteenth-century Cosmati work and a companile of the same age. The interior is ordinary, except for the courtesy done two old pillars whose newer concrete covers have been grooved to let their elderly faces shine through. Below, there is the usual, and always strange, many-columned crypt. Often at this time on Sunday, the long empty interval between the last morning service and the end of the afternoon nap, there will be a few boys batting about, helping the priest. They will show the crypt proudly and efficiently; they know where to find the lights, the corners where sketchy old frescoes hide; they point out the variety of capitals on the numerous pillars. They know how to illuminate the casket that holds the remains of the local patroness saint in the chapel of the upper church.

With a small bribe—ice cream or, better still, the price of the matinee at the movies—three or four of these boys, or their cousins or brothers, will lead you through tunnels of wine smell, down cobbled slopes, into fragments of courts, greeting their friends and, for a dreadful minute or two, encountering a father who sits like a big-thighed Jove frowning down from his balcony. Jove, a suspicious man and a father who must make a show of power, calls back his son, who has already won your sympathy by being considerably uglier than the other boys and obviously something of a gangling, clumsy patsy. The father refuses to let the boy go on with you and the others. The son begins to cry heartbreakingly—catch an American boy of twelve weeping so readily, so fully—and drags his spindly legs back to Jove. If your Italian can manage it, you intervene to say that he is only performing the fine courtesy of guiding visitors through his *bella, interessantissima città.* Il Duce nods his slow, grim assent and you gambol down to the edge of town and across the Cassia highway.

Following the signs that point toward Rome, one soon comes to a wooded path marked "Villa Staderini." The path leads toward tufa walls and, poking out of the vines and shrubs that grow luxuriantly in the tufa, a tiny primitive house with crude irregular windows cut into the stone and a rusty lock that seems to be quite locked. The boys have no difficulty with it, and you walk into the most elementary of basilicas, darkly and unevenly chopped out of its matrix. The anteroom is scored with shallow troughs very much like the communal burial shelves in Cerveteri, and above them, sections of medieval frescoes. The church as church proper is defined by an altar of tufa at the end of rough-hewn columns on which are pasted Stations of the Cross that might have been torn out of a Sunday-school primer. The boys find the lights, which reveal nothing more than details of the extraordinary crudeness and, on the floor, many used flash-bulbs, the souvenirs of a recent wedding, the boys say—and they know.

This church of the Madonna del Parto was probably part of an Etruscan necropolis, to judge from the troughs and the tunnels and niches cut into the surrounding tufa. (The boys demonstrate the frightening pleasures of this exotic playground by climbing up to a pitted, dark stretch of stone, peering into a hole to recoil, shouting happily, "Bones, bones and what a stink.") Later, the site was probably a Mithraic temple and, soon after, a hidden meeting place for the rival cult, Christianity.

Farther along the via Cassia one comes to an "Etruscan" theater, not usually enterable except with the help of the Duomo's sacristan who has a key. The boys can climb over the gate and squeeze through its bars but find this lock too much for their skills. However, it is quite easy to see the stepped seats, the niches for grand chairs and thrones and the square openings that led to subterranean alleys. The almost round theater is not altogether Etruscan, more likely Roman on Etruscan plans. (One begins to realize in traveling through Italy that many things "Roman" were not only Greek but Etruscan as well and feels that the older civilization has been unjustly slighted. But then, the Etruscans probably built their theaters on Greek plans; it was a small and intricately connected place, the ancient world.)

The gates of the amphitheater face a tall, heavy stand of medieval wall, which uses Roman and Etruscan stones, and a rise of auto road that re-enters the town. Immediately beyond a "Dancing and Dining," if it's still there, a narrow, taciturn arch leads toward the vicolo del Vescovado and that into a set of tall, narrow—as if ready to shut—arches. These protect the approach to a tight square with a few small, dusty houses in its corners and the ancient palace of the bishops, whose Gothic eyes stare out over the ponderous wall onto the Etruscan landscape.

Meander in an out, around the Duomo and into the court of the Palazzo Comunale, through the streets and paths that cause Italian tourist literature to label the town *suggestiva,* which here means appealing and evocative, opening the eye and the imagination. Some of the medieval houses are as simple as a child's drawing, their adaptation for modern use limited to a new window or two cut into the yielding tufa or a storeroom attached to a housefront to support a handful of terrace barely capable of holding its profligacy of vines and flowers. Sutri is not a rich town or "charming" in any polished sense, yet somehow—in spite of its dense past, which includes a name derived from the Etruscan version of "Saturn"—it is not a mess, nor too much retouched; dignified, not at all self-conscious, poor and orderly, it is genuinely charming.

Farther southward there is another Etruscan town, Nepi, which rears up dramatically from a massive spur of stone. The Duomo has been so often molested that only its crypt, built over a Roman temple, is of any interest. The truly distinguished Palazzo Comunale of the baroque 1700's dims its other ornaments by displaying blatantly, as if it were a heraldic shield, the big yellow dial of the local phone center. Don't be angry with Nepi for this injury to a fine building; she makes amends in her neighboring vineyards. If you stop to buy a bunch or two of grapes in a vineyard, the lady of the house will help you pick them—"No, don't take those, these are riper and prettier"—and, offering the handfuls of green-gold etched with tendrils and nestled in velvet leaves, she will accept no payment but your effusive thanks. You start back for Rome on a smooth, long wave of affection for her, for the sunshine and the vineyards, the tufa that is hospitable to green and the unknown people who cut a hole in their house in Sutri just large enough to hold one geranium plant.

Viterbo and Environs

TWO HOURS FROM Rome by car or train (and faster via
the Roma Nord bus) reaches a pure and complete townlet of the
Middle Ages within a city that has distinctive fountains, more
stone shields than old walls should be forced to carry, and an
austerely harmonious piazza; not prosperous or pushing, or
showy (there is a polite restraint that is almost Anglo)—Viterbo.

An Etruscan center, certainly, but its important period and the
source of the eye's pleasure was its time as papal enclave, on and
off, beginning in the twelfth century with the flight—part of a
recurrent pattern—of the Pope from inimical Rome, then under
siege by Frederick Barbarossa. His grandson, Frederick II, set
siege, unsuccessfully, to Viterbo in the thirteenth century, when
the city called itself Guelph (the party of the Pope) and welcomed Pope Alexander IV, another refugee from Rome. Alexander established himself, his cardinals, and his entourage in this
papal annex, ready to stay a long while, judging from the Palazzo
Papale on its piazza and the density of the surrounding buildings.
It was an exceedingly nervous time, however, and a succeeding
pope decided to make his refuge Perugia, perhaps because it was
farther away from Rome or its despots less troublesome. The

next pope chose Viterbo again, and the palaces resumed their growth.

To a city so intimate with the papacy falls the distinction of having initiated the first of the conclaves for the election of a pope, now a solemn meeting, sometimes slow and long but never a forced imprisonment, as it was in Viterbo after the death of a thirteenth-century pope. The *capitano* had the cardinals locked in their palace to stay until they had chosen a new pope. Months passed—a subtle show of contempt for the *capitano?*—too much time for a dictator to brook. He had the roof taken off the meeting room, hoping to whip the cardinals with blows of weather. Still immobile, undecided or belligerently stubborn, they sat for many more months. The *capitano* deprived them of food. That did it and, after two years and more, they elected Gregory X. When the papacy left Italy altogether for Avignon in the early fourteenth century, Viterbo returned to the business of family feuds, to continue the tortuous dance of fidelities and infidelities to this party and that, and finally, exhausted, fell back into the arms of the church as a papal state.

Viterbo's recent history was marked by heavy bombing during World War II, which accounts for the presence of two cities, the medieval and the newly rebuilt, melding at a few points: a broken medieval tower with blank sky-blue eyes that clings with vines and cobwebs to a glass-bound bank and a small, primitive church that shrinks from a conquering army of automobiles. One starts in the large, reconstructed Piazza dei Caduti, specifically in the tourist office, to ask for a detailed map, the first ploy, and then chooses any one of the spokes of the piazza hub. If your taste and tendencies lead to museums first—and the local museum is unusually attractive—cross the piazza, go into any of the ancient vicoli that take you across the Corso Italia and the via Mazzini, through the Porta della Verità, to the church of Santa Maria della Verità.

The museum occupies the cloisters of the church, walks covered with slant tiled roofs, cool walls inside neat quartets of arches that surround a sunlit square and bird song. First, the Trial of the Etruscan Sarcophagus, not too rigorous in Viterbo since there aren't too many. Several might interest you: a skillfully draped lady whose red coloring lingers in her tresses; an Etruscan lion who had at least one Assyrian grandparent; a red-faced fat man, walleyed and broken-nosed, who might have been a famed pugilist; a gentleman whose lineaments have all but disappeared, leaving for posterity only his large umbilicus.

The walls of the second level show a diversity of interesting stonework, plaques inscribed in handsome Gothic lettering, one in rhymed verse, a few Hebrew tombstones. One section of wall is incised with graffiti and birds and houses and people, like a communal drawing on the wall of a talented kindergarten. A few lively portraits, several of them boldly Renaissance, accompany Romanesque capitals and bits of frieze. It is easy sauntering that doesn't require awed attention, except for one pair of heads in relief on a marble background of vines and fruit, probably a funerary piece, though the vivid eagerness of the strong profiles defies death. An upstairs inner room is guarded by the red arms and red dark-eyed face of a bright-eyed, happy boy rising from the pit of his own grotesquely elongated torso. Continuing on past a collection of apothecary jars and examples of church crafts, one comes onto a Viterbo specialty, the *macchina,* a lighted tower carried in honor of Santa Rosa on the evening of September 3. The tall, ornate towers drawn by dozens of men were and are redesigned every three or four years; there is consequently a plenitude of models to look at before you pursue religious paintings of the sixteenth and seventeenth centuries interspersed with earlier panels.

On to one of the way stations of the saint who inspired the ingenuity, devotion and strength that the *macchina* demanded, by way of the gate and a right turn on the via Mazzini. The Romanesque church of San Giovanni in Zoccoli (redone, with fidelity) is framed in two photogenic arches and contains a good fifteenth-century triptych by a Viterbese painter. Quite possibly a passerby will stop to suggest you notice that the church is out of plumb. This slight lean, he tells you, was intentional, designed to symbolize the slanting droop of Christ's head on the cross. Such churchly tidbits spill readily from local mouths, whether as symptoms of religious faith or color to brighten a hard-working life, it is difficult to say. Continuing past a gathering of flowered balconies, a palazzo-tenement, a fountain, a modern butcher shop that emphasizes the fresh innocence of its veal with a sculptured portrait of a cow nursing a calf, one comes to an irregular arrangement of street levels that meet at a characteristic bulb fountain in a small square of passive, shy charm. This Piazzetta della Crocetta is a compendium of geraniums and wash and colorful plastic strips at the entrance to a barbershop and as many parked cars as can butt each other below the stairs that lead to the church where Santa Rosa was baptized. Here, too, her "uncorrupted" body lay for six years, until Pope Alexander IV had a dream about the saint and consequently ordered the body sent to its present resting place.

Signs and the street name (via Casa di Santa Rosa) indicate the humble house, with its few minuscule windows, where Santa Rosa lived and died and, close by, her church as it was redesigned in the mid-nineteenth century. The house is part of a six-hundred-year-old convent fallen on hard, agnostic times; the government recently reclaimed the property and now requires that the nuns pay rent. (If your Italian is weak, pick up for this visit an ageless, motorbiked gnome who hangs around the tourist office and claims knowledge of English and French. His confidence is based on four or five distorted words, but he is seemingly a friend—not so much liked as amusingly tolerated—of everyone in Viterbo, and though he acts as if the city were his fief, he expects a tip.) At the end of a small garden, one rings and all sorts of distant bells respond and unexpected hatches, reminiscent of the last act of *Der Rosenkavalier,* fly open.

Admitted, one enters a hall of the nunnery for a glimpse of extensive cloister gardens and a meeting with cases of rosaries, dolls and scarves whose sale helps pay the rent. The first small low-ceilinged room is full of holy images and prints of *macchine* of sundry times. The second has an antique wood-trimmed fireplace and near it, a pile of cannon balls that fell on the city two centuries ago but were deflected, says your polyglot savant-now-also-hagiographer, from their catapults by the saint who averted not only death but damage. Santa Rosa's bedroom, as tight as medieval rooms generally were, is lightened by artfully placed bands of the ubiquitous lace-edged votive silver hearts and the contented smiles and hushed comments of the poor devout from outlying villages. A foreigner is naturally conspicuous and soon approached by the young, good-looking Mother Superior, who doesn't ask for money—one makes an offering in exchange for the book on the history of the convent and its works, which she presses as a gift—but would you please give her addresses of interested organizations in your country to whom she might apply for help? You are, of course, too polite to ask, "What about the Vatican?"

Mounting the steps of the church (careful of the edges chipped out by bomb damage), one comes into the ornateness accumulated around the miraculous remains of Santa Rosa. She lies in a chapel supervised by nuns, encased in a thickly decorated glass casket flanked by silver angels who wear offerings of bracelets, necklaces and chains of rings. Still surrounded by the stout country ladies who scorn bras, corsets, makeup and hairstyling and are fortified by garlic and faith, the savant points out how fresh Santa Rosa looks, the brown of the skin not decay but the result of fumes from a fire in the seventeenth or eighteenth century—he can't quite remember which—and repeats the story that the Mother Superior has already told: the body was examined earlier in this century and the heart proved to be fresh and firm. To adoring eyes, she looks like a maiden dressed in a new robe that covers a pink young heart. To the eye of the curious, she is parched, smoked, flat, with a leathery shrunken mask and the brown, curved fingers of a small monkey.

From the benches among the trees off the Piazza dei Caduti, you may observe the cleanliness of the city and people, the well-pressed neatness of clothing, the simple chic of the girls, and look across to roofs covered with tiles like wrinkled bark, onto distant churches and towers and closer modern buildings surrounding the octagonal Renaissance *tempietto,* Madonna della Peste (plague). Continue the descent from the park along the via Ascenzi to find, at the right, the warm rotundities of Santa Maria della Salute, whose pink-and-white checkerboard stone and portal figures, some of them grouped as friendly conversational couples, can best be seen from the stairs that descend to the via della Pescheria. The portal on that street frames an entrance to the thirteenth century: streets that ramble under eaved balconies and vines and flowers to relieve the unremitting gray, streets that wall in *boccie* players and their kibitzers and a couple of elementary trattorie.

The Piazza del Plebiscito is an imposing space defined by a Neapolitan red palazzo and a palazzo of tan-white, splendid shields, one of them a stone heart whose veins are a tree, and a slender bell-topped clock tower. The Palazzo Comunale, begun in the latter half of the fifteenth century, is the most pleasingly designed of the buildings, with well-proportioned windows and a run of graceful arches, which frame, at their extreme end, the temple of Santa Maria della Salute. The traffic that leaps out of the confinement of narrow streets into the pleasure of tearing through this expanse of space makes gawking at piazza details difficult, but combining daring and alertness, you can enjoy the columns of the Palazzo Comunale portico, the pillar that supports Viterbo's lion and the jungle of shields, lions, palm trees and stone fleece under the clock tower. Across from that superescutcheon a church carries near its portal, like a bulging coat pocket, a Roman sarcophagus jammed with lions, horses and warriors. According to a popular legend, this is the tomb of a twelfth-century heroine, *la bella* Galiana. The most beautiful girl in Viterbo, she was coveted by a neighboring baron who, on receiving "no" for his importunings, laid siege to Viterbo. Reluctantly impelled by promises that if she showed herself on the city walls the siege would be lifted, she walked out and was killed by an arrow from the bow of her suitor. If he couldn't have her no one else would, a popular principle in its time and still active in Sicily.

A slit of street, the via Sant'Angelo, expands to a bell tower and a red wall gaily splashed with late sunlight, part of a building that foams horses, griffons, cornucopias, heaped urns, mermaids and sea dragons. This anthology of mythological figures on the Piazza Mario Fani leads into the via Saffi, a beguiling cluster of fourteenth-century houses, respectfully restored, well proportioned and inviting, in spite of their dour color. The street runs down to the oldest and biggest of Viterbo's fountains set on the piazza named in its monumental honor, the Fontana Grande, originally designed in the thirteenth century, patched up in the fifteenth and in the nineteenth adorned by an improver who decided that four small obelisks were essential to the harmonies of venerable curves and Gothic spire.

The Piazza della Cattedrale, silent and majestic, sits apart from the rest of the city in its own corner of ineffable dignity. The eye is caught first by the papal palace and its loggia, an antique courtly tune and lacy trills wafted from the austere building. A flight of steps that call for the rustle of stiff ceremonial brocades and a glitter of jeweled staffs leads to the denuded great hall left only its wooden ceiling, plaques bearing papal names, traces—according to a few very sharp-eyed observers—of the tent poles erected by the cardinals when their roof was taken from them and, as it must have done seven hundred years ago, the sun pouring through the wide biforate windows. The fountain of the delicate, feminine loggia is in the usual local style, a bit more carefully worked than the others and carved in bishop's miters, as suited its position. Ruins of double pillars face a valley rising to a solitary tower and the immense dome and light campanile of a distant church. On the opposite ledge sit two boys reading comic books, loudly and with stage effects that drown the plashing of the fountain. As background for the Italian equivalents of "Pow!" and "Crash!" and "Zoom!," there is a row of frail double columns enclosing Gothic embroidery and between the columns an oblique view of the Cathedral, the striped campanile and, across the piazza, a Romanesque-Gothic house whose balance of spaces, gem windows and limited size make an appealing contrast to the mighty palace.

The Duomo accommodated through the centuries to its roles as Etruscan structure, Roman temple dedicated to Hercules and church of the twelfth century; it was dressed in a campanile in the fourteenth, refaced as Renaissance, damaged in the twentieth century and remade so that the restrained design sets off well and subtly the contours of its neighbors. Nor is this church of the chaste façade free of the usual ecclesiastical confusion of styles and tastes and periods, a mélange of scraps of fresco, huge mediocre paintings, pagan putti, frozen Virgin, Virgin of the Florentine aristocracy, frantic trompe l'oeil winging way from good wooden ceiling, Romanesque capitals and the tomb of a pope who was killed in the thirteenth century when the walls and ceiling of a room in his palace collapsed.

After contemplating for a while longer the unique piazza ensemble, turn down the via San Lorenzo to peer into courts of palaces with splendid doors, shields and lions. Stop at an overpass (Ponte del Duomo) and look down to a pile of Etruscan stones and a garden where two nuns may be beating carpets with large-gestured Italian vigor, as passionate as if they were exorcising sin. The via Pellegrini, the Piazza della Morte, the via del Cimitero make a montage of stairways bordered by flowers, fountains, arches crammed with secondhand contortions of metal and one station wagon blooming in pink, white, blue, pale-green and red plastic basins and fronds of brooms and brushes. The via del Pesce, the Piazza Carluccio and adjoining tangents are, more or less, an "antiques row," concentrating on old copper. Make your way up and down the narrow paths called via delle Piaggerelle and the via Centoponte if their very private air doesn't discourage you; the meager wineshops, the obscure carpenters' caves, a ceiling of wash and a floor of children who expect neither cars nor strangers to distract them are the rooms of a self-sufficient tribe, and seclusive.

Inside courts and steep alleys, through tunnels and around towers, past the flowery prose attached to the pretty Piazza Scacciaricci, which praises the beauties of this "Quartiere di San Pellegrino," and on to the souvenirs and *objets* on the Piazza San Pellegrino, a telling collection of medieval at its most inviting, cozily angled and nestled in bowers of arches. A seemingly nameless, perfect piazzetta slants to the via San Pellegrino and a shop that spills onto its historic path a flood of copper, stone masks, scraps of mosaic, terra-cotta urns and stone flowers among the fresh; and if there is anything else you might want to buy, they will dig it out of the caverns cut into the slope. The vias Grotti, La Fontaine and delle Fabbriche, with their sprawling children and watchful cats, lead back ultimately to the Fontana Grande and its lions chewing on the tiny spitting obelisks.

After refueling from the *porchetta* stall (a large roasted pig on a spit) on the via Garibaldi you might continue down to the church of San Sisto near the city wall, at the bottom of the street. Antichurch (architecturally and artistically speaking) as you may have become or are fast becoming, this interesting ninth-century church built on a temple (battered classic columns to prove it) and its cloisters make a rewarding short visit.

Diagonally across the city—and not as far as the map, which makes a street of every thread of space, would indicate—is the Piazza Fiorentina, a dignified space made singular by the presence of a vast, empty fortress, a bare, shocked structure begun in the fourteenth century by the Cardinal Albornoz who was the begetter of many such *rocche*. It grew in might and size to be almost entirely demolished by the bombing that left it only a few unusual shields, a high aristocratic loggia and its tower. A neighboring victim of bomb damage, the church of San Francesco, fared better. Standing in a piazza of effulgent pines and hedges, next to a coarse, stirring monument to Sardinian soldiers who fell here, it has been given back its measured Gothic proportions, its long windows and simple bell tower and, in one corner of the textured stone, an outdoor pulpit where, in the fifteenth century, Siena's San Bernardino preached to the populace. In making the necessary extensive repairs no one seemed to bother about lighting, unless authenticity required Gothic dusk that calls for groping one's way from tomb to papal tomb. Instead, recross the piazza of the fortress and follow the via San Faustino (where someone has washed and hung to dry on the street three lambskins—feet, cap, and all) until it swells as market: the colors of fruits, flowers, vegetables, chickens and umbrellas painted on a canvas of gray and white church façade and a cool moist smell of earth from the plants sprayed by the fountain.

Glancing right and left in your progress along the via Maria SS. Liberatrice, stop at the via Santa Maria in Volturno, which frames a stand of towers across the valley and the large church of SS. Trinità. Its omnivorous façade absorbs pillars, pilasters, lifesized saints squirming out of their niches and, along the top of the tall false front, torches like gigantic chess pieces above an explosion of rays, angels' heads and wings surrounding the symbolic eye encased in a triangle. Snoop your way back to the via della Bella Vista, which fulfills the promise of its name, one of a tangle of ancient streets, decayed, restored, stairs worn to bumpy slopes, new paint and old stones peering out of floor matting; a brook of flowers running along buttressed supports, stairs, balconies, medieval and Renaissance portals, to stop near the *tempietto* on the Piazza dei Caduti.

The following short walk might be combined with the Piazza del Duomo–San Pellegrino area. Though efficient, it makes a toomuchness in a small compass, and retracing one's steps is a pleasurable matter of a few minutes. Locate yourself on the Piazza del Gesù, facing the twelfth-century church that wears a smiling lion and a tired eagle near its self-effacing belfry. This was the church in which the younger Simon Montfort and his brother Guy stabbed Henry, the son of King Richard of England (1272), to avenge the torture and death of their father by royal command, an event recorded by Dante rather prissily for a reporter of the Middle Ages: "the sanctity of the place meant nothing to him." A sad beauty veils this neighborhood of useless towers and tired fountains, crumbling stairs and faded market umbrellas, scrawny cats and sagging balconies; a moving, exhausted antiquity whose "new" church of Santa Maria Nuova was consecrated in this corner of "Biterbo" in 1080, whose parishioners heard Thomas Aquinas preach from its street pulpit.

Fornaccio, Crochi, Baciadonne (woman kisser) are streets that echo the charms of the San Pellegrino quarter, though less carefully polished. They lead through combinations of paths to the via dell'Orologio Vecchio, a collection of small palazzi collapsed, collapsing, supported by wooden slats masked by soup and movie ads, tottering toward the Piazza dell'Erbe, whose name suggests that it was at some time a market place. Now it is the place of the bus schedules, of a big fountain and of a view of the clock tower, the stopping and clotting place—and one of the noisiest in Viterbo—for meetings in the course of the evening *passeggiata*. It is the place where new young army recruits hang around and hang around or march back and forth showing off their new military briskness, in unison, and going nowhere. Little boys push toy boats around in the fountain, and young toughs try to push each other in, and everywhere in the piazza not preempted by cars, groups talking and talking, standing through hours of conversation on their admirable Italian feet. After the *passeggiata* is long over the Piazza dell'Erbe voices go on, thin during the dinner hour to thicken at about 10:00 or 10:30 P.M., when diners return to talk through the blatting of motorbikes. The town idiot stands in front of the piazza café, also talking, incessantly and incomprehensibly, and always there is a kind soul to nod, now and then, as if he were listening. The babbling thick voice is big and bounces against the walls of the piazza when everyone else has left, the last voice on the midnight piazza except for the clock, which bongs its full slow strokes.

Viterbo can be explored in one exhausting day. There is, however, another day or rushed half day in the environs worth considering. Directly east, at the edge of the city, on the Orte road, accompanied by an amiable fountain and a slapdash bar that acts also as neighborhood grocery and sweetshop—a bit of this and that and all of it sticky—there stands the stately Renaissance church of Santa Maria della Quercia. A few miles onward, through endless ropes of vine looped on deep green hills and around flat, solid houses of hay capped with eaved roofs, one encounters Bagnaia, a small town of the attractive usuals: clock turret, little stone houses and a discolored, hard-working fountain. On the rise of its hill sits (hardly the word; "cavorts" is closer) the Villa Lante, a late Renaissance–early baroque or mannerist, if you like, illustration of conspicuous consumption, a quintessence of *bella figura*—making the finest possible figure in conduct, dress and possessions. It was a summer retreat of the church hierarchy, its woods stocked with animals for mitered enthusiasts of the hunt. Later tamed to formal park, the area began to take on its present form in the late sixteenth century, shaped by the artists—among them the architect Vignola—who had built the palace-fortress of Caprarola (page 108). According to historians the work, which stretched over many years, was interrupted by severe ecclesiasts who objected to such sybaritic purposes and expenditures (the Reformation had made the Church self-conscious about its luxuries for a while), but the extravagances of designs and money soon flowed on, fed by one rich and powerful nephew of a pope and later another churchman of a potent family.

A small admission fee opens a vast "English" park, carefully planned to resemble unbridled nature, which slopes to a fountain of Pegasus surrounded by a semicircle of terms, statues stuffed and bound into their stone pedestals—a favorite architectural diversion of its time and a lasting staple for formal gardens. Villa Lante (a large admission fee) is a misnomer: there is barely livable house space in the extensive grounds devoted to fantasies of topiary and fountain art. The hedges, as arabesques and geometric patterns, as mile on mile of thin green lines coiled and boxed—always in balanced patterns—gather to an apogee of manicured perfection in a complex composition on a center rise. The huge groups of fountains on several levels are linked by curves of slender channels for purling rivulets of water, the long chain defining a graceful border for the elaborate all-over design. An upper fountain is an Olympus of gigantic mossy river gods and their consorts, the middle an assemblage of circles and semicircles that hold stone oil lamps which raise a screen of high, fine needles of water. The lowest set of fountains is centered on the symbol of one of the papal houses involved in the development of these pleasure gardens. It is supported by two gods (or goddesses; the stubborness of moss, the waywardness of fern and the constant battering by water, have obliterated definition) and surrounded by stone boats, each with one small stone passenger aboard.

The upper stories of the playhouse villas are not viewable at all times; reconstruction after recent war damage and the vandalism of soldiers continues, and, furthermore, a member of the owning family may be in residence. Nevertheless, the lower sections suggest a gaiety of decoration and elegance of furnishings: a fine set of pew seats, massive tables and chests, a round folding table of supple design and, on the walls and ceilings, murals of towns and sea, handsome robust ladies, children and fruits under domes of tricky perspective and skies full of birds. Behind the

houses, one finds the essential dark, moist, romantic-erotic grottoes, inhabited by a Neptune whose trident pours water into a
rectangular pool studded with the heads of rearing horses, a Venus who makes fountains of her breasts and a variety of figures
imprisoned in niches and so maltreated by time and moisture
that men, women and animals have receded to a prespecies, pre-
sex Ur-thing.

One of the two summerhouses built in the style of Renaissance
tempietti is frescoed with a garland of lovely girls, birds and
flowers and gives access to a large rose garden and a fern grotto,
where waters glide and gleeful dolphins' heads and tails sprout
ferns.

NOTE: The hours of admission vary with the season: 9:30 to
12:00 and 2:30 to 4:30 are generally safe. The fee for the park
alone is above 300 lire, for the rest over 1,000, and like all prices,
on the increase.

Traveling northeastward for about twenty minutes or so brings
one to a savage landscape: at one side a high, closed town, on the
other a silent, unused field stretching toward tall, grizzled rocks
that loom like a horizon of menhirs. Bomarzo, and the arrow
that points into the rocks for the Parco dei Mostri.

Somewhere in the park there is a sign that says it is like no
other; quite true. Villa Lante is extravagant, the park at Bomarzo
profligate; Villa Lante is fanciful, Bomarzo grotesque; Villa
Lante is engaged with people and town, Bomarzo sits apart; Villa
Lante chuckles with water, Bomarzo is silent; Villa Lante is, in
spite of its exuberance, the result of controlled planning; Bomarzo is an eccentric flight from the rules, an individual fantasy
that clings to the rim of madness. To the right of the entrance,
past a brook lost in large leaves and ferns, an encounter with the
host, a giant of pitted gray stone. The next *mostro* is a pair of
mermaid sisters; one wears wings and the other has two tails
which embrace a pair of lions, all very large. Soon, an arcade and
a place to rest, a bench shaped of a monumental maiden with
large breasts and behind her, a four-headed pet. Down another
path (the paths are as wayward as the sculpture but there is little

danger of being lost if you stay among the monsters, scattered on a few levels of a limited area), past a giant urn and a bench that tells you, again, of the marvels to see here.

The marvels were ordered by a sixteenth-century Count Orsini, who may have dreamed the idea while gazing from the window of the family palace onto the weird outcroppings of rock, or in the course of hunting among them. It is said that the living rock was cut as gigantic nightmare figures by Turkish prisoners captured at the Battle of Lepanto, but that is conjecture, and little else is surely known except that the park was lost for centuries and only recently rediscovered. And knowing that much, carry on to a superelephant who supports a howdah on his back and drags a dead Roman warrior in his trunk; a dragon with rounded wings, maddened eyes and fierce maw, fighting off two lions, or tigers. A stone tablet and benches were carved inside a fanged mask, on its lip the legend "Every care flies." (You will notice the numerous legends and mottoes that assure you that these creatures were meant to help create a lazy atmosphere of dalliance, of *dolce far niente.*) A moss-covered Neptune, the cavernous open mouth—a small room—of a dolphin, a sleeping woman who is a grotesque caricature of a Michelangelo figure, an enormous tortoise carrying a protesting giantess on his back, a stony Moby Dick yawning to show myriad arrow teeth, startle the bosky paths and diminished trees. One giant tears another apart, head down and roaring, and near the stream that meanders through the menagerie is a stricken face whose nose is a newish faucet.

As you round back, you should come on a man-sized *tempietto* adorned with rosettes and niches and, in its vicinity, an oak tree on which someone, appalled by this frightening world and its pagan messages, has attached a holy image. Not too far from the other side of the entrance, there is another huge mask, with disconsolate eyes and vulnerably idiotic in its basin hat of flowers. In spite of the menacing mouth (that particular Orsini might easily have been a tooth, tongue and tonsil fetishist) he looks like Ferdinand, the reluctant bull. There may be other discolored, mottled beasts lost in the magic woods, but these should do; one gets the idea quickly. In spite of the "Linger, enjoy, let the world and the hours slip by" messages carved into the stone, the six-teenth-century "tunnel of love" décor is less for ruminative wan-dering than nightmare, a dream of being locked in a leafy version of Dr. Caligari's cabinet.

On leaving Bagnaia you probably noticed an unusual number of crudely painted and lettered religious banners hanging over doors and shopfronts; "Grazie Tutte per Me Madonna Mia," for instance, not far from a figure of Christ standing in the sun. It was such fervor that served as excuse when Viterbo destroyed its rival town, Ferento, in the twelfth century. Some zealot discov-ered that a notable crucifix of Ferento showed Christ with his eyes open (Siena has one in the *cortile* of its Pinacoteca) rather than closed. Destroy the heretics! They did, and the city, which had lived a long Etruscan, Roman and medieval life, never re-covered. What is left, other than stubs of various periods, is a battered and lofty Roman theater, as solitary as the temple of Segesta. The high, strong arches cut of blocks of tufa, the stage, its runways for men and animals (and the square holes for ob-serving and prodding them), the expanse of seats, and especially the isolation are strongly evocative, and one can readily imagine togaed dignitaries passing through marble colonnades and the sonorous sounds of classic drama (still occasionally performed during the summer months).

From an upper range of seats one looks out to a breadth and height of hill and a valley of green trees and white cows deep in amber wheat and poppies; below, the intimacy of wildflowers clinging to shattered marble columns and, on the sun-baked stone seats, green lizards and red bugs hurrying in erratic, myste-rious directions through the silence.

At the place where the fork of a nearby road points to Bagnaia in one direction and Viterbo in another, a dirt road leads into woods and the sound of lightly falling water that spills, one soon finds, over bright, orange-red rocks near a deserted farmhouse. Leave the car and walk down a few steps to a broadened shallow spread of water over a table of dark gold-red stone. Pushing aside branches held by strands of wild vine that shiver like plucked strings, you will find a trickle of clear water that breaks into gold-red rivulets. The ferrous red shimmering under the transparent silk of water in bowers of quivering green, the open empty windows of the abandoned house, are the place for a fairy tale. And, as in a fairy tale, the house cannot be approached without peril; not an ogre this time, but snakes to guard the enchantment.

Notes

HOTELS.   Quite close to Rome and not especially a tourist center, Viterbo finds no reason for building—if it can afford to—posh hotels. One of the favorites was a prototype of *the* provincial hotel, more eccentric than most, the Angelo Nuovo, off the Piazza dell'Erbe and one hopes it has remained unchanged. One paced a deep, wide *sala* to meet behind the desk a nearsighted, deaf old gentleman, nose in account books and impatient of interruption. Having forced a room from him, one followed a lady guide through a labyrinth of anterooms and back halls, under ceilings painted to imitate medieval wood, and up the stairs along brown-gravy views of Viterbo, into a remarkable (to use an equivocal word) *sala* where Botticelli's Venus has been repainted on coarse wall cloth by a local hand. The rooms are clean, a number have baths, and the ladies who look after them are efficient and kindly (no English), but some of the walls are paper-thin, which may or may not, depending on your command of Italian, reveal interesting aspects of Italian life and love. With or without sociology, modest in price.

The Leon d'Oro, on the via della Cava, is more modern and has a larger number of showers attached to its rooms, and the price is somewhat higher. For cheaper accommodations, try the Antico Angelo, the elderly kinsman of the Angelo Nuovo, or the Albergo Marconi on the via Mazzini, or ask the tourist office for suggestions.

RESTAURANTS.   The Antico Angelo, which has a small garden in the bustle and noise of the Piazza dell'Erbe (homemade fettuccine in cream and duck cooked in wine and brandy are especially good); the Spacca, at 9 via della Pace, whose specialties are a rococo form of ravioli; La Tuscana, on via della Cava, serves decent beefsteak. Or try the popular Quattro Stagioni in the tight walls of the via Calabresi. (Be prepared for a couple of them to have turned exclusively to pizza.)

As in other cities, one can hire a taxi for a few hours or a day; the cost will be about 25,000 lire for a full day, and often worth it to save the wear and waste of finding one's way through country roads on which there are few signs and fewer people to ask for directions.

Viterbo, an agricultural center, is a mosquito and bird-droppings center; carry insect repellent and keep a sharp eye on the pigeons.

Wear thick-soled shoes; there are few stretches in old Viterbo that aren't cobbled—true as well of the historic quarters of many other Italian towns.

Orvieto

LIKE THAT FAMOUS auto-rental company, Orvieto tries harder. In its attempts to preserve an august Umbrian image, the city posts many polite, antinoise signs: "Please avoid making unnecessary noise." Tilting at windmills. Even in this venerable town perched high, high, on its Etruscan tufa throne, secure in its dusty-yellow Valhalla loftiness, noise remains—like oil and wine—a basic component of the Italian bloodstream. Neither pride in its past as a religious center of Etruria (as almost always in Etruscan studies, there are as many doubters as supporters of this supposition) nor the miraculous felicity of its Duomo façade nor the possession of an extremely potent relic will allay the roaring bulldogs that are small cars and motorbikes.

Some light knowledge of the history of other Etruscan cities makes it possible to improvise a past for Orvieto, and, except for specific names, the result is fairly accurate: a Roman settlement on Etruscan ruins, overrun by the Goths, later taken by the Lombards, involved in competition with Florence and Siena for a way to the sea so that she might more profitably sell the products of her thriving medieval industry, torn apart between the Guelphs (the Pope's party) and the Ghibellines (the Emperor's party) and sung by Dante; scene of continued strife between powerful captains called in for their experience and the manpower they commanded; taken by the church, relinquished, later taken by Cesare Borgia (Valentino) when he was working for the French. And, a familiar detail, refuge for popes.

The common approach, via the auto road, pulls the car into a long spiral of now you see it, now you don't, coiling up to the startling gray-yellow loaf and into the pristine white-gloved hands of policemen who look like naval officers, portly gentlemen who indicate where you might leave the car, and there it is, before you, the glistening Duomo. The approach by train ends with a funicular ride up into expanding and narrowing views, one of the best 500 lire (it may now be 1,000) bargains, and a walk, or a bus trip, up via Postierla, past cranky Renaissance stone and iron grating, a few passive older houses and stands of attractively packaged Orvieto wine, and ceramics of various colorful styles hung on the walls. (You may recoil from the commercialism, but keep in mind that Orvieto is hardly a thriving industrial or trade center—except for its wine—and, in any case, the smiling shine of ceramics brightens long stretches of gray wall, to be respected for their antiquity, but sulky at times and in need of splotches of playfulness no matter how foolish the designs.)

The very best way to arrive is by helicopter, possibly borrowed from a Milanese magnate friend. Arrange to be dropped in the Piazza del Popolo on a Saturday morning, near noon. First, go into a wide, dim doorway next to a minute church. In the semigloom two rosy, generous ladies in big aprons make fat roast-pork sandwiches from a pile of fresh rolls called *rosette* and the meat of two gigantic pigs on spits. This, after a wait on a short line (one of Orvieto's distinctions is that it will, sometimes, stand on line, an anomalous act for Italians, who consider queueing submissively stupid, sheeplike) and an extra slice of pork because you are a *straniero* and how charming and amusing of you to do this indigenous, working-class thing, will cost about seventy-five cents. If you return for a second *porchetta,* the heaping will be higher: you have now combined the lovableness of eccentricity with being a good feeder.

Warm *porchetta* in hand and maybe a chunk of cheese or a tomato bought at one of the market stalls, walk up the stairs to the open balcony of the Palazzo del Popolo and, chewing contentedly, look down upon the market. It is much like other large Italian markets except that few have this enhancing vantage point, which draws the helter-skelter broken patterns of eye-level viewing into a series of brisk paintings. The Grande Albergo Reale, haughtily aloof to Saturday slapdash and noise, is, nevertheless, neighbored by a long orange awning that shelters baskets and flight bags and a green wagon that pours boxes on boxes of shoes. Toward the center of the piazza, white, red, orange, blue and yellow awnings, waves in a fauve sea, lift for glimpses of plastic toys and straw hats, work pants and flowered cotton tablecloths. A *gelato* wagon explodes its shining rays over the dull, brown sacks of onions, and a plastic-covered carrousel top dangles the clear, naïve colors of little girl's dresses. Gay umbrellas, white canvas sails, and orange and green squares shade burred cucumbers, pearls of onion, baroque tomatoes and blocks and bricks of cheese. In back of the pennants of yard goods and the rows of pocketbooks whose arched handles looked like astonished eyes, beyond the signs of "fixed prices" that serve to evoke ardent bargaining and the muddled designs of "Indian" blankets, are the stalls of live fowl, dots of brown chick among the speckled hens and plump, white geese. The noise is not great for a market—a record player demonstrates its skills in a moderately subdued voice, one vendor proclaims his wares rather soberly; the ensemble of sounds makes a low, warm tone that beats with the steadiness of a healthy heartbeat.

Go down the stairs (careful not to disturb the old black-hatted men who sit and watch wherever there is something—and sometimes nothing but the mists in their aged eyes—to watch) and go across the piazza to look back at the palazzo, a beauty of red-gold tufa that, here and there, takes on a greenish tone when the sun saps its color. An ecclesiastical seat in the twelfth century, after that the palace of the *capitano,* it later housed (in the sixteenth century) an "academy" in the Renaissance sense of the word and a theater. The renovations and additions that accrued with changes of use and style were recently erased to bring back the early, androgynous form, sturdy, plain-spoken Romanesque dressed in the ribbons and curls of the Gothic. Under the long balcony there are deep arches that hint of old murals and, above those, rows of stone tatting or ruffles on a stone petticoat (or you might see them as square breasts) that make a rippling, female effect and a curious one for a building meant originally as a stalwart haven for clerics.

Via a gantlet of ceramics and wine, handmade lace, babies' booties and collars few men now wear, one comes on the long horizontal stripes of the Duomo and, then, its façade. Because it is enclosed in meager space and because it is a bazaarful of métiers, materials and styles, it must be explored section by section. (Unless you climb on a roof or are extraordinarily skillful, you will find it impossible to take one full-on camera shot that includes the mosaic-imbedded columns, the bas-reliefs and mosaic panels, the rose window, the statuary, the frail arches and spires.) The basic fact of this overwhelming mélange is that it works, and works better than a number of façades for which it was the prototype. Perhaps it works only in Italy; it might be scorned as an architectural monster in a more chaste, Puritanical country less permissive of wild, gushing polychrome fancies. Whatever, the Duomo lures busloads of square-bottomed ladies in sat-out, shining skirts, Umbrian priests with their eager flocks, young Sicilian priests in twos and threes and heavily camera-laden. From Rome come carfuls of families who take a quick look at the façade and then divide into three groups: the children to the *gelato* wagon; mama to the postcard vendor and immediately to the stone benches on the piazza, where she writes a greeting to the sister she will see tonight, a week before the card arrives; papà keeps trying, from this side of the piazza and that, to center the whole church in the eye of his camera.

The Duomo was built as thanksgiving for the miracle at Bolsena by order of Pope Urban IV, who was in Orvieto as a refugee from threatened assaults, in the swan song of the Swabian empire, by Manfred of Hohenstaufen, the son of Frederick II, the great-grandson of Frederick Barbarossa. Its building was initiated late in the thirteenth century on designs, it is believed, by Arnolfo di Cambio and the construction continued by an unlucky Umbrian master builder for whom the walls wouldn't stand nor the arches hold. It was therefore decided to call in the Sienese Lorenzo Maitani, who set the structure back firmly on its base, designed the façade, and with the help of his gifted sons and other sculptors of the early fourteenth century, carved the supreme bas-reliefs—fluid, open, deeply felt—of the Creation and Genesis, on the first pilaster.

Moving toward the right, one notices that each successive pilaster becomes more crowded, until the fourth is a forest of virtuosities that is still distinguished marble carving, but the mellow rhythms and purity of emotion are quite gone. The intervening ropes of stone and mosaic, glittering and supple, lead the eye up to strong bronze Evangelists and a bronze canopy that shelters a Virgin and Child, the figures attributed to one of the Pisanos, the canopy and angels the work of Lorenzo Maitani. As specific entities, the mosaic panels are disappointingly incongruous, often vulgar, in contrast with the slender, sinuous grace of their bordering piers. A number of the ancient panels were taken off the façade and presented to Pope Pius VI to be replaced by conscientiously inept substitutes while others were entirely "restored" at diverse times from the seventeenth century to the nineteenth; rarely has restoration been so deadly hard-working and off the mark. The mosaics should be viewed as distant, rectangular glow and color, one misty element in the mesmeric whole. (Strangely, *they* are often lauded and two handsome bronze doors, modern but not too abstract, rather like Pisano sculpture in their straight, direct dialogue with the spectator, were for a long time—and may still be—displayed in the Duomo, not yet placed because some authorities consider them not quite worthy of the church.)

The interior is its own showpiece: the endlessly long alternations of dark and light, the even, ceremonial progress of pillars and strong capitals in calm light filtered through stained-glass windows. The two other major strengths of the Duomo are a pair of chapels. One holds the holy relic in a remarkably rich reliquary shaped like the cathedral, designed by Maitani and executed in 1330 by a Sienese goldsmith. This is the ornate box that is carried in procession through the streets on the afternoon of Corpus Domini, a solemn rite that ends on a pagan note. A small

Gothic tabernacle is placed in front of the Duomo, a wire attached to it and strung to the roof of the church of San Francesco. A dove is tied to the wire and urged to slide down, accompanied by the splutter of firecrackers, to the tabernacle where the Virgin and the Apostles wait. If everything goes well, it will be a good year; crops will flourish and the wine flow into dozens of bottling plants. The dove? If it hasn't died of terror or burns, it is handed over to the most recently married couple; the sensible Italian pragmatism has changed the symbol of the Holy Spirit to a symbol of fertility within a few minutes, and if the pragmatic couple is poor enough the dove may change, again, into the shape of a meal.

Back again to the Duomo, however. The frescoes in the Cappella del Santissimo Corporale (the chapel of the relic) are of the fourteenth century, restored with a heavy hand in the nineteenth to stress the story of the miracle that occurred in 1263 in Bolsena. A young priest from Prague, tormented by doubts about the distance between Christ's blood and flesh and the wine and host, is shown celebrating the mass nevertheless. The host he raises turns to flesh and the wine becomes blood that spills to stain the cloth under the chalice, the corporeal. The frescoes maunder on in their overexplicit way as lessons for illiterate congregations, and you might better turn your attention to the Madonna in her serene, fair Sienese world as painted by Lippo Memmi, the brother (some say brother-in-law) of Simone Martini and a devoted follower.

Many visitors come to Orvieto for the façade and the Luca Signorelli chapel and leave, an unjust way to treat a city that gallantly persists in a futile antinoise campaign and designs its marble markers so handsomely. The combination, however, is a rich plenty. The Signorelli chapel, more formally known as Cappella Nuova or that of the Madonna di San Brizio, was first— 1447—entrusted to Fra Angelico, who, with the assistance of Gozzoli and other painters, managed to cover two sections of vault before he was called back to Rome by the Pope. Gozzoli et al. continued for a while until all work was stopped by the murder of a prime power and contributor of substantial sums for the adornment of the Cathedral, a tyrant with the superb name of

Arrigo Monaldeschi della Vipera. Forty years later, Perugino was hired (1489) and left before he could properly prepare his colors. In 1499 Luca Signorelli agreed to finish the job for 180 ducats and regular rations of meal and wine.

Signorelli was one of the painters of whom Symonds says, "What they design they do; nature and art obey them equally; the resources placed at their command are employed with facile and unfettered exercise of power. The hand obedient to the brain is now so expert that nothing further is left to be desired in the expression of the artists' thought." It is easy to understand why Michelangelo, whose tenet was "the hand obeys the intellect," studied Signorelli's frescoes (an influence reflected in the Sistine Chapel) whereas he might not have looked into the chapel at Orvieto had Perugino finished it; "a mindless painter, a block-head," he called Perugino and scorned the repetitions that painter turned out with speed and greed. When he came to Orvieto, Signorelli was near sixty, almost all those years spent in ceaseless study of the structure and the flexible compositions inherent in the human body. (Vasari tells the story that the painter's son was killed quite young, possibly in a street brawl, and that the father had the body brought to his study and in the combined drives—oddly painterly, singularly Renaissance—of passion and study, sorrow and intellect, painted a portrait of the nude, dead boy. Another version of the story has it that the boy was painted as the Christ in the Orvieto panel of the Deposition in the one night immediately after his death.) He could, as Symonds says, do anything, express anything he wanted to with a mastery and inventiveness that encompassed the gamut of realistic normal to brilliant bizarre, as in the unforgettable panels of the world's destruction, of Hell and Resurrection—more closely linked to Dante, incidentally, than to the docile, ordered work of Fra Angelico.

The crescendo of Signorelli's frescoes begins at a panel of the Antichrist, prompted by a demon, preaching to a crowd which consists to a large degree of portraits of contemporaries. In the background is a struggling mass of Christians being destroyed by the followers of the Antichrist; in an upper section the Antichrist is hurled to earth over the heads of friars, warning of the end of

the world; at the bottom left appear two dark-clad, dignified figures, probably a self-portrait and a portrait of Fra Angelico. The
end of the world is a horror of fiery sky and blood-red moon, of
crazed animals and frenzied men, of earthquakes, burning and
floods. People flee, stumbling over naked cadavers, women try
to protect their babies from the avenging lightning and flames
and the death rays sent down by demon astronauts—chillingly
prophetic—with icy white wings and close caps.

The Resurrection is guarded by two enormous, vigorously
masculine angels who look down on the struggle of nude bodies
pulling out of the bare depleted earth slowly, painfully, a few
already skeletal. Some are still in the earth shoulder deep, some
already out helping the others in their struggle to emerge among
the bewildered nude, dazzled by the angels. All are masterful
studies of the nude, yet not so coolly intellectual that the wonder
of one, the agony of another, the sweetness of a third, are ever
lost in the craftsmanship. Hell is a violence of green, fanged and
sow-eared demons grappling with the dead; supervised by armored and sworded angels, they bite, strangle, torture the chaos
of naked, contorted bodies. (A blond of Slavic features and lank
hair falling over full breasts appears as several of the damned
women. She was, according to contemporary gossip, the painter's mistress, and after she discarded him he placed her several
times in hell, molested by a demon that is, supposedly, a distorted self-portrait. When she loved him he painted her as a
Virgin in another area of frescoes.) Heaven is happy nudity, as
skillful and expressive as that of hell; it stands serene and relaxed
or in postures of delighted wonder, under a vault of robustly
beautiful dancing, singing, lute- and viol-playing angels.

The frescoes are more, *in toto,* than should be taken in one
stretch of time. In order not to lose the smaller decorative panels
in exhaustion, it might be a good idea to take a pause in the
Palazzo dei Papi next to the Duomo (the sacristan is always ready
to open and reopen the Signorelli chapel for a small contribution). The palace in which the refugee popes lived and met with
dignitaries is much like the others of its time (the late thirteenth
century), a stolid building despite its Gothic daintinesses and the
thrusting diagonal of its stairway. The upper hall and quarters

were in reconstruction for a long time, but the lower hall is now the Museo dell-Opera del Duomo, a deep and immensely high room full of arrangements and derangements of papal treasure: iconlike inlays from defunct church stalls, a ponderous chunk of painted ceiling, the remains of ancient church pavement, cartoons for frescoes that never happened, Virgins of many periods and degrees of sophistication, resplendent churchly robes, coffers and reliquaries. In wood, leather, cloth, ivory, stone, pottery, marble, one finds bits of church art, expressed in modes that range from austerity to bosomy ladies whose bottoms disappear in leaves and on to flirtatious simpering figures in gilded drapery. There are a number of fine works—a della Robbia Angel of the Annunciation, a Simone Martini, a Signorelli, figures by the Pisanos—and interesting architectural drawings and medallions, etc., etc., in this collection which is neither dull nor insignificant, simply a bit distrait at present.

After surveying some of the glories of Orvieto past it might be time to see the city live, possibly by walking beyond the funicular stop to the Giardino Comunale, a formal shaded park rather in the style of late-nineteenth-century cemeteries (it may remind you of Père Lachaise in Paris) whose neat walks lead to deep, wide views and the huge blocks of tufa and spurs of broken column rising from a depth of grassy steps, which are the remains of an Etruscan temple. A few paces from the polite park of dark gentlemen reading their newspapers and toddlers held in cloth reins by young mothers, there is an expanse of café terrace which spreads from a set of tennis courts and a juke-box enclosure. The ice cream is delicious, as always, and especially vivid in taste after the encounters with Doomsday. One hopes that, still, the boy who serves you is a trusted habitué of about seventeen and the idol of two smaller boys of five and eight; among them they share the pleasure of placing before you a dish of ice cream, one glass of water, one small paper napkin and one spoon. Duties done, they take to the juke box and over and over again play, "My, my, my Delilah; why, why, why Delilah; before we come to break down the door; forgive me Delilah; I just can't take any more." Again and again, increasing the volume to its maximum as if the repeated hammer blows of sound must ultimately shatter the English incomprehensibility and reveal a core of meaning.

Out of youth, light and noise, now, into the historic dankness of the ingenious Pozzo di San Patrizio (the well of Saint Patrick), named for the Irish saint because he lived in a cave in which there was a similarly deep well. The Italian well was built in fear of a siege. Pope Clement VII, who had escaped the sack of Rome, and was afraid that it would extend northward to reach Orvieto, ordered a search for water. When it was located (and some pre-Etruscan matter, too) he assigned Sangallo the Younger to design the well, which he did as two parallel spirals of steps, one for guiding donkeys and casks down and another for ascending.

The entrance is filled with an enboxed lady tightly surrounded by booklets and cards, a plain saint covered with ex-votos. The descent begins immediately, circling on wide, shallow steps of a subterranean tower pierced with openings that are cut too low for comfort. The smell of ancient damp moldiness rises to meet the swift-growing dark and the gelid, imprisoned air. Halfway down the cold is such that one's breath makes small clouds which dissolve in the mist that rises from the bottom of the well, and the well recedes frighteningly, farther and farther away, ominously luring. Circling, circling, groping for the invisible step, fearful of tumbling down, down, down, through an infinity of time in endless gray-green mists and the smell of moss at the openings, no longer openings now but locked cell doors. Few make the complete descent into this minor hell, as you will notice when bodies brush against you with apologetic embarrassed murmurs. Why should you? You have come to Italy for diversion and/or enlightenment, and the well offers limited quantities of either. Make for the roses and oleanders on the via Roma, watch the boys exercise in the yards of the pink barracks, and try to catch glimpses of the Cathedral's stripes as you approach the Piazza Angelo da Orvieto, the well-restored medieval houses on the via Arnolfo di Cambio and, ultimately, the tall white, gray and yellow church of San Domenico. Narrow and handsomely serious, the church has a good portal which once belonged to another church, a highly skilled portrait-tomb by Arnolfo and, its pride, the seat from which Thomas Aquinas taught during his sojourn in Orvieto in the late thirteenth century.

Rounding back on the via Felice Cavallotti to the Corso Cavour, and standing in the middle of the city, you are poised for any direction: toward the majestic clock tower, the medieval Torre del Moro (so-called because of a relief of a Moorish head on a nearby wall), the Loggia dei Mercanti, whose arches fly over vases and tables of fresh flowers and the sturdy ladies who sell them, or the Palazzo Comunale and a golden ten-sided tower. Its shadow cuts across the front of a small, important church, Sant'-Andrea, a simple, patched and shored-up structure of the twelfth century over a sixth-century original whose remains can still be seen in a subterranean area of the present church. The interior is as modest as the façade, a basilica of three naves divided by four and four columns of Oriental stone as old as the second century. There is impressive Cosmati work of the twelfth to the thirteenth century in the pulpit, the roof is a satisfying composition of wooden latticework held in heavy-beamed supports like the bottom of a longboat; a tabernacle designed by Arnolfo encloses an appealing, worn Madonna and Child, and the light filtered through the alabaster windows leaves tiger-skin patterns on the dark stone. It is a very old church, but there are many in Italy, and it has a number of art treasures; others have more, but not too many have witnessed so much medieval history and ceremony. It was here that the Fifth Crusade was announced by the Pope in 1218 and Pietro d'Artois was crowned King of Jerusalem a year later. Sant'Andrea was the scene of the canonization of a local martyr and the place where the Duke of Anjou was crowned King of Naples after the rout of the Hohenstaufens in the latter half of the thirteenth century. Popes and cardinals received their vestments and insignia in Sant'Andrea, and leaders of the commune came to leave large candles as symbols of devotion at the simple portal. Much, much before these events it was probably—in the usual displacement of pagan by Christian—a Roman temple over an Etruscan one. (Proof or disproof of these suppositions should have come to light in the course of archaeological excavations long in progress in back of the church.)

Orvieto's archaeology, almost exclusively Etruscan, was and

still may be divided between two palazzi across from the Duomo. That marked "Museo Archeologico" is a climb through Pompeian fernery to a sign and a room with a chain across the doorway. A bell is rung and a man eager to have his solitude disturbed sells you a ticket (unless you have the stub bought at the Opera dell'Duomo, which serves for both) and lets you loose among the glass cases, a number of them cracked and bandaged in gay yellow tape. This section is of a period when objects were amassed rather than collected and stuck with bits of numbered paper, the mysterious numbers related to a hidden or lost catalogue or one not yet made. The Etruscan mixture is as in other museums, but don't run too fast; there are a number of rewarding objects to glance at, among them, an object which is obviously a fork, not used in the rest of Europe until a later millennium, as witness the comment of an English gentleman: "This form of feeding I understand is generally used in all places in Italy, their forms being for the most part of iron and steel, and some of silver, but those are used only by gentlemen. The reason of this their curiosity is, because the Italian can not by any means endure to have his dish touched with fingers, seeing all men's fingers are not alike clean."

On the piazza two sandaled friars are still trying to get a frontal view of the Duomo and are disturbed, at one point, by two men carrying an enormous strawbound vessel of wine, a common sight in Orvieto as, once upon a time, was the wine cask that stood before many houses, from which a customer could drink for a few lire. An interval on a stone bench to lift one's face to the façade as to the sun, to see how the friars and the cameras are getting on, to watch the broad, straddling steps of the wine porters and then, to continue with Etruria in the Palazzo Faina. Count Claudio Faina, who died in 1954, left to his city an invaluable gathering of Greek vases and a large tract of land, whose yield was to be used to augment the collection and to stimulate and support further exploration. You may already have seen some distinctive pieces of the collection in the first section, or they may have been transferred here. In any case, at this writing the Palazzo Faino contains a fine group of small terra-cotta heads of the fifth century B.C.; a male tomb marker, a lotus blossom that is basically a penis bordered by petals; crude pottery and delicate. Try to find, in the enormous miscellany, a small Venus with an archaic smile, believed to be a Greek's work in Italy, which may account for the ripe, round thighs. Somewhere there should be a group of expressive old men's heads—including a dignified, resigned head wearing a wreath and a vivid, speaking bald head of the fourth century B.C.—a small incised bronze dancer-musician and a bold black vase with a border of lions and wild eyes under whips of eyebrow. In a niche off by itself and especially lighted, a polychrome sarcophagus carved by the hand of a master; among the black "bucchero" pitchers (considered an indigenous style), one that is a staring face, the eyes disturbingly rounded, the eyebrows thin, stylized wings, the slender bearded head, that of a Carthaginian perhaps.

On the way to the upper floor one finds photos of local Etruscan necropolises, their number, density and extent, as always, startling; as always, the conviction that wherever one stands in Italy, it is on the crust of a vast dark honeycomb. The objects of the upper floor continue in Etruscan categories with a perfect minuscule bull, a well-shaped foot, seated figurines, three extraordinary vases of the seventh century B.C. topped with human heads and a cobwebby necklace made of near-microscopic rings calling from the abundance. The famous Faina collection of Greek vases is on this upper level, many of them identified with Greek names still alive in the annals of art, a few of them hair-raisingly patient reconstructions of thousands of once-broken bits. Near the exit, white niches to frame choice sarcophagus covers, a nice gesture of farewell; what better than a tomb cover to close off things Etruscan?

Coffee now and a pause in the shaded outdoor café on the Piazza della Repubblica, eyeing the yellow signs that point to the medieval city and San Giovenale. There is a short, direct way to the church but it is better to meander through the via dell'Olmo, the via del Paradiso, the via Cava, to cobbled walks at the edge of the city, over pinwheels of yellow-gold-red tiles, under embracing archways and paths that may lead to a café whose one table is absorbed in card playing, immune to the clack and crack of nearby *boccie* balls and the animated voices of the contestants.

The via Volsinia I presents a side door of San Giovenale and a late-fifteenth-century bust of the saint over the door. Suddenly an old crone leaps out of the shadow and from between her black beard and teeth stumps begins her rapid chant: this is the oldest church, have you a few soldi (they never say lire, soldi is the more pathetic, poverty-stricken term) and you look very healthy. Coins handed over, blessing received, you enter a truly venerable, quite primitive church confused by groups of pews that face several directions. One has to go out and enter the main portal to have some sense of the design of the church. Before returning, however, go to the wall of the piazza for an Umbrian panorama of precise strips of green and gold field, the higher gold of hayricks, black cypresses screened by the dusty silver of olive trees and, in the far distance, yellow and gray streaks of erosion. Close to, the yellows and oranges of melons and gourds under strings of vine clinging to fruit trees and, closer still, tanks of gas outside a kitchen and a stairway covered with geraniums and a covey of dark-aproned old ladies.

No one will venture to say exactly when the church was founded. A piece of documentation places it at the turn of the tenth century into the eleventh, that date believed to mark reconstruction rather than original structure. The imponderably old and fascinating church is most entirely frescoed by primitive and not so primitive artists, mainly local, of the thirteenth to the sixteenth century. Hard contrasts imprisoned in still outlines repeat and repeat the same subject in the same frame, painted in the same style, one next to the other, as if an early art school had set a limited range of tasks, or proposed a competition. Out of the repetitious and meagerly gifted there emerge a number of striking angular figures and one or two masterly heads. The light and fluid of Siena appears here and there among the dark and rigid, especially pleasing in a small chapel that floats in a wash of afternoon sun.

Via Volsinia I becomes low walls and more views of Umbrian countryside above the grasses that have pushed through the crumbling battlements. Turn back for the vicolo della Caccia, through houses and tiles and tall, narrow alleys that burst open for lush gardens, into the via Francalancia and the via dei Simoncelli, and back into the via del Paradiso under an arch that supports a house. Notice the good-looking doors (many, and good windows as well, in Orvieto) as you follow loose curves under balconies and green shutters into the Piazza Guerrieri Gonzaga, whose houses hide their blots and wrinkles in masses of flowers, and continue through the flattened tile-covered arches of the via dell'Olmo and past the classic foundation of the via Magalotti to the campanile and rosy rose window of Sant'Andrea. (Even churchly Orvieto, which had and probably still has a Communist mayor, cannot keep back the encroachments of feminism; so, not far from the church, you should see a blond lady competently performing surgery and inflation on bicycles and motorbikes.)

One very good reason for staying the night in Orvieto is its display of summer evening light and shadow suffused with the perfume of jasmine. At 8:30 join the *passeggiata* on the via del Duomo, closed to traffic at this hour, and as you stroll up the hill, observe the dusty glow slide from the side of the Cathedral to warm the façade for a few moments and then slowly leave, lingering as gentle glitter on one last strip of mosaic. At about 9:30, the frail last light of evening dissolves the contrasting bands to a uniform velvety gray and the Gothic curlicues become tassels on a dark palanquin. The birds fly around and in and out of the spires, drawing sharp lines on the receding, shadowy mass. A thin final ray evokes a murmur of gold on the side piers and a faint blush on the mosaics as they sink into the night.

As the shape of the clock tower disappears, leaving only the vague contours of the big bell and the metal man who is its mentor, walk through the archway across from the Cathedral, into the narrow streets that sell ceramics and wine, engaging during the day and magical at night. No eager voices, no plethora of things to buy or reject; only the whisper of fountains, subtle street lights, the smell of jasmine, a bench to sit on under a tapestry of flowers, an archway that frames narrow dark sky and one lamp light, a wine flask dangling from a wrought-iron sign, ceramic pitchers in niches, a big barrel in front of a wineshop, a terrace canopied with vines unified in the slow, quiet breathing of an old, old town.

Notes

The preferred hotel in town is the Maitani, neither large nor countrified, almost on the steps of the Cathedral and fronted by a column of sea gods wrestling with each other in a great twist of tail. (Double with shower should be $50; less, if the amenities include only a toilet and basin.) The Grande Albergo Reale, on the Piazza del Popolo, is still somewhat grand and a whiff decayed, the rates a little lower. The Hotel Italia on the via di Piazza del Popolo, is in the same category. In the third category and cheaper are the Duomo and Posta.

A number of small restaurants man their tables with big bottles of Orvieto wine, and serve the traditionals respectably: Da Peppe, gardened and off the Piazza Scalza, and Morino on the vicolo dei Lattanzi, are especially good. For a distinguished meal out of cavernous fireplaces under medieval vaults, go to La Badia, the abbey of Saints Severo and Martirio, a few kilometers below the city. It has a miracle story, frescoes and cloisters and is functioning as an attractive, unusual hotel. High.

Knowing the People
and the Language

WHEN ONE CONSIDERS the number of thinkers and writers who devote their lives to studying their own people, such phrases from three-week travelers as "We want to get to know the people, the real people" or, worse, "We got to know the people" are, to give it a gentle word, touching. The phrases obviously express a traveler's dream image compounded of scenes from Italian films—large, plump, musical, smiling families, napkins tucked under round, contented chins, heaping platters of steaming spaghetti lovingly placed before them by abundant apronsful of beaming mamas and *nonne* and *zie*—and from nineteenth-century romanticism, images of an invitation to tread the grapes in an Italian Eden where the vats shine and tremble under the purple dancing feet of beautiful *ragazze* in embroidered costumes, black hair and ribbons flying.

If it exists, the village is probably not reachable on a traveler's rushed schedule; if you should get there you won't understand the dialect, and the freshly pressed juice you have dreamed of drinking, caressed by the feet of Gina or Sofia, will be too new and sour. But assuming that language proves no barrier and assuming that everything goes dreamily, it is still not easy to know

146

the people, a very complex people. Nevertheless, the slippery quest is an entertaining game. Listen. Watch. Join an Italian tour group in a cathedral or palace if it crosses your line of march. Throughout the tour of not markedly significant art your companions cry gleefully, "*Guarda! Guardi!* See how the arm always points at you, no matter where you go," an always happy, surprised comment wherever a trick of perspective crops up and a good way of commenting on art when one wants to avoid making a judgment. You will observe, as you may have before, the strong Italian taste for the baroque, murmurs of "*che bellezza*" meeting straight on and courageously the most blinding, contorted, gilded excrescences. As in eating and emotions, so in art, Italians have no fear of exaggerations.

The traveler navigating in his cocoon of illusion "Italian" seems often to crack his head on knobby contradictions. How can the seat of Catholicism, the breeding ground of saints, lead the rest of Western Europe in the size of its Communist Party? How can an open, kindly people be so indifferent, so inconsiderate? How can a courteous people trample one another for a seat in a bus? How can men—Catholics who wear conspicuous medals to prove it—who are so child-loving snip their home ties with such ease? Such contradictions are our invention, built of Puritan rigidity and raw newness as a people with little of the Italian's long astute experience. He was born with a caul of doubt and optimism and is infinitely old. He has seen and been Greek, Phoenician, Etruscan, Roman, Norman, Spanish, French and has learned through the millennia that what we think of as contradictions are the mottled, knotted warp and woof of living. He says that animals, for whom he has little love, are too stupid for contradictions; it is only man who is capable of the variations of thought and response that seem to clash but don't, really.

It is often difficult for us not to confuse wide-open Italian Catholicism with dour Irish Catholicism and Calvinism when we are, for example, confronted with groups of boys and men who seem to do nothing but hang around their neighborhood piazze, even where employment is high. We are made uneasy and it takes some forcing of the mind to accept the fact that the familiar scene offers him infinite variety and that watching is a favorite Italian occupation. Furthermore, if one can manage to live without, why work? When he works, he works hard (watch the waiters in a crowded restaurant), and when he doesn't he loosens completely, without any guilt about improving each shining hour; the shine is enough.

We are prone to couple good manners with "mind your own business." The polite Italian's business happens to be anything within reach of his eyes and ears. Ergo, any untoward event draws a crowd, which can quickly explode into big voices, big gestures, hot disputes, a search for the police, all intensely operatic. The books say that Italy invented the opera; one sometimes wonders whether the opera didn't invent Italians. Homemade, instant opera is apt to break out on any street at any time, fully equipped with protagonists, chorus for lamentation or rejoicing and an audience.

Scene: a Sunday afternoon in a seaside town. Action: a boy on a motorbike zooms down the road and lightly grazes the knee of an old woman who is trying to cross. She falls down, instantly, and lies spread-eagled and mute. Traffic stops. Windows and doors fly open and a chorus of women swiftly surrounds the heroine. The mezzos sing a low, rumbling line of *"poveretta, assassino, che sciagura"* while the sopranos keen high and triumphantly, *"È morta, è morta, è morta"* (she's dead), lifting their arms like winter-frozen twigs. Two members of the murmuring bass chorus pick the woman up. She gathers her limbs slowly, brushes her skirt, stares about her blindly—Mimi in her last-act delirium—and releases a trickle of tears. Hand on heaving chest she permits herself to be fed droplets of cognac at a café and, still wiping her eyes, still panting, begins to intone her encounter-with-death aria. She is joined in a duet by the weeping boy standing at his motorbike. Shortly, the chorus takes over to thunder at him. The boy goes off, the chorus disperses, the curtain slowly drops on the old lady sniffing and crooning her terror and pain against the pitying, angry staccato of her attendants.

You need not be told that Italy is one of the noisiest countries in the world, a fact often attributed to the fireworks of temperament, the narrowness of ancient streets. The basic cause is a remarkable absence of community spirit. The only viable Italian community is the family and its expanded form as the tribe that includes café mates and, in working-class houses, immediate neighbors. The result is total lack of consideration in a general, abstract sense, although there is great sympathy on an eye-to-eye level. In other words, nonpalpable people don't exist. Italians like noise, it is company and a symptom of life; silence is loneliness and death. Anyway, a shrieking, weeping quarrel of two washer-women claiming the same strip of courtyard at 6 A.M. is "Italy," which you have come all this distance to experience.

The Italian's pragmatism disturbs those who prefer him innocent, lazy, knee-deep in flowers, *dolce far niente*-ing. It is startling to find that the man who has given one a bunch of grapes, gratis, off a country cart is the same man who, in a chance meeting in the city, has turned impromptu beggar. To the Italian it was a sensible notion at that moment and why not *approfittare* from the presence of a rich and grateful tourist? The visitor's enchantment with hearty, red-cheeked flower vendors falls from him with a thud when he finds the long-stemmed anemones he bought had borrowed their graceful length from extra, nonrelated stems attached to the short flower with thread. His Puritan soul recoils when he finds that the young god who is the helpful desk clerk escorts for sightseeing and profitable dalliance now a smitten woman, now an eager man. But the youth has been speaking of the hometown girl he hopes to marry! How can he service women and men and babble on about a wife, a small rural bar and a house to fill with bambini? "Why not?" he might answer were you bold enough to ask. "Why not? What harm is there in being attractive, in earning a little money by pleasing and, having saved that money, establishing oneself as a pillar of small-town society?" He sees no contradictions, no immorality. If everyone profits, what's immoral?

The day one begins to ask "Why not?" rather than "How can they?" might mark the beginnings of knowing something about these people—any people, perhaps.

For a longer stay and a persistent quest of the people there is no avoiding a knowledge of the language. The phrase-book words, "Does this train stop at . . . ?" "Bring me a clean fork," and the imperious "I think this taximeter is not working properly, I will not pay that amount" will not open villages. So, we study more Italian, learn to be polite on grade one or two level. (Few foreigners can master the higher spirals of courtesy, and if they did, the lack of the proper nods, the rich voice and intimate glance would make the locutions stiff and foolish.) We learn to eat and sleep and shop in Italian, the words appropriate to trains, buses and driving and some of the multitudinous words that describe flat, round, thin, fluted, plumped, short-tubed, long-tubed, curled, bowed, in dots, in sheets, pasta. The same small number of words are repeatedly pulled out of the limited hoard, and one begins to feel more and more, among this mellifluous people, like a retarded child.

We mush on, enamored of Italians and Italian, through a Mandarin terrain that grammars describe and few speak, through the perilous land and mangrove swamps of irregular verbs and their chameleon auxiliaries, into the jungle where the fearful touchy subjunctive lives. It is a nervous little beast that hides in trembling shadows of hope, sorrow, pleasure, doubt, belief that is disbelief and laps at the shores of the imperative. Why? Because you may ask or even order someone to do something, but will he?

We have about run the emotional course of the subjunctive and its hissing tails (*potessi, potesse, potessero*), have nailed down the little pronouns that skip in and out of phrases, now tagged on an imperative or infinitive, sometimes in tandem (when they change spelling), sometimes pulled in to make a phrase more musical, occasionally mating to produce new types of small monster. Good soldiers with severe eyestrain and taut eardrums, we slog on until we have learned it all, or almost. We are no longer frightened or made breathless by the length of Italian words, are fairly adept at sprinkling sentences with *ci, la, ne,* accustomed to the fact that one egg is masculine and two become feminine singular and that polite address to a male makes him "she" and "her." Our vowels are as ripe as August peaches, we can pound out the double consonants clearly, the "r" ripples and trills.

Equipped, we travel, ready to ferret out Italian thought in its own language. The south, however, is determined to speak its own impenetrable tongues. It brings a few of its mannerisms to Rome, which has long had its own nongrammar speech, attractive lazy pronunciations—in Trastevere, for instance, they like to *magniare* rather than *mangiare*—and obscenities and curses that are common, friendly exchanges and hair-raising out of their indigenous terrain. Learned Padua prefers to say its *ce* as *tse;* one pays *tsento* lire for a *capputsino* and greets one's *amitsi* with *"tsaio."* Moving eastward the *ce* and *ciento* stiffen to hard *dze* and *dzento,* and the Venetian dialect closes one out altogether.

In one region water added to your cup of coffee is *lungo,* elsewhere the same amount of water makes it *alto.* The width of a piece of cloth is also *alto,* but if your shoes are wide they are *largo.* A form of the past tense is used commonly in one region and rarely appears in the speech of another, and so on and so on, until you decide there is no mastering a language which is so many languages. You drop the laborious study, slip into the common simplifications around you—*bello* for all things good, *brutto* for all that's bad, *fare* as a portmanteau verb, and give Dante's language back to him and the Mandarin savants.

3

TO VENICE
THROUGH UMBRIA

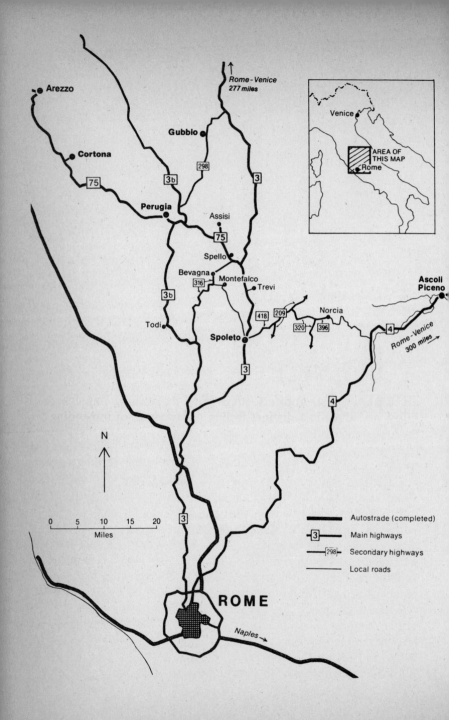

Arezzo

Cortona

[75]

Gubbio

[298]

[3b]

Perugia

Assisi

[75]

Spello

Bevagna

Montefalco

[316]

Trevi

[3b]

Todi

Spoleto

[418] [209]

Norcia

[320] [396]

Ascoli
Piceno

[4]

Rome - Venice
300 miles

[3]

N

0   5   10   15   20
Miles

[3]

ROME

Naples →

Rome - Venice
277 miles

Venice

AREA OF
THIS MAP

Rome

Autostrade (completed)

[3] Main highways

[298] Secondary highways

Local roads

Todi

Hᴵɢʜ ʜɪʟʟ ᴛᴏᴡɴꜱ challenge, dare one to invade and pierce their secret places—virgin princesses sequestered in towers. Like the rest, Todi also lures with its seeming impregnability, and there is a distinct feeling of suspense, of impending drama, as the road winds up and up, passing gates cut into Etruscan, Roman and medieval wall to reach the *centro* and a confrontation with a breath-taking main piazza.

Isolated above the meeting of the Tiber with the River Naia, small, aristocratic Todi was once a bustling Etruscan city and later Roman, vigorous enough for the usual internal strife among parties in the Middle Ages and powerful families during the Renaissance. It had the toughness to fight off Frederick II, to attack and be attacked by Spoleto and Orvieto. Now Todi is a modest agricultural center, a repository of august churches and palaces, patchy shadows of Etruscan and Roman past and a large memorial to one of Italy's early poets, Iacopone da Todi. There is a center of studies and publications devoted to his work; a school has been named for him and a piazza; a monument stands in his honor and his tomb rests in one of the best of Todi's churches. Born thirty years before Dante and only ten years after the death of Saint Francis, he, too, was a product of Umbrian mysticism and a Franciscan. Like Saint Francis he had been a rich man who retired to a life of holiness and poverty (tradition relates that the dramatic change came after he found that his wife, who had died in the course of an evening's festivities, wore sackcloth under her silks), and, like the saint, he wrote religious poetry. However, he infused adoration with an urgency, a graphic immediacy that is intense, almost violent, as witness the lacerating cadences of the Virgin lamenting the Crucifixion: "Son, your soul has left you, son of the lost one, son of the dead one, poisoned son: Son white and red, son incomparable; son, whom shall I look to, son, now that you have left me?"

There is major art in these hill-town matrix squares, called del Popolo, del Capitano, or Signoria or Papale or Comune, made of the same elements—cathedral, seats of government and palazzi of governors. The style is indelibly unique, as identifiable as Mozart quartets, and, in their harmonies of line, texture, color and ornaments, as varied. One or two are a shade more compelling, more perfect than others, and Todi's L-shaped center is one of the masterpieces. It was sketched out centuries ago as the Roman forum; the later composition of towers and battlements, calm arches and Gothic window tracery, a sharp rush of stairs opposed to serene, contemplative rises, is the work of the late thirteenth and early fourteenth centuries, touched by the Renaissance.

Part of the charm is the satisfying expectedness of the design, the knowledge of what the elements will be, but how related to each other, in what felicities or incongruities? We find the Duomo what and where it should be, enthroned on a set of stairs at the top of the piazza (as was the Roman temple before it), its stern thirteenth-century horizontality balanced by the rise of the campanile. The severity relaxes around rose windows and at meetings with intricacies of leaf carved inside the band of pink and white stripes that surround the entrance.

The outer serenity is immediately disturbed, as one enters the church, by a strange, windy, chalky, big mural of Judgment Day in a dust storm. More soothing and accomplished are the smaller, less ambitious figures on a side wall, and particularly, the saints peering out of the capitals of the pillars. To the right as one enters, there is an extra nave of Gothic arches supported by delicate octagonal columns leading to a fourteenth-century Virgin. A more primitive Virgin, in a niche near the Last Judgment, takes on the mood of her neighbor victims of doomsday, her crude wooden head staring frantically, pulling out of her panel in terror. After following the alternation of highly pleasing and appalling that is characteristic of most Italian churches, go out to the right side of the church for a look at the full, tall curve of apse and Gothic windows and ornaments.

The steep rise to the combination of strict crenelated tower and Gothic grace of the Palazzo del Popolo and Palazzo del Capitano leads to the Museum and Art Gallery (Pinacoteca), with the usual collection of religious paintings and local Etruscan and Roman finds. Take or leave the museum to examine and re-examine the squares, to enjoy the lavish expanse of countryside behind Garibaldi's statue. Go around to the left of the church to see the might and confidence of the Vignola archway of the Palazzo del Seminario, or follow the wall down along the via Anzidei, and on the street of Paolo Rolli (a translator of Milton; this *is* a literary town) peer into open doorways that reveal streetscapes of housetops and balconies, trills of stairs accompanying small houses, all against one immense landscape of hills and farms and distant abbeys. Wander, loiter—every prospect near and far pleases in this village—and hang around the main piazza a bit, again. Have coffee and window-shop on the via Mazzini under medieval houses, and take a look at the Teatro Comunale, very much in the nineteenth-century opera-house style. It is reduced to showing westerns, which doesn't seem to have impaired the amiable spirits of writers and composers (the fat one must be Rossini, the bewigged gentleman, Goldoni) who beam out of plates on the façade.

From the monument to Iacopone one reaches the attractive Piazza della Repubblica and above it, the church of San Fortunato; on the way, an enchanting little Gothic building whose shape suggests that it might have once been a medieval tower later dressed in a loggia supported by minute archlets and Gothic windows under a gentle, shallow roof of tiles. (In every hill town there is one house, at least, that every visitor must have; this is the Todi sample.) Nearer the church, quite another expression of housepride, expressed as Pompeian designs, griffons and shields, scrolls and masks, faded to a sepia color. In between, shrubs shaved and clipped to make formal gardens, a stand of regal trees; and at the top, the unfinished, raw face of the nevertheless impressive church of the late thirteenth to fourteenth century, with a grand portal surrounded by numerous receding bands of skillful carving and, on either side, attractive figures of the Annunciation. Other than the scraps of frescoes in the Sienese style and those of a later painter, the essential matters that beckon inside the church are the distinguished woodwork stalls carved by a Maffei from Gubbio and the tomb of Todi's poet in the crypt.

Anywhere now, depending on your next place and when you think you have to be there. Ancient walls and gates and more medieval houses along the via San Fortunato for one; the maidenly charms of the church of San Carlo wearing a tall flat screen as hat and bell tower, and near it, four large Roman niches, part of a once monumental edifice, off the Piazza del Mercato Vecchio. Enormous views drop out of almost any street, some of them enclosing the church of Santa Maria della Consolazione, alone on its green against the fading blues of distant hills. There is some discussion as to whether it is a work of Bramante or not; it might as well be for the remarkable rhythms of its many-sided, domed apses gathered in a Greek cross under a taller, central dome, ornamented with harmoniously balanced and carved architectural detail.

Note

If you can't leave Todi, a likely possibility, or want to make a bid on the Gothic seductress below San Fortunato, you might stay at the Vissaluisa or the smaller, less expensive Cavour. For good eating, the Umbria, whose terrace tables sit on an edge of the town above yet another undulating expanse of Umbrian countryside.

Spoleto—Before and After the Ball

Before time was recorded on anything but knotted string, there was an indigenous people in Spoleto. By the third century B.C. it was an important Roman town, involved in key events of Roman history and personages—including Hannibal, who made no headway here. As an early church center, it was the place from which Constantine issued (in 326) several definitive regulations for the newly organized religion. It was a capital city for the Longobards and the Franks and had the not too singular honor of being ravaged by Barbarossa in the conflict between church (Guelph) and Holy Roman Empire (Ghibelline). When it was a papal state it had particular importance since Pope Alexander VI sent his daughter, Lucrezia Borgia, to act as "governor" of Spoleto. (The intermeshing of reasons for this appointment is fascinating but unfortunately too complex to trace here.) When the French came, they made Spoleto the capital of the province, and from then on it slipped in potency, left with only the power of its beauty and the annual summer transfusion of its music-art-film-ballet Festival of the Two Worlds.

Equipped with the thick sheaf of pamphlets distributed by the local tourist agency (on the Piazza della Libertà), which includes a large, detailed map, hotel listings, a calendar of festival events and picture booklets, make a survey of the cafés that push their flower-strewn terraces into the Corso Mazzini (one of the few examples of people having successfully wrested space from cars) and choose a seat from which to become acquainted with festival Spoleto. An elderly copy of *Le Monde* sprawls with the London *Times* on a table surrounded by medallions and beads, expensive tattered raja coats and Tyrolean jackets. A long and lank-haired lady with the face of a nighthawk preserves her hangover and pallor from the flat slap of 11:00 A.M. sunshine by hiding deep inside the awning of the café. A young Italian (however, one is never sure since the flower look is international and sparse of speech) in a worn suede jacket, curly-haired and languidly graceful, with the facial design that elicits references to Hadrian's boy and Hawthorne's Marble Faun, nestles a kitten in the gap of his jacket, stroking it gently, slowly, as if forever; the world is himself and the kitten and time endless.

Up and down the Corso Mazzini and into the piazza stroll people carrying instruments or scores, people with extraordinary faces—broadly plump Slavic, ascetically Anglo-Saxon and richly curved Italian, many of them clearly the silken, sinuous male camp followers of the arts world. In impeccable white linen suits they constitute the bulk of the audiences for the ballets, the rare films, the theater of absurd or outrage, the chamber-music concerts and the cocktail parties that tinkle out of hotel and palazzo windows.

The shaggy-haired, the coarse-cottoned and raw sheepskin-jacketed provide less decorous and more lively people-viewing. One young man who looks like a peon just thrown out of a Mexico City slum saloon paces restlessly and belligerently through the town, identifying himself as an American Indian and accusing everyone with light hair—Swede, Englishman, northern Italian—of exsanguinating the Third World with his greed. A young English acting company, of a most courageously experimental nature and subsidized by its native Arts Council, decides to put another Buckminster Fuller dome (an unreasonable facsimile of the structure that stands as a welcome to the town and the festival) in the center of the Piazza del Duomo. The piazza is a place of overwhelming dignity, above noticing such matters, or the barefoot walkers who wash their feet in its sarcophagus fountain, or the presence of the crude zebra skins, gaudy ponchos and shaggy Andean rugs hung like barbaric war trophies in front of a cave-shop at one side of its stairs. The festival authorities and the police object, however, and they ask the young actors in Genghis Khan mustaches and orange pants to take down their new home, offering them a polite number of hours for dismantling the structure, which needs only one strong push. The lopsided dome stands; the actors have the right to live, they say, wherever they wish. After the elapsed time, the police begin to take the dome apart while the prospective tenants stand huddled together, laughing. A strip of metal grazes an actor's arm, which takes a swing at the nearest person; a policeman hits the hitter, and a small melee tries to explode. A few drops of blood streak one cheek and the agitated meshwork of flailing arms and legs separates as quickly as it formed. The police carry off the tatters of the house, and the actors line up against the sunny wall as peaceable and flowery as before, a bit dirtier. Later, much later, near a street that shows the same execrable paintings that appear in every tourist center and every "festival" town (judging from their sameness and number they must be issued by a plant as large as that of General Motors, using the same belt systems and the shipping as well organized), one of the actors, now wearing a battered derby, will try to climb a decorative spiral that stands in the windy upper town. Couples up from Rome for the weekend are amused, the other actors convulsed, and the young toughs whose local villages afford nothing but sleep at 1:00 A.M. are awed. But the police stay away and the act is an embarrassed, empty gesture.

An arts festival, crowded into a short season, is a demanding thing. One runs breathlessly up and down hilly streets to see paintings and a show of theater arts, to chamber music at noon and in the afternoon, in thin slots of time, improvised theater. Ballet, films and concerts at night and becoming acquainted with faces that begin to reflect one's own exhausted pallor. Then there are the rehearsals in the Piazza del Duomo for the final, majestic work that closes the festival and innumerable antique shops, galleries and folk crafts—untouched and adapted—to look into. All this to-ing and fro-ing and some minimal eating and sleeping goes on in corners and alleys blocked by television apparatus and film units and maddened with traffic that buzzes and blats up and down the hills through the day and far into the night.

It is not all high art and pure. Schubert quartets thicken to octets and even orchestral works when the accompanying instruments of voices on the street and auto horns join in. The hotels can be merciless, and a reservation made months before may not be honored because one's room was given to a couple who wanted it—and meals—for ten days rather than your meager three. A "large double" can be a maid's cell crammed with a big bed into which one must leap from the threshold.

The Dr. Jekyll face of Spoleto, however, is thoroughly rewarding and worth hanging on for. The final concert begins to release the older, smoother cadences of indigenous Spoleto. Waiting for the music to start, one watches the doves and later the swifts streaking through the pallid daylight while a slice of moon waits for its time to appear. The windows of the piazza are filled with spectators. On one section of wall, perhaps part of a cloister garden, the light catches the white streaks of nuns' habits clustered under a tracery of trees that hold a few agile boys. Daylight slips off the face of the church like the drawing aside of a fragile curtain. At nightfall a new curtain of strong artificial light shines on bright yellow faces and saps the flares placed around the piazza. After the concert, the sky is streaked and torn with thunderous fireworks.

Early the next day the galleries and shops on the via del Duomo fill their trucks with art and *objets*. The primitive paintings are carted off along with the sculptures of mirror imbedded in plaster. Out of the theaters come costume boxes to be hurled into trucks among pianos, fiber trees and a painted gate; once finished with the hurling and the pushing, the drivers stand under the defiled heap in their trucks studying maps for the best way to get out of Umbria. Yesterday's "Big Sale" signs in Italian and English, the old card tables, the antique phones and the two middle-aged cupids who sat in the street on a cinquecento bench have disappeared. So have the banners and many of the automo-

biles, the television and the film cameras. Little is left of Prov-
incetown, Chelsea and New York's East Village, which had become aspects of Spoleto. Their representatives are either sleeping
off the long, busy weeks or are stretched along the highway trying
to thumb rides to Rome, to meet their friends on the Piazza
Navona. The city is again itself and yours.

You might make a fresh start where you began before, at the
Piazza della Libertà, to look at the change of customers, now
predominantly the owners of the shops on the Corso Mazzini out
for one of their innumerable coffee breaks, a lightning gulp and a
half hour of conversation. Stroll down the Corso Mazzini and its
tangents, toward the stairs that lead from the Largo Piancini; you
will probably pass a double curve of stairs that join as one
around two lions with Kaiser Wilhelm mustaches. Nearby is the
Piazza Mentana, which glitters with the shellac shine of twentieth-
century Romanesque and the authentically baroque of San
Filippo. It is not too dizzily ornate for its period, the paintings
please and the high-backed pews are affably curved. The *pièce,*
however, is a glass and gilt box holding the Corpus Petrim,
whose eyes are half-closed in agony. A chaplet of roses sits on his
fair hair and his upper body is clothed in jeweled and gold-orna-
mented silver cloth cut to resemble Roman armor. Below, the
holy body wears a houri's pink knickers and a tasseled petticoat
and, on its feet, sandals like those sold in Soho. How can they,
one asks again, with so many examples of great church art everywhere? They can and they do, with love and hard-earned money.

Down now, into the via Minervio and the via San Giovanni
Paolo for the church of that name and its very early frescoes,
among them one of the first representations of Saint Francis. A
votive painting, protected by eaves of wood, lightens the via
Salaria Vecchia; immediately below this meeting of Madonna
and Child, there is an appropriately placed and almost as suit-
ably old carpentry shop. Somewhere among the shops on via
Salaria Vecchia stands the ubiquitous Arab rug salesman. A shop
owner comes out to the street to pass the time of slow business
and asks the Arab a question. The Arab, with no Italian, shows
the price tag; the owner asks about the size of the rug; the Arab
pushes the tag closer. Now the Italian shouts his question; the

Arab responds by poking the tag closer and closer to the Italian's spectacled eyes. The Italian, no longer casually wasting a half hour and now inspired, as Italians readily are, by the drama and conflict, and almost convinced that he really wants a rug, tries to pull out a corner to judge its size. The Arab, obviously new to the trade (or he would already have opened the rug to show its gorgeousness of design and exquisite workmanship), pulls it back and hustles to meet a compatriot down the street. Together they meet a third, and conversing animatedly they disappear around a corner, rugs smartly riding shoulders like the capes on toreros in a bullfight procession.

Porta Fuga, so called because it was through this gate, or rather an ancestor thereof, that Hannibal fled after his unsuccessful attempt to occupy Spoleto, is a dark, quiet, arched-over street that ties baskets of mushrooms and greens to its twilight walls and spills out of its caverns the shapes and colors of fruit. The mingled odor of baking bread, shoemakers' glue and carpenters' enamels should pull you into the vicolo San Giovanni and via del Trivia and back to the via di Porta Fuga to see that the three Arabs have become four, each blazoned with the identical rug. Before the street becomes Corso Garibaldi, stop before the indispensable shop in town—in all these towns—the hardware, tools, etc., dispensary and this a particularly attractive example of an appealing species. Several windows show scythes, sickles, precision instruments of carpenters and masons, heavy rope and fine cord, screwdrivers and chicken wire, pails, cinches for horses, meat grinders, coffeepots and strongboxes. A provincial shop, in short, that supplies the implements for crafts urban and agricultural—as in other towns, a fair gauge of local activity and degree of prosperity.

In contrast to the alert enterprise of the shop is very old San Gregorio Maggiore on the Piazza Garibaldi, with gaps between its stones and around its tower, red and white barriers marked "Danger of Collapse," the proof in ominous piles of crumbled stones below. The twelfth-century church can still bear your footsteps, however, although it may find its Renaissance portico, gravid with shields and angels' heads, a bit hard to sustain. The portico opens to the Baptistry of the fourteenth century, frescoed with scenes of the life of one of the many martyrs buried here. The cool, utterly simple basilica has been so distorted by repairs and changing tastes as to appear quite nervous, distracted by its mediocre Stations of the Cross, trompe l'oeil trying to look like mosaic behind fake carving stippled with gilt, and a strange faceless nude who holds a scroll against a millefleurs background. What does she represent? Who knows? However, the acorn-shaped front, the floor tiles, and the frescoes near the main altar are worth some short time, if only out of respect for the gallant old cripple.

Out on the big piazza, those rugs on those Arabs, and if you stand with your back to the tower (just where it might hit you if it decides finally to fall), a view of what was once a Roman amphitheater, fortified in the sixth century and again in the fourteenth, and beyond the combination of vast fortress and steeples, high over the city, a green height of Umbrian hill. At the end of the via Pierleone, one encounters the broad pink and white stripes of San Domenico, surrounding a billowy, sugary, bearded-lady Christ over the main portal. The church is an extremely tall, compact example of a thirteenth-century church with well-designed wrought-iron light brackets, a singular Crucifix of wood (fifteenth century) over the main altar and stretches of good frescoes. The most interesting single painting is one of Saint Thomas Aquinas enthroned on a chair equipped with space for books in its arms. Counseled by angels, he is teaching a group of cardinals and bishops much smaller than himself, a device of naïve perspective that emphasizes his superior wisdom and saintliness.

The Duomo embraces the wide end of an ample piazza, whose narrow neck is a shallow drop of stairs. At one side, a piece of incomprehensible modern sculpture and climbing apparatus for children in bright orange, the color of progress and optimism; a misplaced civic gesture, because the piazza resounds boisterously and every child's voice bangs against the palazzi and bounces into the portico of the Duomo. And quite a portico it is, of the Renaissance, and living with the Romanesque church and tower in a symbiosis of beauties. A leitmotif of the church is the shield of the Barberinis, here specifically Pope Urban VIII, who modernized the interior of the Duomo and now sits, surrounded by

Barberini bees, as a bronze portrait by Bernini above the main entrance. Much of what is important to see, except for the surviving stretches of rough, mosaic pavement, is guarded by the sacristan, who opens, successively, several chapels. In one you are shown the work of Pinturicchio and in another accomplished wood sculpture, an appealing Virgin and Child, and a twelfth-century Crucifixion painted on parchment over wood. Elsewhere, a creamy, prosperous Virgin and Child by one of the Carraccis, and in the Chapel of the Icon, a Byzantine Madonna who somehow survived destruction by the iconoclasts and was given to the city by Frederick Barbarossa late in the twelfth century.

The tomb of Fra Filippo Lippi, in gold and white, was ordered by Lorenzo de' Medici, designed by Filippino Lippi, the painter's son, and the inscription written by the scholar Poliziano; all together, an imposing collection of Renaissance might and talents, meeting at a roundel that urges forth an elderly plumpish head surrounded by classical masks which trail ribbons attached to a skull in a neat arrangement of Renaissance motifs.

With the assistance of two other painters, Lippi created his characteristic frail, angelic Virgin in a series that depicts her life. The Assumption has the Virgin in a brocaded gown sitting in a disk of deep blue, and at her side, in a golden circle that flows out as great wavy rays, a child's picture of God wearing a large white beard and a crown. Surrounding them are numerous saints and angels and donors with Botticellian faces in filmy chiffons. (To put it justly, the influence was from Filippo Lippi to Botticelli.) The Annunciation emphasizes the perspective of the small open-arched *tempietto* in which the Virgin waits, and in still another section there are portraits of the painter, his son and the assistants. (The mellow head on the tomb, the ethereal paintings and the title of "friar" all belie—if Vasari is to be believed—everything the man was in actuality. He was sent to the friars because the relatives who took care of him and his many brothers and sisters after their parents died no longer could afford to feed the brood. Filippo left the monastery at seventeen for a life of wandering and adventure, which included capture by pirates from the Barbary coast and imprisonment in North Africa. He was freed because the local Sultan admired his painting. Back in Italy, he became a prodigious womanizer, unrestrainable in his sexual rages—even by a patron Medici—and it has been suggested that he died of poison administered by a woman scorned. Yet he produced religious paintings as serene and innocent as fresh milk.)

Out on the piazza, look up again at the façade, an arrangement of mosaic and minuscule curves, ornamental hooks to relieve the hard edge of the top slopes and, all over the surface, the dynamic wheeling of various-sized rose windows. The neighboring via dell'Arringo, a lyrical, subtle street, surrounds the triple apse and then descends again as a smooth fall of shallow stairs to the Duomo.

The via del Duomo is exceptionally well kept and respectably picturesque; stupendous beams hold up its tunnels, vines curl on its artistic brows, one arch is pedestal for a piece of welded sculpture and another arch hides a public laundering place. The via Saffi is in the same mood, the site of an imaginatively designed art gallery and, a few paces on, a rangy, attractive antiques shop. Through a corridor that leads from the via Saffi one reaches a quiet, sunlit courtyard and the winsome church of Santa Eufemia, which had until recently been dressed to the teeth in frills and furbelows. She is now back in her twelfth-century charms. The capitals and columns don't quite match, only one pillar has been left a patch of painting and only one Virgin and Child remains of a set of frescoes at the back of the church. The altar, however, is a good-looking structure of incised marble and Cosmati work, and above it, well-preserved Sienese triptychs. (As always, study the predelle, often more vivacious than the main attractions.) Santa Eufemia was, some years ago, fired by the Vatican, but in her day she must have been something of a suffragette saint since hers is the only church in Umbria that provided a matroneum—a women's gallery, as in orthodox synagogues—for the ladies.

There is no rational way, as has been said, to plan a walk in a hill town. What appear to be parallel streets on a map may turn out to be a matter of stairs up and down, arches over and under and tunnels that lead to a closed wall. However, one can always try: take the via dei Duchi, which still has medieval shops shaped by wooded doors above, a stone ledge as counter and, below, a protectively narrow slit for squeezing into and out of the establishment. The Piazza del Mercato and its via suffer no kink, no art, no urge to be "with it"; a slow, easy market that wanders from detergents to brooms to shoes, from artichokes and grapes to the slither of fish in battered scales. It pauses for a stupendous fountain, loaded with shields, a huge clock whose hands—mighty rays of sun—don't work, grotesque heads and fat volutes and two startled windows of an old house on which the complex structure was imposed. The via del Mercato ties together, loosely, series of small piazze and alleys (one of them the ecumenical street called Santa Gregoria della Sinagoga, for a church whose remains sit on Roman ruins) that wander, in turn, into secluded minute villages decorated with wash and cats lying in splashes of sunlight.

On the via del Arco di Druso there might yet live a restorer with old things of no weighty importance to sell and a Trattoria dell'Angelo, its totem an angel who flies through the air holding a platterful of steaming spaghetti. The local barbershop is the neighborhood art gallery for homemade paintings in a style that might be called "primitive primitive" and his neighbor makes the musical ceramic angels and little pots encrusted with flowers found in every souvenir shop in Naples. It is a lovable street but difficult to linger on because there are TOO DAMNED MANY CARS on it. Avoid them as you can to stand before the Arco built by local Romans in honor of the son of Tiberius. One of its mighty imperial ends is now sunk deep in a venerable churchyard and the other jammed into, and shoring up, a tired house. Since the arch led into the Forum, sizable pieces of Roman empire lie under the present pavements and help support a number of buildings in the vicinity.

The possibilities out of the arch are, as always, numerous. Find the quiet bends of the via Brignone and the via degli Eremiti and their hidden tangents to the shopping street called Monterone. And there is the Piazza Fontana and its handsome fountain and Palazzo Mauri, now the archives and the library. Or, through the closeness of the via della Trattoria, back into the

Piazza della Libertà, this time not for people-watching but for staring down, through a protective grating, at the Roman theater and its modern relation, the sports stadium, which sit against an ample width of valley. The Corso Mazzini conceals near it posters and cafés and shopping citizenry, several strips of light and dark too insignificant for names: vicolo III is exactly big enough to contain an arch with an urn at its top and an art-nouveau lady fountain; the via Plinio il Giovane (Pliny the Younger) is dark turns and thin straws of sunlight. Another vicolo is interminable grim stairs like those in Piranesi's prison prints while the vicolo Valeria Corvino frames an antique votive painting.

The via Municipio leads to the Palazzo Comunale, its reason for being. The palazzo has only the thirteenth-century tower to prove its age, and, as if to deny the Italian reputation for lack of punctuality, it harbors two clocks, assisted by the tower, which also rings out the time. The steps near the piazza are punctuated by neoclassic urns and a tall spindle of modern metal sculpture that might be a tree, a flame, the spirit of Spoleto's festival. Here we may have *the* Spoleto mixture: modern sculpture, a rush of stairs, a well-made wrought-iron street lamp, buildings used and unused in a mélange of architectural styles, benches to sit on for watching the struggles of a large car trying to ease its way through a steep, narrow path, like a fat woman struggling into last year's bathing suit.

The custodian of the Pinacoteca is also guardian of the Roman house at the bottom of the stairs, and it is he who admits you to it. Tradition says that it belonged to the mother of the Emperor Vespasian; whether that is so or not, it is a good example of a luxurious dwelling of the period.

This may be enough Spoleto for you, or you have forgotten to bring your thickly rubber-soled shoes and have had enough of slipping on stone polished by millennia of feet and stubbing your toes on the cobbles. Whether you stay or go very soon, see the church of San Pietro. Of all the city's ornaments—antique to avant-garde, stern palazzi and engaging churches, wings of stairs and slopes and arches, cats and ornate people—the loveliest is the most neglected, sitting alone and often unnoticed on the side of the road leading to the highway. To be worthy of the link of

Saint Peter's chain brought from Rome, the fifth-century church was enlarged in the 1200's and again in subsequent years. Inside, it is a shambles. Don't bother, even in the unlikely event that the church is open. Concentrate, instead, on the pale-gold façade and its twelfth- and thirteenth-century sculpture. The three unequal horizontal sections are touched with the faint glitter of small mosaic tiles surrounded by precise, elegant designs in abstract, Saracenic style. Two powerful bulls and two strong-winged eagles hold the vigil over the horseshoe portal while Saint Michael bests the dragon of evil; interlacings of grotesque animals and foliage twist around Saint Peter. The rest deals with dire warnings against transgressions. A pair of legs—obviously of one of the damned—sprouts from a caldron; a devil pulls the hair of an agonized victim still in bed (a whore? an adulteress?), her hands bound; and on her abdomen sits another devil reading a Black Mass or a recipe for her advent into the caldron. There is no novelty in the arabesque patterns or the moral lessons; they were the matter required of the medieval sculptor. These, however, are not the flat, passive strings of figure one often sees on early churches; San Pietro's animals and people jump from the stone and call out strongly, vividly, with a certain wit, and in spite of the idiot scrawls of vandals, they remain gems of Christian art.

Notes

HOTELS (reserve well in advance for the Festival). The Gattopone is a small villa at the very top of the town with few—and some quite small—rooms, all well kept and decorated. It looks across to the Rocca (fortress) and onto a tall aqueduct over a deep green valley whose cicadas thunder from fields as evenly spotted with haystacks as old-fashioned candy dots on paper. The food has the reputation of being the best in Spoleto, so you must reserve your dinner. Lunch is served in a vine-covered arbor, food and ambience both attractive. All rooms are double, with bath, and the cost without meals should be $50–$60. Twice that amount and a bit more will cover meals. The Dei Duchi, on the via Matteotti, is the large "luxury" hotel whose rates are somewhat lower. The Albergo Manni, on the Piazza Collicola, has fewer than twenty rooms and a manorial fireplace. A double room and bath are moderate, and meals are easily available in a number of restaurants in the vicinity. The Piazza Garibaldi and its adjoining Piazza della Vittoria have railroad-station sort of hotels; not good, not bad and fairly inexpensive.

RESTAURANTS. The two leading hotels mentioned; the Taverna del Pennello, above the Teatro Nuovo; the Trattoria del Pallone, across from the Carabinieri station and below the Albergo Manni, a place that serves a basic menu under an immense tree whose branches have been woven together to make a green umbrella. There are, as well, many small restaurants in the streets near the market.

Finally, if the above descriptions of slopes and stairs disturb you, be comforted by the fact that buses climb the hilly streets, too. The ski-lift principle works fairly well: a bus up to the Duomo area and then walk downward (map in hand) to ride up again for the downward attack in some other direction.

Caveat: Portions of the above describe the Spoleto Festival at its ebullient height. It has fallen from lustre more recently but, Festival or no, Spoleto is an entrancing town; try to see it.

Trevi

Trevi is a hill town that doesn't clamber or leap from its rock, nor does it hide in ridges of stone to show only gray wrinkles and suspicious eyes. Trevi flows as honeyed icing for a perfect cone, topped with the discreet flourish of a campanile. At night it becomes a mirage of circus tent, a necklace of lights on the dark Umbrian slopes.

Although the people are courteous and hospitable, as they are in most of Italy, the best time for Trevi is the time when all public buildings are closed, when householders and their children have disappeared to lunch and nap between one and four on a not too windy winter Sunday. The town is yours and too small for exigent itineraries; scrubbed clean, scrupulously maintained and every turning a pleasure. A frescoed house swings its armlike arches to link hands with others that pull away to unexpected directions. Secluded corners shelter a cat's cradle of vines or a triangle of balcony and a wedge of red-brown tiles to protect it. Everything has been given care, thought and polish—the arrangement of bricks and stones on the walks, the knockers on the doors, the colored shutters that set off the gray-browns, the pinks and the golden-white of walls and walks. The meticulous cleanliness speaks of an awesome *amour-propre,* an appealing quality in a town that obviously is just getting by.

Somewhere in your wandering through the narrow, serene curves, you should come on a cluster of three apsidal bulges, laced with water pipes, that fill a surprised alley. These rounds and the amazed Gothic faces that ring them are part of the original thirteenth-century structure of the church of Sant'Emiliano, an Armenian missionary martyr. (The Touring Club of Italy guide, the painstaking, encyclopedic successor to Baedeker, records the precise date of his martyrdom as January 28, 302.) From the church, go down, up, around, wherever a shape or shadow calls to you. Ultimately, you will find yourself near the peak, where a patch of space too small to be called a piazza offers you a bench and a view of strict lines of olive trees marching up and up into the hills, undeterred by the yellow stones and unkind earth at their club feet. They waver in the distance, the lines flow together as clouds, then dissolve into endless, amorphous space, neither earth nor sky. In the garden that slopes from the piazzetta, a white puff of Persian cat crouches, sniffs and stalks, her luminous blue eyes searching for a lizard; she is too beautiful-but-dumb to know that the gold on the wall is winter sun and not for lizards. A dignified dog watches her for a moment, then turns his attention to a lean black and white cat who has climbed a vine to look into a kitchen where a woman sings as she bangs her pots. The dog saunters down a hill and disappears, the cats slip away, the woman retires for her siesta; the warm, serene silence lies on the town like a coverlet jerked, now and then, by a rooster who doesn't know what time it is.

Leaving the town as you came (via the Piazza Mazzini) notice as you pass the corner of the via Roma and the via Zappelli a house with monochrome paintings of Diana and Actaeon. Farther along the slope toward the highway, your eye will be caught by a house, once possibly a roadside inn, whose wall is covered with a fresco of a knight in armor riding from a distant castle and gazing toward a ship in a sea of evenly scalloped waves, like those in Chinese embroidery. On the surface of the blue sea, spread in large, clear letters is the legend: *"Amico fedele e sincero. Coraggio. Passerai per questa via del mondo una sola volta. Ogni bene che puoi fare sia fatto subito."* (Be of good cheer, sincere and faithful friend. You will pass but once through this world. Whatever good you can do, do it quickly.)

Even Trevi's homilies are delivered aesthetically.

Note

There are several eating places in the town, but you might enjoy a restaurant in Foligno, a short distance away. It is called da Peppino or Italia and is part of an inn on the Piazza Matteotti. In a vaguely "hunting-lodge" (and a bit of everything else) atmosphere warmed by the smiles and solicitude of the waiter-proprietor, listening to the whispering busyness of two elderly female relatives working at a half-hidden stove, watching mud-covered bicycle riders toil up icy hills on the television, you can surround *crostini* and salami, homemade fettuccini, roast hare or chicken and a large cup of custard topped by a heaping of fresh fruit for little more than the cost of a burger and fries at home.

Poor Relations

A DECADE AGO (and in later years) parts of Umbria were officially declared "depressed" areas. Some towns are barely sustained by tourism, a few on the plain still live off the land as small agricultural centers. A number of the hill towns live as they can, severely, respectably, left with nothing but their old people, their church art and the crumbs of a monumental past; cracked antique cups sitting on the hills. When the cup is altogether shattered, when the few youngsters who play with improvised toys in ruined cloisters leave the towns, as they must, these will be, if they aren't already, the ghost towns of Umbria.

Certainly not worth visiting for their own scrupulously clean, decrepit selves, they provide a few revealing hours to add to Umbrian time, especially if "Umbria" has come to mean for you the brouhaha of Spoleto's Festival of Two Worlds, the beauties of Todi and Gubbio and that pinnacle of church art, Assisi.

Spello is entered via a grand Roman gate and looks down on seas of green, gray and gold fields from an even more splendid gate, the Porta Venere, of the time of Augustus, and named for the temple of Venus that stood nearby. (It can be reached by way of the via Torri di Properzio from the Piazza Matteotti.) Behind

175

the modern arcade of a school on the Piazza della Repubblica—
on the central street named for Cavour and Garibaldi—one can
see the remains of a Roman building. A short distance out of the
town, there is a Roman amphitheater and sections of Roman
wall. The town hall, on the piazza of the Republic, houses
Romanesque vaults and windows and, as in most rural town
halls, sarcophagi and bits of Roman and medieval stone, much
of it undoubtedly from a number of gone or redone twelfth- and
thirteenth-century churches. The most important of Spello's
churches, both on the Piazza Matteotti, are Sant'Andrea and the
church of Santa Maria Maggiore. The façade of the first stayed
more or less as it was. The interior has taken on the tastes and
needs of a number of periods, including modern heaters that mix
strangely with the primitive Crucifixion and the prettily carved
baby columns of the Gothic altar. Santa Maria Maggiore had its
face lifted in the seventeenth century, with the help of some
pieces of its thirteenth-century self still visible in the façade. The
jumbled quality is intensified by two sections of Roman column
standing in front of the heavy Romanesque campanile and, so
that there be no misunderstanding, a cross placed above the columns. Out of season—and maybe in—one must ring a bell at the
side of a yard to the right of the church. A chained dog answers
discouragingly. So, one waits uncertainly in front of the church,
whose door is opened, in time, by a lackluster lady in a black
apron. The reason you are willing to wait is that this is the
church frescoed almost entirely by Pinturicchio early in the sixteenth century. How long you stay depends on how much sweet-
ened enamel you like in your religious paintings, but no matter
how long you stay, concentrate, because the alternatives to Pinturicchio are baroque chapels bulging with mismated elements of
gaud and gilt and distraught flights of large stucco figures
adorned with black dust.

On leaving, you look for the custodian with the limp apron
and expressionless face. She is gone. She hasn't waited for a tip
not because she is rich, but because she is defeated and depressed
beyond an interest in your 500 lire, a mood that will begin to
seep out of the walls as you wander through the town; it will be
the mood of middle-aged and elderly faces that offer a polite

greeting as they pass in the street or, with their sad courtesy, direct you through the town.

Higher on the avenue of the Italian heroes sits San Lorenzo, considerably transformed since its sixth-century beginnings and interesting mainly for its examples of the Renaissance craft of wood inlay. If he is not conducting a mass, the priest will be most pleased to take you into the sacristy to see remarkably skillful views of Spello as it once was and a set of portraits, ostensibly of the prophets, that look as if they were sketched from life and then built up in judiciously shaped bits of varicolored wood.

The rest is Spello itself—winding streets and paths held apart by shallow arches, crumbling houses, and from the Belvedere (reached via a street named for it), the crest of the town, one can see on a clear day Perugia and Assisi and Montefalco. Around you, on this peak of silence, only the clucking of hens penned behind wire stretched over Gothic portals. Down now, with the wanderings of the town, to pieces of Rome and medieval commune, past little shops stuffed with anything inexpensive that might sell and solemn, good-looking, polite women, inadequately sweatered for cold spring damp, their hair in plain bobs that can be handled by home washing. The older women, wrapped in low kerchiefs almost down to the eyes, carry large shoulder-slung sacks for gathering, on the green slopes that slip from their streets, herbs and chicory to be used raw or cooked and a bit for their Gothic-housed chickens.

Equipped with a small unsalted bread of the region, several slices of country prosciutto—somewhat leathery in texture and color and very zesty—cheese, and a bottle of the undiluted local wine ("not sophisticated" is the way it is said in Italy) and consequently fairly strong (all obtainable in a grocery run by a handsome couple in pristine butcher smocks across from Santa Maria Maggiore), one can make a picnic in the fields off the road toward Bevagna. Don't go too far from Spello, firstly because it is an attractive sight from below and secondly because, later on, one runs into farmhouses and haylofts and attempts at new townlets that leave little space for the bucolic, slightly drunken pleasures of Italian picnicking.

Bevagna is gayer, livelier, the shops bigger, the bars more frequent and spacious, some of its streets and piazze wider since it doesn't have to fold itself around a cone of hill, and it has at least one beauty parlor. Ancient Rome has naturally left is spoor; clearly visible, for instance, as pillars imbedded in a house at the end of the Piazza Garibaldi. These were apparently part of a temple, accompanied by baths and mosaics now in a house on the via Porta Guelfa, behind a plain wooden door and difficult to see except with the help of some swift, enterprising local boy—if there are any around. Sitting above the piazza of antique houses and a lively trattoria is a church dedicated to Saint Francis, its face of the thirteenth century, its interior appallingly improved in the eighteenth. Somewhere in the luxuriousness one finds a stone protected by an iron case; this is the stone, they say, on which Saint Francis rested his foot as he preached to the birds.

It doesn't much matter where one goes in Bevagna—following capillaries wide enough to accommodate a slender body, into a street that is a series of shallow arches flattened at the top, pulled steeply down to the light of a small open piazza, a stage set seen through the wrong end of the binoculars. Here and there as in other Umbrian towns a *porta del morto* (page 183) and double arches gently pointed like those in Siena and, at the side of the stairs leading to San Michele, an engaging cluster of houses, all balcony and eaves. And always the fat, white chickens imprisoned under antique vaults and houseware shops in whose windows you can study the complex bindings of fibers that make the long besom used in rural areas. One entity demands to be seen, however—the extraordinary Piazza Silvestri, a compilation of medieval buildings, stairways, a flattened arch covering other shadowy arches at odd, attractive angles from each other to create a setting for a rare work, the church of San Silvestro. Empty, cold and damp, perfectly proportioned and balanced in spite of the rough irregularities of its top, it was designed by a Maestro Binello (he left his name and the date of construction, 1195, at the side of the entrance) whose name should be added, if for this church alone, to some of the other great B's—Brunelleschi, Borromini, Bramante, Bernini—in the list of magisterial Italian architects. An added attraction to San Silvestro is the custodian, about eighty years old with a dancing lurch, bright deep-set gold-green eyes, ruddy cheeks set in gay rivulets of wrinkles, the ensemble wrapped in kerchief, sweaters, aprons and felt shoes. Her interminable monologue is an incomprehensible whistling and splashing through a few teeth that twist in all wayward directions like a derelict fence. She really has nothing to tell you except that the church is dry—you know it isn't—and that the shallow puddles you wade through come only to warn that three days hence it will rain. (It rains that night.) She is as uninformed and lovable as an old rag doll and follows you after the visit and tip spraying a stream of blessings and good wishes.

The church nearby, San Michele, was also the work of Binello and an assistant; it, too, is a majestic work with a grand portal bound in Cosmati work and two Evangels, or angels, staring round-eyed and apoplectic at the much later addition of a row of skeletal heads of oxen whose horns dangle ribbons and flowers. The upper façade returns to its neater time of delicate triple windows bound in modest ornaments.

With another long look at the Gothic Palazzo dei Consoli and, if possible, its tiny theater in early music-hall style, and the swelling apse of San Michele, you have had the best of Bevagna except the lively company of Umbrians not too deeply mired in restrained gloom.

Montefalco, the "banister" of Umbria, reached by corkscrew twists from the plain, *is* a ghost town. Even the optimistic Italian Touring Club Guide uses words like *silenzioso* and prasies it as a "sanctuary" of Umbrian and Tuscan art, which it is not quite. The same authority lists its population as a thousand according to the 1961 census; the present count is less than half that. The town has steadily lost much of its population and, to judge from the scant presence of the young, is rapidly losing more. This was the town important enough to be taken, while it was a free commune, by Barbarossa and later to be sacked by an emissary of his grandson Frederick; it was handed over by the church to the Duke of Spoleto, taken back by the church and in the sixteenth century invaded and again ravaged. During the course of the pillaging and changing of regimes, it gave birth to eight saints, probably inspired in their mysticism by the strange isolated quiet between battles.

If there are chickens in Montefalco, they don't cackle, and the three babies one sees play alone; the few tourists have the determined look of scholars, come to examine the frescoes of Benozzo Gozzoli and the works of Umbrian painters. The museum, once the church of San Francesco, is supposed to be open during regular museum hours but it is usually necessary to call the custodian, a duty that the lady behind the local bar has taken on willingly. All you have to do is ask, pay for the call and as a courtesy buy one of her cups of cappuccino, leaving—as always—a 100-lire tip. The custodian comes, a woman in a black tailored coat, as massive as a stretch of Roman wall, surmounted by a pretty, small head aureoled in fine, silvery hair. She is intelligent and informed and tells you that there is no agriculture money here, no crafts, little tourism, one weaving plant that employs ten people, and because the town has lost so much of its population, even the poor live in large, lordly apartments.

The museum blazes with frescoes—some imported from other churches, most of them indigenous to this temple for Saint Francis—that form a minor encyclopedia of Umbrian painting with the inevitable golden touches from the Sienese, references to Duccio and Giotto and to the dextrous bravura of the Renaissance. The star of the show is, as mentioned, Benozzo Gozzoli, to whom was given the honor of painting the life of Saint Francis in 1452, a fascinating contrast and vivid lesson in the development of Italian painting over a hundred and fifty years when compared with the Giotto series in Assisi. There is everything you expect in these, by Renaissance standards: graceful attitudes, precisely balanced compositions, utter confidence in attacking any technical problem, smooth surfaces, the faces of great men—Petrarch and Giotto and Dante—among an adoring crowd, and the fall to stylish, pleasant Renaissance earth from the exaltation of the early masters and their blond Sienese heavens afloat on the humming of angels' wings.

A Montefalco painter who worked about fifty years later than Gozzoli, Francesco Melanzio, was given several chapels to illuminate, which he did agreeably and skillfully. One interesting

Virgin whose frail, conventional face sits oddly on her large, sturdy body is shown in an unusually literal aspect of her life and works: beating off with a big club a goat-hoofed, dark demon who is pulling at a small figure that clings frantically to the Virgin's lovely gown, pleading for help. One source attributes the painting to Melanzio and another to a painter from Foligno, Lattanzio. In either case, says the lady guide, "We consider this a portrait of the tough, independent, strong woman of Montefalco," still another way the Italian woman makes her life palatable—by seeing herself as Mary, and vice versa.

The custodian, after lighting sections of the walls for concentrated inspection, now gives you the full effulgence of the total lighting, a dazzling, Byzantine-like richness. She mentions, as she has before, her monograph—not a book, she reiterates, just a monograph—on the Gozzoli frescoes, all gathered together, in black and white. Wouldn't you like to look at it? Of course one agrees to look and, under her ponderous presence, leafs through the book. For lack of any other way out of this genteel entrapment one says, "Very nice. How much?" and escapes the hook because she asks 6,000 lire, much too much for what she insists on calling "not a book, a monograph." You start for the door and she says, very politely and yet with a touch of exigency, "I have something interesting to show you, and beautiful," and opens a folder lying on a table. "This is the work, unique, of a noblewoman," and it turns out to be table mats, carefully embroidered so that no rough ends appear on either side, merely superior examples of Assisi's overabundant embroideries. First, a flicker of anger—she has no right to use the museum or you this way—soon stilled by recognition that this is an Italian thing, *carpe diem* translated into any time or opportunity that may present itself. Then embarrassed pity. Why should a dignified, obviously well-educated woman have to be as alert as a hunter, turning here and there, lying a little, to catch a few thousand lire?

Somehow, after this encounter, the silence becomes oppressive, the scars on the faded pink walls become deeper and wider (wonderful to paint and photograph) and the wind colder. The sharp spring wind, the gray cast by a heavy cloud, the very old one-toothed man who shuffles into the piazza to meet a friend and, finding him already gone, weeps a few senile tears, the custodian-lady's dignified desperation become too much. One leaves, with the hope that a few of the boys will stay and help revive the town. With what? How? Ultimately, it is probable, the large valuable collection of books in the Palazzo Comunale library, some of them rare examples of early printing, will be taken to Perugia or Rome and the frescoes detached and placed, along with works in other dying towns, in a great museum of local church art, possibly near Assisi. Otherwise, it must crumble in not too distant time—people, churches, frescoes and all.

Note

Considerable reconstruction, retaining the old style, has begun in the area. Spello, for one, is fresher, livelier, and sports a good restaurant, Il Molino, faithful to local products and dishes.

Gubbio

A BOOKLET ON Gubbio calls it the "Paestum of the 14th Century," a curious twist of pride, since Paestum is dead and uninhabited. Gubbio's *mementi mori* are limited to its Roman theater, almost gracious if one might use that word for a Roman theater, where classical plays are performed in the summertime, and its "doors of the dead," the small filled-in archways one sees in many old houses, reminders of an ancient local custom. The door from which the dead were taken out had to be sealed to bar the return of evil spirits, a fear that long predated Christianity and coexisted with it for centuries. For the rest, Gubbio's medieval houses shake dust out of their carpets, air their blankets on decorative bands of Renaissance stone and put out pretty floral-designed ceramics to dry in the sun. The doors are wet with fresh paint and the slish-slosh of masons' trowels is ground base for their lusty morning songs.

Gubbio seems constantly to be having its face not lifted, but a few of the deeper wrinkles smoothed, filled in, to maintain the beauty she has been for centuries. Thus, she is known as the Siena of Umbria and more dramatic than that Tuscan city because she lies in the tough, russet steepness of uncompromising

Umbrian hills with a tapestry of green-capped rock at her back and, beyond that, folds of mountain streaked with snow into springtime.

The usual opening gambit: find the tourist office, not far from the large market piazza-park, Quaranta Martiri, named for the forty innocent men and women machine-gunned by the Germans before a nearby church, in reprisal for the killing of one German and the wounding of another by partisans sheltered in the mountains. The office is easy to find; look for the conspicuous lettering on the Communist Party headquarters, whose building it shares. Equipped with the intelligently made and attractive booklet, and probably a poster or two, for which Gubbian *gentilezza* will not permit you to pay, return to the big piazza and look up at the towers and tiles, the green of climbing gardens, the pigeonhole windows and the ample arches rising to the Palazzo dei Consoli, the splendid crest of Gubbio. There are a number of streets that climb fairly directly to the Palazzo, but do it some longish way, left and right, and always up, through perfectly undisturbed, unimproved medieval streets. They are not the long gray stretches, sad and tired, that fourteenth-century streets can sometimes be. For one thing, the streets rise and drop and are attractively careless about uniformity of height. Except for lucky towers that weren't razed by enemies or law, none of the houses are tall, but within the limited height there are innumerable gradations of higher and lower and the red-tile roofs slope steeply or gently at angles that leave openings for the Umbrian sun, which turns the stones to blushing beige-white. The via Baldassini, after you've diagonaled your way up, will give you an integrity of medievalism and, under the Piazza della Signoria and supporting it, four enormous arches, reminiscent of Etruscan and Roman grandiosity. Another rising zigzag and you are standing before the virile palace of the consuls and a wall that gives onto a total view of the city—for tall people; the master mason who planned it was either very tall or thought in terms of fortress height and strength, a constant medieval preoccupation. After a time of examining the hauteur of the stars and portal, the shapes of the windows and the high delicate loggia, walk up and into what is now the museum.

The great hall in this fourteenth-century structure is a reflection of the power and riches of the commune, a witness to the fact that the communes' consuls were, like the English barons, tough, shrewd traders and warriors, and this grand vaulting space was their due, appropriate to their might. Standing in corners of the hall are Roman pieces found near the theater, slabs of inscription (it must have been a busy industry, that of carving honors and information into every flat stone in the vast Roman empire), the ubiquitous sarcophagus and medieval marbles. The matter of importance here rests in a room beyond the baronial hall, surrounded by good examples of sturdy unaffected furniture and a many-sectioned chest inlaid with street scenes of Gubbio. In frames on swivels that permit one to see both front and back are the famous bronze Eugubine tables. Found in the area in the fifteenth century, they may some day be the Rosetta stone that opens to the world the Etruscan language. There are seven tablets, of the third to the first century B.C., a few engraved in the maddening Etruscan script of N's and E's facing the wrong way that give the feeling that were one to read from right to left, or scan a mirror image, it would all come limpidly clear. Some of it is recognizable Latin, but both Etruscan and Latin letters shape Umbrian words which describe religious ceremonies and the confraternities that were concerned with them; the Etruscan remains secret.

The upper salons are the Pinacoteca, probably still being filled, because there isn't too much quality in the collection except a few extraordinarily small reliquaries, a rather horrifying, super-realistic German Pietà and a precise, pearly Madonna of the Pomegranate, possibly the work of Lippi or Pier Francesco Fiorentino. Interest lies mainly in the furniture, a good fountain and a wall fountain (the guide tells you this was the first building in Italy with indoor water) and doors that close off what were fourteenth-century indoor toilets.

There is good reason why these advances in civilization belong to Gubbio, at several points in its history an important city. The Eugubine tables would indicate that it was a major religious center of the Umbrians; as a Roman municipality, it not only minted money and provided classical drama but also involved itself in the struggles for power that established the Empire. After suffering the common fate of massacre and pillage by the Huns and slowly, slowly recovering to play the popular games of today-Ghibelline-tomorrow-Guelph and trying to sack its neighbors, it flourished as a free commune. Ultimately it became the fief of the Montefeltros of Urbino, the cultivated family who stimulated and supported the arts here as in their native city. It was in Gubbio that a great illuminator, Oderisi, was born as well as Bosone Novello Raffaelli, the author of the first Italian novel. And while these distinguished citizens were busying themselves with their crafts in the thirteenth and fourteenth centuries, refinements of ceramic making began to adorn the palaces, by the fifteenth century splendid enough to be jewels, the high glazes touched by real gold and imbedded with gems. The ceramics now shown in shops and in well-designed displays on street walls still have a delicacy of ornament and felicity of form greatly superior to many of the mugs, the rooster pitchers, the tiles with bright sayings and lumpish ashtrays that beckon from walls in other towns.

From the ceramics shops near the Piazza della Signoria, it is a step to the Gothic Palazzo Pretorio, the town hall now and the repository of archives and library. The building is usually open to visitors in the morning and worth the visit to see the vaulted rooms, to glance at centuries-old documents and, most important, illuminated books of choral chants painted locally in the thirteenth century, some of them possibly the work of Oderisi.

Along the street that flows from the great austere piazza and the ceramics, look for gateways that one might mistake for house entrances. These are the entrances to a hidden street, the via Galeotti, a long eccentric tunnel whose arches drop and lift, spurt out of each other to accommodate turns or the walls of a house, or pause altogether to let a strip of sun touch the fourteenth-century purity. It may seem like a taciturn place to live in, but follow a mason or a mail carrier to find well-kept small courts of freshly painted doors and, sometimes, paths to other courts suggesting the defensive plan of the Middle Ages, the *castellare* (page 22). Notice the slope of the bricks in the walks, the design of the overhanging street lamps, the interlocking of tiles over a room that stands on an arch and the filled-in doors of the dead. And consider the disappointingly rational cause for their existence: the original fourteenth-century house built with a major door that led to a shop or a small dormitory for traveling salesmen. Flanking the main entrance, there were two doors, both raised from ground level; one was usually decorative and the other served as entrance—with the help of a ladder—to the family living quarters. One authority suggests it was a rash of thefts that caused one lateral door to be closed; another says that advances in domestic architecture and the fact that better and separate inns came into existence made it natural that the main door become the family entrance, one smaller door to remain as window and the other shut as a useless channel for drafts. Both authorities compromise with popular beliefs by conceding that these closed windows were opened to permit the dead to pass through and were then blocked up again.

A gaggle of girls bursts from a green wooden door that opens to a steep slope of small houses and secluded gardens, a tiny village within the hidden village. One of the gardens is quite small—one tree, several sketches of vine, a few flowers, one bench and one stone pedestal dragged out of some ruin or other, and a set of twins, a boy and a girl of about seven or eight, both round, plain and energetic. They are playing "television." He stands on the pedestal, giving the news and comments on the news with an uncanny reproduction of the voice—a bit rough and slow, with traces of a Milanese "r"—and the very words of a leading news broadcaster. Having finished his discourse, he descends from the pedestal to her enthusiastic applause. It is her turn and she goes behind the tree to be announced as a popular singer about to moan the currently popular lament. Having evoked a promise from her brother that he will applaud as vigorously as she did, she mounts the pedestal and gives a frightening imitation of the arms-shaking, the head-tossing and the wails of the chanteuse. A varied, endless economical game that needs no toys or numbers of participants.

On a sharp run of stairs that drops to the lower town, a group of boys with discarded broomsticks and paper caps play war, running up and down the stairs, pointing their sticks and bang-

banging, falling dead, coming instantly to life, until the game ends altogether when one mastermind mounts to the top of the steps and, letting fly a crumpled ball of paper, launches the *bomba atomica*. All fall and stay fallen. One is no longer amused, and the only palliative is to watch a little sister, barred from the game but still hanging stubbornly around, red cheeks smeared, mop of blond hair disheveled, slowly, cautiously, squatting and sliding down the smooth, steep path at the side of the stairs. This she does holding a large, naked doll, her brother's sweater and a small suitcase that contains her treasures and indispensables—a stoneless tin ring, perhaps, a string of plastic beads, one doll's shoe, a comic book which she cannot read—not to be left for a split second out of sight or reach.

However beguiling the children, one has come to see the city. Immediately north of the palace of the consuls is the Palazzo Ducale, built by the Montefeltro family in 1476. Local historians say that this was the place of the seat of government when the Longobards ruled, and here Frederick Barbarossa was entertained, and probably Charlemagne. The palace is, at this writing, still being restored after a long period of neglect and despoiling (superb inlaid panels and ornaments that belonged to the Duke Federigo da Montefeltro found their way to the Metropolitan Museum of New York City, for example), but it is generally possible to see the handsome courtyard.

The Palazzo Ducale shares its piazza with the Duomo, which houses the usual fading clouds of ancient fresco and a Gothic tomb as well as an ornate fifteenth-century bishop's throne by one of the Maffesi, a local family of talented wood carvers and workers in wood inlays. It is, however, the repose of the broad nave surmounted by gently bowed arches, a local style said to be an imitation of hands joined in prayer, that is most appealing.

The church of Santa Maria Nuova, listed in all the tourist literature as an important church of Gubbio, is not. The door is locked and a sign points to a custodian of keys in a local house. She turns out to be a good-looking woman (the people are, as a rule, quite good-looking, although that might be the mote in your pleased eye) armed with a key which, if the tourist season is long past, will not turn in the frozen lock. She returns for a key to the sacristy. This works, and one enters an unkempt warehouse, first confronted by a high, broad and incomplete baldachin, which obviously doesn't belong to the limited space. Two ornate sarcophagi, emptied of the local patron saint, Ubaldo, who inhabited them, stand embarrassed in the middle of the floor. The discarded church is kept open only for the Ottaviano Nelli fresco, now under glass and further protected by an overhang and frame painted in bright blue. This Madonna del Belvedere of the early fifteenth century is said to be the masterpiece of the most famous of Gubbio's painters. It is not by any means a great painting, particularly for a time that was producing masterpieces as if off an assembly line, though the Virgin and Child, the musical angels and the tiny rich donors being introduced to the Virgin, everyone dressed in silks and brocades and placed against nicely designed wallpaper, have considerable charm. More Nelli is to be seen in the church of Sant'Agostino, immediately outside the tower and arches that is the Porta Romana. Here he has covered a good portion of the apse with scenes from the life of Saint Augustine and a Last Judgment. They are conventional but artful and imaginative within the tradition. The curves of the painted surfaces and the dark of the church make examining difficult; this is where the opera glasses you should be carrying come in handy, and if the sacristan is about ask for some light.

Still more churches, most of them with the mellow hands-folded-in-prayer ceiling and a number of them with Nelli frescoes, but you may prefer to leave antiquity to see what might be going on in the big market in the middle of town. You are thrust back, however, into inescapable antiquity almost immediately, because the long, plain, two-storied loggia in the marketplace is a fourteenth-century structure built and used by the weavers' guild to protect their cloth from the sun. It is still in business. It now shades bars and shops, stalls of fruits and vegetables, plastic toys and two or three glass boxes, each wrapped around a brown torso of roasted pig, to be sliced for the *porchetta* sandwiches, here made with big chunks of crusty bread rather than the usual roll. The competition for customers is quick-eyed and noisy, the several vendors dominated and bested by one burly young woman. Keen in catching an interested glance, she makes swiftly for her prey and taking a firm hold, will rush him to her stall, a female Keystone Kop carrying Charlie Chaplin. Take your paper-wrapped *porchetta* to a bar, for a bottle of beer, to another stall for a chunk of cheese, then settle on a bench near the monument to the forty martyrs. Munch and listen to a nervous concert of fragments of rock, Sicilian passion, the oom-pah-pah of street bands and an Italian girl trying to sound like Piaf, wafted by a record stall. Watch pink plastic brooms go by and big tongs and copper vats, an orange baby tub, market bags, sieves, and news-paper-wrapped shoes; and see it all, people attached, try to crowd into the buses that go back up into the mountains or down to the valley.

Peering down on people, buses, bundles and your hard-work-ing jaws is the octagonal tower of the church of San Francesco and its adjoining cloisters. If you look very hard, or imagine it well, you might find there traces of the house in which Saint Francis was sheltered after his father disowned him. Not far from Assisi, this second home of the saint remembers Saint Francis as the tamer of a magically unkillable wolf who terror-ized the countryside. Surprisingly, the major number of frescoes, some very old, some restored, are not devoted to the saint who spoke kindly to his brother wolf, although there are a couple of panels devoted to him. In one apse (here again, you will need your opera glasses) there are numerous panels of the life of the Madonna by Ottaviano Nelli, who painted himself as Saint Matthew. The sacristy is part of the restored house of Saint Francis' hosts and leads into the cloister, where (in the spring of 1983) the most imposing entity—other than the agility of one ten-year-old football player—was a large and lively set of Roman mosaics, not obscenely pagan as at Pompei, for instance, but pagan nevertheless.

And there is this church and that, most of them pleasantly, undemandingly Romanesque; some show Nelli, some do not, and architecturally, San Giovanni the most satisfying of them all. More interesting, however, are the streets to prowl. The via Piccardi, rising from the upper end of the weavers' loggia, is a meander of gray stone under foot, textured stone as walls, and overhead an arch cut out to admit a bright square of sunlight. It

meets the equally inviting and slightly more majestic via Baldassini near the house of Saint Ubaldo, now the Center of Umbrian
Studies, reshaped at sundry times, but still representative of an
upper-class Umbrian house of the early 1300's. The via Baldassini, followed to the left, leads almost immediately into an especially delightful corner (the superlatives begin to fail) of a large
fountain and the perfection of balance and spacing, the justness
of becoming detail, of the Palazzo del Bargello.

It was for a time the government palace, its aura of severity
relieved by the dark gold wood of the doors, and on the lower
wall, plates of a ceramics atelier; no harm done because they
echo the design of the roundels of glass in the windows and the
rotundities of the fountain called the "Fountain of the Mad." It
belongs to all Gubbians who are, they say, at least a little mad.
All you have found is kindness and good humor, and maybe that
is, for the present day, madness. Possibility it is a little crazy for
a card player in a bar to rise, when you ask for the toilet, to walk
out into the cold to his house, to return with a huge key and,
conducting you to a door marked, for no sensible reason, *"las-
ciare libero il passo"* ("don't park here"), usher you into his shop
toilet. Maybe it is slight madness for a woman cooking the luncheon meal to leave pot, bambini and husband to reopen her
shop for the one roll of film you need because she feels sad that
your camera is deprived of film and you of the recorded beauties
of her city. Let them define it as they like; such courtesies, not
rare, are the gold of Italy one comes to seek.

Before you inquire about a house on the via Savelli or a sun-
struck apartment in a palazzo at the top of angled stairs, see what
you think of living in a small house, backed by a sweep of green
mountain that supports a creamy monastery on its slope, near
the little river that slips under the weavers' loggia and reappears
at the side of the via Piccardi. The river must have been extremely useful to the cloth dyers at one time; now it is mainly
decorative, burbling under minute stone bridges that connect the
unpolished houses, probably too old and poor to be usable by
American standards. The mind begins to wander, nevertheless,
among masons tearing down walls to make one room of several,
among electric heaters and newly whitewashed beams, maybe

replacing a tile or two on the roof and asking an ironmonger to curl an ornate basket around a window ledge of flowers; furnishing an increasingly persistent American dream of nestling—somehow, sometime—into a warm corner of Italy.

Notes

HOTELS.   The Cappuccini, on the via Madonna del Ponte, a short distance from town, was a Capuchin monastery. The décor has been kept simple, tranquil and in good taste. The only thing that mars the extensive gardens is a tree near the road that nervously flashes colored bulbs, but you won't see it from your comfortable bedroom or the attractive, monastic dining room. A room for two, with bath, should be about $50 per day.

In town, more modest in price and décor, the Oderisi, on the via Reposati, and the San Marco, on the via Matteotti. The *albergo* Della Rocca is in the hills above the town and has the advantage of views from a terrace, quietude and reputable food. Rooms with bath are comparatively few, but the view is worth at least one bath.

Unless you want to tootle up and down the Umbrian hills or travel on a sky lift (*funivia*), your choice of restaurants will be limited. Try the Taverna del Lupo, or Pierotti, the Federico da Montefeltro, or eat in the market, as suggested.

Arezzo and Cortona

WITH CHARACTERISTIC PASSIVITY—or were they ready
to let their civilization die?—the Etruscans succumbed to the
Romans who shaped of Arezzo a military station to serve one of
the major Roman roads. The military city, its temples, theater,
baths—its whole sybaritic life—was smashed by the crude
hordes from the north when Rome's end came. After several
dark, confused centuries, a commune was formed to be ruled by
embattled bishops, the powerful "Patriarchs" of the Middle
Ages. The bishops were of little help when Florence and Siena
decided to take Arezzo but failed, after a long siege. Twisting,
being twisted, Arezzo ultimately established a commune under a
large group of ruling nobles who built new protecting walls and
put castles in them for their own use and pride. In the mid-
fourteenth century, walls, castles and all were sold to Florence.
Time passed, not without its struggles. When she was invaded by
French troops, Arezzo tried to join with Siena, or Florence—
whichever wanted the trouble of protecting her—and neither
did. Her destiny was that of most of Tuscany, however, until
Italy became a united country in the nineteenth century.

As Vicenza belongs to Andrea Palladio, Arezzo belongs to its artist, Piero della Francesca, though not so exclusively. Arezzo was a producer of arts and artists long before Piero—though admittedly, not quite at his level: Petrarch, the great poet; Aretino, playwright, pimp and talented blackmailer; Guido Monaco, the deviser of modern musical notation; and before them all, Maecenas, the patron of Horace and Virgil. One unique art form that became an industry in Roman times was the famous "corallini" vase of plump, pinkish glazed clay. The early architecture was mainly Lombardic-Romanesque until the 1400's when Florence fostered the changes in style developed during the Renaissance. Arezzo still has a good number of houses built in the sixteenth century, but her most expressive and majestic are the earlier Romanesque-Gothic.

At this writing (early 1983), Arezzo was in a rather nervous state of intense improvement, change, restoration. The office for tourist information, once on the piazza around the statue of the musical monk Guido, disappeared; and maps and pamphlets were distributed by a shining traffic policeman on a shining motorcycle who stood with his sheaf of tourist information near the façade of the Church of San Francesco, which houses the most remarkable Piero della Francesca frescoes. Surprisingly, he would not permit tourist cars to continue up the rather steep streets to the upper town although local cars bounded up unmolested. A number of buildings one had come to see were closed, semi-closed, hung with the green meshwork of reconstruction. It all should have improved when your time arrives: an Ente Provinciale office centrally located, maybe a bus that plies the hill for the sore of foot, directional signs simplified, the green wire fungus gone and beautiful old stone brought back to the light.

Maybe you are determinedly intent on examining the antiques that fill the Piazza Grande (the huge square at the crest of the town) the first Sunday of every month. Or, enchanted with Siena's Palio, come here to see Arezzo's equivalent, the Giostra del Saracino (first Sunday in September; check), a recently revived late-Renaissance contest of eight horsemen in medieval dress and armed with lances, who try to pierce the heart of a shield worn by a Saracen puppet, adroitly manipulated to twirl and evade the lance. Otherwise, your first stop will probably be the church of San Francesco in the lower town. From the time it first appeared, in 1290, it has undergone almost constant change and reconstruction. The façade is shockingly nude, no covering at all. The interior is large, tall Gothic, with long, slender windows, a masterly wooden roof and some aging frescoes that encompass an impressive Christ, of exquisite quality, a rose window by a Frenchman, Guglielmo de Marcillat, a monk whose skill and fame carried him to Rome where he worked in the Vatican at the same time as did Michelangelo. He later settled in Arezzo, which he adorned with his glowing glass panels.

The chancel of the church carries the incredible group of paintings, crowded and chronologically confusing, painted by Piero in the mid–fifteenth century to tell the "Story of the Cross." (The maps and descriptive matter given travelers usually has a chart that names the matter of each panel; a pair of binoculars helps clarify some of that matter.) The strength and color of the frescoes, the composition, the boldness of invention have been universally judged to be among the peak of Italian achievement, notwithstanding the existence of hundreds of remarkable paintings flowing from every atelier in northern Italy at the time. Should the area be crowded with visitors, as it often is, forget politeness and force your way to the "Annunciation" for the magnificence of Piero's earth-mother Virgin. Spend time with the meeting of Solomon and the Queen of Sheba for its regal figures and rich color; and stand for a while with the *chiaroscuro* and strangely disturbing mood of "The Dream of Constantine."

When you've come out of the hypnotic spell of the frescoes, take the Corso Italia which cuts directly up to the higher town and, in climbing, watch for a few distinguished old buildings, some very old, almost as old as Santa Maria della Pieve of the twelfth and thirteenth century, a large and fascinating Romanesque church, a lacework of columns and arches with a tower of dozens of windows which, locals tell you, was inhabited by squatters until very recently. Like so many churches, the Pieve has undergone destruction and reconstruction through the centuries. In the seventeenth century there were actually display places, as shops, at one side of the church; and in front, a figure, like Rome's gossiping "Pasquino," who pointed out crooks and mischief-makers as they passed by. The interior of Santa Maria della Pieve is beautifully austere in contrast to the highly decorated façade. With reconstruction and restoration complete, one of the treasures of the Pieve—a set of alter panels in the Sienese harmonies and charm of Pietro Lorenzetti—should be back on the altar; not, one hopes, too much restored and repainted.

You should be on or near a street called the via dei Pileati, a street of Gothic houses and the remains of Gothic towers, the street of the Palazzo Pretorio which holds the community library, its fourteenth-century facade covered with shields and crests of members of the podesta, the local government, who ruled from the fifteenth to the seventeenth century. A nearby street, the via Albergotti, is ornamented by a knight on a horse, probably taken from an old Palazzo Communale which may also have provided some of the shields and crests on the library. Notice that one of the palazzi courtyards is holding on to capitals of the original Pieve and window sections and ornaments of the façade of an ancient version of the Duomo—to do what with? Something useful, clever and attractive, no doubt.

Sitting high and isolated from the rest is the Duomo, a refinement of Gothic in the Tuscan style, built between the thirteenth and sixteenth centuries but actually not finished until the twentieth. It too is remarkably severe and majestic, grand both in its tall pillars and extraordinary adornments. The Frenchman Marcillat designed the radiant rose window, and among other brilliant pieces, an "Expulsion of the Profane from the Temple." A superb, many-tiered tomb of the bishop Guido Tarlati, believed to have been designed by Giotto and executed by Sienese artists, it has, in spite of its size, the delicacy and fine precision of an ivory reliquary. The Duomo houses many other elaborate tombs, but none like this; nor any figures to compare with the terra-cottas of Andrea della Robbia; nor, among the paintings, an equal to Piero della Francesca's "Mary Magdalene." The Duomo has been given, and gives back to travelers, a generous plenty of treasures.

Now you are at the mercy of the signs. You want to get to the Piazza Grande with its variety of houses, churches and antique shops. You are constantly pushed into a large, indubitably handsome park with great views of the countryside, but you stubbornly want the Piazza. A native, when asked, says it is on the moon. A less fanciful Aretine shows you a short set of stairs below the park, between a set of ordinary houses, that spills you into the vast space. At the side of the piazza—or part of it, not always easy to know among these amorphous borders, there is San Domenico, a modest late thirteenth-century church built by Nicolo Pisano, which has a fine collection of Sienese paintings and a dramatic Crucifix that is one of the earliest known works of Cimabue.

On the street called the "XX of September" is the house of Georgio Vasari who bought it in 1540 and dragged all the top artists he knew—among them, they say, Michelangelo—and his own busy hand, to decorate his mansion, which is an explosion of mannerist exaggeration: fun and visitable. From here, if you have the energy and mood for them, additional pleasing churches; a Pinacoteca Communale for paintings; a museum of medieval arts; a Roman amphitheater that once held 8,000 spectators, and *its* archaeological museum with a collection of Etruscan bronzes, Roman jewelry and many of the Aretine ceramics mentioned earlier.

Arezzo can be "done"—a stupid expression—in one frantic, inattentive day. It merits at least two before you go on, possibly to Perugia which can be reached by train or probably bus, now that bus routes are being busily established between towns.

The Hotel Graverini and the Europea are pleasant and moderate. The Minerva is a fairly large step up. The city's restaurants are unremarkable; The Spiedo d'Oro and the Buca di San Francesco will give you a decent meal at an honest price.

Cortona, truly a Tuscan hill town, possibly the highest of them all, asks a flight up and up through an alluring set of curves and into narrow, deeply arcaded streets; in and out of small squares to the square at the peak, the Piazza del Duomo. Sitting on the old walls, the church, once Romanesque and changed in the Renaissance, shares with the visitor an immense breadth of view into endless fields and rows of olive trees and, close by, a rather cheerful cemetery for a silent, sad town mired in its own early

Renaissance image. In those days, Fra Angelico painted here and the gifted Sienese came. Luca Signorelli, a native son, painted a Madonna with Angels for Cortona's Church of San Domenico and, in the wider art world, the remarkable frescoes of the Apocalypse in Orvieto's brilliant cathedral. Signorelli, it is claimed, was, if not a teacher, a telling influence on Michelangelo.

Across from the isolated Duomo which seems to have little to do with her parishioners, one finds the Diocesan Museum (open the usual hours, but rather slow about it; you may have to wait a half hour or an hour for opening time, time that can be spent with the Duomo view, or with a view of Lake Trasimento from a lower square named for Garibaldi). Once hospitable, the museum rewards your wait with two exquisite Fra Angelico works, an Annunication and a Madonna with Saint. Sassetta, not frequently seen, is here with a Madonna and Child; Duccio represented by a Madonna with Angels; and a remarkable, compelling Christ on the Cross as seen and felt by Pietro Lorenzetti. Most of the rest is Signorelli, all extraordinary, especially a strong, vivid Descent from the Cross. As if to prove it was a thriving Renaissance community once, Cortona keeps well-designed gold plate of an earlier day, in a room adjoining the paintings.

On the Piazza Signorelli, which vaguely marks the center of town (it holds a bar and a shop), a set of tall stairs will take you into another museum, arranged in an enormous sala of a thirteenth-century palace, some of it redone in later centuries. The exhibits are a miscellany of Roman bronzes, imaginative Etruscan fancies and paintings of varied provenance, some of them good, some not so good.

Should you choose to stay in this town of evocative shadows, try San Luca e Ristorante Tonino for modest bed and board and life of the main piazza, Garibaldi.

Assisi

"SAN FRANCESCO (Francis) is the most beautiful and most attractive, the most moving, figure in the hagiography of the catholics, in the art of Giotto and the poetry of Dante; they have bestowed on him an immortal apotheosis." Thus an Italian book, and although a bit baroque like much Italian prose, not unjustified, from what we know of Saint Francis, a most extraordinary man.

The city which dedicates itself to him and his followers is a quiet, beflowered, dignified place, restrained except for the enormous size of its double Basilica of San Francesco. The city was not always so serene. When the Umbrian-Etruscans had it, the settlement was taken by the Romans who were succeeded by the Goths, who were succeeded by the Lombards. For a very short time a commune, Assisi later became a fief of the Empire—contended for by Perugia and, at various times, Urbino, Milano and the Sforzas—and finally became a Papal State.

During the Imperial period, sometime in 1181–1182, a rich merchant who dealt with France named his newborn son Franceso, in honor of that country, or to do his wife, a Frenchwoman, such honor. There are several versions of how the rich merchant's son became so movingly pious that all of God's creatures (lauded in his, the earliest Italian poetry) were his brothers and sisters. One story tells of his imprisonment during a battle with the Perugians, and his sudden enlightenment through intimate visions of the Virgin and Child; and during those visitations, receiving the stigmata of sainthood. Another version of the legend tells of his being accosted by a simple man who proclaims that he will do great, noble things. Yet another part of San Francesco's story tells of hearing a voice from the crucifix before which he was praying. It said, "Francesco, repair my house which is falling." For one of those causes, or all, he left his father's house, his monies and ornaments, and devoted himself to treating lepers and tending the poor, he himself living as the poorest.

In time he and a few followers petitioned Pope Innocent III to permit them to establish an order based on rules of chastity, poverty and obedience. Permission granted, he returned to Assisi and founded several subsidiary groups, "Frati Minori," of the Franciscan order. His vows and views made him an enemy of feudalism and consequently earned him enemies, not only among prosperous landowners, but abbots of large monasteries and bishops of wealth and power. Unmoved, except by his mission to honor all life, he continued to preach and travel. On one visit to Rome he met Santa Chiara and helped her establish the Poor Claires, the second Franciscan order, and then a third order for the laity. Burning with his cause, he turned toward the pagan in the Orient but was forced back by storms at sea. He managed to reach Spain, where he stayed for a short while, and followed that venture with an attempt to convert the sultan of Egypt who would have none of him or his passion for self-abnegation. Difficult to discourage, Saint Francis stayed to preach in a number of cities of the Middle East and then returned to work in Italy, which still needed him. As he grew older and more frail, he stayed closer to Assisi; and when he knew himself to be near death, asked that he be taken to a small piece of naked earth where he chanted the praises of "that dear lady, Poverty." His body was taken, after his death in October 1226, to the church that is now the Basilica of Santa Chiara and shortly after to a deep tomb chamber in the newer San Francesco church. Two years later he was canonized by Pope Gregory IX.

As one climbs and climbs toward the high pink and white city spilling flowers from its windows and balconies and old stairs, the double basilica—actually one church imposed on another— seems almost grotesquely massive in spite of Italian information's telling you that "it is the most beautiful house of prayer, a wonderful reliquary of faith and art." From its very beginning as the first Gothic church in Umbria, and vastly full of fresco space, it attracted the very best of the early painters, from one of the Pisanos to Cimabue. Soon there were Cavallini and Giotto and the masters of Siena. By the time of the great Renaissance painters, space or interest or both lacked, and we have very few significant works of those resplendent years—leaving San Francesco one of the greatest single repositories of early Italian painting.

The compound of two churches, a crypt and an adjoining monastery were designed, it is generally agreed, by a Brother Elias; and the lower church widened shortly after his original work was done. By 1235 or 1236, the walls were ready to take frescoes. The Romanesque-Gothic lower church has a dark, womblike quality, and for a while, seems a confusion of dim, floating forms. With a little time and a few coins that buy illumination, the eye begins to pick out frescoes and stained glass of early times. Those dedicated to the life of Saint Catherine go back to the fourteenth century, and some are as old as the thirteenth, awkwardly and touchingly depicting the life of Saint Francis. A dark area that tries to speak of the life of Christ has painted in its own illumination: a vault of bright stars whose vivid color give life to the whole. The fifteenth-century Cloisters of the Dead quite belie their name; they are fresh and light and provide a contrast to the crypt, which holds Saint Francis's iron-casket tomb. The dramatic legend of the tomb has it open to public view until late in the fifteenth century when it had to be sequestered, hidden from the marauding Perugians. The story suffers a long hiatus, to pick up in 1818, the tomb casually rediscovered, some way or other. Some draw a vivid picture of a group of the devout working night after night of almost two months, breaking through travertine tablets to free the body of

Saint Francis and those of a few of his friends.

Back from the crypt (rebuilt in this century), direct yourself to the first chapel on the left (still in the lower basilica) for the Legend of Saint Martin as painted with great style and sophistication of color and composition by Simone Martini. Although it was of the early fourteenth century, this set of frescoes has nothing of the naïve or primitive about it (remembering his work in Siena, one realizes that Martini, along with the brothers Lorenzetti, was an advanced painter for almost any era). Like other of his works and much of Sienese painting in general, these are not pious paintings, not devout pieces of hagiography; this is painting for the sake of painting as well and as elegantly as one could. Pietro Lorenzetti who painted to paint was also capable of deeply religious expressiveness, here represented in the almost tragic quality of his Passion frescoed on the walls of the north transept. In the riches of painting, which can be overwhelming, try not to overlook (south transept) a singularly august work by Cimabue, "Saint Francis with the Madonna and Four Angels."

The upper church is an explosion of light and color, with much to show, some of it dimmed by an almost forbiddingly tragic Crucifixion by Cimabue and lightened by the twenty-odd frescoes of the Life of Saint Francis by Giotto—not quite so compelling as the lives of Christ and Mary in Padua, but very close in the masterly arrangement of forms and detail and the impact of emotion which also characterizes works in the third chapel based on scenes in the life of Christ, most of those considered Giotto's work as well.

Here there should be a general caveat: the allegories of Poverty, Chastity and Obedience may be, but are not necessarily, by Giotto. The figure of Dante in several panels needn't be Dante, nor did Simone Martini necessarily introduce a portrait of Giotto into one of his frescoes and there is a disconcerting number of "attributed to," "pupils of." This should not put you off; the expressiveness and expertise usually tell the right name, while the struggles of several young hands (although they might be working for Cavallini or Giotto or Cimabue) occasionally betray inexperience or slavish adherence to a master's style, losing the essence of the master's work. Whoever did or didn't do the aggregation of remarkable works, it is a profound pity to see them going and gone as so much of Cimabue's work, for one, has faded into its walls.

As a change of pace to the secular, there is the ride, or fair hike, to the medieval Rocca—built by the German feudal rulers in the fourteenth century and enlarged by later popes—which affords broad views of the countryside and of the roof tiles, spires, and twisting streets of Assisi. If your mood is still churchly, follow the antique houses of the Via San Francesco, with short deviations into the via San Rufino and via del Comune Vecchio, and on to the church of Santa Chiara built in the mid–thirteenth century. A rather simple church, it takes on a majestic air from its deep, strong and surprisingly un-Italian buttresses. The interior is modest, decorated by pale frescoes concerning Santa Chiara and companion lady saints and, of about the same time, the fourteenth century, a huge crucifix at the high altar.

The crucifix of Saint Damian which spoke to Saint Francis is in one of the chapels of an old church incorporated into Santa Chiara's church and conspicuously displayed as an important chapter of the legend, its importance enhanced by Saint Francis' burial here. The coffin of Santa Chaira stayed in the crypt of her church and her presence is made more concrete by a glass case that displays her antique robes and a box that holds her gray curls.

Not unexpectedly, Assisi is well bechurched—in its center and its environs—many of these holy places connected with Saint Francis and Saint Clara and, for most travelers, a demanding pilgrimage. If devotion demands it, however, and time and energy permit, buy an Assisi booklet (sold everywhere) or ask the Ente Provinciale per Turismo for its pamphlets, and follow their leads to the significant places—like the cave-cell in which Saint Francis lived from time to time and the convent in which Santa Clara died—in these extraordinary lives. The city itself acts out its heritage in frequent religious festivals and rites, like the procession of friars who chant their devotions in the streets at twilight on Fridays of the Lenten season. The celebrations for Saint Francis in the fall; Easter Week; all religious holidays, for that matter; and a few medieval churchly observances no longer in general use make one huge cathedral of the many chapels of the city. It seemed quite fitting that, in the spring of 1983, a well-attended World Peace meeting was held in the city of the gentlest, most peace-loving of saints.

Note

A car is always best, but there are train connections and, increasingly, bus routes that reach Assisi. For a small city, Assisi has a good number of hotels and restaurants. The smallish Umbra is favored by some for its intimacy and good meals (high moderate). The Piazza San Pietro is the address of the San Pietro (moderate) and the tiny Berti (modest) and, as well, of an attentive restaurant or two. And don't forget to take opera glasses for those high, dim masterpassages you might otherwise lose.

Ascoli Piceno

THE MOST SPECTACULAR and derring-do way to ap-
proach Ascoli Piceno (unless the difficult stretch between Norcia
and Arquata has been repaired, and even at that it might be
derring-do if you don't like relentless turns into frightening voids
of sky) is to leave the highway at Spoleto and follow the road
arrows that fly up toward Cerreto, Triponzo and Norcia. An extra fillip can be added by leaving Spoleto at about 6:00 P.M.,
when the late summer sun has begun to slip from the taller hills
to lie flat on the lower roads and few other cars are out. The
climb begins immediately as steep curves into blue hills crowned
with pale golden light, the well-kept road equipped with barriers,
reflectors and cement loggie to support the weight of restless
rock. Far below, Sleeping Beauty villages with no visible means
of access peer out of deep woods. High above, white monasteries
float in the blue-green air. Turning and turning through dense
forests of hunting preserve and a growing sense of isolation, the
car suddenly curves into a bubble of human life shaped around a
grocery, a tobacconist, people sitting and standing and going
about their business as if this were truly part of the real world;
and most improbable of all, a man and his wife, one small child

and a baby carriage come strolling down the road enacting Sunday in the park.

Out of the oasis, wondering how it lives and feeds, one comes soon on a sharp slope that is scraped nude, marked with even dark ribs like a newly unearthed monster fossil. Close up, the ribs show as interwoven vine twigs placed in preparation for terracing; a painstaking struggle with the rocky earth, the stubborn will to make it yield that will appear again and unbelievably again as bared, ribbed slopes. They give way, farther on, to leave an open vista at whose depth, sitting on a small cushion of earth, is a miniature village of gold, ivory and whispers of pink, as pearly and unreal in the distance as the Taj Mahal. The gorges soon grow deep and deeper among high angry crags that thunder down to a lively river bordered with wildflowers and poplars. Running in and out of the river's edge, like a blue ribbon slipping through green and gray eyelets, is a one-car train, as incongruous and comforting in the dimming light as the pram several miles back. Very carefully following signs, though they may seem to indicate contrary directions, you arrive gratefully in Norcia, a name which may ring a bell if you've been looking at food shops in Rome. It is the home of "norciana" mountain proscuitto and salamis of high prestige and also a lower-middle-class resort for people who want the mountain air.

The map shows Ascoli Piceno to be a fairly short and ominously looped distance from Norcia. Local advice brings the usual mystification: one citizen says "flat as a table"; another says, tersely, "terrible." Whatever the responses, whether the road has been widened, covered with asphalt, hedged in by blinkered barriers, or not, don't cross it at night. There are worse places in which to spend the night than the Albergo della Posta of Norcia. First, the get-acquainted stroll through the town, whose finest possession is its hills. The rest is an old clock tower, a truncated fortress whose corners splay out like huge arrowheads, and a few shops that sell copper objects and souvenirs. The hotel is a maze of alleys among old bedrooms and new, an uninhabited, musty sitting room, a more alert bar and an undistinguished, unobjectionable dining room where one eats well, and so do dozens of summer ladies—secretaries, teachers, their cousins and their sisters and their aunts and their mothers.

The morning ride to Forca Canapine was (it must have been somewhat improved) a rough, dizzy trundling around unprotected heights into a fresh, treacherous sky that tried to suck the car into its limitless blue. At some impossible point you may meet road workers and their machinery and there is no way around the rough stones they spread, which may bring, along with other hazards, a tire puncture. Admiring and kind, they gather together to push your car between and over the obstacles, and you are free to continue the perilous journey. The landscape, you observe, if you can, has turned to Tyrolean green plush spotted with sheep and the modern bungalows of a winter-sports and summer-air hotel (the Albergo Canapine) above an older, small pensione. The road soon becomes wider, wide enough to accommodate both your car and the indomitable Norcia–Ascoli Piceno bus, and the landscape that spirals downward takes on moderation and familiarity. The dark mosses of mountain forest separate as individual trees, the gray unconquerable bulges of mountain crest melt, terraces of vines and olives and jumbles of roof tiles and church eaves rise to road level. On one golden table of field the hay lies in neatly criss-crossed heaps to pattern a background for a country Madonna who rocks a baby. The valley loosens and flows as softly undulating green to meet the River Tronto at Arquata. The river bumbles in its trough under fortresses and houses, below woods and terraces and forest slopes. In the high distance, the gray masses of furry, blurred mountain suddenly become sharply contoured again, to resemble huge Aztec heads incised in the gray rock. Rock and greenery then take on an alternating rhythm like waves of hard gray sea streaked by thick strands of seaweed. The river soon curves around Ascoli Piceno and separates to make a second watery arm around the city, the Castellano River.

Not the most beautiful, or artistic, or intellectual of cities in Italy, Ascoli Piceno is certainly one of the most easygoing and affable, good to look at without being awesome. It is energetic and worldly, and it eats well.

If you had thought that Tuscan towns and those in Umbria—or, for that matter, anywhere in Italy—had complex, overeventful histories, try a quick dash through this city's past: an indigenous people, the Piceni, conquered by the Romans whose governors they murdered; besieged and reconquered by the Romans (we have already jumped two centuries), who made it an important market center; later conquered by the Lombards and later still, a papal state; fought off the Saracenic invasions that flooded southern Europe. In the thirteenth century it became a fief of Frederick II with the proviso that it keep some of its privileges as a free commune. The church then took control and relinquished it, on and off, and then it was the turn-of-the-fourteenth-century *condottieri* (whom, the tourist booklet says, the citizens threw off, "always in a haughty manner"). Testy relations with the church resulted in a cancellation of civic rights because the church declared Ascoli Piceno too rebellious and unsteady a community. Then, Napoleon's forces, and in the nineteenth century, it became a part of united Italy.

The present bustle one feels and sees has reasonable cause. The city sits at the base of a vast funnel of productive green, of olives, fruits and grain, and, in the valley, a sizable number of plants and factories. Steeped well and busily in the twentieth century, the city has enough that is attractive and telling to show off its past but doesn't segregate them in "artistic" or "historical" parentheses; thus the nineteenth and twentieth centuries live easily with the Middle Ages, the Renaissance and the Roman to make pleasing juxtapositions. The streets sometimes call themselves "via" but most often "rua." like the French *rue* descended from the Latin, and probably a local mark of French influence. Almost any via or rua will conduct you to the central Piazza del Popolo, dominated by the Palazzo dei Capitani del Popolo of the thirteenth century and the Tempio of San Francesco, with its adjoining Loggia dei Mercanti, of a later time. The palazzo, a mighty edifice, is not as invincible as it looks; its choleric people were able to burn it in the sixteenth century, although local apologists prefer to say that it caught fire inadvertently during an incident of "discord among the citizenry." Several reconstructions and additions have given its face rather discordant features, elements of a number of periods that include a soaring Renaissance portal, which supports a pope and two rusty clocks, both accurate (an uncommon talent in old town-hall clocks). The rest of the piazza—we will return to the church later on—is sprawling cafés, shops, and the young, enterprising tourist office that dispenses maps, pamphlets, sound advice and whatever help you might need. The smaller buildings are joined in a unanimity of style at the rooftops—a flourish of Ghibelline crenelations among the tiles, long narrow windows edged with stone tatting—with a pair of towers for backdrop. A later, gaudier house hangs out shields, mottoes and a castle dangling from an arrangement of griffons, sea monsters, sphinxes and Medusas.

The peculiarly stimulating Pinacoteca can wait, so can the museum in the Palazzo del Popolo and the interior of San Francesco. Go, particularly if it is early in the day, past the loggia and into the via Malta to see the facade of the Tempio. It is a joyful thing, the portals held by the slenderest of columns which rise as tiny pagodas that house saints, its lions as happy as lap dogs. (For contrast with medieval control of design look at the dusty, naked green ceramic ladies among the fountains and peacocks that advertise the distinguished quality of a general store a few yards away.) There should be many women with limp market baskets going by to shop in the market that hugs the church, as it has for centuries. Some vendors have stalls under the former cloister arcades; the rest place their crates and baskets in the open and leave their awning-umbrellas, to be used against the later full heat of the sun, in the cloister fountain. Very pleasant it is to see the summer's bounty examined, pinched and picked over by the round housewives, who move slowly and seriously among large flat baskets that spill fields and forests of salad greens, big burrs of artichokes, tomatoes green to yellow to red, pears of pale jade and blood-red peaches. Farther off the street, shrimp, dark-fringed octopus and pink mullet shine and stink—a little—together. And beyond that, still hugging the church, the yawning cartons of aprons and kerchiefs, dwindling to thread and needles and the market indispensables, sunglasses and watch bands. The market makes one last mercantile gesture as a noble shop with flourishes of gold letter on black glass framed in nine-teenth-century wood, and one is back at the piazza and the church.

San Francesco was begun in the latter half of the thirteenth century and was not fully completed until the sixteenth. It might be worthwhile to circle it again, this time disregarding the market and concentrating instead on the design and details of the cloisters, the shafts of light and shade made by concave and convex surfaces in the long columnar divisions, the billow of apse and the portal that parallels but differs from that on the via Malta.

The interior is expectedly vast, compelling but not especially appealing. The church art of the fifteenth and sixteenth centuries is, as often happens, obliterated by other church furnishings, here heavily carved and depressingly black confessional boxes. A modern Virgin makes an unattractive appearance as a nun, and Christ has discarded his crown of thorns for a crown of electric bulbs. The rest is more doughy art in polychrome plaster, except for the apse, which widens to delicate Gothic lacework and, on a doorway, a tendriled fringe of wood carved in Gothic designs. As you leave, you will notice that the most conspicuous poor box begs money for *riscaldamento* (heating). One wonders how much it would take to warm this enormous ecclesiastical barn and how much has already been collected. Not a large sum, one suspects, from the history and present unchurchliness of the city.

Beyond the market area, the via Malta presents a glimpse of a six-sided tower ringed by a balcony, a contrasting modern building of glass and concrete and, a few paces on, elaborate corner chapels held in complicated ironwork (you should be near the meeting of the via Vidaclio with Cairoli) and a row of Renaissance houses or merely ponderous doorways patched on earlier houses. The via Cairoli continues as "picturesque" (poorly lit and musty) shops—a shoemaker, a mender of clocks, an upholsterer—to the rua Simone Cornacchi, a medieval swaying and bending and the touching of roof overhangs. If you haven't yet been flattened by the merciless traffic, you should soon be standing on the large irregular Piazza Ventidio Basso, and at your left the myriad glass circlets that fill the windows of San Pietro Martire. The church is big and ambitiously bastardized to surround a squat "classic" entrance; its heavy weight drags through the interior as thick columns and sentimental paintings in sententious chapels, relieved only by flights of putti. The church exterior simplifies and improves as it moves with you along the rua delle Donne. Under the subtly leaning towers, now, on the via delle Torre and into alleys that reach toward the via dei Soderini, a compound of medieval and Renaissance buildings whose carriageways have become tiny crafts villages which orchestrate a steady clanging, buzzing, hammering and sawing. Where Soderini joins the rua dei Longobardi, it shows two distinguished tower-palaces of the twelfth century, the usual dourness indigenous to these towers brightened by engaging detail.

The green-clad river nearby flows under a Roman bridge, accompanied by sprays of tower and several palm trees. You can pick your way over slanting patterns of cobblestones onto the bridge at the thirteenth-century Porta di Solestà, or pass it, to peer down on the river's greenery—the fig tree that clambers up to greet you, the dance of vines, the screens of poplar that mute the river to a pale-green flicker among the nodding branches, the Rousseau jungle that sometimes hides it entirely except for a faint gurgle. The river's sounds and the rustling of its trees are joined by the music of the rua della Musica, the scraping of a file used by a metalsmith to round the edges of his iron and copper, utterly alone in his obscure alley.

Turning back to the Piazza Ventidio Basso, one meets the chaste white boxes of travertine of the basic shape of the church of Santi Vicenzo e Anastasio, begun in the eleventh century. The squares were frescoed centuries ago, but as in Greek temples, the loss of color has created another form of beauty. Above the recessed wooden door there is a short upper story of biforate windows and at the side of the church a triangle of trees and benches, the daytime home of a dozen of the oldest women in Italy. Having examined the very dark and primitive Virgin and Child between two saints, the portals and courtyards, and had another guess at the possible aggregate years sagging and gabbing on the benches, explore the Largo dei Parisini and the rua Pietro Dini and any vaulted tunnel that leads toward the center—perhaps, the street of the seven thresholds (Sette Soglie), whose narrow sky is crammed with tiny, plump balconies and their explosions of flowers.

Too many men and boys are trying to set an improvised stage on the big piazza. The first performance by a once-popular singer of his version of a Pirandello play has been announced for that night, and nerves are frayed. The scenery is uncomplicated, elementary, screens of leaves and fernery and an insubstantial door, but the men argue in booming voices, trip over and sever snakes of wiring, place the frail door, take it somewhere else, arrange and rearrange—shouting all the time—the screens of plastic leaves. A good place for watching this harried, inchoate process is the café nearest the church, whose specialty is *affogato* (stifled or suffocated or drowned). The name of catastrophe represents a tumbler full of rich chocolate ice cream topped with a dark cherry sauce (*amarena*), which costs about $1.00 and is a corner of paradise for chocolate-ice-cream fanciers. Bored or deafened by the confusion on stage, you might take your coffee in a café at the other end of the piazza, a splendid establishment adorned with an Art Nouveau spiral staircase, art-moderne chandeliers that might be Lalique and a genteel "Parisian" air rarely found in Paris.

The Palazzo del Popolo is likely undergoing repairs, but viewable by way of scaffolding and a tall Renaissance court. One comes, soon, on a few attractive mosaic panels and, in an extraordinary assemblage of polychrome ceramic busts, a most extraordinary ceramic boy. He is surrounded by white birds who seem to be eating the little red fountains near his feet and pecking at the boy himself; an awkward version of the young Saint Francis or a character strayed from a Tennessee Williams play. The Museo Civico proper is on an upper floor (closed Sundays and after one o'clock on other days) and, unless it has moved to the larger quarters it was hoping for, a diverting hodgepodge of local history and prehistory. Among the numberless fibulae, there is a safety pin that is about a foot and a half long; of the Middle Ages, a few pieces of highly sophisticated jewelry made of gold, enamel and gems. One unique display is a caseful of pellets shaped like clamshells and inscribed with names; they were used by special Roman forces to subdue rebellious locals in A.D. 90. Another singular Roman object is a famous mosaic at whose center a minor god smiles benignly or frowns in startled horror, depending on where one stands.

The equivalent of via Malta on the other side of the Piazza del Popolo is the via Trieste, a good place to be at about 6:30 P.M. Everyone is out, greeting, meeting, windowshopping, with a slab of pizza or an ice-cream cone in hand. A theater covered with masks and muses admonishes "Carpe Diem, Lumen Vitae" in large carved letters, and the people heed, filling the main streets and squares with rollicking sounds. Northward, the via Trieste presents, again, the easy partnership of modern banks and office buildings and the erratic billowing and retreating of ancient houses, one so bold a sparsely windowed cliff that it pushes away the narrow sidewalk, forcing pedestrians into the traffic.

The beckoning church of Santa Maria inter Vineas, near the river, is a travertine jewel joined to its bold tower by a minute bridge; below it, an ancient passageway to the river. Recent restoration has unearthed late-medieval frescoes on a few of the pillars, and a Virgin and Child near the main altar demonstrates a common early combination of low relief and flat painting. The most conspicuous ornament in the small church is a funerary monument—big, nervous, crowded, crude—that is a good example of naïve art of a time (the late 1400's) when Donatello and Jacopo della Quercia had finished working their stone miracles.

The river shows itself again, now nude, its greenery discarded, as companion along a route of medieval windows on an arch of the street named for Charlemagne (Carlo Magno), one princely palace, a number of bridges and a coquettish loggia on the Porta Tufilla. Across the river, a vision of modern housing as a marriage of Scandinavian and Japanese styles sealed with Italian red-tiled roofs and beyond a handsome tall-arched bridge, the baroque Tempietto di Sant'Emidio alle Grotte, dedicated to a martyr who, like Saint Denis of Paris, carried his head to this place where he consented to die and be enshrined. It is a fair distance out, and it might be better to turn back toward the Piazza Cola dell'Amatrice to find the nearby Palazzetto Bonaparte. (You may have to ask permission of a shopkeeper to stand in his doorway for a look at the palazzetto; the alternative may easily be ignominious death dealt by a miniature Fiat.) The palace is an engaging collection of Renaissance charms and mannerisms, its neat harmonies of rectangular and square windows framed in classic borders, the spaces between nicely filled—not mobbed—with plaster grotesques and the doorway well proportioned.

Centuries disappear quickly in the short distance to the beguiling twelfth-century baptistry, the crest of its octagonal form wreathed in a pretty loggia. The Duomo frowns on a wilderness of traffic that screams around its broad haunches and the fruit and angels' heads and plumes plastered to its side. With a few remarkable exceptions, a Duomo is a Duomo, usually better outside than in for the simple reason that it is easier to paint, replaster, regild and often uglify an interior than it is to rebuild serious, authentically regal, aged contours. The Palazzo Comunale, which shares the Piazza Arringo with the Duomo, is much more entertaining. It has a grand inner court and formal gardens that spew forth exotic palm trees like heads of curly green hair, which nod at stony white statues and brilliant flowers. The Pinacoteca represents the nineteenth-century ideal of what an art gallery and museum should be, and the zippy city will undoubtedly modernize it one day which would be a pity. As it stands, it is a supreme example of greedy, omnivorous show, repellent and amusing, a monument to late-nineteenth-century taste. Through staggering rows of inlaid, gilded, contorted furniture one goes, under the threat of uncontrolled ornateness in glass chandeliers, past brown-gravy paintings, a bust of Rossini, whose features are liquefying into fat, a naked lady who, like most Victorian naked ladies, doesn't look naked at all. Then, more glass flowers and curlicues in the arbors of chandeliers, more red drapes over lacework curtains, the glitter of several superb Venetian mirrors and still more art—religious and kitsch, always conventional; more big salons and long galleries puffing red velvets and stuffed brocades.

It is a longish and diverting calvary to the treasures in this eccentric assortment, gathered in a room of older church painting and objects. A large cope made in England in the mid-thirteenth century consists of embroidered, tufted and drawn-work circlets that tell the life of Christ and many saints. It is a remarkable example of dedicated skill, each robe and its ornaments different from the others, each face an individual face animated by its own particular emotions, each figure moving vividly among the others. Here, too, is the young man who *is* Ascoli Piceno, who postures from every tourist-office poster. Part of a Crivelli triptych, he is the quintessence of Renaissance dandy: a red cap on his smooth blond pageboy bob, a short tabard of brocade with sleeves of contrasting brocade and inserts of filmy linen from elbow to wrist, long, decorative Mandarin fingers, a nose that is disdainfully sharp and a tight-lipped mouth. Above the smart red cap he wears a halo; lightly, casually, he holds an arrow that may or may not be imbedded in his meticulously pleated chest. Certainly, the arrow disturbs neither boy nor costume. Besides being the perfect Renaissance courtier he also happens to be Saint Sebastian, the most insouciant of Renaissance saints, who maintains, from painting to painting, the same languid stance, whether as nude pincushion or wrapped in figured silks.

Stay on the Piazza Arringo for a while. It is a vibrant agora where people study bus schedules and notices of job openings while their children dabble in two vivacious fountains of large, fiery bronze sea horses rearing and spitting, of pigs spurting, of dolphins poised on their chins and gills, forcing water out of their brains, but still smiling and smiling, as dolphins should. The vivacity and action diminish along the via Achille Argenti and the rua del Mattonato to become a stillness at the narrow rua dei Tre Re, which owns a strip of piazza that holds one cat, one café table and two citizens, one small newspaper kiosk and the front of a house where the peripatetic Garibaldi stayed.

Find your way to the Largo Carlo Crivelli and its neighbors for their architectural wonders. The Post Office, for instance, is Mussolini modern (1928) sufficiently Herculean to support everything—a colony of hero-sized nudists walking resolutely through stone embroidery, masks, cupids and the essential shields. The lower story of the Cassa di Risparmio, at the corner of the Corso Mazzini with Africano Tito, it held up by elephants, while the upper section is left to the care of sturdy rams. On the other side of the Corso two pensive men hold up a smaller, more modest house graced with a pretty balcony and plaster fruits. Nearby, a fountain of worried lions who have to spit the water through iron rings or they lose their jobs.

On the Piazza Roma stands the apogee of maternal stone ladies protecting the fallen of World War II in a mist of enamel and glue smells wafted by a cabinetmakers' alley, the rua della Seta. The side of the Piazza Roma nearest the Piazza del Popolo turns its back on the lady to concentrate on stalls of shoes and nothing but shoes, casting only an occasional glance at the church of Santa Maria della Carità, designed by a local artist, Cola dell'Amatrice, in the sixteenth century. Its calm, judicious design gives way to "fountain art" in the upper section, where volute eyebrows over window eyes at either side of an obelisk nose form a mask. The frantic amassing of gilt, plaster babies and fruit on a gray-green chalky base make a Wedgwood bowl of the inside. Skip it and go on; into the via Alvitreti, perhaps, to walk its oval cobbles leading to and from puffy Renaissance doors in oddly angled houses; into narrow neighboring paths under stone and ivy and eaves that fold on each other like reposing hands. Or back to a main shopping street to catch the news broadcast, local and worldwide, that issues from the loudspeaker of an automobile. It is not permitted in Ascoli Piceno to be indifferent or ignorant or, that dread word, provincial.

Notes

Some Ascoli Piceno time should be spent in eating too much, particularly of the specialties: *crostini,* which are bits of bread toasted or fried with mozzarella, prosciutto, mushrooms, local pâtés, in combinations or singly; and an especial specialty, large olives stuffed with ground meat, rolled in batter and fried. The favorite restaurant is the Vittoria, on the via Bonacorsi, at Number 7, not far from the Duomo. The stuffed olives are delicious; so is the green sauce served with the boiled beef; and the bread is singularly well flavored. Another quite satisfactory restaurant is the Giallo d'Oro on the Corso Vittorio Emanuele, about a block beyond the Duomo.

The few hotels in the center of town occupy corners of voluble traffic. Should you be given a front room at the Hotel Artù on the viale De Gasperi, the noise will be as great or greater, but you will have the consolation of a view across the river into terraced hills and bouquets of trees. The price here should be about $40 or $50 for two and lower in the other hotels.

Il Treno

TRAIN TRAVEL in Italy has the potentialities of a large subject; we must condense and, to begin with, quote a sign that appears in every train; polite, realistic and forgiving, the Italian style. In Italian, French, German and English it quotes an extract from the Royal Decree of 22—11—1925 N. 2175 modified by the L. of 12—7—1961 N. 603, *con rincrescimento* (with regret): "Whosoever damages or dirties the Railway carriages or their fittings is punishable with a fine varying from Lire 800 to Lire 8,000 in the case of saloon or 1st class carriages and from Lire 400 to Lire 4,000 in other cases. When the damage done is clearly not deliberate, if the offender declares himself ready to make a payment equivalent to the minimum fine in addition to paying for the damage done, the Official will collect the sums due and give a receipt for them. This payment will extinguish all penal action."

On a mysterious scale computed by miles whose details shouldn't bother you, the farther you go in one direction the cheaper the train fare per stop. In other words, if you know your ultimate destination will be Milan with stops on the way, it is wiser to buy the full ticket from Rome, rather than from point to point. (Check time limitations.) Although fares are normally inexpensive, beware the supplements that mount with degrees of rapidity and luxury. Categories of speed are rather like American classifications of olives—nothing smaller than colossal in olives, nothing slower than *accelerato* in trains. The Settebello that glides—all soft reserved seats, pretty pictures, plenty of ashtrays and portly gray-suited businessmen—from Naples to Milan, making only major stops, will cost about twice the usual sum plus a reservation supplement.

The joys of Italian train travel are well known: miles of benign scenery, spurs of campanile and castle, blue sea and tawny wheat; the myraid possibilities inherent in eight passengers pressed into a second-class compartment—the eager sharing of lunches and sweets, the lively curiosity (one of the best symptoms of intelligence) and ready exchange of vital statistics. Where are you from, where are you going, how long are you staying, are you married, what is your profession, how many children do you have and what are their ages and don't you find Italia beautiful?

Then your pleasant lay companions will leave you, with sprinklings of *piacere, buon viaggio* and *auguri,* to be replaced by several nuns in sturdy winter habits over well-pasta-ed bulk. The elderly leader has the calm dignity, the wise hooded eyes, the slow voice and serene gestures of Dame Edith Evans playing a Mother Superior. A younger, plain woman with the intelligent, vulnerable face of Rembrandt's *Lady with a Fan* is monitor for the gaggle of five round excited young nuns, two of them already wearing light mustaches and all spotted with adolescent pimples. They carry black reticules like outmoded medical bags and, having deposited them (with much hesitancy and discussion; obviously it is an unaccustomed occasion) in the overhead nets, begin to strip off sections of their black and white wool: detachable sleeves easily pulled off; pieces of mantle and headdress deftly lifted out of place; it is less peeling or undressing than the dismantling of a complex structure. The new shapes—no longer as wide as a church door but, for bulk, they will serve—settle themselves in, careful not to press the *straniera* drowning in the billows of black wool farther into her corner. A few minutes of awed silence, a burst of chattering and, in the immortal manner of the young on outings, complaints of pangs of hunger. Dame Edith remonstrates, seconded by the Rembrandt nun; they couldn't possibly be hungry so soon after lunch. But being assailed by an appetite is a serious condition in Italy (hunger is a vivid nightmare memory, and, furthermore, the flesh is an intelligence, a sentient entity with judgments of its own to be respected), and the older nuns relent. Down come the black bags and are snapped open to produce a child's meal. First, the garish orange soda to wash down sweet biscuits, then the apples and pears followed by chunks of dry cheese that shed white-yellow pebbles on the floor, then coarse slices of bread and disks of garlic-studded salami; a backward meal, as permissive and adventuresome as riding in a train. The Mother Superior looks on smilingly as her flock chews and chirps. When asked permission to open the window a bit and smoke (the odor of salami and warmed woolen gowns in the closed compartment soon becomes over-ripe) she looks long, too sweetly to be accused of staring, nods her assent and as the cigarette is put to the sinful female mouth, crosses herself quickly and inconspicuously, to perform the necessary gesture as tactfully as possible.

The reverse of the coin shows (one of the fouler habits of life) in trains, too. Ebullient companionability often means luggage and standees in the narrow aisles so that one cannot get to the toilet or off the train without high-stepping, stumbling, babbling futile *scusi*s and *permesso*s, tearing by obdurate backsides and bellies. On the other hand, riding in first class (except in the holiday season, when it is likely to be as crowded as second) not only costs more but it can mean sitting alone in a compartment or staring at two anonymous legs rising to a wide newspaper clutched by two anonymous hands.

No class of train travel, mobbed and convivial or comfortable and taciturn, is free of one distinguished hazard; though signs for the *sottopassaggio* (underpass) abound, the stations are shy of speaking their names, nor does the conductor always call them. Thus it is easy to pass a small station, catching its dimly painted name on the far—and wrong—end of the platform. Sometimes, worried eyes jumping from map to landscape might pick up the name from a local warehouse, but night riding erases this chancy possibility. The obvious recourse is to keep asking neighbors, who will take to themselves the responsibility of putting you off at the proper time and place. Or, ask the conductor to call a warning and hope he will not be at the other end of the train when your moment arrives. If your Italian will not stand up to asking questions and assistance, buy an Orario dei Treni—in condensed regional versions and one large pan-Italian version— at a station periodical stand. You can then check off each station as it passes and anticipate your own. Besides, the Orario is a scholarly work and fascinating for the precision and logic of its lists and symbols: two indexes for finding your connections (pay no attention to page numbers, the important numbers are those of train groupings), what sort of services are available, what change points you are likely to encounter. It also offers the delight of reading Italian place names, hundreds and hundreds of them, that evoke olives and grapes and umbrella pines, and makes a cherished souvenir for carrying home to leaf through on a wet winter evening, the nostalgic tears dripping on Bruzolo di Susa, Casella Molinotto, Funghera, Calolziocorte, Acquanegra, Montelupo Capraia, Villa Bartolomea, Occhiobello.

4

ZIGZAG FROM FLORENCE TO LOMBARDY AND VENICE

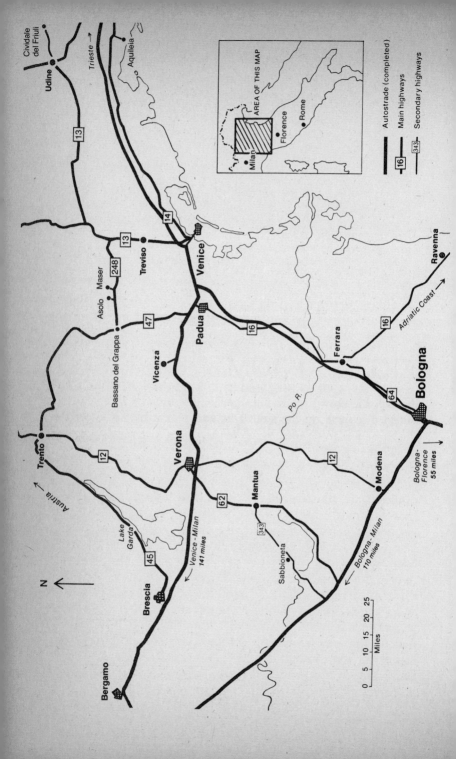

Ferrara

AT NOON IT IS almost impossible to thread one's way through the crowd of middle-aged Ferrarese who stand in animated discourse on the sidewalks and piazze that connect the Castle of the Estes with the Cathedral. At the first warning of winter they gather in their heavy coats—some dating back to a style that called for belted tweed and a fur collar now balding—and dark hats to examine minutely and at great length the events of the day. It is an immediately noticeable Italian habit, particularly marked—and somehow foreign, too southern, here—in Ferrara. As in all Italian towns, the men separate for dinner and a nap at about 1:30 to reappear, in smaller numbers, at about 6:30. By then, the women are out shopping or finishing their tea in an old-fashioned, low-tabled upstairs *sala* of one of the innumerable bars and cafés that just barely leave room for a shoe shop, a dress shop, a branch of the ubiquitous small department stores. At nine o'clock on an early spring evening that still remembers how to blow wintry breezes, the city is deserted—except for a few intrepid scholarly tourists in the city's leading restaurant, two or three young men pacing like caged cats, the pale illumination of a shop that hopes to share an affinity with

Sloane Square in its display of belts and sweaters and names like "Tombstone." The rest is a silence that hangs like bats in the endless, low arcades.

Unlike other cities that keep their shows of antique splendor and arts in one or two colossal gatherings, like gigantic museums, Ferrara disperses her gems. Such and such a palace or museum is therefore a long walk from another (plan carefully, and save time and energy by picking up a taxi near the Palazzo Comunale diagonally across from the Cathedral), in an alternation of narrow old streets twisted around each other and wide, strict avenues. These broad, flat roads may explain why Ferrara seems to have more bicycles, more bicycle purchase and repair shops, more signs with instructions about where bicycles may and may not be ridden or parked, than any other Italian city. The young ride bicycles, and the old and middle-aged, with and without market baskets slung behind or over the handlebars. The dominance of the bicycle (a constant, silent character in the novels and stories of the Ferrarese writer, Giorgio Bassani) may be traced back to the resplendent Este family, whose strong, skeletal fingers still hold the city. Ercole I rebuilt the city, opened broad, straight avenues studded with palaces at the end of the fifteenth century, and added a public park, an extraordinary concession to plebian life for its time. Thus, Ferrara is often cited as the first example of urban planning in Europe.

Denys Hay, in his *Italian Renaissance in Its Historical Background,* points out that a study of the "reception of Renaissance values in Italy should begin not with the great princes but with the little princes. The first clear adoption of humanist assistance in the arts and graces of life and in the day-to-day administrative machine is to be found in the small tyrannies—of the Carrara at Padua, of the Este at Ferrara, of the Gonzaga at Mantua." The Estes established themselves in Ferrara by the usual strong-arm methods of the thirteenth century and stayed in power, burgeoning in several degrees of splendor until the fall of the house in the early seventeenth century. Its highest period, following the parallels of similar houses, was the Renaissance. Quite early in their careers as sponsors and enhancers of the arts, the Estes invited Italian troubadours, who wrote in the then fashionable style of

Provence and also copied out Provençal poems to be read in court. Petrarch was a guest of the court, which later sheltered the great poets Ariosto and Tasso. The Estes married into the leading families of Europe: the French royal family produced one wife and the Borgias another, the justly or unjustly infamous Lucrezia, daughter of a ruthless pope and sister of Cesare, the demonic, perfidious yearner after power. For the embellishment of their palaces and to show off at their magnificent court receptions, they called for Pisanello, Piero della Francesca, Cosmé Tura, who left their mark vividly on the work of local painters. They sent emissaries for foreign artists, and so the Flemish painter Rogier van der Weyden found his way to the court of Ferrara as did the Flemish composer Josquin Duprès. Ferrara had a University, founded by the Estes, in the fourteenth century, and its court educator, Guarino da Verona, who was trained under the same master as Mantua's Vittorino da Feltre (page 263) and devoted to the same enlightened principles of education. (Professor Hay, again: "It was in Mantua and Ferrara, not in Florence, that humanist education theory was given practical illustration: we are still directly influenced by the curriculum there established.")

One might begin exploring the meshwork of the city by picking up a thread of its learning. On the Piazza Sacrati, a few steps from the indispensable *Ente per Turismo* and the moated end of the Castle that broods at the entrance to the old city, one finds the church of San Domenico. Following the bulge of its apse one comes into a neatly arranged small courtyard hung with a few sketches and photographs of portrait prints that tell the history of the university. It was here, in this section of the church and cloisters of the Dominicans, that savants gathered, as early as 1200, to exchange knowledge and views. Later, under the Estes (1391–1567), it became a university of the arts and medicine whose professors were the Guarino Veronese already mentioned, described as a "Hellenist"; a foreign professor of medicine (*clinico*) named Giovanni Caius di Norwich; the Italian humanist Pico della Mirandola; Erasmus of Rotterdam; the anatomist Vesalius; Paracelsus, whose other names were Teofrasto Bombasto; and a German pharmacologist who must have known his business to keep himself alive, according to one of the tablets, from 1423 to 1514—an awesome list and only part of the impressive stable of intelligence and skill gathered by the Estes.

Walk into the low, fumbling shapes of the arcaded street of Santo Stefano and the alleys of sunless brick houses that look like failed warehouses which run parallel to that street: the via della Sacca, Cortevecchia, Vegri. Any one of these will lead to the long, hooded tunnel of the via delle Volte, a shapeless, stirring thing of dusty workshops, lumber yards, large studded doors leading to heaps of gnarled scrap iron and apartments above, to judge from the blanket airing in a window and domestic garbage below. It seems impossible that such discouraged houses have the energy to stand, but they do and have for centuries and, here and there, managed to lure a new shop and a small hotel that justly calls itself "Piccolo." At some point, maybe by way of the via Boccaleone, which seems to have excessively sharp cobbles—maybe no one has walked there for centuries—take a look at the old shops and once-grand doors on the via Ripagrande and the ex-churchly via San Romano. Continuing on the street of Mayr, you will meet a respectable tamed street called the Sciences (Scienze) that will take you to the via del Paradiso, where the later university stands. A rise of marble stairs mounts to classical figures and plaques that speak of Ariosto and Paracelsus and of Copernicus—astronomer, mathematician, philosopher, physician and jurist, who took his degree in canon law to crown his other accomplishments, particularly that of studying the "vertiginous heights of the infinite." The library is full of students who don't seem to find it too difficult to read and study under the stern eyes of red-cloaked cardinals.

The next door on the court opens to a vestibule and a frail iron staircase, which leads to the old anatomical theater. Apply in the office near the entrance to the garden. Keys are quickly found, and someone or other, always polite, shows you into the apple-green and gilt coil of ledges against which the students leaned to look down on the anatomy table and across to the high seat of the professor. The corpse was passed in one door and out another, but you are assured by a typewritten sheet attached to a paddle that the teaching was "theoretical and didactive." One doesn't ask why a table and anatomy theater were needed in that case, at a time when corpses were hard to come by and dissection probably illegal. However, any other corrections you care to make in the "Englished" version on your sheet are gratefully accepted and, since no one can resist being an editor, the sheet may by now have undergone sufficient changes to make it more garbled than the original version.

Another stretch of antiquity lies immediately to the east of the university, loosely bordered by the via Mazzini. The street leads into the side of the Cathedral and the vicinity of the Castle, neither to be neglected even if you have begun to loathe the castle-fortresses that stare down at you—big, bloodstained, glowering dolts—in almost every Italian town, or find that your response to church art is turning off and tuning out. It takes a good deal of effort to disregard their dominating presence, and in any case they share, within a few yards of each other, several interesting to magnificent things. Crossing the large moat of milky green, under a structure of deeply incised stone that helped lower the portcullis, past a set of iron bars which established Ferrarese measures, one reaches a deep court. Most of its surrounding space is used as government offices, but you are soon led through a few large halls that have lived a long time and in that long life have kept and discarded several periods of decoration. Of the castle built by Niccolò of the Estes, mainly its own indomitability stands, a shield here and there, an old window filled with circlets of glass. The visible rest is largely of later times, such as the ceiling paintings that portray Antique Games, one of them a combination of football and pig-sticking, the pig represented by an inflated skin. All the men seem to be too old for games; all of them, and there are many, are naked and most of them overripe. (Some Este or other had the tastes that would now buy "health, strength and beauty" magazines for men.)

Adjoining a terrace once used by Este ladies, there is a room, at present in restoration, which seems to have muraled walls of *fêtes champêtres* in bucolic landscapes with orderly, sweet classic ruins. Moving through this sacked warehouse of spectral luxuries one comes on an attempt at revival with a repetition of the Schifanoia murals (page 238) copied on these walls fairly recently, the stubborn, lustrous presence of Venetian glass sconces, and in one room, a spoor of persistent legend. It is a small mirror in which, they say, one of the dukes could see what his young second wife was up to in an apartment across the court. He found what he must have suspected, that she was having an affair with his son of a former marriage. They were immediately imprisoned and soon executed.

To reach the prisons, the guide leads one out into the court, up a brick ramp and down through a trap door to sets of low dark stairs and the cells. The guard puts his lantern outside one stone cell to show that almost no light entered from the minute barred window, nor from the flap that admitted food through the iron door with an immense, unforgiving lock. Another section of the dank stone corridor stops at a heavy wooden door, inside that another wooden door at least a foot thick and inside that a third iron door. Here the unfortunate and imprudent Ugo was executed with his stepmother Parasina and, centuries later, the political prisoners who were supporters of Garibaldi left their names, mottoes and dates charred on the low-vaulted ceiling.

What is left of the original Cathedral predates the Castle by more than two centuries. To the usual expansions and the pressures of changing styles that affected the church must be added the vicissitudes of earthquake and shifting soil. Entrances were closed and opened, frescoes were painted over, masterpieces of early sculpture were lost or imbedded in new paving. The campanile designed in the Renaissance and redesigned later is not yet finished and bears no relationship to the façade and sides. The interior is neither to be dismissed nor lingered on; it is an enormous gathering of trompe l'oeil, dozens of big chandeliers, derivative painting and that indispensable sign of church self-respect, the twisted columns from Bernini out of classic architectural decoration. With opera glasses handy and a prayer that the restoration of the central panel of the façade has been completed and finally relieved of its cover of straw matting, concentrate on the outside. Replacements have scattered extra lions in the approach, the relatives of those who bear medieval Atlases who, in their turn, hold up the knotted columns that support the outer arch of the portal (copies of the originals kept in the atrium of the church). The eye is carried up to the gaiety of multitudinous arches in many sizes separated by pairs and bundles of columns flat, round and twisted, to openings cut by the busy, ubiquitous Gothic stencil and to breezy grace notes trilling up and down that close the lilting rhythms of the façade. As becomes instantly obvious, the concentration of sculptured ornament is in the panel that rises above the portal and in the portal itself. Imbedded in a succession of columns, and themselves columnar elements, are two prophets of the early twelfth century, attributed to a Niccolò who had, apparently, some knowledge of the pillar-saints of France. The narrowing, receding arches are made of columns and bands of floral designs and abstractions, of grotesques, animals, birds and leaves gathering to enclose a lively Saint George, his alert horse straddling the dying dragon. A band of legend calls to the onlooker to admire these works of Niccolò, their creator, and of the row just below, naïve and extraordinarily convincing panels of New Testament scenes. The clearly Gothic section above, worked like an ivory reliquary, is of the thirteenth century and a work of keen observation and imagination. It is a Last Judgment, Christ enthroned displaying his stigmata, surrounded by personages and symbols of the Crucifixion and, in the eaves, an angel chorus of elderly, bearded angel musicians. Angel trumpeters separate the serene and saintly from the naked, tormented damned; agonized, crying, one tearing her hair. In an accompanying lunette, the agony, the shrieking and the contortions of pain increase as clawed and horned devils push the bodies into the maw of a monster while the heads of the already cooked and damned stare out of a caldron. As literal as comic books—which early church art was meant to be—they are explicit, compelling lessons in the wages of sin.

The atrium, as mentioned, is a premuseum of sections of displaced portal; the museum proper is at the top of a few flights of stairs. Wandering through the stimulating miscellany, one comes on an interesting accumulation of illuminated volumes of church music and a superb stone relief of a male and female profile, almost undoubtedly Roman, who face with serene dignity an enormous embroidered, puffed, stuffed, complicatedly stitched cloth made of gold thread. (Its weight, you are informed by the helpful, intelligent custodian, is about 85 pounds and it has been used, since its presentation to the church in the late nineteenth century, as a spread for the high altar during Easter week.) Near a long stone covered with decorative Gothic engraving and small pieces of older needlework, there is the masterly Madonna and Child with Pomegranate of young Jacopo della Querica (1406), a development of the earthy naturalism—now brought to high skill—of the earlier sculpture of the façade.

It isn't always easy to examine Romanesque capitals *in situ,* and here, for close scrutiny, is one that tells the story of Herod with a maximum of adroit detail crowded into limited circular space. King Herod, Herodias and a rabbi with his book are seated at a shallow table. Near the king stands the hard-faced Salome and behind her a servant carrying a vessel; around the other side from them, a soldier and a shaggy mass, which is the sheepskin worn by John the Baptist, and below, the bearded, distraught head of the saint, very recently lopped off and lying upside down on the ground.

The small museum of several wonders continues to surprise with four panels that once formed the organ case of the cathedral, painted (1469) by the most important and influential of Ferrara's artists, Cosmé Tura. These unearthly, pale, long-fingered personages set in classic perspectives against mysterious, dreamy fantasy landscapes out of Chinese paintings are not to everyone's taste, nor is the almost mannerist chiaroscuro (exaggerated by the fading of colors) defined with chalky white lines. Seductive, mesmeric, they appear to have been hallucinated rather than painted.

The works that sit with Cosmé Tura at the pinnacle of this collection are sculptures of the early thirteenth century that surrounded a Duomo portal demolished in the seventeenth century. They are a unique set of Months, a common enough motif in its time, here depicted with rare vivacity and richness of detail. March and April are a young male Spring in a flowered chaplet, accompanied by an older figure—the last of winter—blowing a horn of winds that stand his disheveled hair on end. December is a handsome young peasant ready to cut more wood for the caldron that stands under a row of hanging salamis. June is a youngster pulling on the branches of a laden fruit tree, and August is about to pick ripe figs from a branch to put them into a carefully observed and carved bucket. July's frisky horse tramples sharply defined bundles of wheat. The set of months and symbols of rural life is incomplete and one's delight is stained with disbelief and anger to learn that the eighteenth-century contempt for the "crude," "unformed" work of the Middle Ages impelled the artistic mentors of the church to turn the panels face down and use them as paving blocks. Those in the museum were recovered about thirty years ago, and one hates to think of what happened to the rest, supporting sewage pipes and auto tires.

From proletarian life in the thirteenth century, a ten-minute walk down a plain and not unattractive shopping street called Porta Reno (look as you go for one princely hardware store, broad and tall, wearing vermilion iron ribbons) leads directly to an aspect of today's daily life in Ferrara, the market, less satisfying aesthetically than the earlier panels but as lively. It rambles along an edge of town, drifts into a parking lot, and climbs a plateau that is very like those used as fairgrounds all over the world, space no one particularly wants to use for anything more important. After you push your way through the bikes and the greenery and seeds of the lower market into the new and old and army surplus camouflage clothing, and stand immobilized in the clot of bodies pressing to go down or up on the dirt path that connects the two levels, and squeeze past thousands of shoes and shoes and sausages and cheese, you will find, as climax and grand finale, a symptom of fairground—the track and bright, tinny baby autos for miniature racing. Don't rush to see it; it is not half as interesting as the quick lesson in local economics offered by the clothing of the customers and the edging and trimmings they select to go with the inexpensive yard goods. Nor as interesting as the calls of the vendors—"Shoes beautiful enough to wear as hats," "Come, come, all you beauties; come to see, come to see what I have to give away at ridiculous prices"—nor as interesting as the yearning looks cast on a group of garish rugs spread along the slope, nor as stimulating as the sight of two nuns drooling over bright orange and green, high-heeled, cork-bottomed sandals.

The market is not far from the university and the via delle

Volte (page 228) if you prefer to do it this way and a not impossible distance from the via Savonarola, a street of palaces. One of them housed the royal wives of Ercole II of the Estes (Isabella of Aragon and the other, Renata of France) and another, bristling with plasterwork, armor and shields, is still haughtily belligerent despite the tempering of the weather. Look for the occasional beautiful formal garden behind screens of ironwork, for bold doors and portals and the reminders of native sons. Boldini, the painter of tall, enameled ladies, was born on this street, though he had to find his fame in London and Paris. Savonarola, too, was born here and came to fame elsewhere. (The plaque blurts it out angrily: "spent his first twenty years here and was burned in Florence.") You will notice how quiet these streets are, how few cars and cafés there are, only the endless, silent flight of bikes as you follow the street of Savonarola on its dignified course past the large church of San Francesco to the Casa Romei.

In spite of having spent most of its life as a monastery and the presence of some church art—Byzantinish paintings, medieval stone, a pretty fifteenth-century Virgin—it is a light, graceful mansion, a fair example of a ducal residence of the 1400's. The deceptively snug entrance leads into a large, low house ranged around two handsome courts, a somewhat Saracenic effect created by the two tiers of round arches on slender columns and, in one court, an ornament of colored disks. The once-splendid furnishings, except for the stately fireplaces, are long gone, supplanted in part by a well-arranged panel of photographs of the art and sculpture of Ferrara and environs, and shields and tombstones of the Estes, the Romeis and the Barberinis' three famous bees. But there are echoes of playfulness in the traces of floral paintings, loosely enlaced in fluttering ribbons and mottoes that run through sections of the court; a taste for the peculiarly playful appears as a tree which is also a snake with many heads from which stream multiple bands of legend. Grotesques dance daintily on the Pompeian borders of several of the remarkably varied ceilings—diamonds of painted wood set into diagonal bands; ornately painted paper applied to wood; a ceiling that looks like a tapestry, another like tooled and colored leather. In all, an exhibition of the invention and craftsmanship that, along with the major arts, burgeoned in an optimistic new world that trumpeted man, especially a rich man, as a splendid being.

It would appear to be easy, from the map, to continue on to the Palazzina Marfisa and the Palazzo Schifanoia to the east and then southward to the museum in the Palace of Ludovico il Moro and the nunnery of Sant'Antonio in Polesine, but it would require precise planning according to hours of opening and closing and superhuman concentration and energy. (One often begins to dislike a town that seems to demand too much, although the fault is clearly that of a harried, omnivorous vacation pace.) It is probably time to rest but before you return for blank, comfortable sitting at a café in the center, or in the minute park near the church of San Domenico, to watch the bike-polishing that preoccupies even the very young, walk into the via Madama. If it chooses to disclose itself, you will see a very old, rural house-stable combination in an antique yard, which may have been part of the Jesuit garden where Montaigne, according to the attached sign, saw a rose garden that yielded a different bloom each month—one of the most beautiful of the many beautiful things he saw in Italy.

Onward, now, to a remote edge of town, where Ludovico il Moro, the Milanese overlord who married Beatrice d'Este, built and had decorated a section of his palace. It remained unfinished, according to the guardian, when Ludovico was imprisoned, to die a prisoner. The ambitious plan for a large palace reveals itself from the garden, obviously meant to be the court surrounded on four sides by halls and rooms. The two completed sections give plainly enough the seignorial quality of the palace: the fine details of the arcades of the entrance courts, the plaster plumes and streaks of gilding on the fireplaces, the glitter of old mirrors, the coffering and studding on wooden ceilings. One ceiling is a painted balcony crowded with little angels and musical people—one holds a lute, another a viol—looking down into the room, an attractive version of the Mantegna invention in Mantua (page 265).

In recent years, the palace has been used for finds (exploration is still going on and will be for a long time) from the Etruscan necropolis of Spina, drowned in the marshes between Ravenna and Ferrara and first detected by low-flying army planes. In a grand hall of windows looking down on the entrance court, among old map paintings, there are newer maps and aerial photographs of the Spina area. Near the entrance, more charts and maps that show the broad extent of the necropolis—suggesting again that Italy is one vast Etruscan and Roman sepulcher—and photos of finds just emerging and the wet, dirty work it is to pull these treasures out of the mud. The collection, awaiting additions, possibly may not yet be neatly organized, and some of the most remarkable pieces are taken out from time to time for study and documentation. There is still a plenitude of singularly interesting objects even if, by this time, you feel you've had quite enough of ancestor-worshiping Etruscology. There are pairs of figures very much like Indian bronzes and clever ornaments in animal forms from Asia Minor, frail Alexandrian perfume flasks, Phoenician objects and much from Greece, actually or by imitation. From Greek bowls and vases, through great bronze candleholders, bronze and terra-cotta figurines, beakers with negroid features and beakers like curly rams, through hooks, pots, alabaster perfume vials, down to a wooden comb—it is all there, always the same, always different, always evocative, this residue of a mysterious civilization that left so much and still remains mysterious. (If your time is limited make for Room XV, which seems to have a unique selection, a bit of everything in the gamut, and each piece extraordinary in its category.)

In a lower gallery, near the room of the ceiling fresco, a guide, maybe lonely but certainly concerned that you don't miss a thing, will take you to see the Roman boats carved out of enormous trunks. And that guide—or another—forbidden to take the tip he doesn't expect in any case may walk with you in the formal garden, past its maze and through the bower of roses, pointing out bits of unfinished wall and the gratings over tunneled cellars that lead to the Castle, smoking a forbidden cigarette. You light up also and offer him a few for after lunch. He takes one but firmly declines a second and third and you realize that this is characteristic of the city; it accepts no admission charges, or very little (usually accompanied by apologies), and its attendants, though no better paid than in other places, act like curators rather than servants. You will meet this noblesse again, should you ask the man at the card and booklet desk where you might find a cab. He will telephone, invite you to sit down and refuse a coin for the call.

By way of via Beatrice d'Este and continuing eastward toward a bastion of the old city wall, one approaches the nunnery of Sant'Antonio in Polesine. It faces a neglected court inhabited partially by a scramble of small houses supervised by a half dozen giant cats of different types, as if some fancier had searched out the biggest black, white and tortoise-shell cats he could find. Someone or other will be looking out of the window—the most important furnishing, when the bed and table are not in use, of a working-class Italian house—to indicate the bell you must ring to be admitted. After a pause, during which all but two nuns disappear, a little grate opens. The password is *affreschi* (frescoes), and the door is opened by a combination of a youngish, broad-faced nun, still a shy girl from the country, and an old good-looking woman, warmly curious and confident, with alert blue eyes and a lithe step; no country girl, she; a descendant of the bluestocking Isabella d'Este, one decides.

The frescoes she shows are thirteenth-century examples of that enormous, inept school gathered in a big lumpy sack labeled "Giottesque." They obviously show close, devoted study of Giotto's frescoes, so close as to repeat the famous yellow robe of Judas in Padua and to move in the same range of colors. But the attitudes make stiff caricatures, and for emotion all eyeballs are turned to the edge of an eye slit in the manner of Giotto, who added to this one device many others, particularly genius. Another section of paintings, less tutored, more naïve, is also more engaging and wonderfully literal. Things were really spelled out here, as in a panel of Mary sitting on a shell in heaven, and as if she were fishing—in a way, she is—she lowers a long loop that connects her with praying figures below; the prayers come up on one side of the cord and the Virgin's responses, the prayers answered, go down the other side. Simple, reassuring.

The variety, for a fairly small church enclave, is stimulating. It includes some remarkable heads and saints' figures among the naïvetés, a few worldly, later pieces of blue distant air behind

romantic trees, in the Bellini manner and, at the other end of the
scale, an iconlike Madonna and Child wearing a silver crown.
While you inspect, the older nun, having noticed that you did
not genuflect each time you passed the altar, speaks with affectionate amusement of the innocent, literal symbolism in the older
frescoes, rather like a professor of art who shows you something
that beguiles him although he has no great respect for it. She will
then take you proudly to the big vineyard and plastic-bowered
garden that provides the nuns with vegetables all year round,
and later conduct you to a full-length silver image of a nun with
a golden face, the reliquary for the bones of the woman who was
the founder of the nunnery. Below, there is a space for a dented
zinc sheet that drips water into a basin during several consecu-
tive months of each year, no one knows why, nor whence. It is a
miracle; the holy water cured a deaf woman, not so long ago, a
woman who hadn't heard at all for many years. Doctors hadn't
helped her, nor could they explain the cure. There is no indul-
gent apologetic smile now. The painted miracles were for primitive, lovable ignorance; this miracle is here, now and thoroughly
credible, to judge from the exalted solemnity with which it is
described.

In the aristocratic Ferrarese manner, there is no request for
money, nor even a meaningful look at the discreet box for offerings near the door. As you slip some money into the box, out of
the pretty, blue-eyed, wrinkled face comes "Thank you" in English, and if you speak a little Italian a request that you add to
her English vocabulary, if it doesn't displease you. How do you
say *tanti auguri* in English? You tell her that it might be "all
good wishes," which she writes down, accurately, and memo-
rizes instantly, offering you a smiling sample of your linguistic
gift as you leave.

Returning toward the long central spine of the Corso della
Giovecca one comes to the Palazzo Schifanoia, ambitious to become a civic museum, which it may or may not be in your time.
Some of it is closed off for repair, pieces of fresco taken out for
restoration; the usual "civic" hodgepodge of ceramic lamps and
old stones lies in disorder. Nevertheless it is worth the walk, or

the taxi ride, and the time. As usual, the present uncommunicative building requires a forcing of the imagination. One must see it as the pleasure palace, the "delight" it was meant to be, a short distance into the country, not too far from the center of business and politics, and devoted to festive entertainment, great balls and dinners in a sybarite's luxury of art and furnishings. It should be surrounded by gardened space and ceremonious entrances and peopled with the luminous guests of the Estes during the late fourteenth and through the fifteenth century. The glamour and luxury, the grandeur of Estes—particularly the fifteenth-century duke called Borso—are immortalized in the remaining frescoes of Months painted by several fifteenth-century Ferrarese but attributed, because other names lack, to Francesco Cossa, who undoubtedly had a large hand in their making (and maybe, Cosmé Tura).

Like many wall paintings in neglected palaces and churches, they had a shocking history: for a long time abandoned and marred by vandals, they were whitewashed in the eighteenth century to cover their messy uselessness. A century later a few traces were brought ineptly to light and then turned over to a more skillful hand, which carefully restored and retouched two walls. The rest is sketchy and pale, blotched with white patches of obliteration that release, here and there, echoes of ebullience and shadows of gracious personages, their houses and countryside. That which is clearly visible is a deft setting of the glorified Borso d'Este as huntsman and benign prince among classical figures, signs of the zodiac and castles and churches in Ferrara's seasonal landscapes. Against a group of clearly defined brick houses, a company of farmers—one of whom has the same profile, oddly, as the Duke Borso—are defining March by polling trees. The fecundity of April is an abundant compendium of Spring and love, through which Venus rides on a float drawn by two white horses toward groups of ideal lovers—kissing, talking, playing musical instruments, all blondly beautiful, all exquisitely coifed and dressed. What is left of May repeats the bouquets of lovely girls of the same fair mold, differentiated by a variety of hair style and texture and color of gown, this time accompanied by a triumphant Apollo. The primary pleasure in the frescoes is, along with the enchanting subjects, the Renaissance joy in rendering the goods of the earth—the nervous grace of hunting hounds and horses, the fresh curves of young cheeks, the eager backs and ears of nibbling rabbits, the folds of brocaded gowns and pleated velvet tabards, the shape of a lute, the density of leaves, the mask of a swan, the play of the breeze in white pennants—delicate, idealized and happy with a vision of life that is a not impossible Eden.

It is difficult to say what else might be visible to you, guided by the sadly amiable custodian and his cat, but booklets do describe a hall of bronzes set among pieces of seventeenth-century furniture, a collection of local ceramics of the fifteenth and sixteenth centuries, a room devoted to numismatics, a hall of Virtues imbedded in rich plaster work, and somewhere in that room, a terra-cotta Virgin whose rounded, serene young face makes her sister to the girls in the Months.

Another country "delight," near the same stretch of wall, is the Palazzina Marfisa, the house of one of the Este ladies and her husband, built in the mid-sixteenth century and still whispered about as a place of curious activities and practices. The custodian won't explain further, probably because he knows no more. This summer palace, devoted solely to entertaining, has spacious airy rooms that lead to a garden and, beyond that, to sleeping quarters, which are now nondescript apartments. None of the original furniture is left; the present furnishings seem to be wardrobes and refectory tables brought from extinct churches. It is the Pompeian designs that curve softly up to the ceiling, the handsome lattices of wood (possibly modern) at the broad windows, and above all the decorous minuet of doorways leading from room to room and the effulgent light that bring one here. Only one panel of frescoes remains of the many, and several ceilings are dimmed because this *delizia* was used at one time as a warehouse and at another as an ironworks whose smoke fumed the walls, but the essential quality of a little summer villa, an ornament to adorn a luxurious life, unmistakably remains.

A walk back on the Corso della Giovecca, accompanied by elderly gentlemen and their wives, who wear that emblem of middle-class elderly respectability the dark-velvet toque, is a walk in Main Street—shops, cafés and houses bringing themselves up to date. One of them, at 131, was threatened by scaffolding, but it may have been able to rescue the plasterwork and iron of the art-nouveau façade with its watery scenery of bending reeds and gracefully convulsed water lilies.

One of Ferrara's prides for centuries—and it may still be—is the avenue named for Ercole d'Este I, the city planner and remotely the begetter of all those bicycles. It runs northward from the Castle and is, like many streets inhabited by Renaissance palaces, stern and heavy, aloofly don't-you-dare-touch-me-or-even-come-close, a street armored with thick walls and massive ornaments, lightened only by the tall old trees that insist on escaping. From some distance one begins to discern the bulges, the studded armor, that covers the Palazzo dei Diamanti, so called because the entire blistered surface is made of more than twelve thousand stones cut like diamonds. It may have been a charming fancy in the designing, but as it emerged seventy years later, in 1565, its myriad stone points shrieking into the street, it is a bellicose building. Now Ferrara's museum of fine arts, the Palazzo includes a collection of local painting, galleries for modern shows and, near the back of the court, a Boldini museum.

Boldini's pearly portraits of latter-day Gainsborough ladies were commissioned and painted elsewhere in Europe, leaving Ferrara only one sleek, full-length beauty. The rest is mementos: Boldini's Empire bed, his cane, a death mask of the painter taken from a toothless, imponderably old face and work one rarely sees, done for his own pleasure rather than the salon—a couple of self-portraits, an attempt at sculpture and many sketches. He drew his studio table and his bed, a corner of a piece of furniture, a profile in a café, on scraps of bill, on a waiter's pad. There are a few small paintings that are distinctly like Turner's, a little painting of a doorway, of a corner of a street, a fine small portrait of a man and a diversity of women's heads lovingly sketched in a few gentle curves or as economically and coolly derived as Matisse portraits. The enthusiastic guardian—whose enthusiasm will become joy if you understand Italian—especially likes an amusing "studio" painting that shows, in the foreground, the back of a woman who has obviously come to see the progress made on her portrait in the background, but the amazing sketches are the crown of the engaging collection.

With a second look at some of the doors that acclaim rather than invite, wander through the unassuming streets that lead back to the via Cavour and listen to the local chimes that describe seven o'clock by banging 4, 4 plus 5; or 5, 5 plus 4 or 5, 5 plus 5 but never 7. Look into the frail cloister arches that hide behind a big insurance building (Assicurazione), and facing that, the big postal building whose structure is Mussolini yearning for the Roman Empire. Here the city begins to trail its weight of modern buildings and automobile road toward one defenseless, unaccompanied skyscraper and the anonymity of the railraod station.

Notes

The best hotel, and not expensive (about $60 with bath for two), is the fairly modern Astra on the via Cavour. The Touring, on the same street, is also fairly modern and satisfactory. The rest are smaller; the Hotel San Giorgio on the Piazza Sacrati, and a few scattered through the center of town. It would be best to ask about these at the Ente Provinciale, or explore for yourself. Ferrara is an exceeding clean and self-respecting city, but its rooming standards and yours may differ.

For eating there is one old, famous place, across from the Castle, Da Giovanni, and always safe for the quality of its food (the *bollito misto* is a favorite) and service and immutable air of Ferrarese refinement. Or try Max, behind Da Giovanni, or the Annunziata; chances are you'll keep returning to Da Giovanni.

Mantua and Sabbioneta

SIDE BY SIDE with the Roman column, the papal tiara and crossed keys that are among the conspicuous symbols of Italy, there should stand the old lion that supports the portals of medieval churches. He might act as the particular totem of old lions of towns, once mighty and now emasculated and exhausted, like Pisa, like Ferrara, like Mantua, especially Mantua. It is not a convivial town, though always polite, nor especially comely, and although it can be lively, there is, under the liveliness a heavy silence, a mood of courageous resignation.

The Palazzo Ducale, the seat of the Gonzagas, is a place apart, not quite like any other place. The stolid marble-faced monuments to progress and Fascism, frowningly repeated in a number of piazzas, are distinctly Italy of the thirties. And yet Mantua's redbrick archlets, awkwardly Gothic, remind one of Gothic Revival buildings in Victorian London; the loss of cover and grace of ornament, the nudity of falling brick and empty windows made some of Mantua look like London dock streets several years after the bombings. The damage was not new or raw. Fresh damage has a certain sharpness and cleanliness; here the clarity of shapes and color was gone. If one's references were not London but rather New York, the echo of abandoned El stations might return and from some obscure corners the whimper of neglected streets that bordered El terminals. (That these impressions were not the result of one's morbid sensibilities alone, there was the testimony of a show held, appropriately enough, in the house of the Gonzaga court painter, Andrea Mantegna. It was called, "Mantua, a city that needs saving.") Much has improved but Mantua will never be merry.

Before you've done your duty as a tourist to the famous, bizarre Gonzaga palace, to the church of Sant'Andrea, tried to get into the little round church of San Lorenzo, rambled through the market and its surrounding arcades, peered up at the towers and admired the swallow-tailed curves on the government palace, take an hour in the Mantua that is not so much taciturn as quietly ruminative. At the north end of the market piazza (Erbe), look for a flat wooden-beamed tunnel that seems uninviting, but not to Mantuans who have placed here an art gallery, a doctor's office and, to keep the medieval franchise, a melting house under a broad swing of arch, waving laundry and the leaves of potted plants out of a half-closed door. Out into the light again and under another arch into the via Roberto Ardigo, a calm street except when youngsters swarm around the scholastic institutions to which the street is dedicated. All the buildings are "noble," ponderously good-looking, and one of them, the state archives, holds a treasury of Gonzaga information. Beyond that, a building of the eighteenth century, originally planned by local Jesuits for a university and now the site of a community library, schoolrooms, lordly stairs, and palatial corridors for children's running feet. On the wall immediately inside the entrance is a plaque for Maria Theresa, who founded the library in 1780 and expanded her taste for culture to the Vergil Academy on the next street, her beneficences there too advertised in large letters. Look back as you stand at the edge of the patch of green across from the Archives building to see the cupola of Sant'Andrea and the old tower that holds, high up, a cage of iron for malefactors (considering the intensity of seasons in this area, no one could ever have served a long sentence, almost all punishment must have been capital) and, under an arch, a medieval tangle of low houses embracing each other as in a children's game by Breughel. In the park, Dante, holding his quill and tablet, dour as usual, threatened by towers in front of him and in back.

The eighteenth-century Academia Virgiliana is a building with large sores scratched down to brick, only the capitals above its pilasters still uninfected. To continue the game of similarities, it looks like the discarded city hall of a small American town. Attempts have been made, and are being made, to save the "Scientific Theater" inside, a fantasy of 1769. One rings the bell at the side of a Belle-Epoque gate of bent iron and is directed by a pleasant woman (she, too, is drying her hands on her apron, in the usual show of busy housewifeliness which seems to consist, at all hours, of laundering) to tiers of minute boxes that fan out from a narrow end, in the shape of a shallow vase rather than the traditional horseshoe. There are tiny columns and arches, big columns and large arches that end in scrolls, swags, paint, an ornate ceiling, everything ribboned and curled in the nervous fussiness of its period. Still, because of its surprising presence behind the worn façade, and because it has the quality of a miniature—it might be tasteless were it larger—it is thoroughly appealing, and one can easily picture the silks, wigs and jewels shining out of the minute boxes as they listen to the young prodigy, Wolfgang Amadeus Mozart, one evening in 1770.

Turn into the via Pomponazzo, a street of tearful palaces which, in spite of bruised rustication and disappeared plaster, still holds on to its well-made doorways and windows, then into the vicolo Carmine, a London dock street again, of massive stones and unused windows in dusty brick that leads to a pleasant breath of open, loose yellow-gold arches in a monastery garden. Off Carmine, the vicolo Corridore, a humble dockside street, is doing its very best for its houses with pots of bright paint. Back on via Pomponazzo, at Number 23, stands the Palazzo Sordi, built in 1680 by a Flemish architect, and one would like to know why, with so many Italians available, a foreigner who worked in the Italian style was needed. At any rate, it requires special permission to go through the palace, and all you may do is enter the vaulted portico hung with martial emblems and stare through the gate at the wreathed and colonnaded curve of court

that surrounds a group of classic statues, the center group either
Persephone being carried off by Pluto or a faun and fauness playing a sexy game. (Although those ever-present opera glasses
might help, there is a perverse, voyeur feeling about scrutinizing
so minutely and fixedly a stranger's house, so you may never
know just who they are and what they are really doing.)

In and out of the vicolo this and the vicolo that and through
the vicolo called Barche one reaches the dock of Porto Catena,
named for the chain that closed off the harbor when Mantua was
a busy port city. It doesn't seem particularly active, although it
may derive some business from the tanks that glisten across the
waters or from a long, glass factory building suspended on two
concrete bridges, very much a Nervi design. Standing on the
stairs along the side of the dock building one looks down onto
the leavings of the canal that surprises from back streets as it
drags its slow way across the city. A longer view of the canal,
from the bridge on the via Massari, is reminiscent of the back
canals of Venice, down to all the noted details—raffish pictur-
esqueness of irregularly jutting houses, distant bridges, greenish-
yellow waters too laden with objects to move and a few pieces of
laundry out to catch the dimmed sun; good to look at, however,
if you can hold your breath and resist thinking of what it might
mean to try to sleep in these rooms during a humid heat spell.
Then, by way of still, still streets near the canal to the blossomy
court inside 24 or 26 on via XX Settembre, and on to the via
Pescheria (fish market), a pair of long, narrow porticoed buildings designed in the early sixteenth century by Giulio Romano
for the fish merchants of the city. Soon, a small triangle of park
rimmed with whitewashed stone, sitting in the shade of a late-
medieval bell tower. Along with the few babies and the ice-cream
vendor and the old gentlemen who seem to own park benches,
you may see a sturdy bearded man wearing a monk's hood, rubber boots and a yellow tabard, talking to himself. You may see
him, now and again, anywhere in the city talking reasonably to
himself or praying near a vigorously realistic new Pietà in one of
the chapels of Sant'Andrea. After his prayer, he drops a coin into
the offerings box. He is never molested, or even approached, but
there seems always to be a young priest who busies himself in the

near vicinity for the duration of the visit.

If the sun is shining, unstained by clouds, the big café on the Piazza Cavallotti will have fanned out its innumerable tables and chairs and begun to rush large cups of ice cream served in a variety of colors and ornaments. Have a *coppa* and then, with another look at the canal that makes an unexpected appearance behind a neighboring flower shop before it disappears under the piazza, make your way to the modern arcades diagonally to the left. There you will find a bus marked "G," which finishes its run at the Sanctuary of Santa Maria delle Grazie. The bus zooms past the railroad and bus stations, into new housing and a few old villas trying to shield themselves from the impudence of small industrial plants, toward a big cemetery with the walls of a fortress and a sententious portal of the thirties. It then slips through farmland scored with irrigation ditches and studded with brick farmhouses in the pleasing, traditional style of family quarters and animal shelters united as one long building with wide openings and inventive brickwork screens for airing beasts and hay.

At the last bus stop, the eye is caught by a frail iron portico, now quite rusted, that echoes, as do a number of shopwindows and cafés in town, a wave of prosperity and adornment at the turn of this century. A long unpaved street accompanied by a row of apple-green, cerise and blue houses—a curiously Mexican effect—is stopped by a broad façade with the same red-brick attempts at curves that recall Victorian London. The total effect of the generous portico is inviting, an effect immediately canceled by the frescoes under the arches, which were painted by someone who tried to do like Mantegna, but couldn't. Luckily, much of the frescoes has been scrubbed away by those stern critics, the years. The church was built as a sanctuary for votive offerings by Francesco I of the Gonzagas in the early fifteenth century, to give thanks for the passing of a plague and, one suspects, because the Gonzagas could not stop building. Baldassare Castiglione, the author of *The Courier,* lies here, his tomb engraved with several choice words by another Renaissance writer and scholar, Pietro Bembo. One room holds several cases of suits of armor and the rest is thousands of ex-votos. Some are old and embroidered on fine silk laced through with silver threads; some are crude handwork on the stamped cotton found in rural markets; the walls grow a silver fungus of votive hearts, and crutches shape a small, dreary forest. Votive paintings describe miracles in the shocking straightforwardness of all primitive paintings: a child not quite run over by a car is observed and saved by the Virgin who looks down from the sky; a man who has fallen off his bicycle in front of an onrushing train is rescued from death by saints who braked the train in time.

The grand finale of this accretion of souvenirs of miracle and gratitude is found in the main body of the church. Under the floral ornaments of the vaults, there are large niches that resemble a closely set group of tight opera boxes. Emerging from the boxes on two tiers are near-life-size figures made of papier-mâché and wax that depict people of various moods, stages of coma, agony, or mayhem. The opera glasses mentioned constantly are needed here to see the fine painting on the clothing of the ladies and knights, the distortions of head ineptly attached to body, the looks of hauteur or surprise or bewilderment. A man with a big stone around his neck is either being pushed into a well or pulled out of it by two happy little angels. One fiend, bursting with malicious joy, is ready to crush what might easily be a head with a heavy mallet. A coarse-faced seated figure in a torn coat, one arm extended, is either begging or protesting the fact that he has been put in stocks. (The uncertainty results from the occasional incapacity of the artist to render forms precisely.) One of his less fortunate neighbors is in dusty shroud white, thoroughly and grotesquely hanged, while another is praying his last with the noose already looped about his neck. Lacing together these nooks of sinners, courtiers and ladies is a wonderfully peculiar decorative band. The upper areas of the band mingle rows of breasts and hearts; the lower sections let the hearts go to concentrate on breasts, innumerable breasts bordered by lines of hands, breasts and hands in a whitish yellow that must have attempted the color of flesh. The mind immediately re-records primitive forms of punishment that cut off the hands of thieves and the breasts of whores and then moves toward a montage of the heaped flesh of historic massacres. The sight is perverse,

amusing and evocative when one considers that these works of
the sixteenth and seventeenth centuries were crafted by priests
dedicated to the gentle, abstemious precepts of Saint Francis.
Perhaps three or four centuries of sweet abnegation must crack at
some point and emit little psychological demons, like a worldful
of breasts and hands that approach them but never touch.

Astonishment soars to utter bewilderment (and there is no one
to explain, except for a taciturn monk who sits in the sacristy
making rosaries to sell and clearly unwilling to be disturbed as he
bends over his beads and wires) as one looks up, beyond the
figures, to the graceful Venetian glass chandeliers and find hanging among them a stuffed crocodile.

The bemused trip back on Bus "G" will leave you where it
picked you up, in the center of a web of interesting directions
and possibilities. It would seem reasonable that the street named
for Giulio Romano should hold his house, or some form of vice
versa, but this was not subtle enough for one fine Italian mind
and it appears on the adjacent strip called via Poma, a good
street with several fine houses on either side of a row of trees and
the playground of diabolical motorbikes. Romano's house is at
Number 18, expanded and somewhat changed from his original
design but still light and engaging, necklaced in cool garlands of
fruit and flowers and Greek ornaments that guide to the niche of
a winsome Mercury. The Palace of Justice on the other side of
the street has been blamed on Giulio Romano for certain resemblances to the decorations in the Palazzo del Te (page 250), but
whatever the original mid-sixteenth-century plans were—by Romano or someone else—centuries of odd taste have left the
building one of the most fascinating and ludicrous. Twelve caryatids strain under the weight of extravagant stone, and what
caryatids! They may represent the horrors of injustice, or the
seven deadly sins plus five extra, but whatever else they are, they
are incredible. The huge heads are stupid or greedy, gleefully
cruel or glowering in misery. They are male—one looks like Moses gone mad at the sight of the Golden Calf—and female,
among them a stunned Brunhild. The torsos are square, doughy
and sexlessly alike with long, contorted valutes or eels (the slip-

periness of justice?) as arms. For sex organs (reminders of sex crimes? of vengeance heaped on illicit love? of the torments of venereal disease? your guess) there are small monster heads, inventively differentiated in a much greater and more colorful diversity than nature's two dullish combinations; one monster has crazy flamelike hair, another sports tusks, still another dangles enormous, pendulous ears and several of the stone genitalia share combinations of these ornaments. The once delicate, playful Pompeian grotesque, a faun in a funny mask, obviously suffered a long siege of elephantiasis to produce such overgrown Baroque fancies, stone echoes of Bomarzo (pages 125–7).

Toward the end of town, at Number 47 via Acerbi (don't forget the rubbernecking in courts and alleys that is the right, pleasure and even duty of every traveler), there is quite another kettle of building, the house of Andrea Mantegna, on a piece of property granted him by Ludovico II of the Gonzagas. It must have been a very attractive house, originally set beyond the edge of town, and though cleverly designed, it is quite unpretentious. A circular yard that leads from a number of rooms is surrounded by an open square of building whose windows give on the court and a fair-sized garden. It has been restored and it seems a pity that no use has yet been found for it (perhaps an art school) except an occasional exhibition.

Continuing in the same direction (there is a bus from the center, however, if the feet have given out) one reaches the Palazzo del Te (the word may mean huts or a type of tree, no one seems to be quite sure). It is near the sports stadium and the race track, quite justly, because this was the palace for fun, feasts and games, for housing mistresses and providing pasturage for the blooded horses that all the Gonzaga dearly loved. The country palace was not too far from the palace of business and family, yet at a good psychological remove since the land was then part of an island. The building was one of Romano's first ventures in Mantua, though he was by no means a novice; as a star pupil of Raphael and considered by some to be his artistic successor, Romano was already a successful painter-architect. The pleasure palazzo is a calm, classic square ranged around a court which opens to formal gardens held by a pleasing curve of arcade.

The frescoes in the many rooms were very likely the product of committee work: a committee of Renaissance savants and writers to select subjects from the classics and another committee of painters working under Romano to carry out those suggestions. It was probably Federico who decided that the walls of his banqueting hall be used for portraits of his finest horses set in Arcadian landscapes, among references to classic fables.

The tour of the classics, some of it a bit stained by time and accident, wanders through Ovid's *Metamorphoses* and on to a fairly complete pictorial biography of Psyche, the twenty-odd panels finishing at a great feast of the gods celebrating her wedding to Cupid. Once they are married, to live happily ever after, we pick up the adventures of Venus and Mars, of Acis and Galatea, and on and on into an enormous, seething minestrone of mythology, including portraits of the winds and signs of the zodiac. King David attends and the weighty presence of Julius Caesar; on the ceiling of the master bedroom Phaëthon re-enacts his fall in a virtuosity of light and shade, of movement and complex perspective. Around these tons of naked flesh and exaggerated musculature supported by strong wings fly arabesques, medallions, friezes and sumptuous ceilings—entertaining for a while, boring for a longer while (we have been subjected to four hundred years of repetitions of this matter, after all)—until one is brought up short at the famous Room of the Giants. It concerns itself with Jupiter's defeat and destruction of rebellious giants, when the heavens cracked open, great rocks fell and huge columns crumbled to crush the ugly crouching monsters with coarse, brutal faces who seem, however, to be more annoyed than terrified. The stamp of Michelangelo's Sistine ceiling is unmistakable, but the room has an odd, stupefying courage of its own.

Some years ago the large garden of the palazzo was used as exhibition ground for the agricultural uses of plastics—dark plastic coverlets for cosseted seedlings and long, shining caterpillars of plastic for the protection of sensitive plants—neatly arranged and decorated with a profligacy of flowering plants. It seemed a reasonable way to use an unused pleasure palace on the edge of the city. However interesting the show may be in your time, don't forget to look into the small rooms at the end of the curved colonnade. Fanciful and miniature, equipped with a grotto and a pocket handkerchief of hidden garden, the rooms were, in all likelihood, the apartment of the Duke's favorite and longest-lasting mistress, Isabella Boschetti. He also paid her the compliment of decorating the palace with salamanders and the legend, in the slanting, gnomic manner so much admired in the Renaissance, to the effect that "that to which he [the salamander] is immune, tortures me," which means that while salamanders cannot be burned, the Duke, on the contrary, is consumed by the fires of love.

It may be time to try, once again, the door of the Rotonda of San Lorenzo whose sign says that it receives between 10:00 and 11:00 A.M. and between 3:00 and 4:00 P.M., though it sits obdurate and impenetrable in the market brouhaha, except for Sundays or the time of a wedding ceremony, for which these small, ancient churches are in vogue. Open or closed, San Lorenzo is an important structure, not only as a vestige of the might of the vigorous Countess Matilde of Canossa (Lombardy's Eleanor of Aquitaine), who caused it to be built in the eleventh century, but because it is the core of the old city, the hive that sends forth the market buzz and color. There should be, hugging its side, a pet shop as tight as a newsstand. One minute section is given to a tank for goldfish, a few inches provide space for white mice, at the other side, cages of canaries and blue, red and speckled birds, tiny and mindlessly restless. Trailing off, still hugging the curve of the church, a display of pink and yellow cages of glistening plastic, and almost as restless as the birds, children examining potential pets, if choices were offered them. Skulking, swaying, hoping, disappearing under the stall, reappearing for a hungry look at the unattainable smörgåsbord, waiting, watching, is a large black-and-white gangster of a cat.

An early-rising fruit and vegetable stall stands a few yards down the street; in back of the church a sturdy, weather-beaten country couple lift down crates of eggs and chickens from a truck. The top of the shallow flight of stairs leading to the portal of the church splashes the market scene with plumes and fronds and cups of flowers. Under the clock tower more vegetables, fruits, cheeses and a wonder of order and efficiency—a shining, pristine truck whose side opens to reveal antiseptic rows of olive jars, vegetables in vinegar, glass vats of anchovies placed in un-Italian orderliness. The truck is always busy, not because its goods are cheap—they cost less at the corner grocery—but the ladies are fascinated by the unaccustomed precision, the Americanness of it, as if it were a super computer. This, along with a few piles of children's socks and aprons and a big-voiced record stall makes up the usual daily market. On Thursday morning there is a sudden outcropping of dark mushrooms, the black hats of rural merchants and farmers who make thick clouds on every piazza and around the grain merchants' exchange, a thunderously ugly and diverting building. The market swells in noise and size; eggs and chickens multiply overnight, the cheeses put on weight as they teeter on slender planks, new heaps of blankets, ceramics and pink-cheeked ornaments appear, lengths of lace and edging hang like drying pasta over remnants of yard goods. Supported by a tower an enterprising gentleman stands high before a wall of sheets and tablecloths and one doesn't need Italian to follow the universal litany: "Forty-six hundred lire for this gorgeous, big, colorfast tablecloth, washable in the machine [a piece of subtle flattery] or by hand. They are worth 6,000; I myself paid 5,000, but today I'm letting them go for—no, not 4,000 but 3,500." The tablecloth paid for, napkins are offered, but one cannot buy them immediately, the actor on the cotton stage must speak his lines "not 3000, nor 2000 but 1000 for these lovely—look at the delicacy and color of that pattern—napkins." Should you find yourself near the market at about 1:00 or 1:30, closing time, you will see the pavement grilles opening to swallow stall supports, crates of cauliflower and bundles of fennel that await, in their medieval sepulchers, the early-morning voice of one merchant whose lusty, tuneful singing calls the market awake the next day.

San Lorenzo, red, round and imperturbable as a brood hen, creates a significant halt and start in the rhythms of the city, the bright spot on the canvas that catches the eye and directs it on. At the northeast corner of Mantua, near the bridge that divides the Lower Lake from the Middle Lake—two of three arbitrary divisions of the waters that surround the city—there is a watery ruralness of row boats and sheds for swimmers and fishermen, a few modest houses that front the lake (though, in that inward Mantuan manner, they seem not to be looking at it). Around the corner, returning toward the Duomo, there is a refurbished house that has been named "Rigoletto's"; the deflating truth is that there was no such humpbacked jester whose daughter was carried off by the Duke of Mantua, as Verdi wrote it, and, in any case, the house has been a womanless adjunct of the Duomo for centuries. Then the long, weary, darkly beautiful Piazza Sordello named for a Provençal poet, dragging itself gallantly toward a medieval jumble of towers and arches, Ghibelline crenelation, the shut eye of a closed rose window in the church of Sant'Andrea and slices of red brick that buttress its sides. Out of place and rather surprised sits the eighteenth-century dome of the church, which had been designed (later changed and rechanged) as a classical temple by one of the most sternly classical of Renaissance archtects, Leon Battista Alberti, who died in 1472, when the actual construction of the church was begun.

Away from the lake, going toward and beyond the big piazza of ice cream, choice foods and Bus "G" (page 247), there are the shopping streets, several of the shops still supremely provincial—in no pejorative sense at all—dressed in glorious lettering and feminine bent woods of the turn of the century, shops that sell corks and corks only, and one authentically Edwardian bar that names itself the "Caffé Sport." Since no town can call itself the major place of a district without them, Mantua has a supply (not quite as large as Ferrara's) of shops full of trusses and surgical corsets.

Their number has dwindled to give room to symbols of prosperity and up-to-dateness that stem from the light, lucrative industries burgeoning on the rims of town. Ergo, clothing shops that feature Missoni woolens and Gucci shoes, Fendi bags, antique and freshly blazing jewelry. But cheek by jowl with the big-city wonders, there are still pharmacists who concentrate on what gives your horse a bellyache, what makes your sow sick (do pigs ever get sick?) and supply the panaceas. With them, hardware stores that supply the ropes and pails and knives and axes bought by the farmers and vintners who come on market day.

Let us assume that you have had enough market-watching over breakfast from the vantage of the bar of the San Lorenzo hotel, that you have finished working out the balances and counterbalances, the diagonals and curves of the architectural composition before you. It might be time to go up into the Palazzo della Ragione, the thirteenth-century seat of law and archives, much restored now, and its great hall used for exhibitions. The shows are usually well arranged and always pleasing enough for a bit of time, but save some attention for the style of the pitched wooden roof and its supports, and vestiges of antique murals—a few stiff, saintly figures and a piece of battle scene with figures in the style of the Battle of Hastings Bayeux tapestries.

The seat of government in the thirteenth century was the massive Palazzo del Broletto on the piazza of that name. At the base of its tower, a butcher has reduced his window to the size of a jewel case to show three perfectly spaced, perfectly matched calf carcasses. On the side of the tower facing the piazza there is an attractive Renaissance house and near it, in a niche of Romanesque columns and ornaments, sits a smiling thirteenth-century Vergil wearing a medieval cap of learning, his hands resting on a book; a rather anachronistic monument for a man born in 70 B.C., engaging as a work and as a gesture of the free commune proud of its native genius, born near Mantua.

Off the piazza, on a street named for a "lion of gold," there was once the "university" of the merchants (the word means guild or association) whose buildings remain—without banner, emblem or importance. (Notice as you go the shops and cafés named for the Gonzaga, as well as cakes; a street named for Rubens à Gonzaga protegé, and butter stamped "Vergil.") The via Cavour begins its course with a palely painted palace of the late fifteenth century and the tower that held the cage for malefactors then passes a few more mansions and a happily proportioned and gay palazzo. Observe the stillness of the via Mainoldi, the crookedness of the properly named vicolo Storta, and follow the medieval and Renaissance meanders to the Piazza

Matilda di Canossa, cracked open by the aggressive pressure and weight of the late seventeenth-century Canossa Palace. Look at the houses on the via Fratelli Bandiera, the slit of canal in front of the church of San Francesco, the good houses on the via Marangoni, full of law offices and sometimes hiding, sometimes not, spacious courts and gardens.

The street ends at the enormous café under the classic pediment of the Teatro Sociale (1822), and if you have checked the bus schedule with the capable and well-Englished lady at the Ente per Turismo near the market, maybe there is time for the short walk down the Corso Vittorio Emanuele to the cul-de-sac where you will find the bus that goes to another Gonzaga extravaganza called Sabbioneta, a half hour's ride, depending on the duration of stops, from Mantua.

After the bus driver has dropped a package at the bar of one hamlet, left a few riders at another, stopped to exchange a few words with a crony at a third, the bus halts at a walled town with a tall Renaissance portal. It opens on a long main street much like those in any rural town, except that it is broader and its tangents are in straight rows, a sign of city planning. There isn't much movement in the town nor much to inspire movement; few young people, always one policeman and a starer into space, waiting for the skies to drop a miracle, if only in the form of two tourists. In the tourist office a buxom young woman hands out Sabbioneta pamphlets in the appropriate language and asks that you wait for the gentleman with the keys. Before the tourist office was open, the arrangement was do-it yourself, free-form. One asked at the post office for information about seeing the town's attractions and was directed to the house of a woman in an apron and the kerchief that is a second skin to country women. She handed over a massive bunch of keys, pointed vaguely in the direction of the places the keys would open and closed her door. You were on your own, in sole possession of the shadowed antiquities of a Renaissance fantasy. Now the gentleman of the keys arrives, courteous, good-looking but rather approximately informed. He will tell you that the ornaments that catch your eye in the Gonzaga chapel are stone inlay; they are plainly in the same trompe l'oeil that characterizes the rest of the church, substituted for carved marble and plasterwork not only because that show of virtuosity was fashionable but cheaper, and even Gonzaga money couldn't go on forever. He will tell you that the very first indoor covered theater is that of Sabbioneta, but denies that it is considerably like Palladio's (in Vicenza and an earlier work), which was completed after Palladio's death by Vincenzo Scamozzi, the designer of the very theater in which you stand.

Be that as it may, he will take you to a few fascinating shards of splendor in several stages of decay, some of it so wispy that you will have to weave up loose strips, repaint the walls, restore the resplendent illumination and fill the halls with the whisper of silks and the clank of armor as you go through this "Small Athens" created by the hubris of Vespasiano Gonzaga. His father, Luigi, of a collateral line of the family, was a handsome, aggressive warrior and politician and extraordinarily strong, an attribute he liked to show off by destroying a horseshoe and cutting through a tree trunk with one blow. Sabbioneta was his, and he passed it on to his less sinewy but equally impetuous, hot-blooded son, who had, moreover, been brought up in the strict formalities, the Don Quixote knightliness and the intense religiosity of the Spanish court. He pursued his first wife with implacable insistence and ardor and arranged a secret Romeo and Juliet marriage at dawn in a not too distant town. He grew tired of her, accused her of infidelities and, as some biographers kindly say, "set her aside." Soon afterward he married an Aragon of Spain and seems to have spent enough time with her for a magnificent marriage ceremony, to collect a lavish dowry and to father two children. Then he went off to wars and adventures leaving her to languish, bored and homesick, and ultimately to die alone in a gray fortress-castle where she had been virtually a prisoner.

His "iron will," more like insane willfulness, killed his own son, who had not obeyed his father's order to dismount from a horse. The father kicked him in the genitals—a form of suasion or correction that seems incompatible with a prince brought up in the Spanish court—the kick so fierce that the tissues were ruptured and became infected and the boy died.

This maniac, it must be kept in mind, was also a Renaissance gentleman, devoted to the arts, to books and their contents and to vying with other courts where culture shone. Ergo Sabbioneta, an inconsequential village, transformed into a town of orderly streets, palaces for winter and summer use, churches, and the famous theater whose audiences were members of a distinguished court. He founded a notable library and museum, established an "academy" to attract and hold scholars, maintained a mint and supervised a press run by a colony of Jews who produced unusually fine books, religious and pagan, in several languages including Hebrew.

The press was closed by order of the Inquisition in 1598; the mint lasted almost a century longer, by which time Vespasiano was long dead (1591), the glamour dimmed, the slide down to walled semi-ghost town already well in progess. Now the village is trying to patch and shore up what might be salvaged. The theater has been dusted in recent years, the statues of its classical arch and niches are less darkly spectral, though the scenery tends to become disconsolately limp. The Ducal Palace, a comparatively simple structure for its type, once had a façade that was a marvel of decorated woods, bronze and frescoes. Nothing of that remains and the interior seems hardly capable of revival. A marble fireplace or two still stand, a number of gilded and carved wooden ceilings are still splendid, a certain indomitability breathes from the big equestrian Gonzagas sculptured in wood and the curious gallery of Gonzaga portraits in stucco reliefs. (There are copies of the portraits in the ducal palace in Mantua.) The rest is not far from rubble; gaps and great cracks, discoloration and tomb coldness.

The Church of the Incoronata, the family chapel, is, as already mentioned, decorated with "fool the eye" effects and is of interest primarily because it encloses the mausoleum of Vespasiano. The marble figures and the bronze statue of the Duke, much gentler in death than in life, owe a conspicuous debt to the Michelangelo figures in the Medici chapel of Florence, but only the seated bronze figure, bearded and wearing a suit of armor, has caught a strand or two of the inspiration in those works.

Beyond the park and its enormous magnolia trees sits the summer palace, the Palazzo del Giardino. Bouncing, vivacious designs on classical themes and in boundless variety fill the rooms of the lower floor; frescoes and stuccoes, a frenzy of grotesques and curlicues, full-bodied ladies and mighty warriors gambol in the sunlight that pours through the many windows. A glowing hall of mirrors under a rich ceiling calms down to pastoral scenes. The gallery above is a long, welcoming hall pocked with empty niches and lengthened by a perspective game of columns and open space painted at the ends. It was in this hall, now used for exhibitions (what sort of exhibition is mounted here and where do they get the viewers?), that Vespasiano arranged and showed his reputedly priceless collection of Greco-Roman art. The treasures were taken to the Ducal Palace in Mantua late in the eighteenth century and subsequently dispersed, victims of wars and the gyrations of Fortune's wheel.

There are other palazzi and traces of the fortress with which the summer palace was connected; nothing, however, quite as intact as the small synagogue, restored and kept well dusted and polished, not for the Jews of Sabbioneta, which has none, nor for the infrequent visitor, but rather as a memorial maintained by a descendant of the old colony. It is not difficult to find one's way to the via Prato Ranieri, but where next? One of those men who supports the corners of buildings will respond when you say "Sinagoga" by knocking on a local door, which bursts wide open to frame a smiling lady whose teeth are like the Ducal Palace—strips of gold on decay—and who wears the sort of straw hat once worn by peddlers' horses. On her chest there is a conspicuous crucifix; "please make no mistake," it seems to say. In a joyous, ceaseless babble she conducts you up several flights of stairs and unlocks the door to a little temple whose ornaments are bits of bronze and fiery lettering on the doors that close on the Torah. Your hostess shows the doors proudly, whisking the end of her apron over a speck of dust on a balustrade, and then points out the matrons' gallery. She is astonished when you tell her that there was a *matroneo* in early Catholic churches and she stands looking blank, for a while, in order not to look skeptical. She starts briskly again, talking and running, and opens a storage room to point to a rusty set of iron gates that her husband rescued from the Jewish cemetery—poor things—when those terrible people began to rummage through Jewish graves for jewels and dentures. In her big kitchen-dining-living room below (there is an abundance of living space in these semiabandoned villages) she points to a portrait of her grandson in his First Communion suit, painted in the techniques and colors used for plaster saints, and soon hands you several small notebooks to decipher the address of some *inglesi* who send her countless presents, constantly. A bit guilty for not having the spirit or pocket for such largesse, you overtip her and leave, the sound of her voice carrying on cheerily until you are well out of sight. The man who might be her husband is back at his job of holding up the corner of the street.

After all this, why go to Sabbioneta? There are older and more beautiful synagogues in Italy, grander ruins of many periods, better art and architecture, less desperate palazzi, the classical theater in Vicenza infinitely more splendid. It is walking through the dream of an Olympus dreamed by a madman, moving through quiet left by extravagant ghosts, that is the lure. So alluring, in fact, that a worldwide meeting of philosophers was fairly recently held in this flat, penurious never-never land where, perhaps, they played out *their* dream of returning to a time when philosophers were courted by courtiers.

From the shelter of the ramshackle all-purpose café that guards the roadside bus stop for Mantua, one can often watch a revealing game. A group of local road workers in tar-smeared boots, a miscellany of sweaters and foolish, jaunty caps, plays a well-practiced, noisy game which they call "Sabbioneta billiards." The equipment consists of a kitchen table with shortened legs, a hole cut in its center, and a set of disks. Basically, the game requires standing behind a line and twirling the disks into the hole, simple enough for men who have perfected a technique over the years. For this very reason they invent variations; the table slanted at different angles, the line moved back, obstacles introduced. A favorite obstacle and obstacle-placer is a good-looking man, a Don Giovanni, the organizer and life of the party and probably a bully. It is his role to sit at the edge of the table and place a saucer over the hole, to remove it as the twirling disk almost touches. His timing is superb, unhampered by his steady

stream of obscene challenges expressed in country wit. He
doesn't always remove the saucer in time, not in error so much
as in mischief. A great howling results from these maneuvers,
and counterpoints of obscenity and insult, but no one really
minds at all. It is a thoroughly Italian happening: the inventiveness, the passion for noise and words as noise, a wit that is salty
and robust rather than finespun and ironic, a capacity for intense, concentrated enjoyment, for total immersion in any moment (one sees it in conversation, in eating, in the eyes that love
a child), and above all, admiration for the boldly crooked if it is
carried off with style.

It must happen eventually, the visit to the somewhat forbidding Palazzo Ducale of Mantua, after you have checked viewing
hours and days (usually closed on Tuesdays, but things change).
It might normally have had the usual appeal of palazzi found in
the central piazze of old towns, an aristocratic mellowness, a
sturdy, simple might; this one is too long, too much like a secretive wall. Or is one made uneasy by the contradiction of plain,
unrevealing façade and the knowledge of erratic building it
seems to protect, the knowledge of the opulence it chose not to
betray?

There are several contenders for the title of "greatest Renaissance court," in the sense of unlimited wealth which brought art
and artists, scouts to seek them out, musicians and goldsmiths,
philosophers and wits, dwarfs and buffoons, anyone and anything it cast its glittering, restless eye on; the pattern set in Italy
and repeated by the great houses of England in later centuries
and, near our time, by the Morgans and Fricks. Some historians
insist that the honors go to the peripatetic court of Frederick II
the Hohenstaufen of Puglia, often called the "first Renaissance
man." Then there was the Montefeltro court at Urbino, that of
the Estes in Ferrara, and of course the Medicis in Florence,
among a number of dazzling others. It is a silly game, the rules
too easily bent by particular emphases and tastes. Whatever the
measure, though, very near first place is always given the court
of the Gonzagas, which flourished from the early fifteenth century into the beginning of the seventeenth, when the money

went, the last of the direct line of the dynasty died, and plague and wars took their place.

The section of the Gonzaga Palace that fronts on the muted piazza was not originally theirs. It was fought for and won in 1328 by Luigi Gonzaga, then the *capitano*—safely translated as war lord—of the city who took it from the Bonacolsi. The Bonacolsi had, in their time (the late thirteenth century) imposed a dictatorship on the former free commune during a confused and bloody period of Guelph-Ghibelline conflicts. Established in the medieval mansion, the Gonzaga improved it (the Gothic windows, for example), began to build additions and continued building toward the lake edge—fortress, church, courts and gardens to lead in and out of something like five hundred rooms and halls. To embellish the early, sprawling Versailles, emissaries were sent to bring Pisanello and, later, Mantegna; several leading Renaissance architects, among them Brunelleschi and Alberti, were called. Prominent writers and scholars were invited to stay, to enjoy discourse with each other and members of the family, among them Isabella d'Este, the wife of Francesco II, who was one of the more cultivated women of her time. Giulio Romano came and Tintoretto and later still—shortly before the fall—a violist named Monteverdi, who had been hired originally to accompany feasts and entertainments, saw his operas *Arianna* and *Orfeo* lavishly produced in the Gonzaga court.

It was not, obviously, a three-century blaze of splendor; there were dimmed periods. The main Gonzaga line were, however, energetic, intelligent men and shrewd politicians, as small princes had to be to survive in dealing with the more powerful city-states, and they managed to keep Mantua—already safely isolated and protected by its waters—a peaceable, flourishing city during a time when other small cities were being torn to bits by contesting powers in the intervals when those powers were not too busy starving each other out. Among the steady and responsible there were a few men of genuine cultivation, like Ludovico II of the midfifteenth century, the sponsor of Alberti and Mantegna, who repaid the Duke's generosity by immortalizing him and his family.

Something of the family balance, as well as its taste and learning, may have stemmed from the precepts of the educator Vittorino da Feltre, a founder of modern western education. His school at the court, the "Casa Gioiosa," the "joyful house," has been called "the most famous school of all time." It was Vittorino who taught Ludovico II how to be that confident, curious, athletic, sophisticated warrior–art connoisseur who was "the Renaissance prince." The children were well grounded in the classics and mathematics, which alternated with periods of play and exercise and affectionate, persuasive lessons in ethics and morality. The lessons were offered and absorbed in an atmosphere that was itself a basic lesson in Renaissance Christianity—the need and duty of man to respect the potential grandeur of man, and woman. Thus, the Gonzaga girls were taught along with their brothers and with the poor boys Vittorino insisted be included and treated as equals. Additionally persuasive must have been the simplicity and unassailable integrity of the man himself, who, the story is told, would make no promise to stay if the court lapsed in conduct or principles. It speaks well of the court that Vittorino stayed on until his death.

As in Sabbioneta and many other palaces that have long lost the reason for their immense, rambling size, whose gilded coffered ceilings seem to be drifting on a tide that has already washed away companions in magnificence, one must sketch into the voids figures of popes, royal visitors, scholars and artists, princes and dukes, and, behind them, brush in backgrounds of paintings and sculpture to replace those that had wandered circuitous routes to other places. (One set of adventures concerns Charles I and Oliver Cromwell. The English king was a connoisseur and active collector who bought a considerable number of art works from the Mantuan court at a low period of Gonzaga fortunes. After Charles was beheaded, it was deemed proper by the succeeding Puritans that luxurious frippery like art be exiled and so, via England, some of the Gonzaga collection reached the Louvre and the Prado.)

Because it is an endless maze and because several sections are closed for restoration—a heroic enterprise that has been going on since the beginning of this century, when the enormous enclave was hardly more than ruins—a guide must lead the way, taking a fair-sized group for each trip. One is led almost immediately into what it is hoped will be a *pinacoteca*. At this writing it is more optimism than art, with two exceptions. One is a vivid painting that flashes gallant white horses and warriors in red hose who fought the battle between the Bonacolsis and the Gonzagas in the piazza and shows the cathedral façade before the eighteenth century got to work on it. The other is patched-up Rubens accompanied by a diagram that shows the number and shapes of sections sliced by French troops in 1797.

You may or may not see—depending on the time, the devotion of the guide, places closed off for work in progress—what is left of the numismatic collection, the Greco-Roman sculpture, the engravings. The guides almost always like to point out, however, a portion of the old building where, they say, the founding Gonzagas kept the body of Rinaldo Bonacolsi. Enlightened as they later became, the early members of the family preferred to know that the body of their victim was safely encased and in their possession, reducing to a minimum the risk of wandering, avenging spirits.

In a growing haze you will trot through an innumerableness of apartments for popes and princes and halls for court entertainment and the display of art. You will pass under deftly carved wooden ceilings and ceilings painted like trellises, ceilings of calm deep blue on which float the signs of the zodiac and ceilings agitated by the drapery on allegorical figures. The unleashed fancies of dozens of artisans created "fish" rooms and "bird" rooms, a room of Moors, biblical rooms, mythological rooms and a hall of "months." The eye loses its thickening glaze, shocked by the dour prisons and the complex of cubicles, quite empty now, which made up the "Dwarf's Apartment." It has a fairly large number of rooms and although one knows that dwarfs were fashionable accessories to royal courts—see Velásquez paintings, for example—these seem excessive, even for a time and place of excesses, and may have been ordered, as much of the decorations were, to stupefy visitors. (Later theory has it that they were not dwarf's apartments at all.)

Acres away from the sinister dolls' house is the small, enchanting apartment of Isabella d'Este arranged for her after the death of her husband. It once held several of her private and choice collection of paintings, now hanging elsewhere or completely disappeared. Fortunately her tastes and interests remain in the mottoes and symbols, a few of them incomprehensible symptoms of occult studies or private superstitions, that weave through the golden ceiling and in the remarkable panels of inlaid wood brought here from her earlier apartment in the Castle.

At some point in the visit you will be taken into the Castle, built at the end of the fourteenth century as a fortress that also served as family mansion for successive generations from the middle of the fifteenth century to the middle of the sixteenth. It surrounds an open court with sections of portico attributed to Mantegna and a ramp designed for mounting to upper rooms by horse. One of these rooms discloses the heart of the palace—the Camera degli Sposi—the Mantegna frescoes of Ludovico II, his wife, Barbara of Brandenburg, their children, members of the court, servants, animals, on the two extant walls. There is no need to describe them, they are too famous and, in any case, it is useless to try to pin down the magic of a masterpiece. A less well-known grace note of the frescoes is the circular painting imbedded in the ceiling, an opening to sky and clouds above a ring of balcony on which putti with gossamer wings perch and climb among a group of ladies and a glossy peacock who peers down into the room. Of itself, ringed in a luxurious garland, it is a delight; its historical importance lies in the fact that it is the first attempt (1474) of endless perspective straight up into the sky, used and overused in later church art.

Leaving the verity, the accessibility of the people in the frescoes—no one, especially Barbara, has been sullied by flattery, and everyone is about to speak or gesture—one turns toward the lake, through the via San Giorgio for a look at the medieval mass of the Castle and by way of the Piazza Castello into a strangely shaped square sustained by good arches and, centered around the court church, Santa Barbara. The square is a curious, mournful ghost, but the church is no longer worth your effort or the custodian's. Mount the slope leading to the Piazza Paradiso instead, for still another view of the restless, irregular clottings of palazzo buildings in an alternation of density and openness. The via Corte, skirting a small public park, shows a plaque commemorating anti-Fascist resistance; in the park itself, there is a monument to a Mantuan hero and, nearby, something that looks like more of the same, a tomblike structure in elaborate stonework. In a ready mood for looking at remembrances of non-Gonzagas, one approaches it to find that the stone openwork screens a number of large, male heads; you are examining an elegant pissoir.

Find something else to examine, something that will not stare back, like the "Rabbi's Palace" on the via Bertani, near the back of San Lorenzo, which should have been restored to its former sixteenth-century graces of good proportions and delicate scenes in stucco. Or San Lorenzo may be willing to show its primitive blandishments of thick columns, shallow arches and scraps of twelfth- and thirteenth-century frescoes. And you may not yet have seen the Duomo, nor walked through the triumphal-arch entrance into the classic serenity of Alberti's Sant'Andrea, whose immense size keeps the altar at a long, indifferent distance from the young children running back and forth in the large spaces at the back. Mantegna lies in Sant'Andrea, and a respectful bow to his bronze tomb portrait might be a fair and fitting gesture on which to leave Mantua, but not before greeting Pisanello.

For several centuries lost, recently discovered and readied for public viewing in the Palazzo Ducale are the remarkable-to-unbelievable frescoes painted by Pisanello in the early fifteenth century when he was also modeling the famously beautiful medals he made of members of the family and their tutor.

The frescoes, in various stages of work and some destroyed by time and accident, deal with a gigantic battle based on chivalric myth, possibly a battle of rivalry between Lancelot and Tristan. Unfinished, marred, it is yet a great work that encompasses several masterpieces of portraiture, particularly two blond women and a Moorish knight.

Notes

HOTELS.   The San Lorenzo, immediately in the center, has no dining room, although it does have an inviting bar–breakfast room, and the rooms and hallways are nicely appointed. The

Jolly is an older hotel taken up by the Jolly chain and consequently not so bristling new as some of the others; "clean and
usable" about says it. Or try the Italia, on the Piazza Cavallotti.
All moderate.

  The best food, surprisingly good by any Italian standards, is to
be had at the "Garibaldini," or the "Tre Garibaldini," as some
people prefer to call it, in the street across from Sant'Andrea's
façade. Three small restaurants in the arcades behind the market
serve unpretentious, well-cooked meals at reasonable rates. Seating is limited; go early and have the local Merlot, a light, pleasant red wine.

Bergamo

THE PAIRING OF "upper" and "lower" townlets in one city is quite common, the creation of topography and its use by history. There is usually a linkage, via shops or streets, between the divisions as in Arezzo, for instance. But Bergamo, near Milan, is distinctly two small cities, in character, in mood, in looks; and is linked only by steep roads, a funicular, a name and handsome pride.

The logic of chronology makes it almost imperative that the visitor drop his valise in his hotel or, if it's to be an exhausting one-day visit, in the depository at the station and then, near the station, find a number 1 bus. At the end of a ride that soars up the hill, turning in and out of varied and attractive landscapes, and bus ticket still firmly in hand, he continues on a funicular which leaves him at the end (or entrance) to a long, narrow, meandering medieval street that leads to the astonishments at the peak of the old town. Or a number 3 bus, also near the station, will do as well. It meanders through the lower town, then up past country villas, old ramparts and romantic niches to an arch that leads into another arch and the winding old brick-paved street that is the spine from which smaller antique streets dangle.

The center of this "Citta Alta" is the ample Piazza Vecchia, replete with restaurants, antiques and a touring office. Through a couple of archways at one end of the Piazza, something dazzles, sparkles, teases; something as shamelessly, beautifully decorated as the façade of the Cathedral of Orvieto. You move toward it, stopping for a moment to admire a peculiar fountain; it is a conglomerate of spitting sphinxes and lions and snakes and chains, rather like one of the gigantic ornaments the Victorians (and Italian Victorians) deeply admired. And look back at the large classical building that carries a few monsters in its arches, in the style of Gulio Romano whose influence was wide and strong in his Mannerist time.

The alluring pink-and-white shine beyond the sphinxes and snakes has been called the most beautiful square in the world; beautiful it is, but not exactly one clearly definable square since it breaks up into a maze with churches and chapels piled on each other. (See it all from a nearby street called Mercato del Pesce, the onetime fish market.) The two dazzlers on this Piazza del Duomo are the façade of Santa Maria Maggiore, a loveliness of tiny pillars holding delicate archlets and the carved elements of an overall pattern of pink and white mosaic stone. The jewel next to it is the Colleoni Chapel.

Santa Maria Maggiore was built in the twelfth century and organized as a charitable institution in the thirteenth. These are about the times of the building of the Palazzo della Ragione in the Piazza Vecchio—much changed over the years but still marked in history as the first communal building in Italy. Each century made and remade portions of the church, but its interior style is mainly that of the ornate baroque of the seventeenth century. The south entrance of the church remained simple fourteenth-century Gothic, its modest portico resting on lions that look more Assyrian than Venetian. (Of the same time, supposedly, the baptistry has lost its Gothic directness, and with its combination of red and white pillars and statues of virtues shaping an octagon, manages to look like a large piece of marzipan, a nineteenth-century confection, possibly.)

The interior of Santa Maria Maggiore is a superabundance of riches. Nothing lacks—not tapestries of various ages; not old frescoes made at about the time of Giotto, more primitive than his work and quite appealing in their simplicity. There is a baroque confessional that, in contrast, appears almost decadent in its piling on of skill and symbol: the Virgin Mary, Saint Peter, the Holy Spirit, and others unrelentingly crowded and convoluted in the carving. As another contrast, look for the inlaid wooden panels, one covering another (the sacristan is pleased to show them), designed by Lorenzo Lotto and executed by fellow artists who achieved remarkable balances of light and dark, strength of movement and fineness of detail in the difficult, limited medium.

The Capella Colleoni was dedicated to himself by Bartolomeo Colleoni, he of the Verrochio equestrian status in Venice, "the captain general" who ruled Bergamo. Begun in 1472, it grew slowly. The gilded wooden statue, high in a niche over the porch of the chapel, was the work of a German craftsman of the early sixteenth century, and the frescoes in the deep dome waited for Tiepolo. We move back again in time to the style of the tomb of Medea Colleoni, supernaturally long and slender and ineffably elegant, very much like a fifteenth-century lady of Laurana. As you leave, notice those lions that worked so hard through many decades sustaining pillars and the lightness of the two balconies and their figures above, and if you have been to Verona, the resemblance of this enchanting chapel to the stunning Scaligeri tombs which were older and probably prototypes.

The lower town gathered its size, importance and increasing governmental and economic functions in a Victor Emanuel—or Edwardian, if you like—period. Banks and official buildings luxuriate in the size and confidence of neo-classicism; the older hotels are equally large and broad in their way and, like honored hotels in Monte Carlo and Nice, display large flags to welcome visitors of all nations. The streets are wide and handsome, seemingly fashioned on Parisian boulevards. All of this has left an attractive, old-fashioned smartness touched here and there with modern chic. An imaginatively arranged shop of breads and pasta is called the "Boutique di pane" (bread); on the same prosperous street, shops of salamis and cheese are decked out like fine restaurants. Ice cream is "crafted," and sweets are advertised as the work of "artisans." To prove that it is in this "now" world, there is a "punk" shop whose dresses are printed with skulls and whose T-shirts bear arcane messages in something like English.

The most impressive, and in its way important, single entity of the lower city is the Accademia Carrara, a smallish museum that encloses remarkable quality. (Take a taxi or check the possibilities of the number 9 bus.) When Giacomo Carrara died in the late eighteenth century, he left his collection to his art academy. It was added to by other collectors and still finds donors to help fill the dignified building. Simply to list the paintings would be excessive and possibly meaningless to those who are not encyclopedic in their knowledge of paintings. (And who, but a very few, are?) It might be better to tell a reader that here on view is the exquisitely aristocratic and unforgettable portrait of Leonello d'Este by Pisanello. In company with a lovely, delicate Sienese Virgin and Child set in their golden, ethereal background by Bartolomeo Landi, and a sturdier, down-to-earth Virgin by Signorelli, we come on the famously unattractive, powerful profile of Giuliano dei Medici as painted by Botticelli. Giovanni Bellini's simple peasant Virgins are here in a gratifying number, displaying the influence of his brother-in-law, Mantegna, who worked in the court of Mantua and undoubtedly suggested that his other brother-in-law, Gentile Bellini, paint the portrait shown here of Gian Francesco Gonzaga of Mantua, quite fat, like several of the rest of his breed. Carpaccio's women attending the birth of the Virgin are almost as attractive as his more worldly Venetian ladies. And there is work by Crivelli, Vivarini and more Giovanni Bellini. Lorenzo Lotto is represented by a languid, sleepy-eyed boy, not unlike a number of his other portraits; Cosme Tura shows us one of his strange, other-world, sickly Virgins. Some painters like their saints unadorned; another cannot resist a beautifully rendered pearl headdress on Saint Catherine. There are two or three distinguished Raphaels, a telling portrait of an elderly man by Tintoretto and even an El Greco beginning to show his eccentric and very personal coloration of people and objects.

Not to be too parochial, the collection includes Dutch paintings, a magically painted picture of a puzzled, frightened child by

Velasquez and then returns to later Italians in portraits, in the facile and charming sleight-of-hand of the Tiepolos, in a carnival painting by Longhi and a most admirable group of small paintings by Francesco Guardi: small capriccios, Venice bright, Venice under a fading sky, Venice with an imagined set of antique arches, and the boatmen of Venice, brilliantly achieved with two or three strokes.

Not an inconsiderable city this one, that, though small, encompasses so impressive a collection of Italian art and an equally impressive collection of medieval architecture and decoration and, altogether, boundless charm.

Note

If the opera and particularly Donizetti mean anything to you, there are many places in Bergamo where you can pay him your respects. Although much of his activity was not in Bergamo, he was born and he died here, and there are a number of places in the city that invite you to his birthplace, a theater dedicated to him, a museum, a park monument, and in Santa Maria Maggiore, a tombstone whose weeping angels destroy musical instruments while his Muse weeps.

The Excelsior San Marco flies the bravest show of flags in the Monte Carlo manner, asking for the show somewhat more (highish) than does its rival nearer the station, the Grand Hotel Moderno, not too markedly "moderno" (moderate). The simpler Del Moro (moderate) has a highly respected restaurant. Bergamo eats well, and if your stay takes you through several meals, inquire about other places with imaginative menus.

Brescia

On an eastward journey—a pause between Bergamo and Verona, for instance—you might decide to spend some time in Brescia, a city of no great wonders, which makes it something of a wonder in Italy. Its wonders are about two and one-half small ones and worth long, interested looks. Otherwise it is an active, bright-eyed town with the sense to keep its artichokes, its asparagus and cheap sweaters flowing around its chic and old greens market, possibly of medieval times, which stubbornly stayed and spread. It makes a pleasant set of contrasts of forms, tones and meanings.

In its enthusiastic propaganda, Brescia recites an eventful, but not unusual history: conflicts between church and empire. Into those divisions slipped with their spikes and swords barons who created more local woe and permitted covetous, powerful neighbors—della Scala of Verona, Visconti of Milan, among a few others—to exsanguinate the town. The attitude toward this fairly typical Lombard set of events is exemplified by a note in a historical pamphlet: "A *long* peace marked those years, which were disturbed only by the terrible siege of the Visconti troops in 1438, by the French domination (1509–1516) during the pillage

273

of Brescia (1512)." Among the historical personages that Brescia remembers is Charlemagne, the great ninth-century emperor who chose one of the local monasteries as a place to leave his wife, and there she died while he continued mastering Europe.

The first half-wonder is the curious shapes made by time and tastes in the Duomo and its piazza and the newer Cathedrale which leaves one with uncertainty about "Duomo-Cathedrale"; aren't they the same? Here the problem is settled by speaking of the "old" Duomo and the "new." The old Duomo is truly old, a rough building that dates from the eleventh century, built on the site of an even older church. (Incidentally, the Duomo, its paintings, its reliquaries and its crypt of tombstones are closed to the public on Tuesday rather than the customary Monday.) The not-quite "Duomo" next door, the Cathedrale, is an enormous white super-baroque building whose heavy large columns bring the eye up to ornate Corinthian capitals and heavy ornaments that echo the rest of the heavily decorated building, begun early in the seventeenth century but not considered complete until 1815. A few paces beyond, there is the truly distinguished Broletto, the first seat of the Commune, built in the twelfth to thirteenth centuries and whose antique bell still rings for meetings. Essentially medieval, with accretions from the Renaissance and even Mannerism, it is a mixed-up, interesting complex, still in government use for some municipal services. Across from the Broletto, two low, medievalish arches lead into a cleverly designed, elegant "Italian modern" shopping arcade made more appealing by its showing off and obviously cherishing its Roman and medieval stones, melded with the modern design.

The shopping street you've reached, the via X Giornate (10 days) takes you into a wonderfully animated square full of everything: grotesques, arcades, fountains and a somewhat incredible Loggia. At your left, a continuous line of white, dignified buildings in two attractive styles—early and late Renaissance. In both periods they were the Monte de Pieta (pawn banks) of the city. The piazza opens to a number of diverse streets, but its name and distinction derive from the tall, deep, broad, aristocratic Loggia. Titian had a hand in its making; so did Sandsovino, and certainly the deeply rounded roof was devised by Palladio. As in

loggias elsewhere, these walls record local suffering and sacrifice
and the bravery and charity of Brescia's citizens. It also shelters a
good spread for benches supported by sphinxes from which one
may watch much of Brescia following various paths out of the
Piazza—to denim pants, to redolent cheeses, to skeins of wool,
to tomatoes. One is permitted to enter the Loggia building, to
admire the fine ironwork decoration, the patina on wooden
doors, the broad and tall curves of stairs and graceful panels of
delicately abstract grotesques. The great meeting hall is gathered
under a wooden ceiling, its shape modified by sets of pink brick
columns that emphasize unexpected curves at the windows—a
Palladian fancy?

Out of this proudest of municipal halls, wander into the nearest market street swelled with the strong voices of market wom-
en and notice the ancient decaying houses, narrow enough to
suggest that they were all once towers, as in other towns—San
Gigmignano in Tuscany, the last of these belligerent and protective clusters of tower. In another direction from the loggia (you
have a map from the tourist office or hotel), you should come on
the Piazza Vittoria—an important square, judging from the
structures which honor it: a Post and Telegraph building whose
façade consists of enormous square pillars in alternating dark
and light stone—tall and heavy and strange enough to suggest a
super-production of *Aida*. Lower on the piazza, a large, attractive
(also expensive) street café and a piece of sculpture that pleads
ineptly for peace. Three bronze figures—Mussolini, Uncle Sam
and Hitler (probably)—are melded into one as they thrust a bay-
onet into a dying soldier. Because the faces are grotesque masks,
and almost humorous, the emotional, moral tone is feeble, elicit-
ing neither admiration nor a passion for pacifism.

The second full wonder of Brescia, after the Loggia, is the Via
del Musei (C bus from the station), which leads up a small hill
past saints suffering in *grisaille* and a couple of old palaces.
(Look in to their courtyards when you can.) Walk past a doorway
flanked by mighty eagles and thick window frames, the Questura
(police), and enjoy the gleeful rococo church just beyond, a playground of baby angels and dolphins coiled on each other fairly
amorously. And suddenly the presence of ancient Rome, the

ruins of a Capitoline Temple of 73 B.C. Several columns reconstructed of material found at the site and aided by sections of modern brick speak of an enormous temple, while inner spaces witness the modes of the time—several carved panels devoted to the popular god Mithras; skillfully molded swags of fruit and bull skull (revived and used extensively as decoration in the Renaissance); a particularly delicate relief of a simple wine ewer.

Up and up, endlessly up, in a modest building concealed by the tall ruins, achieves the Museum of the Forum. The display is not unusual, as these collections go, but the quality is frequently outstanding: curiously rough Etruscan vases stare out at beautiful Greek heads as copied by Romans. Some of the small bronze figures are unusually good, and one or two bronze hands compellingly appealing. From one wall stares a group of Roman worthies, including the lady in the curly fashionable wig frequently seen on dour matrons of her time. On another wall a stimulating though incomprehensible photo reproduction of a thirteenth-century map. Its original eleven segments now joined like a Chinese scroll, it purports to represent a sort of military Roman map dug up a very long time ago. Not too informative, not one of the roots of history, the wonder is that it exists. Much more overtly understandable are the lovely round belly and legs of an Aphrodite, the rest of her physically gone and yet the juicy image all there. At the very end of the museum rooms, standing alone, a large bronze image—imperturbable, invulnerable, and superb—of the Winged Victory, one of the finest extant and unforgettable, Brescia's last and best gift to you.

Notes

You are near lovely lake country, with Lake Garda fairly accessible. For all sorts of information about timetables, campsites, motels in the countryside and at the lakes, write the Ente Provinciale per Turismo, Corso Zanardelli, Number 34, Brescia. Give them a very long time to answer your letter unless you can make arrangements from Brescia itself.

For a short stay in Brescia, the Igea hotel, near the station, might be convenient. It serves carefully prepared meals of a classic menu. Both meals and rooms are in the moderate category. (A basic meal should cost about 20,000 lire in your time, should prices continue to fly upward.) The Vittoria, in the center of town, is more luxurious and expensive, without a restaurant. La Sosta, in a genuinely old house in a quiet neighborhood, asks for its worldly service and menu worldly prices; yet, compared to the cost of the same meal in New York or London, not particularly high.

Verona

Some say it is like Florence for its museumlike quality, its multiplicity of treasures gathered in a small compass. Others compare it to Rome for its monuments of Roman times and the spreads of café seats and babbling customers who speak many languages (a look at the map will confirm its position of easy access to and from the rest of Europe). It has been weakly compared to Venice, possible because it was dominated by that city for centuries and its back alleys and their Venetian-Gothic ornaments show some resemblance. Those caught in an unfortunate, interminable deluge—and Verona drained of sun is a city drained of blood and lymph—say it is an English invention by William Shakespeare on the suggestion of old Italian stories. It is none of these; it is singularly itself, Verona, and, like Siena and Gubbio, rejects comparisons.

The opening moves are usually two. First the complex of Guglielmo Shakespeare: the house of the Montagues, the house of the Capulets and Juliet's tomb, all three assigned skillfully (the houses seem right for the time) but arbitrarily, since there are no confirming records of the people or places. Second, a performance of *Aïda* in the Roman arena that sits surprising, big and stolid in the enormous Piazza Bra, which is strewn—at a respectable distance—with a sea of international ice-cream eaters. Between Shakespeare and Verdi they walk the endless *passeggiata* of the via Mazzini to look into the shops and to enjoy the rare pleasure of strolling in a main street closed to traffic. They stop for some coffee or souvenir hunting in the market square, the Piazza Erbe, and back again to the tables near the flank of the arena.

It is lovely to sit in the sun, to watch the prams and the fat German and French guidebooks go by, to try to figure out the next move of the torpid, sack-laden, bearded youths supported by a lamppost and each other, to admire the waiters' adroit manipulation of body and trays through slits of space, to wonder at their comprehension of orders spoken firmly and loudly—it always helps people to understand if you shout at them—in foreign languages. It means missing, however, masterpieces of unknown architects, one of the most brilliantly arranged museums in Italy, a complex of noble squares, a virile river and meshworks of engaging streets in a mixture of moods and style that creates a singular harmony.

The via Roma leads from the gate at the lower end of the Piazza Bra to the ivied Ghibelline walls and turrets of the Castelvecchio, the fortress built on the edge of the river by the overlord Cangrande II della Scala in 1355. Many conquering hands destroyed, rebuilt, rearranged (Napoleon built a miniature fort inside one of the courts), but restoration has brought it back again close to the fourteenth century, and the Napoleonic fortlet, supplied with attractive windows and doors rescued from destroyed local houses, now has the innocent look of a late-Gothic summerhouse. Before entering the portcullis gate labeled "museo" walk across the fortress bridge, the Ponte Scaligero, a massive feat of fourteenth-century engineering. Such a heavy, narrow row of medieval weight might be dour, if it weren't, as this is, of red brick that turns rosy gold in the sun; if it weren't scalloped in paired curves of battlements, if it hadn't put on the white of stone and the tracery of iron torch holders. From a river edge nearby, a view of strong arches and tower piers breasting the swift river in a contest of matched strengths, particularly satisfying after you have watched the summer-sapped Tiber and Arno exhaustedly nudging their unconcerned bridges.

The museum beyond the deep, ivy-filled moat is a remarkable work—the old and the new used to produce sources of generous light, contrasts of level and textures, imaginative, thoughtful spacing—that is of itself worth a visit. The collection deserves its surroundings, beginning with rare pieces of medieval art and early crafts moving toward extremely expressive sculpture of the fourteenth century (a Martha supporting the inert body of Mary, for example), and painting of the thirteenth and fourteenth centuries. Early Renaissance paintings include a Madonna of Jacopo Bellini, a Madonna of the Rosary by Stefano da Verona, very much like a flower-strewn tapestry, and Pisanello's exquisite, fairy-tale-princess Madonnas. A number of Dutch masters give way, again, to the Italians: Bellinis, a Crivelli, some works by local painters, several panels by Andrea Mantegna, a few lively, naturalistic paintings by Caroto (look for a boy with a drawing of a puppet). Somewhere in the stimulating progress between rooms and court, you will find projections of bold-angled slabs of cement, the pedestal for the stunning medieval statue of Cangrande I, sheathed in chain mail and, spurting from his back, a hard helmet with spurlike plumes. This is the original of the figure in the group of Scaligeri tombs (page 284), and it might remind you of the Simone Martini painting of Guidoriccio da Faliano in Siena, which was painted a year before; the same intimacy and mutual respect of man and horse, the dashing erect posture, the not quite suspended motion.

The collection ends at the Olympus of Venetian painting that consists of Paolo Veronese, Tiepolo, Tintoretto and Francesco Guardi, whose fresh, swift paintings mark the chronological close.

The "sacred way" of the Romans, now the Corso Cavour, is at first glance an ordinary, heavily trafficked shopping street. It requires some poking into, some circling around to the backs of houses on the riverfront, some stubbornness to hold one's position on the busy sidewalk, and it repays the effort. Almost immediately on leaving the Castelvecchio, a Roman arch, the Arco dei Gavi, rears its height, not in perfect shape but a Roman arch nevertheless, which once stood in the middle of the road, nearby; the gift to the city of a Roman family. A few steps and several centuries away, there is the small church of San Lorenzo, indented, as if moving back in retreat, from the modern avenue. The fifteenth-century portico looks on pieces of much earlier church that loll in the minute court; around the side, two round Norman towers that were the access to the women's gallery and four Roman columns, which may have supported the first portico when it faced the river. Not very large, and with an air of being forgotten, San Lorenzo has a dignified, undistracted purity of tall pillars and arches given a fragile shimmering quality by the local building style of alternating brick and tufa in horizontal bands.

Leaving the Romanesque and Roman, one leaps ahead to the Baroque in one palace that still retains vigorous twists of iron and traces of distinctive plasterwork and returns to the Renaissance with two palaces, by Michele Sammicheli, of the first half of the sixteenth century, whose large courts gaze on the river. Then, back to the Gothic hiding behind a few biforate windows. (The signs in courts that warn about the dog or dogs—*cane, cani*—are sometimes to be believed, sometimes not; ergo, watch out.) After the Corso takes the name of the Porta dei Borsari, for the remains of a medieval tax gate built into a Roman portal, time becomes more consistently the present.

Streets grow narrow and houses less spacious, relinquishing their street levels to bustling, effulgent food shops, particularly excited and showy in the days of the Easter weekend. Mounds of rice-stuffed tomatoes, strips of pepper, artichokes peeled to sleek green buds prove their affinity to the market nearby. Among the butcher shops that display one huge hanging carcass, inevitably reminiscent of the Rembrandt painting, a windowless cavern surrounds its entrance with a pendant deer, pairs of rabbits, matched and facing each other or arranged in loops like unfashionable fur pieces, a fence of hares with pop eyes, black and white peonies that are bunches of pigeons and, as a final flourish, a flame of pheasant feathers.

Meat, cheese, tobacco, banking and pizza are displaced by antique shops as the street approaches the church of Sant'Anastasia, the largest church in the city, planned late in the thirteenth century, replanned, modified and expanded through two hundred years and consequently odd and arresting. The unfinished façade—was it irresolution, boredom or lack of funds that left uncovered the brick sinews of these churches?—is disconcerting; tattered marble at the base, two immensely long windows and thin towers at the sides, a long screen of brick rising at the center, these spare nudities surrounding a remarkably worked double portal curtained in colored marble.

There are attractive areas inside the church; basins for holy water resting on the bodies of straining humpbacks, a late-fourteenth-century fresco of the Cavalli family before the Virgin enthroned, an interesting struggle of accustomed concepts trying to reach naturalism in a fun house of perspectives. The frescoes of the fourteenth and fifteenth centuries, skillful and appealing terra-cotta panels, sections of carved wood, the floor and the tall, painted ceiling are all pleasing; but they seem to be diminished, almost obscured, by the height and vastness, as if the church were scorning its ornaments—actually hiding, in the sacristy, its most beautiful and rare ornament. It is the large remnant of a panel that includes the famous Pisanello "Saint George and the Princess of Trebizond," whom he has rescued, or will rescue, from a dragon. Full of exquisite Pisanello details of animal drawings, of men hanging from a gibbet against a disconsolate landscape; the pale, very pale knight and the ineffably beautiful princess in the large headdress that makes her face so delicate gather as a strange, disturbing picture. It has the strangeness of sad fairy tales and myths of chivalric knights and their Guineveres and Isoldes long gone.

To the left of the church, a fourteenth-century canopied tomb, and to the right a medieval pathway that leads to the via Sottoriva, which follows the bank of the River Adige for a short distance. Some ancient shopfronts and strips of arcades are inhabited by antique shops; but older, less splendid shops have not yet been invaded. They remain dusky caverns of carpentry and shoe repair. The street weaves drunkenly and picturesquely, the line of roofs rising and falling, tottering to its meeting with via Mazzini. Before going as far as Verona's Fifth Avenue, however, en-

ter the via delle Arche Scaligere, and very close to a wineshop
with a sturdy sign, "Vino del Duca," find the house appointed to
Romeo Montecchi, affixed with a quotation, in English and Italian from the drama that spurs a great number of romantic visitors to Verona. (It would be amusing to know the precise percen-
tage of the tourism brought to this city by a sixteenth-century
Englishmen who in all likelihood never left his island.)

That tiny church whose cloister you have seen as a slotted
white ornament in the sweep of hill up to the castle (one of the
best of Verona's views, from the back of St. Anastasia) is part of
a small museum of antiquities. A modest museum that has the
courtesy to offer you the use of a lift (rather than the interminable flights of stairs indigenous to too many public buildings in
Italy) incorporates what is left of the church, quite faded except
for the worldly, vivid ceiling. The rest is the appealing cloister,
and in spaces around it, a diversity of objects of Roman times,
most of them found in the near vicinity. The Roman theater
below, still in occasional use for modern performances, has left
the museum mosaics that seem to portray theatrical characters
of, possibly, gladiators. In the common diversity—Etruscan
bronzes, vials, pots, pearly glass and vessels—you will find a
good number of unusual and masterfully made objects: mosaics
of girls' heads of considerable charm (one head, in bronze, is a
double image and particularly appealing); walls of mosaic in sophisticated patterns; torsos draped and undraped, most of them
not unexpectedly mutilated by man and time. Of the time of the
cloisters, there are vestiges of fresco, a fine carved basin, the
flowerlike capitals on the pillars and the archlet ornaments and,
almost best of all, the modest, girlish air of the cloister itself. And
in the praising, one must not forget the lift man, who also seems
to be guide and curator eager to show and eager to please, sin-
cerely.

(Go before 1:30 P.M. and never on Monday.)

Below, across from Romeo's house, a stunning group of Gothic
tombs introduce a regal, harmonious complex of medieval
squares and peaks of funerary art. A mesh of strong, yielding
patterns of ironwork attached at one end to the small twelfth-
century church of Santa Maria Antica, the Scaligeri chapel, ex-

tends to enclose the ancient churchyard in which that family was buried. One porch of the church is the tomb of the Cangrande I della Scala, who died in 1329, surmounted by a copy of the equestrian statue now in the museum of the Castelvecchio. It is difficult to see except in photographs, but the horizontal Cangrande has the same gleeful smile as that of the statue, a smile that we shall meet again, a Veronese specialty. And he had reason to smile. His short life was an exceedingly accomplished one: wily politico, great captain of armies, a connoisseur of the arts and learning (like his brother before him, he was the eager host to the exiled Dante) and, despite the fact that he was a medieval tyrant, a popular leader elected to remain in power.

The monument of Mastino II, who died in 1351, under its peaked canopy is richer, a soaring of columns, of several figures, arches and aspiring finials directed toward an equally masterful equestrian figure, more massive, more heavily armored, the face concealed in a visor and helmet that bears sharp wings. The horse also wears a visor and, like Cangrande's horse, is covered in brocade, still visible as lightly carved patterns. It is a powerful, faceless portrait of invulnerability in horse and rider. The tomb of Cansignorio of about 1375 shows less skill or care; the result is a characterless fat-rumped horse and stodgy lifeless rider. Supporting them is a frenzy of Gothic which, detail by detail, is not as satisfying as the earlier tombs. Still, it is quite a structure to bump into around the corner from a quiet street. To give the tombs their full splendor, one must imagine them as they were originally—brightly painted, the contrasting colors and shapes exploding yet contained by the narrowed, upward shapes and muted by the patterned shadows of the grillwork.

The facing arch empties into the Piazza dei Signori, an inviting outdoor room that has frequently been called the "salon of Verona." A pensive Dante stands among several extensively restored buildings that form a nucleus of Veronese history and architecture: the Palazzo of the Scaligeri, which sheltered Dante; the gracious Loggia del Consiglio of Renaissance design; the Palazzo Comunale, a mixture of the striped Romanesque and Renaissance; the Palazzo del Capitano, handsomely classic in the Renaissance style, and some Baroque to broaden the stylistic range. To complete the picture and the range of styles involved, there is an area being excavated for its promise of more medieval and even Roman structures. Along with buildings and Dante, pigeons, children on tricycles, children with balloons, the tables of dispensers of snacks, pizza, ice cream and coffee, there is a most determinedly nineteenth-century café, the Dante, the leading salon of the middle-class and the middle-aged and older of Verona. The tables are marble; the chandeliers and sconces are of Venetian glass; the small, ornate mirrors gilt-framed; and the red plush on banquettes and spindly chairs is worn down to bald pink. The time to go is between 6:00 and 7:00 P.M. to see ladies, all dressed up in their new velvet toques, exactly like the toques they have been wearing for years, and the old gentlemen, extending admirable grace and charm. In one back room, a group of six or eight men used to be bent over cards, oblivious—by a trick of Italian genes or rapid adjustments in infancy—of the noise. Still deeper in the back, plainer, smaller rooms protected the *jeunesse dorée* who come for Coca-Cola and a look at television. Not gone, but going with the snows of yesteryear. The elderly have become too old to maintain their numbers at the café and the young find Coca-Cola anywhere and everywhere else and have their own television to watch. Fortunately, the pleasant anachronism stays, defying time and the expansion of the pizza dispensary that now almost hides it.

The arches in the square invite to open rooms of vaulting, the remains of bold-patterned polychrome decorations and mellowed marble. The most splendid of the inner courts, hidden by the façade of the Palazzo del Comune, is that of the Mercato Vecchio ("the old market," which once sat in this core of medieval city), trimmed with round-arched windows, the usual neat little round bites at the upper ledges, and a tall, stately stairway supported by small, taller, wider, then tallest and widest, arches that disturb and bring to life the four-square striped horizontality of the Romanesque walls. As you admire the arches, the tower, the stairs, see if you can find a quiet, dark little tenement set into one of the aristocratic walls; a symptom of the Italian talent for inventing and accommodating.

Assuming that you have not yet been assaulted by the verve

and color of the Piazza Erbe—its sea of overlapping gray-white market umbrellas that shade postcards, toy gondolas, giant rosaries of plastic, foods and flowers, bordered by the multicolored café umbrellas and shop awnings—it is immediately available via the ceremonious exit of the Arco della Costa. The chatter of visitors at the street tables, the voices of juke boxes and vendors, the confusion of color and crowds tend to drown this evocative, shorthand panorama of Veronese history punctuated by three monuments which struggle out of the spreads of canvas. The Virgin who stands above the fourteenth-century fountain, wearing classic drapery and a crown that appears to have been made of spears, was a Roman statue, placed to adorn and guard the Roman forum, the ancestor of the Piazza Erbe. A square structure with a peaked stone canopy (the Berlina) marks the site of an antique shelter where appointments to public office were made and celebrated. Near the upper end of the square the column of Saint Mark holds a lion, the symbol of control by the republic of Venice.

Behind the lion of Venice, the strong, heavily ornamented seventeenth-century Palazzo Maffei rises to a parade of pagan gods marching against the sky; nearby is the brick Torre del Gardello built in the fourteenth century by the Cansignorio of the fanciest della Scala tomb. Walking in and out of courts when you can, look at the medieval houses squeezed against each other, the stolid form of the early-fourteenth-century merchants' building, the exceedingly high tower of the Lamberti, begun in the twelfth century to rise very slowly to its completion three hundred years later, a house (Casa Mazzanti) of the late Renaissance that still bears the strokes and shadows of frescoed figures out of classical mythology.

Emerging at the end of the piazza as it meets the via Mazzini, turn into the via Capello for a look at the "house of Juliet," an authentically thirteenth- to fourteenth-century house wrapped around an appealing yard with a pretty, feminine balcony and a quotation from Shakespeare. There was a pat appropriateness in the gesture that once put the Ente Provinciale here; that very informative office has since moved nearer Juliet's tomb.

The other end of the Piazza Erba leads back into the Corso

Porta dei Borsari. By winding through retiring alleys pierced with Venetian Gothic windows, occasionally neighbored by cheap lace curtains in grand Renaissance windows (you will have noticed before how much of working-class Italian life is lived in decayed palaces), via streets called Rosa, Egido, Forti, Porta Pietra, Vescovado, Duomo and Pigna, you will reach the bridge called the Ponte Pietra, a Roman bridge touched up in the Middle Ages with patches of stone in the brick. A thirteenth-century tower over the gate at the far side of the bridge soon leads to a tree-screened fortress-castle, once Roman, then Lombard, and in the fourteenth century, the castello of the mighty Gian Galleazzo Visconti of the Milanese family, the scourge of Pisa (among other places) who controlled Verona, too, for a time. The present fortress was built by the conquering Austrians in the nineteenth century. Immediately below stands Verona's other Roman theater, backed by a wall of tufa and being nibbled on by a tiny tenth-century church (page 283).

It is not the habit of cathedrals always to sit in churchly squares among houses that suit their mood and venerable age; years of crowding and rebuilding often muddy the serene air they need. Not altogether so in Verona: although the atrium is a density of parked cars, the surrounding streets breathe at a slow, calm pace. It was born Romanesque and rose as Gothic, its portals sit on the backs of weather-scrubbed lions; and saints gesture out of its façade. The ropes of varicolored stone and a pair of elongated warriors—said to be imported French heroes, Roland and Oliver—that enclose the front portal make it warmly inviting, as does the lovely porch above, sculpted by that shadowy grandfather of modern Italian sculpture referred to as Niccolò. The Gothic interior soaring out of clustered pillars encloses the usual collection of styles and centuries. For lingering with are the fourteenth-century tomb of Sant'Agata, an iconostasis that closes off the altar with marble carved by Sammicheli; and a rich, stormy Assumption by Titian. Recent explorations have opened a "Zona Archaeologico" that now consists of the columns, niches, low arches and tombstones that appear to be remnants of a very old, perhaps the oldest, version of the church. Poking around in the immediate environs of the Duomo, one comes on the Biblioteca Capitolare (Piazza Duomo 13; open few hours), considered the oldest library in the world, since it contains documents and illuminated manuscripts that go as far back as the fifth century. You will be told by one authority or other that the library has moved, will move, to a new building very close to Juliet's house. Doubtful, but check and check again.

Even the most meager of tourist pamphlets offers a long list of churches to choose from. Whatever the decision, San Zeno Maggiore, reached by a long walk from the Castelvecchio following the river, or a short bus ride from the same point, must be seen. It sits where it has been sitting, in smaller and older guises, for about fifteen hundred years, on a vast piazza, guarded by a crenelated medieval abbey tower and its tall, slender campanile. The felicitous blending of early twelfth century and later styles is expressed in glowing, creamy stone textured with shallow, frail pilasters and tiny scallops that lead to a bold rose window. The interior interrupts its high narrowness with an iconostasis that screens the raised altar and acts as upper ledge for the entrance to the crypt. Local painters of the thirteenth and fourteenth centuries frescoed sections of the walls and placed long figures of saints on the pilasters. The altarpiece by Mantegna, once lifted by Napoleon's assistants, is again in place. The crypt is hushed webs of hanging lamps in low vaults—some of them frescoed—supported by dozens of columns with the usual enthralling diversity of capitals and old tombs, including that of San Zeno. The cloister is again as usual, and as usual a docile charmer that offers a view of the side of the basilica and the flight of its campanile. Back in the church, there is the superb wooden canopy of ceiling to look at and an enormous Roman saucer of porphyry, which local tradition insists was brought here by the devil himself because no one else could transport it. Not far from the altar, to the left, is San Zeno himself, polychrome and smiling the gleeful smile of Cangrande.

Contented with his fourteenth-century contentment, thinking that his must have been an enviable time to be in Verona, one returns to the portal, the essential reason for visiting San Zeno. On either side of the indispensable lions (out of the Near East, where from times archaeological they guarded tombs, later converted to Christianity as guardians of churches because, according to old legends, they never closed their eyes) that hold up the portico, the work of Niccolò, originally created for an earlier version of the church. The reliefs by Niccolò and a master known as Guglielmo depict the expected scenes from the Testaments and a few lay figures out of legends that seeped down from northern Europe. Above the door sits San Zeno and a group of horsemen surrounded by months, signs of the zodiac and ornaments incised with deft vivacity. The wonder of San Zeno, however, is its bronze doors. Mainly of the early twelfth century with some additions of the thirteenth, they intersperse grotesque heads, strips of tiny saints and boxes of bronze cording with biblical scenes that have a sureness, a directness of impact, a clear crude naturalism that creates a very real world—the Bible as literal, factual history seen in devout medieval terms. They naturally lack the polish and sophistication of the Ghiberti doors in Florence, but in their own idiom and for their own time are their peers.

Evening is gathering now. On the Piazza delle Erbe, middle-aged paunchy and respectable gentlemen absorb papery cones filled with the neighborhood specialty, *panna montata,* which turns out to be whipped cream, plain. One café blessed with television is gathering in the evening's audience, and in the Piazza Bra the evening gowns and fur stoles go through one entrance to the arena while side entrances swallow the besweatered and corduroy-trousered young who climb to the upper rings of seats. The favorite opera by far is *Aïda,* as it is in Rome's baths of Carcella, and for the same reason: the scope it permits for massive, exotic décor, for eye-boggling pageantry and a provinceful of extras to wave peacock plumes from vertiginous heights of Egyptian walls. Good voices have no difficulty sounding through the arena, but it takes great voices and artistry to claim the attention that keeps wandering to marvel at the size of the Sphinx' head, to stare in terror at a turbaned figure who seems to be tottering, along with his large Egyptian totem, at the very edge of an impossible height. It has, in short, certain aspects of a three-ring circus. However, the roster of artists is impressive, the opening ceremony of a moment of total dark illuminated only by myriad match lights is lyrical and the exaggerations are fun. It makes a summer night's diversion that lends one's face and being the smile of Cangrande and San Zeno, a good souvenir to take away from Verona.

Notes

The hotel Due Torri, on the Piazza Sant'Anastasia, near the river, is furnished with ample public rooms and impressive antiques and, as suits the choicest *albergo* of Verona, asks at least $100 for a double with bath. The Colomba d'Oro, behind the Piazza Bra, is cordial, well kept, and asks less for good, undistinguished accommodations.

The Dodici Apostoli, on the corticella San Marco, is highly thought of, and for good reasons: its position in a tiny independent enclave above a set of stairs, the very merry decorations in its abundant flow of space and the polite, English-speaking waiters. The kitchen is very competent and its treatment of mushroom soup, served in a large bowl, is the absolute quintessence of mushroom. Or, see and taste the delicacy with which they handle a rather common dish, Fegato a la Veneziana. By no means a cheap restaurant, but not more than the American pocket can bear.

Il Cenacolo on the via Teatro Filarmonica, Number 10, is full of charm and flowers and has no menu. What you eat is decided for you in a long, swift parade of dishes—maybe more than you want, or don't want at all. The bill will be reasonably high, but it is an experience.

The pizza and pasta on the Piazza Bra will be more expensive than elsewhere, but just behind the spread of the Listone there are several small restaurants—a number with outdoor tables—that will feed you decently for comparatively little. Particularly satisfactory—large menu, nice waiters—is the Piccolo Listone.

Vicenza

Not far from London's airport, at Chiswick, there is a classical villa built in the eighteenth century by an English gentleman as a retreat for the arts and learned, witty conversation among his gifted friends. The plans were based on architectural precepts and sketches of the seventeenth-century architect Inigo Jones, collected by Lord Burlington, a student and connoisseur of architecture. Jones had been a devoted student and follower of the sixteenth-century Italian Andrea di Pietro della Gondola, dubbed "Palladio" by a Renaissance scholar and patron.

That remained the architect's name, the name attached to his houses and his influential books on architecture. It echoes through many later voices in many languages out of state capitals, the façades of large museums and libraries, out of pillared porticoes of churches and houses. The Capitol in Washington, the Metropolitan Museum in New York, the National Gallery in London, and a host of government buildings and buildings of high, dignified finance may not have had their present shapes were it not for Palladio. He must not be blamed for their excesses, however, since they are sometimes coarse swellings on what was an elegant, judicious style, for all its classicism hospitable and humane. Palladio's sources were, obviously, Roman architecture, but the elements so rearranged and balanced as to become unmistakably, singularly "Palladian." Particularly good examples are the villas strewn like jewel boxes—some concise and formal little palaces, others loose and easy houses—through the countryside that spreads in an irregular fan from Rovigo to Vicenza and its environs, north to Asolo, and curves back via Treviso to Venice. The wedge of the fan is ornamented by the dazzling white San Giorgio Maggiore, which rises from the waters of Venice, somewhat tarted up by later, eager hands, Palladian nevertheless.

The majority of the white villas whose curves and planes glow and retreat in the aqueous light of the region (the Veneto) are privately owned and have restricted visiting times: the Villa Maser, for instance (near Asolo), decorated by Veronese, is open, currently, on Tuesday and Friday afternoons, but a holiday weekend may throw that schedule off. There are, however, Palladian tours that can be arranged through the tourist offices of Padua and Venice which include a number of villas. Vagaries disturb these schedules, too, and those of the Palladiana available by canal steamer from Padua to Venice, or vice versa (page 329). Get current information from the Ente Provinciale di Tourism near the Olympic Theater, or your hotel, and be sure to give yourself and Palladio two days.

Born in Padua, possessed of a meager education, the young della Gondola came to Vicenza as an assistant to stone carvers. He was set to work on a classical villa, an innovation for this area though others had for some time been reviving the antique style. The scholar, writer, architect manqué and leading intellectual who had ordered the villa also formed a "school" in the Renaissance tradition, to which he invited the young Paduan and there opened to him studies in ancient architecture and related areas of learning. Palladio came to know, through his mentor, the Count Tressino, a number of scholars and thinkers who had lively ideas to exchange on the arts and architecture. It was for a few of these men and less intellectual warlords and Venetian landowners that Palladio built his houses. Between villas and churches and palazzi he traveled, endlessly, not only throughout Italy, but across the mountains into southern France—studying, sketching, deriving principles, designing, redesigning.

Vicenza is a town with a reputation for extraordinary *furbizia*—shrewdness, a quickness to size up and take advantage of a situation—belied by its rather slapdash center, quite contented to let a few good pamphlets and Palladio do all the work. Something of her story might help explain the quality of the town, the casual provincialism lying at the foot of—and almost overwhelmed by—classical palazzi, none of them quite finished as they were originally planned. Vicenza has little history as her own town. Controlled by Verona's Scaligeris and Lombardy's Visconti in the late Middle Ages, she later put herself disastrously under the wing of Venice. She become the field of conflict when the ancient Guelph-Ghibelline Vivals made a concerted attack on Venice in the early sixteenth century. Vicenza was pillaged, diminished, her arts and architecture inert while much of the rest of Italy was in its Renaissance blooming. Her sense of timing seems always to have been poor. She began to rebuild extravagantly shortly before the collapse, in the latter half of the sixteenth century, of the Venetian economy, which had been sliding for some time as a result of the competing wealth of the Iberian peninsula swollen with gold and silver from the Americas and the emergence of England as a maritime power—to mention only two major causes.

For this reason, the palazzi of Vicenza are often enormous screens, façades on immense, shallow caskets that contain practically nothing: fit companions for the most theatrical of theaters, also a Palladian thing.

The Piazza dei Signori, the central piazza of the gathering of old powers and now possessor of a broad, mighty café which sometimes seems to hold everyone in town and all talking at once. It is not one of the great Italian squares or especially attractive, but it has an enormous worn dignity expressed mainly by the "Basilica" in Palladian terms—strong, courageous, its eccentricities expressed frankly and openly. Fading bits of painting touch buildings here and there, and baroque carving cuts into everything in the square. The old Monte de Pieta (the government pawnshop) has lost its once flowery charm and uses. And although the great patriot, Giuseppe Mazzini, sits in the center of the piazza, Andrea Palladio sits modestly off to a side, a subtle criticism of his strange works—no longer fashionable in the nineteenth century, the time of Mazzini.

Across the square, at the meeting with the street called Monte Contra Porti, one is faced with a building very reminiscent of those in Mantua by Giulio Romano. It is the Palazzo Thiene, attributed to Palladio with a possibility that Romano had a hand in it—and that possibility seems convincing when one observes the heavy rustication and the rough, effective decorations around the windows. Almost directly facing is another, later and more independent work of Palladio, the Palazzo Barbarano (about 1570), quite unfinished, distorted by later additions, suffocated by narrow space and yet essentially a simple, confident design enriched by a light-and-shade tissue of balconies and plasterwork. The same street holds the earlier Palazzo Iseppo Porto (about 1550), and the main cross street called Corso Andrea Palladio leads to two tall, gallant bays of another unfinished palazzo, Porto-Breganze.

The town is, as said, full of aborted Palladian palazzi, but a dozen make an easy, rewarding visit. Assuming an interest which is neither professional nor driven, it might be enough now to go to the other end of Palladio's Corso for the agreeable, colonnaded Palazzo Chiericati, its double tiers of columns rising to statues and giant stone chess pawns. The building—only the façade, as often in Palladian buildings—houses the town's art museum, which has a respectable collection of Venetian masters and a few of the Dutch, one a magnificent Descent from the Cross by Memling, and a charming parade of dolls in sixteenth-century costume. However, the most startling and grandiose of Palladio is still to be seen. Across from the miscellany of the museum, including the inevitable Etruscan and Roman bits, there are the Ente Provinciale and the Teatro Olimpico, introduced by a kind of pagan-wilderness garden, a playground or madhouse for a collection of broken statues, "classicky," but hardly the real thing; startling and theatrical enough, though, to serve as introduction to a quintessence of the theatrical. There were other wooden theaters built in the Renaissance, now gone, and the architect himself had built two theaters before—one in the hall of the Basilica and another in Venice—but this one, remarkably, still exists. The problem of what sort of roof to put on an imitation of an open Roman theater was arbitrarily solved in the nineteenth century when a flat wooden roof, painted to look like the sky, was stretched over it. Palladio didn't live to see the theater finished (he died in 1580), and a number of changes, particularly the impassioned emphasis on scenic perspectives, were introduced by his successor, Scamozzi, the builder of the theater in Sabbioneta.

Though there is basically little invention here, the impact is forceful. The scheme is of Renaissance interpretations of the Roman; rising arcs of seats, colonnades interrupted and surmounted by heroic plaster figures, and a proscenium that holds a large colony of forceful Romans. The scenery—purportedly the city of Thebes—with its illusions of long columned streets ending in arches and adorned with statuary is exceedingly clever, but manipulations of perspective in wood, plaster, bronze, paint and marble were well-practiced cadenzas by the late sixteenth century. *Insomma,* as the Italians say, you are facing another entity of Renaissance grandeur out of Roman grandeur built by order of still another Renaissance entity, the "Olympian Academy," which prepared an optimistic program of classic comedies and tragedies for its new theater. A wave of censorship washed the comedies away, and the only play given for a long time was Sophocles' *Oedipus Rex* (hence the imagined streets of ancient Thebes), whose first performance, according to contemporary reports, lasted for eleven hours. Now, four hundred years later, the theater still offers classic dramas—and music that concentrates on Vivaldi, Pergolesi, Albinoni, Monteverdi, suitable to this stage.

It might be a good idea at this point to hire a taxi to see one or two of the villas at the edge of town which turns quite hilly as it climbs toward the mountains. (There is a taxi stand outside the theater.)

The Villa Capra, usually referred to as the "Rotonda," is *the* Palladian symbol that frequently appears on pamphlets and cards. It is a fairly early work (1550) whose theatrical scheme of four imposing entrances held by a shallow dome—a candid formula readily encompassed—and its isolation on a smooth rise of fill, make it exceptionally photogenic. It was not a land-working villa nor has it much living space; rather, it is an elaborate platform from which to admire the undulating countryside that flows from its regal columns and stairs. The villa was built for entertaining and for show, which were the purposes of Lord Burlington when he modeled his Chiswick villa on the Rotonda. Check with the Ente Provinciale for hours of visibility. At other times it is necessary to push one's begging face against the iron gate for a glimpse that is frontal, aristocratically stunning, as the horizontals of stairs and verticals of columns, the serenity of pediment and unobtrusive dome, flower out of the long slope that echoes an approach to a temple. A hardly livable "folly," it keeps itself on the long rows of crops which flow to a distant horizon.

On another sweep of hill, giving on a diversity of tamed and untamed landscape, there is the complex—stables, guest house and main residence—of the Villa Valmarana, built a hundred years and more after Palladio and worth visiting (check hours and expect to pay over 1,000 lire for admission) as an example of how these villas were decorated. The walls of both houses were painted by the Tiepolos, Giambattista and Giandomenico, in the mid-eighteenth century. The main house devoted its walls to mythological scenes enclosed in the Venetian manner by classical columns that mark off endless blueness of sky, as if each scene were being enacted on a Roman stage or, better still, on a Venetian balcony. The virtuosity is so impressive, the flesh so luminous, the robes so skillfully light-struck, that one is more moved by the craft than by Agammemnon as he prepares to plunge a knife into Iphigenia. Nor was one meant to be moved; these are charades for an evening's diversion, possibly to be accompanied by music. The guest house, mainly the work of Giandomenico, is in the entertaining, imaginative confusions of chinoiserie: lovely crazy hats, exotic fruits and flowers, misty distant pagodas, an Italian pine tree, a slant-eyed goddess sitting under a canopy that drips beads. No one with normally healthy

curiosity need be told look around at the furnishings; certainly
not what they once were, and quite poor and worn in some
rooms. Family photos stare back with the sorrowful, slightly accusing look of funerary portraits, and, most surprising—one
wonders if it could be the same taste—there is a large collection
of books in French and as large a collection, scattered over table
and desk tops, of little ceramic dwarfs and cute children and
bunnies.

The full name of the house includes the word "Nani"—
dwarfs—and they were conspicously there as finials on a wall
that leads off from the back of the house. They are caricatures of
barristers, nuns, nurses, courtiers, soldiers and a vengeful set of
eighteenth-century etcetera.

Sweeter matter rests in the church of Santa Corona in town. It
was built in the 1200's and holds a Bellini and a Veronese, not
too well lit. In full light there stands a stone elephant carrying a
clumsy pyramid, something like the more appealing version in
Rome. One asks a man polishing the church floor what it is,
what does it mean. He doesn't know or won't say.

Minor closing notes on this distinguished, odd city: Both the
Teatro Olimpico and the big cafe Garibaldi on the Piazza dei
Signori have "Turkish" toilets, strange in a country that likes
shining new toilets and treats them well. Also, there is a U.S.
Army base near Vicenza, and you may at first be startled to hear
"country" English and see black faces. Should you see a pregnant
black girl, who speaks with the gentle accent of North Carolina,
looking adoringly at a Virgin in the museum, you will probably
not forget her, nor the thoughts she arouses about living black
and pregnant so far from home.

Note

LUNCH.   The Jolly Hotel, the Continental, Al Pozzo, Tre Visi
offer satisfactory dining. You might prefer, instead, to go into
one of a number of bars that is turning itself into a sandwich
shop, *tavola calda* and pizzeria.

More popular than pizza and the fastest of foods are the great
variety of sandwiches—refined, coarse, slender, fat, toasted, un-

toasted—that contain combinations you might never dream of and that are surprisingly good. (Mayonnaise, be warned, features heavily.) Standing at the bar, pointing and chomping fast, will cost less, often markedly less, than service at a table.

Both the Jolly Hotel and the Continental are undistinguished but satisfactory as hotels; both are moderate, with the Jolly running a small bundle of lire higher.

Bassano del Grappa
and Asolo

YOU MAY NEVER have seen a ceramic old-fashioned straw
hat, shining white and wired for use as a lamp. You have seen
porcelain flowers, as used on Provençal graves; delicately painted
tea sets scattered with pansies and cornflowers; cleverly molded
ceramic caricatures. Surely you've seen them and their relatives—fine or gross—as gift objects everywhere and, come to
think of it, in great numbers and all your life, back to the first
Humpty-Dumpty milk cup. A startling number of these objects,
exquisite, junky, foolish, delicate, coarse, come from Bassano
which insists that you also remember its fiery brandy (grappa)
when you speak its full name, Bassano del Grappa (a drink as
impassioned as French calvados). The city is also an ardent vendor of large, dried mushrooms, beautifully boxed for shipping,
and jars of honey display themselves in considerable variety.

But Bassano is pottery, in tight rows and on each end of the
bridge over the Brenta river, a favorite with sightseers, not only
for its eminent usability, but as well for its odd looks—although
it is characteristic of the area. The bridge is made almost entirely
of wood, substantial, trustworthy wood, and yet manages to look
like a huge toy of crisscrossed support bars, a Leggo structure

(attributed by one or two enthusiasts to Andrea Palladio, with no conviction). As you walk across the bridge, notice that the lettering of names and shop decorations are often themselves of luminous, witty ceramics. And stay with the river to admire its palaces and the chalets in northern style, bearing long wooden balconies; weeping willows languishing toward gentle waters that catch the fleeting images of clouds and mountains.

Within the town, the images are older, tireder, some with remains of paintings, as once in Venice, on the venerable houses. A house of the Piazza Liberta carries an apogee of fanciness as a clock, two crucifixes that tend to scorn each other; neighboring shapes and building gestures fall, in their melting ways, into art-nouveau patterns, unintentionally. The Piazza Montevecchia is also a bewildering compilation of painted houses, now pale storms of what was once bold, almost bellicose, designs.

To match its river views and shop signs and painted houses, Bassano's museum holds to its own special style. It begins its voyage, as many museums do, with antique pieces, some clearly Greek, rather like the Magna Grecia pieces in Taranto, and others more difficult—transitional in style—to place. The stairway to the major portion of the museum is made merry by a large, welcoming, beaming Goldoni, Italy's favorite playwright. The immense collection he introduces—much of it quite entertaining—includes engravings of Jacopo da Ponte (we know this Jacopo of the Bridge as "Bassano"), innumerable Canova drawings, and some brilliantly toned chiaroscura painting rather like those of other northern painters, among them Vivarini. There are works by old "Anonimo" who was often highly skilled, and works that have the look of German carving, a close and strong influence. And, of course, choice ceramics. To complete the conpendium of art in Bassano, find the tracery that was fifteenth-century painting in the pretty Romanesque-Gothic church, San Francesco, which adjoins the museum.

Bassano's history is one of the clichés in Italian history; a robber baron took and held it in the Middle Ages and somehow let it be wrested from his mailed glove by neighboring robber barons until the giants moved in. The powerful Visconti of Milan were inevitably followed by tenacious Venice, which held on and ex-

erted its influence for four centuries. Then Napoleon briefly
made his mark, followed by Austria. Ultimately very late, Italy
became a united country. The Venetian influence shows, as mentioned, strongly in the architecture and its decoration. The rest is
a long and engaging history of various kinds of craftsmanship—
wrought iron for lanterns; carpentry as a subtle skill; the innumerable drawings and engravings in the museum, some impressive weaving and, of course, the ceramics. And *sui generis* are
the flavors that enhance the colorful bowls—the large porcini,
the king of mushrooms; white and green asparagus, in season,
that are thick or thin, tamed or wild, and treated in an ingenious
variety of ways. Floating among their green, earthy odors, the
strong breeze of grappa.

Proud of its table, Bassano arranges a series of dinners in May
at different restaurants to honor its very singular asparagus and
use it most inventively. One restaurant, prized in the area, under
the remarkable name of Al Sole da Tiziano (not *the* Titian, but
the honored father of the proprietor), serves them touched with a
delicate drop of oil, or half buried in polenta (corn meal), the
whole baked in a rich sauce. But the subject, though large, grows
self-evident; and there are, incidentally, snails to consider, little
birds (why Rome has more bird song than the Italian countryside) cooked with mushrooms, and the raw mountain ham.

Al Sole combines several local virtues by seating you among
good-looking lamps and furniture, and placing on its handsome
credenza some unusual pieces of good pottery. Around the windows are clustered groups of grotesque, porcine figures, ridiculous and clever and probably the vestiges of old carnival fun.
The Bacchus of this funny horde is a huge sun-figure, drunk,
almost drowned in grapes, the whole figure accomplished in a
ragged, lively, sure technique. The Bassano principle that treats
food with respect, that serves it politely and in its proper, enhancing setting, functions in other local restaurants as well, led
off by the Sun of Titian, which seems to have appointed itself
curator of food, drink, pottery and enticing odors, a noble position.

Almost as if theatrically arranged, the earthiness of Bassano
strongly contrasts with the *tristesse* of its neighbor Asolo. Most

cities postcard themselves in deep Renaissance colors or those of
ice creams; even Romeo and Juliet in the worst of Verona cards
manage to look like fancy sundaes of several "gusti." A postcard
of an Asolo street, however, puts on dark and darker veils—the
result a wailing wall vaguely etched as doors and windows. The
postcard lies a bit; although it is a town of sad Muses, no place
that calls itself a "city of one hundred horizons" and swings
through heights and depths in a restlessness of exquisite scenery,
can be more than occasionally dark. Asolo seems primarily medieval, although an important time in its life was the Renaissance, when a redoubtable lady, the Queen of Cypress, and no
saint, held court for twenty years in the dominating castle-
fortress, la Rocca. Besides the lady and her ladies, there was
Pietro Bembo, a power behind the papal throne and a Platonic
lover of Lucrezia Borgia. Much later came Robert Browning,
who lived on a picturesque little hill and for whom a street is
named; and later the couple to whom the town seems to have
been dedicated.

We must build up to them, in several senses. First, the large,
ambitious Duomo with a huge altar painting and ornate baldec-
chino and a few impressive paintings by Lotto and Bassano.
Then one glimpses a deeply arcaded street and small shops and
down and up again past villas that show a spot of elderly paint
here and there. It is time now for the core of the town, the Museo
Civico which has the somewhat peculiar attractiveness of many
provincial museums of the turn of the century. This one chooses
to introduce you first to a mammoth's tooth and follow that with
Egyptian figurines, Roman mosaics, paintings "believed to be"
by masters and a Canova funerary piece that incorporates a stun-
ningly callipyginous boy.

Upstairs we come on *the* serious matter of the museum and
the town. These are rooms devoted to the writer Gabriele d'An-
nunzio, displaying his political manifestoes, his red shirt and
epaulets, and photos of his stern, heroic face. The rooms at an
upper level are devoted to his collaborator and lover, Eleanora
Duse, who acted in his plays as well as those of Shakespeare and
Ibsen—superbly acted, to judge from contemporary reports.
There is a rather full collection of her own gowns as well as her

costumes, of paintings and photos and interesting photos of theater scenes in which she appeared.

Your first farewell to Duse in this town of perpetual farewell is to go back to the small square that fronts the Cathedral and look down one of the myriad horizons, on light woods and fruit trees and the gardens that surround a children's playground and, above the school building, a magnificent stand of cypress trees that shape their own, funerary horizon.

It is not a long walk up a steep hill (if you feel especially devotional), or more than a short taxi ride, that will take you to the local graveyard that overlooks long views flowing toward distant hills. Among the colorful tombs covered with blossoms, there is one, Duse's, that stands apart in its own green copse, a broad and simple tomb on which there is always a spray or two of fresh flowers. Asolo never forgets Duse, almost, were it not for its own intrinsic sad beauty, its prime cause for being.

Because of its quiet loveliness, a fair number of Italians use Asolo as a sort of retreat. Those who can afford it stay at the Villa Cipriani (related to the hotel of the same name in Venice) and bask in the landscapes and the products of a talented kitchen. There is a much more modest hotel named, inevitably, The Duse, which provides no meals but points you to neighboring trattorie. Between the lush and very modest, the moderate pensione, Bella Vista.

Villa Maser

ALTHOUGH THE SPLENDID MUSEUM of Palladian work, Vicenza, is not a great distance away, the Villa Barbaro, generally known as "Maser" for the land on which it luxuriates, is closer to Bassano and Asolo, about equidistant from them. The Bassano road will offer you the sight of an enormous villa, probably inspired by Palladio, now being restored, and also the rhythms of distant hills aspiring to be mountains. The road from Asolo threads its way through lyrical woods, and in any case, Asolo is a more romantic place for departure to a Renaissance-Mannerist palace, essentially very romantic.

As you mount the steps, with a classful of children sliding about on the broad flat slippers they put over their own shoes which might soil and mar fine woods and stone, turn and observe the size of the huge park, some of it planted, some of it still treed alleys. Should you have had an exterior view first, you will have noticed not only the vast space that the villa dominates, shapings of space that suggest maze-like formal gardens and the windy (drapery substituting for skillful delineation) statues that punctuate the mazes. The generous façade with a sundial scratched into it spreads gracefully to broad, round ends.

The Villa Maser was built by the brothers Daniel and Marcantonio Barbaro. (Daniele is mentioned as a Patriarch of Aquileia, which may have become an honorific title by the sixteenth century; Venice and her Doges and Councils held the power). One of the later owners was actually a Doge of the Manin family. It then went to an industrialist and is now the property of the Count of Misurata, Giuseppe Volpe. Judging from the restoration going on and objects—photos, for instance—of the present day, the house is being kept alive and vivacious.

Veronese and his associates left hardly an inch of the Villa unpainted, enjoying the play of curious perspectives and trompe l'oeil at which they were consummately skilled. One sala is devoted to women musicians—there are references to music throughout the house—and a hint of games with doors; one door opens to a child, another to a man. One ceiling is a ripeness of grape lattice, another bears a balcony of women and animals. One wall is a genre piece of guests, horses and carriages arriving at just such a stately home as Maser; another is a set of fanciful landscapes, not lacking Palladian villas. Adjoining one big sala, there is a pool fed by minute fountains and with them classic statuary, and a river god half-hiding in a grotto—the essential fashionable bit for a late Renaissance villa.

The burbling of color and movement and play of perspective are engaging everywhere in the villa, but be careful to leave enough time and attention for a remarkable set of gods disporting themselves—Bacchus naturally among them—on Olympus and the almost incredible perspective that presents a knight, handsome and graceful, about to go (or return from) hunting. At what seems an enormous distance away, down the illusion of a very long hall, another door opens to a view of a well-dressed woman wearing a small face mask. It would be interesting to know the actual distance between this set of doors, probably quite short. With his brilliant manipulation of perspective aided by the alert charm of his figures, Veronese has created an admirably convincing resetting of space, an almost magical piece of trompe l'oeil trickery.

The Friuli

THE REGION called "The Friuli," a name linked in its eventful history with Julius Caesar, possibly to honor a conquering drive toward the Adriatic and into the Alps (but which sounds like a bird call), is all sorts of green, freshened by rivers that flow from its mountains. The dense woods produce a thriving industry of furniture, and the vineyards threaten even the railroad tracks; consequently, lots of good wine and grappa; and although the weather in the spring may carry a misty cold from the gray shadows of mountain, the flowers are brilliantly sturdy and rouse themselves early in the year. And surely you've heard of the mountain ham, the prosciutto, from San Daniele del Friuli?

Sometime in your Friuli journey, possibly from or to Austria or Jugoslavia, you will come on the energetic (they actually all are) town of Pordenone which has one particularly humane and Italian distinction, if one is to believe the locals. Like most old cities, Pordenone began its life as a cluster of church, market and governing palace, the central core. The old church is now the headquarters of a music society; the market moved a short distance away; and the outer edges, the newer town, occupied with schools and offices. The antique Palazzo Publico stands where it always had stood, but with a new brand of inhabitants rather than the prosperous merchants and lords who were once the government. Now entertained and entertaining gaggles of old men and women call to each other from the windows on which they lean, call even more eagerly to the schoolchildren and the women with the market baskets and the men with leather cases as they bound in various directions across the square: to an old bocce crony carrying a new grandchild, to an old neighbor—to the world from which they have not, as many of our old are, been disconnected. You hope it's what you think it is, and a local newsvendor says it is—the old people's home. Who needs another palazzo that has to be kept in repair—for what? Let the old have the pleasures of noise and curiosity and intimacy, while they can.

The Friuli towns have each their dominating color (the mood is always good-natured and active); bits of their ancient history still decorate them: one more clearly Renaissance, another still Longobardic, and yet another speaks in Roman accents. Although Venice sings you her golden Lorelei song, Florence calls from her endless horizon of forms and colors, Rome's monumental dignity waits to be admired, try not to rush too fast through the Friuli. The local roads are well-made and well-marked; the trains efficient and frequent and a network of buses connects the towns with fair efficiency.

Udine, the largest of the Friuli cities and most central, is a refreshing confusion of towns. Very much recovered from its recent earthquake (unlike those lazy Neapolitans, they say), the city looks untouched, although Sunday teams still do repair work on water mains and power lines in the city and the hilly countryside (seen, incidentally, from the crest of Udine's fortress-castle, a handsome palace achieved by walking many steps). For a long time, 1238 to 1420, Udine was ruled by the "Patriarchs of Aquileia," a committee of bishops that maintained a feudal rule while much of the rest of Italy was living under the more sophisticated early Renaissance form of committee rule and certainly less subject to ecclesiastical tenets and orders. Then, the common local refrain, Venice took Udine and kept her.

A few steps from the quiet palace path, a crazy mixture of

bicycles, motorbikes, cars, buses, pedestrians, beats up a wild froth of activity, especially on Saturday afternoons, a busy shopping time among surprisingly classy shops, with intervals for eating gelato in shining palaces like our resplendent ice-cream parlors of a time when going out to eat ice cream marked special occasions. The arcaded streets, as heavily trafficked in their way as the broader open streets, just as curved, as erratic, pause for a moment of quiet at a piazza or two, and absolutely still at the Piazza della Liberta, a large area, mainly Renaissance, which cannot altogether define itself—a not uncommon condition in piazze which have been added to and added to, the amassing not always harmonious. To accompany the finials of swallowtailed walls placed as signs of ownership by the Venetians, there is a fair brood of Venetian lions, fiercely Saint Mark in spirit. On one side of the Piazza there is welcoming café space under a Gothic building of buoyant designs and light color, especially enhanced by its stone shields. The Gothic Loggia del Lionello, a serene building and among the several others less serene that witnessed Udine's history (including the arrival of Napoleon), there is one structure that bears the two Moors who strike an ornate clock, as in Venice. Also, a fountain with spitting old fauns' faces at its sides. At the top of the square, an ample goddess, quite Victorian in looks and drapery, dedicates herself to a former ruler and, as guardians of it all, two strange men, one of them a displeased Hercules and the other with the face of an unsuccessful prizefighter; both gentlemen, however, carefully dressed in fig leaves. It means well and patriotically, the Piazza Liberta, but confusions do beset it.

After pursuing successfully (opening hours are playful) the Tiepolo frescoes in the Archbishop's Palace and his confident, airy work in the Duomo, explore—always on foot (there is no other way)—the wheels of streets, in the pattern of the Middle Ages. Take care to look up every once in a while to admire neoclassic fancies near roofs, at least one a very tragic mask. Also examine bus stops and their destination and look out for taxi stands— very few—since the spokes and arcs of these wheels can make long walks. Fortunately, the Via Mercato Vecchio and the Piazza

Matteotti, centers of vivacity, are quite central and there is always another overflowing dishful of melon and nougat (torrone) ice cream swimming in dark cherry sauce (amarena) to comfort you and your feet. Try Ristorante Vitello d'Oro, via Valvason 4. High moderate.

Venice stamped one of her gates on the city of Aquileia, a few miles to the south of Udine, miles of flourishing Friuli corn and wheat, swinging vines and heavy olive trees. Aquileia was once the Roman glory of the region, attested to by the large sections of column and other broken pieces of Rome lying on the sides of the road that approaches the city's renowned basilica, a repository of medieval history that holds shards of the older antiquity. Authorities tell you that since the earthquake of the late seventies, there are still areas to be remodeled, that not all treasures are yet displayed as they deserve to be, and so on. Nevertheless, the basilica yields considerable information and pleasure.

The basilica was built in the eleventh century by an ecclesiastical ruler, the patriarch Poppo, and restored three hundred years later. Recently unearthed, although they stem from the fourth century, are a group of mosaic heads which may have been attempts at portraits of the ecclesiasts in control and possibly builders of the basilica. Their structure may again be sinking as it had probably in times before; square modern bricks do little for arches which may once have been supported by Roman marble. Consolation for this rests in staring at the remarkable high ceiling of gilded boxes arranged as long, harmonious curves. The absolute wonder of the broad basilica and its crypt is the floor which buckles and waves like a gentle sea, home to the many and superb mosaic fish sporting in its mosaic depths.

The early medieval world shone with mosaics in an almost frenzied activity, continued from the high interest (and skills) of the Romans. Left us here are winged fishermen (a composite Saint Peter?) casting a net among fish-monsters and octopi and aquatic birds. In another section of the wondrous shining floor, large-eyed, moving heads that closely resemble the Roman-Egyptian funerary paintings of Fayum. One distinguished head—a saint, a goddess?—wears an elaborate wreath, still and heiratic, while birds flit and fly about her, they themselves halted by abstract symbols which, one assumes, had religious significance. And don't miss Jonah being engulfed by a sea monster.

The Cripta degli Scavi is an even greater astonishment of paleo-Christian mosaic. Peering over a shoulder of one of the surprisingly many who come in large busloads to see the basilica and its wonders, you notice that these subterranean sections of antique buildings grew like vegetable beds rather than architectural space. The badly decayed columns which evidently flashed with mosaics are saddening, but relieved by the flowery, flossy hat decorations (or so they seem) around the old bones in reliquaries.

Here the mosaics are more varied, more lively, more controlled than on the basilica floor: a jungle of goats, rams, kids, chickens, snails, flowers as flowers, flowers as designs, peacocks, lambs, lobsters, a ray, a fox—the earth's fullness, and none of it to be overlooked—rendered with consummate skill, as are the portraits, each in its own design of frame, the frames separated by birds on fruited branches.

The basilica's twelfth-century frescoes may or may not be in view in your time. Have a walk, instead, behind the basilica for another elderly pleasure: a neat, cheerful graveyard, each grave its own pretty garden. The new, imposing Archaeological Museum offers several impressive Roman heads, among them several of Tiberius and Augustus when young. Not unexpectedly, here is a bold, active Mithras in his windy drapery and a competition goddess—more than a bit battered—Astarte (Isis?) of the many breasts, and, achieving a peculiarly ecumenical effect, a copy of a copy of a Greek Venus. A full-figured portrait of Tiberius has him wrapped in "sacred vestments," and one wonders what sinner needed them more?

The prime charm of the museum is its gardened space that holds arrangements of cemetery urns, quantities of gravestones and sarcophagi, more bits of the mosaics that lived here in such profligacy, chunks of ornamental building stone—the miscellany you might expect, including an Aphrodite with neither a head nor a greatly beautiful body. It is the magnificent, triumphant trees that lend life to some of the stone they shade; the curved green walks they shape, now open, now shadowed, that make the museum so extraordinarily attractive.

An aesthetic and historic companion piece to Aquileia, and flanking Udine by a half-hour's ride to the northeast is Cividale del Friuli, beginning to show an enormous wall of gray hills, some of them still snow-capped in the spring. The impressive, rather operatic name stems from the fact that it was the Roman Forum Julii, and for a long time the independent fief of the Patriarchs of Aquileia.

Cividale, the center of the first Longobard dukedom, is civil, even courtly, a small city that held pieces of brutal history and flashes of extraordinary beauty. In the eighth century, the forces of barons against ecclesiasts, the murderous quarrels between Arians and Christians were, as often appears in art history, the troubled ground from which grew some of the indelibly beautiful. The Duomo is the repository, in two of its sections, of these accomplishments of the "Dark Ages," undoubtedly affected by the inevitable takeover by Venice and certainly, more recently, severely damaged by the 1976 earthquake. The earthquake seems also to have injured the Duomo's clocks or her sense of time. Scheduled to be reopened on Sunday at 2:30, it may still be closed at 3:00. Walk, while you wait, into the small town and look for its tragic muse—Adelaide Ristori, "the Genio Tragico," a great actress, they tell you, and sculptured in the tragic veils that suit her genius. Examine some of the houses as you return to the Duomo; the variety is a melding of Swiss chalet, modest twentieth century, and Italian medieval, with a selling counter that was pulled up at night and maybe a door for the exit of the dead above that, as one still sees the house in medieval cities like Gubbio.

If the Duomo is still napping, take a chair and coffee in the neighboring café and listen to animated reviews of yesterday's soccer games. One near neighbor will be Julius Caesar, on his plaque a version of the word "Friuli" that grows increasingly mysterious—still birdlike and pretty—except to the Latinist. Finally, admission to the moving church, simple and stark, a noble structure of broad arches holding immense columns that encompass the Gothic into the Renaissance. A slender Christ, somewhat in the exsanguinated Spanish style, hangs over the high altar on which rest several twelfth-century gilded pieces of Venetian design, disturbingly obscured by a row of shining nouveauriche patriarchs.

Attached to the Duomo is its museum, built around two masterworks of Lombard sculpture. The baptistry of Callisto, with its enormously large (possibly for total immersion) bowl, was a place of baptism, twice a year, for those being received into the church. It was a formal, solemn ceremony accompanied by impassioned symbols echoed in the carvings. The Four Apostles, flattened and broadened a bit crudely, yet carry emotional power; the less imposing objects—candlesticks, birds and animals—are less awestruck (made in a later time?) and, consequently, more naturalistic and more simply pleasing as etchings in stone. It is the raw quality of the symbols of the evangelists and the abstract figures that surround them that carry the strongest impact, echoed by the companion piece here, the Altar of Ratchis. Three sides of the altar are devoted to the Ascension, the Adoration for the Magi and the Visitation. The Ascension, for example, works beautiful patterns around a flat-faced Virgin in Byzantinish draperies, who is framed, held, supported, embellished, by gently floating angels with strong, elaborate wings, surrounded by stars and flowers, the details naïvely appealing, the composition extraordinarily sophisticated.

A search for the Tempieto, which is open sparse hours and those only when the owner permits, makes another, quite different experience. Arrows at the back of the church point to broken earthquake rock, up past a few houses—chalet type, medieval type, but not the unavailable Tempietto. Instead, a view that is its own landscape painting of rushing falls cutting into overhanging rocks; a bordering walk; and a few yards from the gushing waters, a little church both bright and faced with a tiny campanile clinging to it—a winsome picture to close off a very engaging old place.

Notes

You will very probably use Udine as center for short Friuli trips, staying at the Continental or the Casa Bianca (both high moderate) or one of several others your agent may suggest. Wherever you stay, look for the Trattoria Alla Vedova (near the Continental) on the via Tavagnacco. It was once a coaching inn and has the conviviality of such a place in equal portions of Italian and Teutonic friendliness and well-being. The orders are generous—as witness a plateful of prosciutto San Daniele and helpings of the local mushrooms and unusually inventive salads. Not too cheap, nor very expensive, and every mouthful worth the cost. (Reserve: 0432/470291, or ask your concierge to help you.)

Treviso

TREVISO IS A WATERY CITY, and like most watery cities, enormously attractive. Intersected by canals, like Venice, no great distance away, there is little of the sybaritic here, the glitter or languor. Its practical, busy mood links it northward, toward the cold Alps. And the limit of its allure is the easy pleasure of wandering across its canals, staring up at the many painted buildings, admiring skiesful of balcony exploding with flowers. You may encounter the Piazza San Andrea, a triangle of old houses being refurbished; a few Renaissance palazzi putting on new window frames and balustrades. One antique in an earlier style may go back—with some propping up and retouching—to a semblance of what it was in the thirteenth century when Treviso was a power. Or you might find the Corso del Popolo where civic pride has put a very new small fountain, a clever modern Italian confection of boxes of water at several levels, each box accompanied by its small walk—a nice thing, but then most things in Treviso are nice.

The Piazza dei Signori, the meeting place of the town's leaders, holds a large, heavy medieval building and the Loggia dei Cavalieri, also mighty and seriously Romanesque. The square continues on to proliferate as a series of arcades that stop at broad streets. Among these starts and stops you will find market, bits of new shopping streets and of very old; space flows into space in a stimulating mélange of eras and their characteristic modes—the new, the old, the passive, the thriving. One of these inviting streetlets, St. Vito, leads you to its small church which a busy lunchtime populace seems to step into and out of quickly, as a sign of respect it would seem, rather than for a full ritual. Some of the frescoes are gone, some almost, and some glaringly restored. This minute prison building, turned into a church in 1389, is something of a showplace for the small, strange figures on the Gothic altar; they might have been the governing bishops but have much more the belligerence of Crusaders, which they also might have been. The cheerful companion campanile seems newer and has managed to retain a beautiful painting of Christ and Saints over its portal.

Peer and, if necessary, snoop. Stare up at roofs, at stairways, at gardens on high slopes; and possibly find, in the border garden of one canal, the remains of an old windmill.

The "big" church is San Francesco whose frescoes by Tommaso da Modena suggest an advanced boldness in size and manner, some of it difficult to discern clearly now. The tall apse arch shelters a slender, aristocratic Christ and a number of other objects worth some time. It appears, however, that most visitors go to San Francesco for its literary associations. Pietro, the son of Dante, is entombed here; and so is Francesca Petrarca, the daughter of the great poet, not too curious a coincidence. Both the poets and Treviso were important in their day, and entombment of their children here one of the honors they and the leading church merited. If you are moved by the naïve yet advanced qualities of early painting, spend some time with the work of Tommaso da Modena and his associates, of the fourteenth century, and look for frescoes in one of the chapels of San Francesco and more in the church of Santa Caterina.

Because you like the town, you'd like to show interest in its L. Bailo Museum whose contents—dignified murals taken out of defunct churches, a few attractive genre studies, a good portrait by Lotto, another by Titian, a Giovanni Bellini and a few faded decorative pieces that may once have adorned villas painted by Veronese or his followers—do not add up to enough for the effort of walking long rooms (in an admittedly attractive building). Offer your regrets (or take a chance: Treviso is passionate for self-improvement) and lend yourself to the shining streets again. (Again, be sure to carry a map, provided by your hotel or the Ente Provinciale. Like many old towns, Treviso wheels and whirls confusingly.)

Note

The Carlton, Al Fogher and the Continental are favored (high-moderate) hotels. The restaurant often chosen is the Beccherie, with Alfredo's considered, not a rival, but an equal. Reserve. Across from the Beccherie there is (was?) a bar with a small dining room attached that made no demands of any kind. Soup only? Okay, but they've prepared artichoke soup and hope you like it; you will. Never had wild asparagus? Try some. (Not quite so good, but worth the try, particularly since the price is very low.) You might decide to take all your Treviso meals here because food, clientele, chef and waiter are each, in various ways, quite interesting.

Padua

STRIVING, AMBITIOUS, lining its streets with modern shopping arcades that embrace smart Englished shops—a "Dickenson," a "Lord Taylor"—thrusting skyscrapers into the Veneto air, Padua is stretching itself out of shape. It is startling to come with a montage of images of the city that claims to be the oldest in Italy (founded by Antenor, a wandering Trojan, it says in some booklet or other), of a university founded early in the thirteenth century where Galileo taught, of a café that Stendhal frequented, of a luminary among miracle saints and, above all, the house of Giotto's masterwork, and fall into the frenetic newness of the city. One expects a slightly musty town, laden with serious bookshops, soberly lit by students, church art and traditional market place. And it *is* there, hiding from the huge signs of competing department stores, the palatial new marble banks, the glitter of shops springing from the arcades, the crowds of shoppers and congested traffic in the restless, determined center.

The flight back into a less confused time—if there had to be only one reason for coming to Padua, this might be it—should begin with the Scrovegni chapel in the park ringed by chunks of Roman arena, off a central spine of street which has five names, here Corso Garibaldi. The chapel is the simplest of church boxes, so clearly designed for frescoes that it has been suggested, probably mistakenly, that Giotto himself was the architect. Enrico Scrovegni's father had amassed the largest fortune in Padua through usury, and for that Dante placed him in hell. His heir built the chapel as an act of expiation, called in the favorite artist of his time to paint it (1304–1306?) and had himself depicted in the Last Judgment, on bent knees, offering his chapel to the Virgin. These attempts at sanctity did not prevent him from being cast out of Padua, but must surely have propelled Giotto straight up into the forefront of the blessed.

The most famous of these panels of the life of the Virgin and Christ have been reproduced countless times, the artfully lined sections described and analyzed by art historians in numerous languages: the broad sweep of Judas' yellow cloak, the coarseness of his profile as it approaches the ascetic profile of Christ; the bitter pain of Joachim when the priest turns him, and his offering, from the temple; the weight and mass of Joachim's sleeping body contrasted to the alert wonder of the shepherds with him; the gentle joy of the Meeting at the Golden Gate, its subdued drama heightened by one hooded dark figure among the light, glad tones; the grave elegance of Mary's cortege; the woman weeping over the exsanguinated body of Christ and the chorus of agonized angels; the ineffably lovely Virgin and Angel of the Annunciation divided and linked by an arch. No color prints, no book of faithful reproductions can substitute for standing immersed in the aura of the small chapel. It is easy to pick out, if you have the experience (or the patience to trace it), the uncanny technical skill that melds space, movement, rhythm and emotion with the most economical palette and lines. It requires no technical search, though, to be subdued and overwhelmed as those around you are, connoisseurs with powerful opera glasses and much time, as well as rushed, uninformed tourists. Rarely will you be in so limited a space with so many people and hear so little sound.

There are artists who inspire wonder and awe, like Leonardo, and some an awed fear, like Michelangelo. Some lure one into a perfumed pleasure garden of grace and veiled opulence, like Botticelli, and others—many, and here nameless, not to tread on personal bias and sensibilities—who seduce with smooth, creamy trickery. One simply, purely, directly loves Giotto. Anyone who has seen his work knows the feeling: the quiet happiness, the unwillingness to leave, the need to return and return and return again. It leaves an indelible and cherished mark. And one is pleased to know that he was loved and appreciated in his lifetime, a great friend of Dante's and devotedly respected by the poet, and admired by Petrarch, who owned a Madonna by Giotto which he mentions in his will: "The ignorant do not comprehend its beauty, but the masters of the art wonder at it," and in a letter, "I have known two painters of greatness, not of mere prettiness, Giotto of Florence, whose reputation is immense among contemporary artists, and Simone of Siena."

There is a reasonable tendency to leave with the Giotto forms and colors still sweeping across one's mesmerized mind and eyes, to forget to look beyond the room of frescoes and thus neglect the Virgin and Child and two flanking figures on the altar. They are of the time and spirit of the frescoes and worthy company, the work of Giovanni Pisano, one of the giants of Italian sculpture.

From a triumph of art, one falls to tragedy at the nearby church of the Eremitani, bombed in 1944, and in the wreckage, sections of Andrea Mantegna frescoes. The church was rebuilt but still has an unused, empty look. The torn roof has been repaired in a careful repetition of its original thirteenth-century style, a play of opposing curves that meet above the alter to make a frame of wavy stone decorations that descend from the pink, white and ocher stripes of the walls. For some reason, a quintessence of the loss of the irreplaceable is expressed by an old battered clock on one wall and on another, a substitute whose utilitarian brightness was meant for the hallway of a modern school. Nevertheless, it is still, as it must have been, an awesome church.

Some of the work of the young Mantegna, who was a Paduan apprentice shortly before he was discovered and called to work in the church, is in hopeful restoration, some already restored and one panel intact only because it had been removed before the bombing. The chapel of Mantegna may still be closed off by a locked grill and you may peer at the murals like a caged prisoner, deriving only slits of view here and there, but enough to show the strength, the knowledge of, and passion for, classical detail, the largeness and impact of movement that mark his style.

After Giotto, Pisano and Mantegna, other art may appear to be a watery drink. Go instead, if it is still early in the day, to the market nestling below the regal old buildings of the city's medieval center. Having brushed and bumped your way through the sea of color and sounds, try the lower arcades of the Palazzo della Ragione (the Palace of Justice) to dawdle, if the crowd permits, before butcher shops and fish markets, one lit by lamps shaped like fish. Look at the varieties of sausage and the immense repertory of pastas, each named and its filling identified, at the foods prepared to take out and the flowers. The upper loggia of the palace is the place from which to get the *tutti* of the open market below. Pigeons squat and grumble on the supports of the white awnings not quite wide enough to contain in their shadows the spill of orange, red-orange, of greens that merely whisper green and greens of dark miniature forests, of long-handled pearls as spring onions, of myriad colors as silky reeds, as hairy beards, as bristling shrubs, of mushrooms like baroque plasterwork. Beyond the piles and heaps of clothing, cages of pigeons and canaries, billows of white chickens blinking out of low, circular baskets, and everywhere the lilt of flowers springing from metal buckets.

The vast frescoed hall of the Palazzo della Ragione is almost empty except for an enormous wooden horse, a copy of Donatello's horse of the Gattamelata statue (page 324) and, because of an easy leaping to conclusions, believed to be a work of the master. It was carved by someone else in the fifteenth century (the present head is a much later fixture) to serve as a carrousel horse, in all likelihood the biggest, most Renaissance carrousel in the world. The murals are a continuous amalgam of religious figures, signs of the zodiac, the activities of various "months" and savants of the church. There is some order here—an apostle usually acts as a division between the months and their symbols—but it doesn't matter much. Nor does the quality of the painting, although there are pleasing, amusing and bewildering bits in the diversity. The total effect is strange and interesting, as if these four hundred squares and oblongs of color and the curved wooden roof were a painted coffer for the lonely wooden horse strayed from his merry-go-round. (Watch for occasional art shows here.)

The outdoor market slips into side streets and minor piazze to spread its clothing and housewares in the adjoining Piazza dei Signori with *its* splendors of Renaissance loggia and Palace of the Captain. Irrepressible, the market then seeps through the columned arch that divides the building and supports a tower whose highly educated clock of the fifteenth century (the first of its type in Italy) is capable of indicating, along with the usual information, the passage of planets through the zodiac, the course of the sun, the waning and waxing of the moon. Having eluded the clock tower, the market now sits in the shade of a bower of trees, an attractive glade in which to rummage for inexpensive bags and shoes. The market and its piazze have finished their long diminuendo; it is quiet on these streets that close off the turbulence of market and central city to become another, a retiring small town.

After coffee or lunch at an eating and talking and billiards-playing café run by a hospitable woman and her son directly beyond the end of the market, turn into the via dell'Orologio. You will notice how very low these arcades are, a diminution of the arcades in Ferrara, those considerably reduced from the porticos in Bologna. They may seem a bit oppressive, though Palladio approved of them as comfortable and useful: "But if one wants to separate the place where people walk from that which serves for the passage of carts and beasts, I should like to see the streets so divided that on either side porticoes be built along which the citizens might pass under cover to do their shopping without being bothered by sun, rain or snow. Almost all the streets of Padua, that venerable city, noted for its University, are of this sort."

Passing a piece of old wall in which small apartments have snuggled, daring the barking dog—usually chained—who guards a semiconcealed frail loggia on thin, coltish columns, examining the closed doorways that probably served as entrances to ancient shops, one reaches the Duomo. The façade has its broad pigeon-ridden space, but offers no particular grandeur, since it is the barest of primitive church faces, standing like a solid barrier to obstruct the adjacent Romanesque drum of baptistry and the church dome and lantern. The Duomo took two centuries to build, supposedly on designs by Michelangelo. Not much was used of his intentions, but the interior has a pleasing serenity of proportions achieved by the full arches that support a light dome, the cool pilasters warmed by rich sconces and marbles. Serenity flees from the thirteenth-century baptistry, a subway crush of late-fourteenth-century frescoes infected by Giottoism. They repeat the life of Christ, add the life of John the Baptist and Old Testament events and the holocausts of the Apocalypse. The jammed, breathless gamut spirals to a climax in the dome as Christ Triumphant, circled by hundreds of identical heads within a ring of saints that flank a stiff, broad Virgin with a small head. Though it is fixed on Giotto, repeating compositional elements and symbols of characterization, the effect is of much older, naïve art, deeply admired by Padua's country cousins.

The via dei Soncin mingles with the street of Saint Martin as funnels of arcade from which darkly emerge the sounds of carpenters' saws and the clang of metal on metal of ironworkers. Among the low doors, occasionally dressed in pieces of surviving marble, there is one that indicates the "Israelite Center," very likely the core of a depleted ghetto. You will notice that the name of a Rabbi Viterbo appears on the panel of the house, another example of the fact that Italian-Jewish names were often those of places: Pacifici, Parigi, Fiorentino, etc. Skirt the university, the be-Gothicked house that claims Dante in an oblique way, the tomb of Antenor, the big, well-marked Questura and a glimmer of canal; go into the via Rudena. The crescendo toward the center and the decrescendo into shy streets leads to the via del Santo and an immediate, startlingly Eastern sight of bulbs and cones and slender campaniles. The Piazza broadens, edged by the white of stalls that sell religious souvenirs and large candles and, looking beyond stalls, pigeons, pilgrimage buses and tourist caravans, the equestrian statue of Gattamelata by Donatello. Just as San Giustiano, the earliest Duomo, was replaced in the ninth century by the present Duomo, so that church has been replaced as vital religious center by this ornate, Near Eastern complex, the church of the miraculous Saint Anthony of Padua.

Its atmosphere of unreality, of airy fantasy held to earth by complex embellishments, continues on behind the Romanesque façade, here not so much an impediment as a calming shore for the bounding tide of domes and turrets and the bewilderment of chapels (churches within a church) in the interior grandiosity. The most appealing of the chapels is that of San Felice, whose Gothic embroidery surrounds a stepped altar leading to a Frenchy Virgin and saints. (The frescoes that purportedly describe the life of Saint James cannot be reported on—neither execution nor incidents—since they were kept in darkness.) Saints, tombs, frescoes of several periods and nationalities and architectural vestiges of an earlier church fill the immensity. Ornate baldachins droop like Spanish moss. Parties of monks sweep out one area while services go on in another. The sides of confessional boxes trail dozens of contrite feet.

The crux of this matter and the magnet is the combination of the chapel of Saint Anthony's tomb and the large, luxuriant Chapel of the Reliquary that sits center stage. The former surrounds a green marble stone, surmounted by tall candelabra, which contains the coffin of the saint. On one slab of the green stone thousands of hands are laid in prayer, especially the hands of solemn, well-instructed children. On another side of the green box hang photos and crude paintings of persons saved by the saint and, at one corner, a pile of crutches, braces and several long-beaked student caps. From sharp reliefs of the sixteenth and eighteenth centuries one learns what the saint has done, and obviously still can do, and begins to understand why the praying groups bring their children here. Saint Anthony restores the foot of a man who had cut it off in remorse after having kicked his mother. (This should tame any recalcitrant child and put him on the path of momism-Mariolatry that makes and often imprisons Italians.) He causes a young baby to speak that he might tell the truth about his unjustly accused mother; he revives a drowned boy and a drowned girl. It becomes abundantly clear why Saint Anthony is a divine guardian of the young and a close ally of overprotective and adoring Italian mothers.

The gleaming Chapel of the Reliquary closes its golden doors, as the church covers some of its paintings and sculpture, during Easter week. At other times, the baroque chapel leads slow oozing crowds past cases of heart-shaped ex-votos to a triple set of windows that display stupendous jeweled containers which hold the seven-hundred-year-old tongue of the saint, bits of hair and cloak, his chin and, to fill out the miraculous gathering, splinters of the True Cross and thorns from Christ's crown—indispensable basics for any such proud collection. (How many heads could the thousands of thorns encircle, how tall and wide must the Cross have been to be able to shed a million pieces?)

The high altar is the work of Donatello, whose figures have his characteristic repose combined with the promise of imminent, dignified movement, and above, a masterful Crucifixion. (With the usual contempt of the seventeenth century for fifteenth-century art, unsatisfactory in its plain, open statements and lack of whorls and whirls, the altar was taken down. The sculptures, fortunately, were not destroyed as the rest was, and were put back in their original position in the last years of the nineteenth century.) If you are permitted to look more closely—not always easy—there is also a profoundly felt Deposition by Donatello, a panel of anguish and lamentation for the sinews and bones of a suffering death.

Walk around the piazza, to follow curves and bulges, to look at the faces of adjoining buildings and the eager pilgrims, to realize that this is the important pilgrim center of the city, with trattorie and bars and small hotels for the less sophisticated and less affluent visitor. Then return to spend some time with the Gattamelata, the powerful *condottiere;* an indomitable conqueror astride a magnificent warrior steed. Beside its own immortal strengths, intrinsic to the subject and Donatello's art, it speaks tellingly of the Renaissance, of its devotion to classical sculpture, as evidenced by the fact that the Gattamelata echoes the bronze Marcus Aurelius who rides the Campidoglio in Rome. Yet it is a careful portrait, expressing a specific personality, hardly idealized, with a large, flattened nose and a severe tight mouth. (Weathering has done a strange thing to the invincible face; it has whitened two furrows, like tears.)

There are several repositories of art adjoining the Basilica, in various stages of rearrangements: the Oratorio of San Giorgio, the Scuola di Sant'Antonio, frescoed by the young Titian, and the Museo Civico. Whether you visit these depends as always on the appetite—eager or sated—for more church art, on what you have already seen, and what you expect to see in the great collections of the bigger cities. Whether or not, continue down Luca Belludi street, turning back occasionally to the church ensemble that balloons out of the end of the street and on to the oval Prato della Valle, an eighteenth-century, and properly formal, park with little bridges that vault a canal and dozens of statues of worthies related to the university. The precise shape and the cold, learned white men erase any memory of this rather remote, passive area as the raffish fairground of the Middle Ages that had as ancestor a gaudy center of the Roman city.

At the far end of the big piazza sits the venerable Basilica of Santa Giustina, on the site of the earliest church in Padua, built in the sixth century. Rather like Saint Anthony's church in its clustering of domes on various levels behind an unfinished, flat façade, it lacks the appeal of the other building—the bubbling of domes not quite so lively, the tall façade too restraining, the fantasy dulled. The interior is as broad and high as you would expect it to be, vaulting over a good many baroque tombs, and in the apse a heavy, thickly carved choir attributed to a French master of the sixteenth century strongly influenced by the sharp, agitated virtuosities of the Germans. An adjacent freshness of Veronese colors on an exuberant spread of space makes the welcome contrast. Near the right of the altar, a door leads to the core of the Basilica, the sixth-century chapel, a completely restored, appealing and gentle place that encloses the tomb of the sainted founder, an inscription that verifies the founding of the chapel and a few ancient architectural elements.

Round back on the park for a meeting with statues of Giotto and Dante against a background that is a serious mistake of the late nineteenth century, a remotely Gothic loggia, ponderous and very red, accompanied by several other striving buildings in a mess of styles and burbling of ambitious bad taste, such as—to choose one—the demented villa near the street of Luca Belludi. Much better is the pharmacy one hopes you will meet approaching the via Umberto I, a glowing example of turn-of-the-century ironwork, wood-embraced glass and florid lettering. Most of the milky lamps must be gone, but stretches of painting that spread out to the street vaults should still be visible, enthusiastic and inept. The street arcades slip lower and lower to enclose repair shops and garages that appear as tubes connecting with other streets in the huddled, frightened pattern of the Middle Ages. Where the via Umberto I becomes the via Roma, the trees still fly out of walled gardens, and then, nearing the center, trees and gardens hide to leave the stage for shops; one of them, on the corner of the via Roma with the via Marsala, a bulging, glistening Eden for gourmets and gluttons. Off the via Roma, on the via dei Servi, there is the church of Santa Maria dei Servi, not too unlike other churches except that it owns a baroque altar which may be the most elaborate outside of Saint Peter's: bronzes imbedded in a storm of stone, marble trailing through frenzies of plaster, fronds like jungle plants growing up and up, swelling as they grow to yield fruits as big as heads.

The front entrance is closed except on state occasions, but one can see from behind the gates the solid rows of shields of university rectors from many countries and centuries. The Bo, so-called in honor of the former inhabitant of the site, an inn whose sign was the ox (*bue*), was founded in 1222 by a few scholars and their followers from Bologna, the first Italian university. It may have been an act of dissidence, one radical master leading his scholastic entourage to establish a new seat of learning, as happened not infrequently in medieval schools. Or they may have been lured with various benefits by a prosperous community that felt itself worthy of a university, as Siena lured teachers and students from Padua and Bologna in her time. When the sixteenth-century courtyard is closed off by the curlicued iron gates, walk around the corner to the newer court decorated in the thirties with superheroic statues and plaques that remember Mussolini,

Duce, and Vittorio Emanuele, Re. A broad stairwell decorated with murals in the Mexican manner (a just borrowing since *they* learned fresco art from the Italians) rises to an upper floor brightly painted with panels of university caps, a tree of famous scholars and churchmen, books and globes interlaced with ribbons of legend, views of the city and maps in the old "mappamondo" style. A gentleman at a desk in a gold-buttoned, long tail-coated uniform rises to greet you and asks you to wait for his colleague, who soon arrives, similarly dressed, to take you through several rooms. The progress into rooms with fine old globes and not so fine, or old portraits of professors, leads to the large Aula Magna, a sixteenth-century hall arranged for lectures, and climbing up the walls into the curves of the elaborate ceiling, hundreds of crests, one reputedly that of Copernicus—but you haven't brought your glasses nor does the politely brisk attendant have the time for verification. A small room was the study hall, an ancient one to judge from the ceiling, of forty foreign students, and on the wall are portraits of foreign notables who attended the university. One is not too surprised to find Harvey, a student of Galileo's, who traced the circulation of blood, a little more surprised to see the Walsingham, who was secretary of state to Elizabeth I of England, and quite astonished to find Oliver Goldsmith, so very English, so far from home. The next stop is at the condensed, steep anatomy theater, the oldest in Europe (1544), concentric circles of wooden rail that leave space only for the slenderest of bodies on the smallest of feet. A narrow spiral staircase with low openings at intervals allowed for entrance at several levels. At the narrowest end of the wooden funnel stands the anatomy table. There was usually a case under the table into which the corpse was swiftly dropped and a model put in its place if the authorities became nosy. After the illicit corpse had been fully studied, it was cut up (a process graphically, juicily described by the gentleman in the dignified tail coat and gleaming spectacles) and burned in a primitive crematory that still stands outside the hall. Somewhere in the visit, he points out a structure of rough wooden stairs leading to a chair which was the *cattedra,* the seat of a professor; this one happened to be Galileo's. The gentleman gives you a little time to stare at it, to let your hair stand on end and then flatten to normal, and soon whisks you into another hall, where oral examinations for the degree in medicine are held—and have been for a long time.

As the visit seems to be coming to an end, you begin to wonder how one tips so knowledgeable and noble a functionary, very near a host. He solves it by offering two sets of postcards. When you ask how much they cost he says, "Whatever it is worth to you," so you add 1,000 lire to the sum you had been prepared to beg him to take.

A few paces away, a neoclassic portico, a screen of half-columns and the shadow of a tower announce the town's famous Caffè Pedrocchi, built in the early nineteenth century by a coffee dealer whose descendants, some sixty years later, turned it over to the city. In these enormous rooms, at one time without doors for easy access and symbolic of hospitality, intellectuals of the town and students used to gather; an uprising against Austrian rule, led by a student movement, exploded here. Lately it has had a lady attendant whose domain is the phone and toilet, as in the great cafés of Paris; its prices seem to have outgrown the pockets of students and intellectuals, and the café appears too vast and empty. However, there may still be in the maze cheaper and chummier sections, and the classic-friezed terrace is a good place for watching Paduans tear through their day when you have finished tearing through yours.

Notes

HOTELS. The leading first-category hotels are Le Padovanelle and the Plaza (high). The Europa, on the Largo Europa, is moderate, quite satisfactory and, on its street side, intensely noisy. The Grande Italia, somewhat older, is on the Corso del Popolo not far from the station; moderate. There are a number of small hotels which the Ente per Turismo Riviera Mugnai would be glad to tell you about. One seemingly delightful *albergo,* recently redone, on a minute piazza off the via San Martino, is the second-category Majestic Toscanelli, out of the hub bustle and yet central; high moderate. The Igea, a bit out on the via Ospedale (near a street called Fallopia), is sometimes careless, but good-natured and inexpensive.

RESTAURANTS.   The favorites are the Isola di Caprera, behind the Pedrocchi café, and the Dotto, on the corner of the vias dei Soncin and Squarcione. For the rest, there are any number of good large and small restaurants, far removed in quality and décor from what is usually called "provincial," which Padua is not. And try the market for sandwich stalls; hearty and fresh.

Padua is a good place to buy leathers—bags, suits and coats— well made and for the quality cheaper and in better supply than elsewhere. Also, the via dei Soncin might prove to be a fruitful source of antique jewelry.

Don't drive in Padua; most of the streets are one-way; the truly conspicuous signs direct out of the city. It is much easier to find one's way to Bologna or Venice than to the Duomo. Walk or take an occasional taxi or bus.

To Venice by Boat

One upon a time there was a beautiful canal barge glittering with colorful ornaments, resounding with laughter and the clink of glasses. It glided between Venice and Padua to deliver passengers to the luxurious (a few Palladian) villas whose assured façades were reflected in the quiet waters. A recent gesture, tourist-luring and romantic, has put into service a modern *Burchiello* for lacing the cities together and glimpses of the façades.

The ride offers a number of pleasures: group tripping with Italians, some of them from as far away as Caltanisetta in Sicily, a pretty girl guide who speaks good, clear Italian and a convivial day, all for about $20–$25, and that includes the price of a large, indigenous lunch. (Theoretically the trip can be made from May to September, theoretically a number of times a week, but in practicality, it usually plies the slow water only on Saturdays, from Venice, and Sundays from Padua. Check with the Ente Provinciale of either city for details.) The voyage has one marred virtue, it proves once more that you can't go home again. Although the boat is new and comfortable and fitted with a bar for drinks and coffee, it is no glistening Venetian courtesan. Although your fellow passengers are an intelligent, well-informed and amiable lot, they haven't the saturnine romantic looks of Byron or the wit of Goldoni. The saddest loss of all: many of the villas are in mournful decay behind an auto that smears a dark nervous band on their Niobe façades. It is, though, a pleasant way to expand a twenty-minute train ride into a long, dreamy day.

For Women

—particularly those old enough to have been bitten by a film called Summertime, *wherein Katharine Hepburn lived the apogee of her flat-chested, American life*

INTOXICATED BY the mists of Venetian canals, her American guardedness lying at her feet like discarded robes, our heroine was ready for Italian Love. It came as a married and undivorceable gentleman of soft-spoken, persuasive charm whose smooth energy was endless; he minded the store, his family, his American love and could, as well, welcome in the dawn on San Marco's piazza. The *Summertime* mirage is still pursued—now timidly, now boldly—by a good number of women. Emphases and pace differ, of course, depending on provenance; the sexually bored Scandinavian may head for southern Italy, where the approach is direct and unequivocal; no prose, no misunderstandings, total Lib. American women, those of a certain age, prefer the slower unguents: the lingering eyes, the world-well-lost-for-love stance and beautifully absurd, unexpected gestures, when the exigencies of job, bambini and card playing permit.

The opening moves are easy. All that is required is a small flag of receptivity, a look that answers a look, a smile that returns a smile. Whether you play the game or stay a spectator, you will find the field immense and variegated and the game capable of diverse moods from ridiculous to mildly funny, from lyrical to bewitching and even—this is rare—menacing. Basic equipment includes, besides nature's gifts, an understanding of a few profound male convictions and how they operate in Italy. One assumes that foreign ladies, English and Americans particularly, because they are tremulous, neurotic bags of bone reduced by sexual malnutrition, find all Italians irresistible. Gentlemen who agree with this premise are often to be found in hotels during *festa* times when numerous visitors, to-ing and fro-ing at odd times, create a nice smörgåsbord. Don Giovanni prowls the hallways, listening to accents and watching the sway of buttocks. He selects a recipient for his gifts and tracks her down to her door. He knocks and keeps knocking, asking for one small moment, pliss. If you've glanced at his wares and found them resistible, lock the door and don't answer. In time he will tire of your silly intransigence and go on to offer his golden moments at another door.

Conviction two: if she wanders the streets alone at night she is offering or selling; consequently, many car doors open to invite her in. Sometimes, she is invited to get the hell off the street, and *subito*, by the pros whose beat she has invaded. The eventful and rarely dangerous night walk, trailed by panting autos, can be quite a sporting event. Try, for instance, a main street in any city, the larger the city the better, and best in Florence and Rome at about 11:00 P.M. The fun is merrier should it be raining; only a *zoccola* or a *troia* (you havè just added two extremely base words to your basic Italian) would be out this late in such weather. In small cars, big cars, all polished, one man, two men, three men ride in posses, peering through the slow arcs pulled by the windshield wipers. They spot the quarry, wipers hesitate, hang; the damp purring of tires squeaks to a stop, the door opens. An invitation is voiced as "Don't you want a lift, out of the rain?" with an innocent, host's smile, or "Can I take you home?" with a smile that is a middle-aged, slant-eyed memory of Rudolph Valentino. Occasionally it is a flat "Come on in" using the familiar *tu*. It can be, if your mood is for it, a stimulating half hour's entertainment that encompasses every car on your side of the street, several dozen men in a broad range of ages and looks, a grab bag of becks and nods and leers and never discouragement. Your refusal doesn't send them home to wife, mother and kiddies (who have all decided to agree that he is playing cards). If you won't, the next one will.

Since nothing in Italy is useless, and the male mind always alert for adventure, an open umbrella—yours—might serve as first trysting place. Suddenly a head forces its way into the shelter, complaining winsomely through its shining teeth that its newly pressed suit is being ruined, offers to carry the umbrella, an extraordinary flourish of gallantry, and you're off. "Didn't we meet in Paris?" in vaudeville English, though hackneyed, is still a useful ploy for a woman alone in a sidewalk café. The flattery implied wafts both parties into clouds of international glamour, although his natural horizons stretch from Naples to Rome and hers, normally, from Newark to New York. Already showing symptoms of the *Summertime* syndrome, she sees herself in a Paris salon, speaking exquisite French in a company of enameled gentlemen and jewel-studded odalisques. (Her references are usually old-fashioned literary, leaning heavily on Proust.) While she floats toward Baron Charlus, her new acquaintance eases himself into a chair and *they're* off.

A railroad station is also fertile ground. While you are looking for a cab or bus, showing the usual uncertainties of a stranger, a man appears. Are you looking for a hotel room? He offers to take you to a good inexpensive *albergo*, centrally located, clean and respectably run by his good friends. Be prepared, if you accept his company and advice, to share the bed with him and if he is hard up, as he is likely to be, some of your lire.

Naples seems to play its game with shocking candor; anywhere on the street, "Wanna guy, lady?" What the men are trying to say, however, is "Wanna guide, lady?" In less worldly parts of the south there is no game but the hunt. An unknown woman alone, or two driving a car, are out for sport, surely; especially promising if one wears her hair long and loose, still a prostitute's

style in some places. And more especially if one of the women
smokes cigarettes. That unleashes the pack. They follow relent-
lessly, on foot, on motorbikes and cars. They wait at the entrances of museums and restaurants and give chase—passing,
permitting themselves to be passed—in nerve-racking, drunken
rhythms until they force your car to the edge of the road, all in
the serious endeavor to persuade you to go out with them that
night. As you turn up the windows and bolt the doors, the
thought crosses your mind, where is "out" in this hamlet? The
cinema that features a western with John Wayne, young? The
"dancing," to be shown in triumph, Cleopatra with the local
Caesar, to the girls in their homemade, timid dresses? An abandoned stone farmhouse for love among rustling bats and scurry-
ing mice? Worse still, the narrow back of their car? Each couple
to take its turn while the other stands patiently behind the car?

Let us assume that you haven't turned up the windows, you've
let the tendrils of attraction creep in and coil about you. What
then? The quick mount, sometimes, a practice that derives its
satisfactions from how many rather than how well. Several paths
of possibility open thereafter. Don Giovanni never shows again.
Or he does return and if he is young, full of troubles that may all
be soluble with a little cash. His new transistor fell and is irrepa-
rably smashed. If he had the money to repair his brother's car, he
could go to Bari, where someone promised him a good job. He
can't go to his sister's wedding in his worn old suit. If the man is
older, the woman sometimes pays in bewildered blank hours
while, in addition to other pressing obligations, he must attend
his wife's sister's boy's First Communion and tomorrow he must
drive his mother to a miracle Virgin in a distant town. Sunday
the whole family is driving into the country for a picnic. Monday? His son returns from the university. And so he goes. And so
does she, unless we are treating of the anachronism (who should
never be loosed on a Latin country) still capable of wailing,
"How come he do me like he do do do?" while she hangs on the
poisoned cord of a silent phone.

It isn't necessary to pay, always, and there are profits other
than sex. A woman may be told repeatedly, with fine Italian tact,
that young girls are dull little sprigs of grass; it takes care and

time to make the perfect, full rose. For a woman whose native society considers five pounds of avoirdupois the equivalent of five pounds of leprosy, it is a warm boon to hear a man say that he likes a *buona forchetta,* a joyous eater, as he keeps stuffing her the same way his Saracenic ancestors stuffed their women.

Before leaving the subject with much remaining to be said (but this is hardly a manual) several unsung heroes should be lauded, the unconquerable who struggle against incredible odds for a bit of love. There is a superman in Lucca who slows his tired, uncertain bike to stare at a woman, to examine carefully, to make purring noises. At the point where he must dismount or fall off, he speeds up, dashes around the block, returns, slows, slower, slower, inviting, burbling, cooing like a turtle dove. And around the block again, to catch up with his doe on a farther stretch of street for the repeat performance. He cannot possibly expect to carry a woman off on his two-wheeled, one-seated chariot; he looks too poor to afford the opening act of a proffered apértif and no romance was ever launched on a bottle of mineral water. Undaunted, invincible, he keeps on trying, warbling and wobbling.

An old man with a too-short pegleg haunts the station of Vicenza, a fair walk from the center of town. He picks his lady love from among the descending *turiste* and follows her from station to Palladian palace after palace. Tap, drag; tap, drag; tap, drag; from palace to museum and on to the Olympic theater, whose admission price shuts him out while his Beatrice, his Laura, takes a good, long time over the details of scenery and classic gods. He waits, ready to tap-drag up the hill, always keeping the same distance, to the villas at the top of town. Amused, annoyed, pitying, impatient, his lady returns to town, and, chancing on a funeral cortege about to enter a church, hides in the ranks of the mourners and waits out the service. Futile effort. There it is, cap, leer and wooden peg, waiting. Nothing to do but return to the station and bury one's head in a magazine at the bar until the train makes its rescue.

Then there are the old, old men, who, because their sight is failing, come up close, very close, to stare and drool. You can dismiss them with *vecchio sciocco* (old fool) but that would be vandalism; they are about the last shreds of romanticism, proof that hope still springs eternal. Proof, too, that you never need feel alone in Italy. Ten feet away, around the corner, or observing your reflection in a shopwindow, someone is watching you, if only one of the half-blind, doddering optimists.

So much for *amore.* How about the renowned male *cortesia italiana?* It doesn't exist except as verbiage. Two gentlemen may be all compliments and flirtatious roulades as they stand with two foreign ladies in the anteroom of a small auditorium, but if seats are not reserved they will rush into the hall as soon as the doors are open to sit in the last available chairs while the ladies stand.

A man in a first-class train will compliment a foreign woman extravagantly on her insipid Italian, will look deeply and lovingly at every part of her dress and tear it to shreds with his eyes; advise her about restaurants and hotels, search his *orario* for her train connections. The stop arrives and the time for separation from one's new loving friend, the time also for lifting the heavy valises from the rack above and pushing them out of the window to a porter if there is one close by, or dragging them through the aisle and down the narrow, perilous train steps. If friend is staying his face is lost in the magazine which interested him not at all a half hour ago. If he is leaving, he sits out your struggle and, at the last moment, swings his briefcase down and walks briskly by, without a glance, as you crawl down the platform. His name is Legion. Mrs. Legion, if she is traveling with him, will suggest he help you, the gesture of a member of the no-card, no-fee, universal women's union. The union is strong in Italy. Nevertheless, travel light.

5

SOUTHERN ADRIATIC COAST FROM ROME OR NAPLES

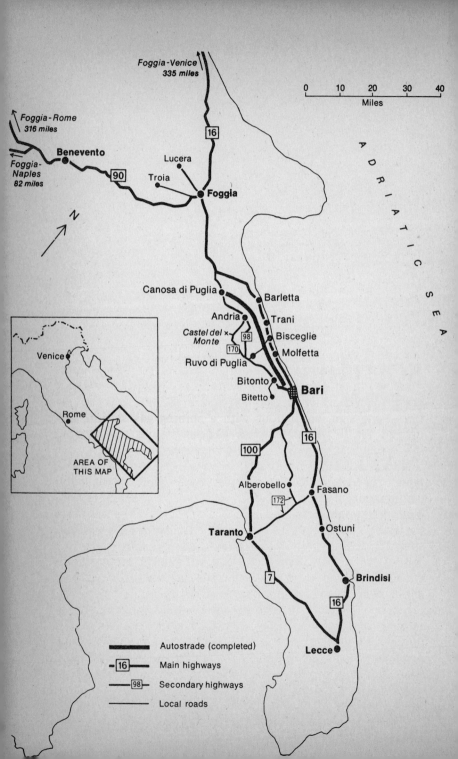

O N THE BROAD highway that parallels the Adriatic coast for a way, then opens approaches to towns with tiled Moorish domes and evocative names—Molfetta, Barletta, Bitonto, Bitetto—one sign, contiguous with a shining gas station, announces the "Dolmen of Bisceglie." A gas attendant escorts the mad foreigners who insist on seeing it over a path of white stones to a locked fence, piles up rocks as stepping stones, lends assistance to superannuated fence climbers and waves them along the continuation of the rough white path. The May sky is Guardi blue with tumbling clouds driven by a wind that twirls and turns the leaves of the olive trees into a soft, shimmering cloth of paled silver. Swift, tiny green lizards streak across the white stones like spills of mercury to disappear silently, without stirring one small stone. The song of a solitary bird melts into the silvery rustling and rises again, to stop with the nearing sound of feet crackling the stones. The olive orchard is endless: crippled trunks hobble in every direction and though the earth under them is newly turned and smells freshly of the morning's rain and cut wild herbs, there is no sign of the tenders of the gnarled trees. It is a short stumbling and sliding on the sharp stones, though it seems endless in the hypnotic rustling and the noiseless darting of liz-ards, and there it stands, the dolmen, a large rock worked to uniform flatness supported by similar flat rocks carefully placed around a shallow ditch. A grave? A ceremonial cave? What and who constituted the society that used it and other local dolmens? One stands wrapped in clouds of time and silence, trying to pierce them, to populate the cave with a priest, a shaman, a holy fire and awed communicants, and almost succeeds when the horns of a party of cars demanding gas rip the frail tissue of imagination.

There are odd towns here, with the slovenliness, but not the warmth, of the south and towns like well-tended hearths. One town crowds its sea front with baby carriages, large odalisque ladies oozing softly, passing men ogling avidly, children in fresh shirts running before and behind their calm round mothers like tugs bustling about a transatlantic liner. A few yards beyond the busy *passeggiata,* in the dimming evening light, a dog ferrets out a rat burrowing in the stones of a neglected strip of waterfront and several little boys slide out of the cracks of a tall, blank casbah wall that stares across the sea to watch the fun. Another town sports clusters of toylike houses, which are possibly—and possibly not—of prehistoric design. Yet another prides itself on the stateliness and lustrous articles in its shops (jewelry, fine leathers, clothing from Milan and Florence), on its broad squares and developed taste, and is devoted to obese, greedy fantasies of baroque palaces and churches.

Every town is frantically automobile-plagued, no car daunted by the webs of souk alleys inherited from the Levant. The con-tentedly unemployed young men stroll through the streets bent with the weight of large earrings of transistors. Sputtering motor-cycles rip through the heavy-laden air that may crack, they say hopefully, to relieve the drought. Older citizens ask if one has come from New York on a train; it must be a long ride, they add sympathetically. And, as if they were still in the country with great fields of wheat and olives to shout across, they greet each other with a coarse, roaring "Ho!" though they actually may be as close as blades of grass. They address strangers in the familiar terms of *tu* and *voi*, as they did in the village where all confrontations were with relatives, close friends and close enemies. The polite forms of *Lei* and *Loro* are sequestered in banks, government offices and a few large shops.

This and much more is Puglia, a repository of Neapolitan wash in the streets, of Sicilian *cavalleria*, of Saracenic houses, of ports abandoned and ports crowded with passenger ships and freighters. It is a place of endless wheat fields and gray-green seas of olives, of Romanesque cathedrals with Norman Gothic curves and touched with Moorish lace. There are streets made of carpets of dirt pressed down by automobile tires and streets of stone scrubbed and polished to satin by age and local pride; there are poor towns that howl and poor towns that live in silent *amour-propre*, tending their boxes of flowers and splashing fresh whitewash on crumbling walls. People look like Sicilians, like Arabs, like Greeks, like the Irish. They are red-haired, blond, dark; blue-eyed, gray-eyed, or cherry black; sturdy, abundant and vari-tinted broods left by the Greeks, whose "Magna Grecia" this country was, and by Saracens, by the Normans and the Swabians, and the hordes of Crusaders who came and left through the Adriatic ports to do battle in the Holy Land.

Like most regions of Italy, Puglia has a complex, exotic history, possibly more than others. First, the Greeks, then the Romans; the void they left was filled by Byzantines (Greeks, mainly) in constant battle with the Arabs who controlled Sicily. A number of legends tell about Norman pilgrims on their way to the Holy Land stopped by a prince or an abbot who asked them to help fight off the pagans. The truth of the matter probably rests in the surge of conquest, shortly after the death of Charlemagne, that fired the Scandinavians (Norsemen, thus Norman) who conquered northern France and, having established their fame as warriors, were invited by popes and princes to join *their* battles. By the eleventh century, the Normans held many fiefs and controlled vast areas of southern Italy and it was the Norman de Hautevilles who became the kings of Sicily, a title claimed in the early thirteenth century by Frederick II, the grandson of a Norman king and of the Swabian Emperor and the shining sun of his unfortunate country, who so loved Puglia that he said, "Jehovah would not have sung the praises of the Promised Land so much had he known our country." A short time later the Anjous took over, but not so addicted to Apulia as the Swabians were, they moved their capital to Naples, and the abandoned region sank into poverty-stricken listlessness. The fields died and the many ports fell under the control of the maritime powers to the north, Venice and Genoa. In the fifteenth century, the house of Aragon ruled. Attempts at conquest by the Saracens and pillage and siege in the war between the French and Spanish for control of the kingdom further depleted the area. During the two centuries of Spanish rule (1503–1707) there was rigid discipline but little economic improvement; the fields again returned to grass, the coastal strips became malarial, the ports were closed. Then, insurrections, suppressions and, finally, the unification of Italy.

Although it seems remote, even to Italians, who tell you they've always wanted to go but somehow never quite got there, Puglia is not difficult to reach. Boats for Jugoslavia and Greece leave from its ports, planes serve the region, and a meshwork of good roads and superhighways make Foggia, a provincial capital and a major gateway to the area, a shortish drive from Naples and a long half day from Rome.

As the signs begin to announce Foggia, the green and yellow and red tapestries of field flatten to an immense plain of wheat and olives. This is the Tavoliere, one of the richest agricultural areas in Italy, cultivated from prehistoric times. (As proof, scholars point to several hundred neolithic villages, detected but not yet unearthed.) Foggia, like all these towns of frenetic refurbishing, startles with a welcome of slabs of instant housing and modern churches so replete with southern aspects of "fantasia Italiana" that they often resemble the wrappings of ice-cream confections, blue fluted brims on cones splashed with *gelati* colors a favorite. The city then unfolds its large avenues, the *centro* of usable hotels, cafés, shopping and the restless molecular movement that invades most Italian cities at certain times, in certain streets. Anyone who has tried to walk in Rome during the prelunch and predinner window-shopping-and-people-appraising *passeggiata* knows the Latin intimacies of these hours: the jostling, the bump of a child's head, the thump of a broad hip, the patient waiting on a narrow sidewalk as a gathering of friends who parted only two hours before fills the space and air with lusty greetings and broad vigorous gestures, the sometime necessity for moving with graceless ruthlessness through this twice-a-day carnival crowd. For the towns of Puglia add an even more leisured southernness, bigger voices, greater pride in the new car shined up for the *passeggiata,* a large population of men of all ages who seem to spend their lives as immobile appliqués on backgrounds of sunlit walls, more and bigger outdoor cafés from which to survey the crowd and roar witticisms at passing friends; in other words, denser, noisier, warmer than the displays of best suit and fine shirt in Rome and certainly a world apart from the decorous, cool progress of the Sienese.

Once settled in Foggia, thread your way to the highway (or take a bus or train; there is constantly improving public transport), on which you have seen signs pointing to Troia and Lucera, each a few miles away. Let us choose to begin with Troia, whose past and present might serve as prototype for a number of these small Pugliese towns: taken by Hannibal after the battle at nearby Cannae, retaken by the Roman forces, lost in desuetude for some centuries, rebuilt as a Byzantine fortress on the Roman ruins, taken after a long siege by the Emperor Henry II. The roving Normans who had conquered much of Sicily (then a designation for southern Italy as well as the island) took over and then were fought off, and for a while the Pugliese had their time of ascendancy. Through these vicissitudes and reconstructions, the city became an important government and ecclesiastical center—almost synonymous terms in early medieval Italy—and a place of splendor until Frederick II destroyed it in 1229.

Now, surrounded by poppy-strewn wheat, olives and umbrella pines, it presents a poor thin face and back-country manners. Its men, as usual, seem to have little to do but stand in quiet groups on the main street; the younger men strut and call to the girls; the little boys, consumed with uninformed curiosity, stare closely at visitors—nose to nose—touching, following noisily, pummeling each other and hooting their uneasy combination of excited interest and xenophobic disdain. The curiosity is soon exhausted and they regroup for a favorite game of bouncing a large, hard ball off the buttocks and back of a boy bent against a wall. A ramble through the narrow alleys leads to wide views of the plain, then back to an encounter with several long-haired goats being urged into a doorway, to paths bordered by plump black-clad ladies on straight-backed chairs, gossiping and shelling peas, and then to the exquisite cathedral, one of the few remnants of the glory that was Troia and a quintessence of the local style, Romanesque judiciously tinted with the Saracenic, the Byzantine, and suggestions of the cathedrals in northern Italy.

Troia's cathedral now stands as the early-twelfth-century culmination of several expansions and alterations of older churches. Here there is no Gothic thrust of heights, no ambitious soaring of spires to wipe out the sweet approachability of the Romanesque. The low, wedded-to-earth modesty is content to keep all its elements in easy view, as if to compliment the craftsmen who adorned it with a constant audience, to keep its symbols always in instructive view. The eye is instantly enchanted by Troia's famous rose window, a fragile stone flower whose petals each have a different pierced pattern, reminiscent of harem windows or, if you prefer, Byzantine ivory work. Above, a wide ledge holds a wealth of ornaments and acrobatic animals and tastefully, sparsely spread along the façade, the ever-present symbols of bull, lion, eagle and angel that proclaim the Evangelists Luke, Mark, Matthew and John. The lower section is a mellow set of rounded tall arches, the tallest embracing an extraordinary set of bronze doors of the early twelfth century, whose biblical incidents and holy figures are accompanied by chimeras from the Near East—large staring gorgon-lion heads mouthing heavy rings, two winged griffon-snakes richly coiled across sections of bronze, their fierce teeth closed on heavy door pulls. The interior is simple, almost severe and, other than the treasures of precious metals, of ivory and ancient documents in the sacristy, holds little except a pulpit of the second half of the twelfth century, a classic of its period, which dictated an open stone box held by leafy columns, an eagle supporting the stone lectern and, around the box, bands of abstract designs and the shapes of fruits and flowers. Troia's pulpit enhances the convention in one rectangle of pattern that encloses a curious and remarkably sculptured panel of animals interlaced in a design of chewing on each other.

Weaving your way through the long-haired black goats, out again for their *passeggiata,* go on to Lucera, a short distance to the north. The city's historical background resembles that of its neighbors except for one anomaly. After its time as a Byzantine fortress ultimately (about 1070) taken by the Normans, it became in the thirteenth century a castle-fortress-court site of Frederick II. Like the Normans before him and rulers after, he was constantly menaced by Muslim invasions and the growing strength of Muslim strongholds already established in Sicily. Frederick pursued them to their lairs, conquered them and, together with Arabic pirates captured off the coast of north Africa, marched them off to Lucera. The records say that the combined population was about 15,000, settled in agricultural and crafts communities. A good number helped build the fortifications, some plowed and reaped, some made the armor and ornaments, others were house servants. A few experts in these matters took care of the Lucera branch of Frederick's harem and connoisseurs in other fields helped augment his collection of classical antiquities. A sizable body of Saracens formed his army; the troops he used, paradoxically, to fight off the heathen Saracens in the Holy Land when finally, reluctant and excommunicated, he launched a Crusade the Pope insisted on.

The ruins of his fortress sit inside the ruins of a castle of the Angevins, who succeeded the fallen line of Swabian Hohenstaufens. It is a large, walled area, standing on a promontory that looks down on the plain whose smooth green and gold are dotted with a few stone farmhouses and the giant tooth marks of local quarries. A caretaker guides one through an immense inner field of wildflowers—poppies, white stars of Jerusalem, lavender, thistle, buttercups and the gold of strayed wheat—that spring around blocks of Roman marble and sections of classic pillar and carpet the floors and pieces of wall fallen from the Angevin fortress. Off to one side, there are traces of foundation and a stretch of low wall left of Frederick's building.

The guardian shows one the great cisterns of both periods, the systems of aqueducts and the mouths of subterranean tunnels, which afforded escape in case of siege. In one corner, along with the Roman marble, there is a mound of immense, crudely rounded catapult stones that once flew over these walls, and in one nook of what is left of the Swabian castle, a section of room with a vaulted ceiling. Nothing else remains but the indomitable walls with their round and square turrets pierced by the narrowest of arrow slits, standing among the wildflowers.

The town of Lucera is a self-respecting one of good, well-polished door knockers and lace curtains. The usual frieze of old men in dark suits and hats, walking sticks hung on their kitchen chairs, occupies the street wall facing the cathedral; the usual coveys of youth wait for an event, any event—a flat tire on a foreign car, a request for a hotel or restaurant or simply directions—any inexpensive diversion. Neither the old men nor the youths nor the hard-working women nor the modest, wary girls look particularly Moorish, as one might expect. Many of them are quite fair, a result of the infusion of French blood imported to replace the Saracenic blood spilled in a general massacre after Frederick's death, when the Arabs refused to be converted to Christianity.

The Duomo is large, not as appealing as many Pugliese churches, but nevertheless an interesting example of the Romanesque yielding to the Gothic of the early fourteenth century, the time of the Angevins, and crammed full of many dark, large confessional boxes that prove Lucera to be either very sinful or frightened.

The town has a Roman theater, but Italy is as full of them as it is of triumphal arches, and whether to look at it or not becomes a personal choice; they are symptoms of an extremely important historical fact but not, after you have seen six or seven, in themselves particularly rewarding. The Museo Civico Fiorelli is another matter, a small, attractive and not much frequented place (the guest book shows gaps of five or six days between visitors) situated on the upper floor of a villa, which was apparently kept up to date with changing styles through the addition of art-nouveau windows and there gave up. The Museo Civico is what a regional museum should be—limited in the number of objects, though not necessarily in scope, an undemanding showcase of what the area has yielded of its past.

The courtyard takes one to a headless colossus thought to be the Emperor Domitian, but who knows? Roman Emperors liked to be translated into colossi with perfectly formed, strong muscles, and the headlessness makes an ideal rather than a portrait. Near the gigantic him there is a Roman copy of a Praxiteles Venus with an odd sullen mouth, and because the notion of being alone is chilling to Mediterraneans, her lone nakedness has been lent a putto and a dolphin. The collection on the upper floor is a pleasing, modest exemplar of what you will find in many museums. The walls and floors display stretches of Roman mosaic and, among the Roman inscriptions, one in Arabic. The Greeks show their skill in the swirling drapes of small female figures caught in a dance step or turn, clearly echoes of Tanagra. There is loving workmanship, and some high art, in the little heads of babies, children and youths, and precisely made hands and feet and genitals, very probably ex-votos. A charming young boy sits on an ox, or a ram, or a pig, but an unaccompanied ox is the best of the animal collection.

Another section is devoted to vases in the Greek style, of which there must be several million extant. They were made in great numbers in the home country and in the Greek cities of Magna Grecia by Greek craftsmen and the indigenous potters they taught, and later for the Romans by Greek guests or slaves and local artisans familiar with the style and techniques. Consequently, no Italian museum that deals with antiquity lacks rooms full of Greek vases, foreign and homemade, not each of them a "still unravished bride of quietness" and yet an extraordinary number remarkably designed and executed. In some sense more interesting than the vases, though certainly not as artful, are the primitive ceramics, much like the early pottery of Mexico or the Orient, suggesting that every civilization took the same fumbling steps in the evolution of a distinct style. After a look at a number of stone heads, some of them badly chipped, yet fine works, one enters a room that holds still a few other strands of the Puglia mixture, an ancient flat wooden Virgin as dour and darkly magical as Byzantine icons often are and a staring negroid head that echoes something of the large-eyed Fayumic funerary paintings, caught in the startled, saddened but not yet resigned confrontation with death.

Another look at the good-natured town, the convoluted streets ending in miniature Romanesque churches, a cappuccino at a café (the coffee in this part of the world, unlike the mediocre food, is superb), and perhaps you might choose to spend the night in a small, elementary, clean hotel above a bar-restaurant near the city gate, or go back to Foggia.

It is possible, and often a strong temptation when the weather is its warm, well-advertised Italian self, to spend a few contented days going from café to café under the canopy of deep trees on the street where your hotel is likely to be, the Viale 24 Maggio, or one of a number of other broad avenues. The coffee, as mentioned, will be delicious and almost hot if you ask for it *bollente, bollente,* the waiter will be pleased and pleasing, the loitering children will sidle closer and closer to stare at you. And if no other amusement offers itself, there is always the ripe, sonorous male voice and the energy exuded by an Italian crowd, which can mean three Italians in Foggia.

Or, if culture urges, go to the museum that hides in an old part of the city (the Piazza Nigri) near an arch imbedded in a wall, all that stayed of Frederick II in Foggia, where his heart once was, figuratively and literally. The heart reposed, old reports say, in a golden case placed in a sarcophagus at the side of the main portals of the Cathedral. It was brought down by the earthquake of 1731 and has since disappeared. The museum is unreachable if you depend on directions from local citizens who don't know what it is, much less where it is—or why, when there is eating or sleeping or talking or sexing to do, you should want to immure yourself in a museum?

Forget it and go back toward the center to the Cathedral, led to, logically, by the via del Duomo. (If you must ask for directions don't ask for "il Duomo" as you would in Siena or Ferrara; Puglia prefers the feminine "Cattedrale.") The approach from the via del Duomo leads at first to the side of the church and a small arch that shelters a dark corner, an open-air urinal. Then, into the full light of its irregular square, a glittering star on a rural stage, steps the delightful amalgam of Arab, Pisan, Romanesque, Norman and much later Baroque. The whole façade was once baroque, as a result of the reconstruction that followed the eighteenth-century earthquake, but subsequent treatment removed much of that to bring back the medieval face. Now it is Pisan alternations of dark and light, saw-toothed doorways, sweeping strokes around a baroque window, reminiscences of Arabic design. Over the main portals, the restorers have released a cortege out of a medieval bestiary: a few animals right side up, many upside down. A bearded god struggles in the grip of sea serpents, an upside-down lion–sea monster looks across at a gentle heron neighbored by a fleur-de-lis; homunculi, newts, lizards, creatures turned, coiled, lifting, crouching; in all, a fairy-tale jungle. Over the portal of the north side of the church, two angels proclaim the miracle of a World War II bombing which shattered their baroque entombment and brought them, untouched, into the air and light through which they now soar awkwardly and gaily.

The large, unremarkable interior hasn't much left to show after severe damage but a brilliant gold frame around a small, miraculous icon and a full-length wax Christ, picturesquely and realistically bleeding, one of the many dozens encountered in Italy, and particularly exaggerated in the south, where the bleeding is more bloody, and weeping more tearful, the suffering more painful, the stigmata more numerous, the jeweled offerings heavier and gaudier and the images always more imminently capable of miracles.

Look back on the Cathedral from the via Arpi, back on the lush baroque tower and façade. At this point, the clattering, odorous market begins to send out its noise. Follow it to its source, then continue on to the retiring little Piazza della Addolorata with a graceful, smiling toy of baroque church, and into the small piazze and streets of the old city. The spine of this area, the via Arpi, will show you a gutted old palace or two whose heavy windows support classical busts and yet another local classic, the stout elderly gentleman in carpet slippers and pajamas, his costume for sitting out all day to watch the passing show, a performance he knows minutely well and still finds fascinating. Off the vias Arpi and Ricciardi the alleys explode with children just out of school and old people roaring good-naturedly together like playful bears and everywhere the tapestries of laundry—above the windows, below, and at street level, more attractive than the film advertisements they might be displacing. As you must have noticed, the laundry is extremely well washed and abundant. Might a row of crisp white sheets and carefully scrubbed boys' trousers represent the best, the most facile display of *bella figura* that a working-class housewife can indulge in? Is there, in poor households, one set of clothing and sheets never used except to be bathed and hung as banners that advertise devoted housewifeliness and solid prosperity?

Barletta—most of these towns seem to have musical names—is a lively center for the products of the local vineyards and olive and almond groves and yet not the lustrous place it must have been in the Middle Ages, when Frederick II held court here to appoint his son Henry inheritor of the crown and Empire should be (Frederick) fail to return from his Crusade (1228); when his favorite illegitimate son, Manfred, chose the city as the center for his work and pleasures; when it flourished under the Anjous. It has a slapdash merriness and a profound courtesy that are "southern" at its alluring best. One traffic policeman on a motorcycle, portly and equipped with 1930's aviator-movies goggles, for an example. Address him in French, if possible, asking for the Ente per Turismo. Expanding with pleasure, he will leap on his motorcycle, scattering people and cars and babbling very Marseillaise French, making of you a VIP and of the short, noisy trip a celebration. Once at the building, he bounds up the stairs, opens the door and ushers your royal self into the presence of several young people, one of them an extraordinarily beautiful girl, who are as warmly hospitable and enthusiastically helpful as the traffic cop.

Aside from its intrinsic charms Barletta is a good place to stay, equipped with a couple of decent modest hotels, and a center from which to explore small, inland towns nearby, the caskets of an architectural gem or two. Not truly a gem, rather a singularity, is an enormous bronze figure, about three times life size, that glowers on the Corso Vittorio Emanuele. He is supposedly a late Roman emperor, of the fourth century A.D., severe to menacing despite the spindly wooden cross in his colossal metal fist. The theory is that he was brought back from Constantinople by the Venetians in the thirteenth century and after a shipwreck was carried by the sea to the Barletta shore. The Angevin Charles II gave a group of friars permission to take the arms and legs for melting and reshaping as church bells; the present limbs are the work of a sculptor of the late fifteenth century, hired to complete the mutilated statue when it was decided to place him here, at the long side of the imposing and confused church of San Sepolcro.

The museum on via Cavour is the mixture as before—local archaeological finds, ceramics, early Christian art, old tombs—with one exception. There is a wreathed, draped bust in Roman style whose nose, forehead and mouth are badly dented. The alert turn of the head, the sweep of the jaw, the strong neck and the damaged mouth that seems to be speaking have convinced admirers of Frederick II that this is his portrait. There are grave doubts, but if one needs a portrait to go with the vigorous, confident image, this might do as well as any for a man called Stupormundi, Wonder of the World.

There is always a via del Duomo, and Barletta's leads to a Romanesque-Gothic combination, retouched by the Renaissance. Near one of its portals there is an inscription to the effect that one, Richard, donated the money for the cost of the entrance. This Richard is believed to have been the Lion-Hearted of England, referred to again by his full title in a mysterious piece of lettering near the bell tower, and it seems reasonable that the Crusader King, on his way to or from his encounters with the infidel, should have made a contribution to the building of the Duomo. About half the interior is distinctly Romanesque and the rest French Gothic, and below is the crypt that reveals the three semicircles of apse of an earlier church. Notice the elegant altar tabernacle and the good thirteenth-century pulpit and, particularly, the fourteenth-century Madonna della Disfida, who was carried through the streets after the victory, in 1503, of thirteen Italian knights over thirteen French knights. It was a fight to the death for control of the town under siege by the French. The Italians won, the siege was lifted, and that was the efficient way gentlemen fought wars in those aristorcratic days.

About 20 kilometers inland sits Canosa di Puglia, a defeated town, tiredly indifferent, and except for the innumerable curious children it shows no sign of its former enterprise as a prime manufacturing center for vases of distinguished craft and of a high-quality wool. But that was many centuries ago, before the birth of Christ. Now its fame lies in the sections of necropolis whose rich contents are to be seen in the museums of Naples and Taranto (page 365) and in the local Museo Civico (open irregular hours) and in the Cathedral.

The church is a complexity of baroque façade slapped onto a multidomed Byzantine-Romanesque of the eleventh century. The interior is washed by a pale glow that derives from the long rows of ancient columns in several tints of stone and their acanthus-leaj capitals of white marble rising to the cupolas. The tall, slender pulpit is an aristocratic for its early time (the eleventh century) and, in its decorations, unmistakably Arabic. A piece of the same period, and much more fanciful, is the restored—as was the pulpit—bishop's throne, a strong, broad chair of marble carved as eagles, vines and animals' heads that rests on the backs of two elephants, surely an Eastern reference. On the right side of the church, not far from the apse, is a miniature church that is the funerary monument for Bohemund, the son of the Norman mercenary and conqueror Robert Guiscard, who died in Antioch in 1111 after the First Crusade. The bronze doors share the highly developed quality of others in the area and distinctly represent the Pugliese combination of Saracenic and Christian elements. Between raised disks of pattern there are Latin inscriptions in praise of the dead hero and one that mentions a candelabrum provided by a Rogerius who might have been—or so says the sacristan—one of the Norman Rogers, kings of Sicily. Nothing is known of the fate of the candelabrum, nor is there any certainty of the identity of the figures incised in the bronze. One school says they represent biblical figures; another identifies them as Bohemund and his stepbrother Roger, Bohemund II and his princely cousins Tancred and the William who became the Duke of Apulia. The rest is pagan emblems and patterns, one especially lovely bronze plate an endless braiding of formal Arabic calligraphy around minute animals. Inside the doors, a length of stone bears only the name "Boemund," a plain, square statement with no qualifications, as if the name itself must evoke awe into eternity.

Andria's primary importance to the visitor is its proximity to one of the most pleasing of Pugliese cathedrals, in Ruvo di Puglia, and to the incomparable Galahad of castles, Castel del Monte. The determining factor for which comes first should be the light; the Castle is best in full midday sun when it shines like a great crown of pale gold and the winds that usually whip around its heights seem to be napping.

Nikolaus Pevsner speaks of the Castel del Monte as the "most accomplished" of the many castles of its time, the thirteenth century, in all of Europe, "an octagon with elements from ancient Rome as well as the French Gothic... the appreciative treatment of Roman motifs (antique pediments) side by side with the novel rib-vaults of France." The Castle, as one approaches it through an avenue of pines, seems to sit in an aura of deep serenity, gathering to itself the slopes of green field, basking in ancient sunlight. Walk around the Castle, follow the rhythms of flat areas alternating with octagonal towers marked by horizontal bands of white stone to vary the texture and tame what might otherwise be harsh verticals. The blond stone between towers is cut by Gothic windows while the well-proportioned, dignified entrance returns to Roman pilasters and pediment and the ubiquitous Romanesque lions, one of them now headless and the other worn smooth to resemble a seal.

The inner courtyard is a place of quiet enchantment, not too large and singularly inviting. The golden stones create a texture of raw, nubby beige silk; shallow arches etched into the stone surround broad windows finished with slender columns under delicate capitals; here and there a niche enfolds the remains of a

sculptured figure. The inner rooms show the same care for restrained, tasteful luxury in vaulting supported by alert, amiable
crouching figures, in mosaic patterns on the floors and, to brighten
the rooms and create contrasts, fan-shaped inserts of colored
stones in the wall and around windows. Because of the shape of
the castle, the rooms are unusual rhomboid forms, many of them
with tall, narrowing fireplaces and in the floor of one room, four
holes that may have led to dungeons or might have served, according to the guide, as bathrooms. The upper rooms, although
of the same height as those below, seem taller and lighter and
gayer because the windows are larger and the arrangements of
decorative bundles of columns and circular Gothic patterns are
more vivid and playful. The top story is closed. From the unadorned windows and shallow height one assumes it served as
quarters for servants and soldiers.

Astonishingly alive and hospitable as this masterwork is, it
still must be peopled, the procession led by Frederick himself, a
man of no great physical beauty but mesmeric charm, who takes
his cosmopolis of Moorish, Jewish, Sicilian, French and German
visitors past tapestries brought from across the Alps to show
them a unique Greek vase, a lustrous bowl from Persia, a bronze
figurine of classic Rome. Speaking Greek to one and Latin to
another, Arabic when that is appropriate, and Hebrew, German
and French when those are needed, he guides his guests to rooms
of Indian sculptures and paintings from China and a large collection of priceless books. Like a strain of fleeting, distant music
two rustling, veiled dancing girls pass an upper window. Below,
the ladies of the court in silks from the East and the communes
of northern Italy stroll in the courtyard, stroking the tensed dogs
straining for the hunt, admiring a young peregrine falcon sitting
on the wrist of one of the Saracen guards. From an upper chamber comes the voice of a troubadour reading the latest poems
from Provence. Out of another window, the words of a Greek
explaining the principles of Aristotle to the young Manfred, and
floating into the sun-struck blue, the slender voice of a dulcimer.
Refilling the empty castle with such sound and shapes is no great
effort; the castle speaks so eloquently of an elegance of mind, of
art, of dress and discourse.

Although the Cathedral of Ruvo di Puglia was enlarged and restored, as was usual, it retains its essential twelfth-into-thirteenth-century style, here the Gothic lift subdued as sharp slopes to the solid Romanesque. The little ornamental arches that scuttle down the edge of the façade and run along the sides dip to an engaging virtuosity of heads—a king, a bearded elder, several ladies, a lion whose feelings have been hurt. With an unerring sense of spacing that told them what to put precisely where, the builders opened the plain, dark space with windows screened by metalwork ribbons and placed the Evangelists in the guise of their animal symbols on deep-shadowed ledges, to exhort out of the stone. Ruvo has its big rose window, too, quite like that of Troia except that it lacks the simpler delicacy of Troia's lace. Above the window sits a sturdy peasant, probably the saint to whom the church was dedicated, and below him, an angel whose wings fill the round space above two alabaster windows. The main portal is complex, crowded and wondrous. The mannerisms and details are familiar; it is their execution and groupings that make them unusual. The seal-lions are, as almost always, here, and so are the crouching men who support them. Above sit their inseparable companions, the griffons, of a sturdier race than the lions, still predatory, wide-eyed and ready, their dreadful claws clutching the pedestal at either side of a desperate human head. The rounded, receding bands that lead to the door are a profligacy of ornaments, and the top band, on which a third griffon sits, is an arrangement of cursive vine that holds together a squeeze of saints and martyrs and angels, a vision of the kingdom of heaven as crowded medieval warren. The best of the interior is its height, the gentle light that filters through the alabaster windows and the sculptured figures like those at the outer portal.

Ruvo's emblem is that of a Greek amphora, a reference to the face that it imported from Greece and made locally a notable number of vases. Over fifteen hundred of these, in various stages of development, have been collected in the Museo Jatta, whose visiting times may be limited, but try if you like. Since Ruvo lacks a fortress, poor thing, there isn't much else to see.

All the towns in this part of Puglia hold hands across short stretches of olive orchards and it doesn't much matter how you link them, but there is some vague geographic reasonableness in heading north now, to Trani, on the coast, a town of remarkable things that acts as if it had nothing. Centuries ago it was a principal port, the scene of splendid ceremonious embarkations, and its regal Duomo the setting for royal marriages. The almost-closed ring of port now shelters fishing boats etched in green and tan nets, a few small tankers, several modest freighters that carry out the local wines and olives. The palazzi that surround the port, once the homes of seafaring mercantile powers, have descended in the social scale to become barracks and tenements swarming with people as only a southern Italian house can swarm, flying the southern flags of sheets and pants. One barracks-palazzo spaced around a pleasant garden had a gate that was tended, or rather haunted, by a yearning Ariadne who was the stout Greek wife of an Italian soldier, brought out of the raucous gaiety of Piraeus to this fallen, stilled town. Twenty-five years later, long married, surrounded by children and grandchildren, she eagerly offered coffee, flowers from the garden, a visit through the barracks—anything—to hold a stray visitor who might listen to her weepy homesickness told over and over again. She may still be weeping.

Trani's Castello, built by Frederick II to protect the port, underwent a number of transfigurations to finish up as a prison, a common and logical use for these strong-jawed buildings. Of the several churches that nestle in the narrow arched-over streets of the old city, the most appealing are San Francesco and the Templar's church (Ognissanti) of the twelfth century. The former grandeur of the city, its might and luxury, is symbolized by the Cathedral, in its idiom as imposing as the Castel del Monte.

On this site wading into the sea, set against a ceaselessly changing backdrop of cloud and sky, there was a church as early as the seventh century. The present structure was begun in the second half of the twelfth century, finished a hundred years later and subsequently marred and messed. It was recently restored to its original *purezza e eleganza* as the Italian booklets have it; a

grave church, inventively and chastely ornamented, introduced
on the bare piazza by stairs shaped like a bridge. The main portal
is surrounded by figures—a nude man struggling with a bird who
is biting his ankle, a lady centaur carrying off a rabbit—all enclosed in a supple run of tendril and leaf, but not entirely enclosed; an arm or hoof extends into the next twist of ornament to
make a dynamic continuity. The shallow arches at either side of
the portal are less agitated, simply chains of stone beads and
joined fronds of extraordinary grace. The Pugliese style expresses
itself again in the rose window, the lions, the griffon-eagles, the
pensive simple-minded on their well-spaced platforms and, as in
Canosa, two elephants who stare out on the piazza from the
frame of a high window.

Return to the end of the piazza to enjoy again the perfect
ensemble of church and campanile, and around again for a look
at the triple curves of apse, the rhythms of tall, lordly arches
sheltering arches and especially to examine the mastery in the
twelfth-century bronze doors. The solemn march of interior double columns (unique in Puglia) lifted by the lighter, smaller columns of the women's balcony, the austere balance of length and
weight, are jarred by a modern panel of Christ at the altar. It is
not too noticeable, fortunately, when the dark reds and pinks of
alabaster in the windows throw tongues of flame onto the floor
and the bases of the columns.

You quickly reach Bisceglie and decide to skip it, having already seen its dolmen. But there is something that compels one
to stay, if only not to miss one of the beads in the coastal strand.
It may be late afternoon. You stop someone in the energetic
mainstreet crowd fortified by lunch and a long nap, and ask for
the Ente Provinciale. No one knows, very cordially, what you are
talking about. Azienda Turismo? Ah, that's the police, over
there, at the side of the square. Police? The informant is right
and soon there begins a polite, stubborn argument with a number of uniformed gentlemen. "We would like to see the church of
Santa Margherita, please." "What in Heaven's name for? It is
old and ugly. We've got some gorgeous new churches we'd be
happy to show you." "But we want to see it because it *is* old."

"Oh, come now!" "We do want to see it." "Really? O.K."

A young policeman, the current rookie, is called and on foot he opens a path through the traffic to lead his eccentrics to the utterly plain, miniature church on an obscure street. Locked behind a gate and a stretch of sandy earth stubbled with crab grass, it is a little mummy, washed and dressed up only for special occasions, but worth seeing as an example of how minute some of these churches were originally. The young policeman, now that he has digested the idea and caught, if only as a piece of Italian politesse, your strange enthusiasm, leads you to still another, older antique of the eleventh century, the church of Sant'Adoeno. Then it is your turn to be polite, to express surprise and pleasure at the sight of *his* preferred gem, a new, fresh, ornate job that shines like tubes of newly cleaned intestine in a butcher's window.

Night has deepened, and before you, as you approach Molfetta, lies one of the most attractive sights on this section of the Adriatic, the hazy mellow illumination that seems not so much directed on but emerging from the cathedral towers and palazzi near the edge of the sea. In spite of the dim casbah alleys behind a high silent section of wall, Molfetta is a lusty, laughing, ice-cream-eating town, its *passeggiata* near the sea a relaxed version of working-class resort boardwalk. The Cathedral sits near the sea in a confusion of surrounding houses and that is probably the reason why its actual size and possible grandeur seem diminished. Like other churches in the area, it is an arrangement of three low, conical domes, two octagonal and one four-sided, and flanking the apse, a pair of good-looking towers. Yet, it seems to lack something. It makes up for the lack when you go through a gate near the reconstructed palaces on the sea walk to find yourself in a square of polished stone that shapes an enchanting miniature piazza. One side leads to an unusually good seventeenth-century portal and the almost square interior of the Cathedral bubbled with arches and domes; complexly Oriental and curiously irreligious. Another side of the piazza tunnels into an attractive meshwork of medieval streets and houses that lead back ultimately to zesty, tireless coming and going on the sea front.

Someone, sometime, had the idea of placing in front of the carved box that is the Cathedral at Bitonto a sturdy pillar plastered with shields and ornaments. All right. Then it was topped with a Christ figure surrounded by metal ivy leaves and light bulbs, like a fake Christmas fireplace in a small-town general store. Never mind. Turn your back on it and examine the Cathedral, where Frederick lay in state on his way to burial in Palermo; like the others and singularly unique. The flowers and tendrils and animals, the supple weaving of ornaments, the bursts of rose window, the procession of portal saints, the large serenity of arches are old friends by this time. A number of the side arches enclose tombs, one of them that of a man who seems to be falling eagerly out of bed directly into death. A variation on the Pugliese church theme shows as an arcade of slender columns with flaring capitals, each unlike the others, each deftly designed and sharply cut, the complex again unmistakenly Saracenic in inspiration.

Not far from the entrance to the church there are a couple of niches that hold vases of early Christian times inscribed in what might be Hebrew or Aramaic. Beyond are two pulpits, one of them a justly famous masterpiece signed—you will see it on the book that rests on the eagle's head—by a Nicolaus Magister of the early thirteenth century. Examine the feathering of the eagle, the rosettes set among designs of polychrome marble, the twists of the columns, the marble inlay patterns on the book, everything; all the details are superb. On the side of the stairway leading to Nicolaus' lectern there is an enmeshing of roundels, fruits and marble braid, held in a rising scale of archlets. In this enchanted wood sits an enthroned, crowned man holding a fleur-de-lis scepter; next to him a knight without a crown yet obviously of prime blood because he is accompanied by another crowned figure who holds an orb with the head of a fox on it. High up, above a large bird, a more disdainful knight holds the same sort of orb. They are said to be the Hohenstaufens: Frederick Barbarossa, his son Henry VI, grandson Frederick II and his son Conrad IV. A recent piece of scholarship turned up a sermon preached by a "Nicolaus" (who was not only a "magister" but also "sacerdos") that extolled the holy ancestry, via a worldly twisting of lines, of the royal family. The supposition is that the pulpit was erected to welcome Frederick II back from the Crusades, part of the praise heaped on him for his efficient conquests. Another possibility suggests that the pulpit was built as an expiatory offering by Frederick, trying to improve his figure in the eyes of the Pope, if not God. Other scholars cannot accept the incongruous picture of the mercurial Frederick (as atheistic as a man of the Middle Ages could be and culturally at least half Arab) in an act of expiation, and anyhow the dates of the sermon and the Emperor's return to Italy don't match properly, they say. Be that as it may and even if the supposed row of Hohenstaufens were actually a scene from a church pageant, it is a supreme work.

Amble around Bitonto, past aged palaces—one of them shored up by equally aged crutches—with strong Renaissance doors and good window detail, peer under and around street arches, cross a variety of piazze and the façades of a number of churches; it is an inviting town, conducive to ambling.

Bitetto's Cathedral lions look like orangutans, and over its portals a group of angels floats among a saintly chorus. The rest is pretty much as before except that the whitewashed town of strong light and deep shade, of outer stairways and ironwork balconies overflowing with geraniums, has distinctly the look of a town in southern—Moorish—Spain, with the difference that Bitetto sports an extraordinary number of redheads and blonds, with gray and green and blue eyes. It must have been, in its time, an irresistible place for Normans and Swabians and crusaders with Anglo blood and coloring, who seem to have lingered, if only long enough to dazzle and take a good number of careless girls.

The town of Alberobello carefully points out its "zona Trulli," a turn off an ordinary street of ordinary shops into a startling view of hundreds of conical houses—bigger, smaller, shorter, taller, one white square, or several, supporting clusters of cones—of whitewash and gray slate. They are authentically usable houses and have been for centuries, but they look unreal, the inventions of a playland. The zone is clean, bright, with a central walk (cars must be left outside the area) that is a steady line of souvenir shops, the vigorous salesmanship their most satisfactory product. Shops are trulli, and the church with medieval arches wears a characteristic cone; the doorways and windows have the flowing, softened contours one finds in Moorish houses, rather as if the trulli were carved of blocks of not too solid material and the edges polished away.

Fasano is still trulli country, and you will observe that like skyscrapers and some people, the cones don't do well alone; they need the proximity of their peers. Martina Franca, toward the south, abjures the primitive shapes and dresses herself in the tinkling ornaments of the rococo, a piquant contrast in this mellow rolling countryside that brings back, as it flows seaward toward Ostuni, those cones again. Now they have white-knobbed tops and look like teakettles, interrupted in their placid, uniform pace by a tired-to-death-of-this-traditional-gray-and-white maverick who puts a pink or yellow or orange lid on his house. An outright revolutionary keeps only the white box and paints the rest purple and red, as bright as the wheels of the high carts that crunch the side of the road.

The country flattens to vines near Brindisi, whose road of black cypresses and sprays of oleander, of dismally poor villages and uninspired new industrial villages, leads to deep-green clouds of umbrella pines and the gates of glistening, plump Lecce. She likes to be called the "Apulian Athens," the sobriquet of a long time ago, and the "Florence of Baroque," a more recent name and, in a lopsided way, justified. A large blond hostess, she spreads an ample welcome of sprawling cafés and roomy shopping arcades off her main square, the Piazza Sant'Oronzo. Lecce is a knowing town, a well-dressed and well-furnished town (notice, for instance, the fittings of the small cafés) shining of self-respect, and sun on its buxom, fair stone.

It is just as well to follow the classic progress, first the Duomo and its extremely tall campanile, accompanied by a set of more reserved and better balanced baroque buildings. The Palazzo del Seminario is on the same piazza, possible the best of Lecce baroque because its details, though too much for some tastes, are finely made. The *portiere,* whom you will tip when you leave, will usher you (say *fontana*) to a dizzying fountain. Mounted on three disks, it is a busy scramble of pomegranates, garlands of leaves and flowers and putti heads; the style and density of design makes wings of the leaves and indented oranges of the putti heads. The whole has the slow, simmering, rolling movement of sugar and chocolate and nuts and raisins bubbling in a pot, preparing to be candy. At the top of all the turmoil stands a pretty young Virgin who looks a bit tired, as well she might be with such tumultuous neighbors, and at the bottom, a new complex of shapes and movement, that of overactive fish.

Leading gradually up to *the* Lecce apogee, one might next see Sant'Irene, of the end of the Renaissance well launched into the Baroque, coiling, dripping and voluting to hold a large, windy saint modeled on Santa Teresa according to Bernini, the ecstasy here less intense, less equivocal. Above the saint there stands an animal—a lamb? a donkey?—holding a large bunch of artichokes under a crown. This may be the Lamb of God, but one cannot be sure. Lecce baroque is much more interested in accretions than exactitude, more addicted to games of exaggeration, of eccentricity let flow and only partially restrained (which makes it one of the "amusing" styles) than to faithful rendering.

One of the "required" places to see is San Nicolò e Cataldo, spoken of as "Romanesque"; it once was, back in the twelfth century when it was built by Tancred, one of the late Norman kings. Don't drive there; Lecce has the most exasperating of one-way systems, all one way and none the other, and it requires a little time to realize that the indigenes beat the system by paying no attention to barriers and arrows. The taxi you should take leads to a war cemetery and, in adjacent cloisters (a remainder of the Romanesque), the trembling, blinking inhabitants of an old people's home. Next, through a neglected neoclassic church to a good-looking façade that obscures its few Romanesque bits with much baroque, principally a number of stern, monumental figures that seem to ride against the sky like the Valkyrie when the wind is strong and the clouds pulling against each other and the windswept saints. The taxi driver, staring up with you, says,

"*Scusi*, but please tell me, what's the beauty? These poor old crocks in there, that cemetery, and we got too many churches anyhow. We're a progressive city; who needs them? Why did you pay the taxi fare to get here, if you don't mind my asking? Where's the *bellezza* (the beauty)?" You point out the proportions of the façade, the carvings in the doorway, the tempestuous movement of the figures. He listens respectfully, keeps nodding and then, with no conviction at all, "*Può darsi*" (could be).

Immediately off the big piazza, via a curve or two and the help of a beautifully fitted perfect gentle knight of a policeman (all Pugliese police are polite and helpful but those in Lecce are downright princely) you arrive at the horizontality, massed with embellishments held in control and proportion, of the Prefettura and near it, the pride of Lecce, the acme, the first place mentioned and the first ordinarily shown. It should be the last, because beyond this there is no place to go in the Baroque. The church of Santa Croce is unashamedly curved, curled, voluted, rose-windowed, bestatued, colonnaded, gargoyled, fruited, puttied, belioned and beshielded, and it also carries columns, urns, griffons, bowls, men, horses, and maternal naked ladies, none of them particularly well made. There is a melting imperfect quality that derives either from the soft fair stone or the speed with which artisans had to cram the city when the Baroque rage struck, which left the ornaments crude and the figures dumpy, lacking altogether the long elegance of the Bernini figures they were trying to echo. The interior is equally rich but less confusing because it is confined in rows of ornately capitaled columns interspersed with old hanging lamps and the ceiling enjoys the peace of repeated designs. As in other Lecce churches there are flare-ups of frenzy, but the white and goldness is, in the main, delicately, meticulously made. The main piazza lures, again, with its cafés, a Roman amphitheater, an attractive square building which seems to be its own excuse for being, and a column that once marked the end of the Roman Appian Way at Brindisi and used in the mid-eighteenth century as pedestal for Sant' Oronzo, who, it was hoped, would rid the city of the plague.

The city has a nice mood of respectable, not too showy opulence, reasonably good food and a couple of satisfactory, moderately priced hotels: the largish President and smaller Delle Palme, and then there is always that coffee. You might as well stay, take a walk, choose to see what's left of the fortress or not, glance at a few more fair and fat churches and palazzi and go to bed early because the museum in Taranto closes at 1:00 P.M. and it's best to make an early start the next morning.

Taranto doesn't put its best foot forward; perhaps it hasn't any left to extend, having lost much of its best over the centuries. The Spartans took it in the eighth century B.C., from the indigenous peoples and made it the richest, most productive city of Magna Grecia. It was a center of art and philosophy worthy of a visit by Plato. Then came the Romans, by which time the city was already diminished. The Saracens in their turn (927) crossed the seas to capture the city, which was retaken by the Byzantine Empire; taken again, retaken once again, et cetera, et cetera. Like a number of seaport towns in the area, it was severely damaged during World War II; since then it has had a remarkable and speedy revival. It is now so busily, enterprisingly modern that the scenic situation of the old city, an island between two swells of land, is hardly noticeable and when noticed seems a piece of play acting, an affectation.

The road from Lecce carries one into strict squares neither handsome nor ugly, not particularly prosperous or poor, with surrounding streets not quite wide enough, except for the boulevards along the sea. The traffic, as in all Italian towns, is erratically designed on baroque curves, the favorite Italian style. You may find yourself going around and around on the sea road, obeying signs that all point to the Post and Telegram Office as if that were the essential organ, the blood-pumping heart, of the city. Several turns on the merry-go-round will ultimately show which turn-off approaches a swing bridge that may be open long enough for you to examine the stalwart Aragonese fortress, a later model of a fortified site in Roman times. Once you've crossed into the Città Vecchia (the old city) be careful not to be shunted onto the next bridge, which leads inexorably to tanks and factories on the mainland. Leave your car and walk to the Duomo.

It should be as pleasant as walking in Molfetta or Bitonto but it isn't. There are too many children in the streets, the very young tumbling in orange peel and lettuce leaves and crumpled pages from old comic books. In spite of the gleam of new refrigerators near dark doorways, and the stately forms of dimmed Renaissance palaces, there is an atmosphere not so much of poverty as underdevelopment, of not knowing what to do about dirt except to leave it where it falls, of not knowing what to do with a stranger but suspect him. This is one aspect of the "southernness," the "primitive" that frightens so many northern Italians. It is part of a naïve coarseness that can, in the individual, be quite engaging; in the protection of the pack it can become piercingly derisive and threatening. One begins to understand why the hysterical dance, the tarantella, derived its name from Taranto and begins to believe the stories of snake cults and bloodletting during Holy Week processions.

Circling back from the vicinity of the second bridge along the sea wall, one passes a characteristic little forest of poles bearing ropes of mussels that jut out of the sea and, recessed in a nearby alley, the eleventh-century church of San Domenico Maggiore. But one doesn't come to Taranto for its once-lyrical separations and meetings of land and sea, nor for its churches, nor for its shops and the sailors of its naval base. Taranto, by no means an art town—nor does it care—has an exceptional and important museum of the antiquities of Magna Grecia. If you have been doing your homework in the museums in Puglia, you needn't look at every vase, every figurine, but here is the pick of the crop—the loveliest terra-cotta dancers, the most perfect heads sculpted of stone, remarkable jewelry, a magnificent medallion of a sea nymph riding a sea monster, among hundreds of rarities. The total is a fascinating assortment of Greek things (some of them very early) and native works from various parts of the region, splendidly arranged in light, airy, attentive space. As mentioned, the museum was not open in the afternoon at this writing, and it is not likely to be. However, the advice about spending the night in Lecce needn't deter you from staying in Taranto, if that is more convenient. In spite of some of its streets and their tough owners in the old city, the citizenry is amiable, the park of Villa Peripato good for strolling, the Ente Provinciale well informed. There are a number of satisfactory hotels and at least one restaurant (Gambero) on the sea front that does miraculous things with sea food, and the police worry about tourists like neurotic parents.

Brindisi, like Bari, has its old city. There are grottoes and dolmens strewn through the countryside, as well as little churches of ponderous age. There are towns that make pottery and towns that press wine, towns that have miracle fountains and saints; towns whose houses are like caves or like bright cubes; towns that sit in the sea and others in wheat fields. And to the north, the Gargano, there is a wilderness, fast being tamed, of forest and islands and ancient monasteries. Thus, the above serves only as a sampler, an invitation to an Italy that is not remote from the others though quite different from them.

Hotels in places where you might be likely to spend a night or two:

Foggia—Palace Hotel Sarti, moderate; Hotel Cicolelle, high moderate with good kitchen

Barletta—Royal Hotel, low moderate.

Bari—Palace Hotel, high; Grand Hotel e d'Oriente, moderate; Jolly, high moderate.

Taranto—Palace, high moderate; Park Hotel, high moderate.

Finally a word of warning. Though the map might show a good short cut from here to there, follow principal, well-marked roads. It may be an adventure but rarely fun for long to find yourself faced by several forks of country road in a sea of olive trees; no signs, no one to ask and daylight fading.

Buon Viaggio: A Bouquet of Reminders

REMEMBER THAT THE FIRST phrase to learn in Italian, before "how much," "where is," "toilet," "hot water," is "Ente Provinciale per Turismo." These local tourism centers can, at best, be invaluable—maps, handsome brochures, people who talk English well or semiwell—and, at worst, ineffectually simpatico.

In summer, one should reserve at least from town to town. Although they often stay only one night, tourists disgorged by buses that come from France and Germany and Denmark and, seemingly, from Japan are already there in great behemoth herds the day you come to town.

Those traveling alone, usually the most foot-loose and planless travelers, have the worst of it. Some places have no singles and won't let a double go because, in high season, they require that guests take some meals and one in a double room cuts down the revenue. The singles available are often afterthoughts squeezed into the noisiest corner of the hotel and closing the window cuts out air, energy, will and enthusiasm, but not noise. *Pazienza:* the capacity to endure with serenity.

Remember that everything is subject to change—museum and gallery hours, and prices, which are rising steadily. If there were rigidity it wouldn't be Italy; don't fret, don't set tight limits on time or lire, don't eat your heart out if some art goal or other is closed on your day, or most days, for lack of personnel. Normally, closing days are either Monday or Tuesday and safe times are 9:30 to 12:30, 3:00 to 5:30, though there is considerable elasticity about closing hours, depending on the season. About prices—like all prices everywhere, soaring. Fifty to sixty-five dollars for luxurious accommodations for two (at 1500 lire to the dollar) is about as high—and that rare—as small cities ask. In general, $30 to $45 for two, with bath, would be as high as you need pay. At the other end of the scale a room without bath would be about $20; the price range between should buy you various forms of decent comfort. As in hotels, restaurant prices are lower than they are in big cities, though not by very much, since meals in most of Italy are inexpensive. In the leading restaurants of Verona, Padua, Mantua, Ferrara, Siena and cities of similar size and fame, $20 will cover the cost of a bit more than you can eat and drink. In smaller towns, and in lesser restaurants of large towns, $25 pays for a full meal for two and it often can be done for less, especially if you choose your meals from the tourist menu that flaps in four languages at the doors of numerous *trattorie*.

Keep in mind that buses—whose drama, unlike the limitless theatrical riches produced by trains, is limited to fights between those afraid of a draft from an open window and those who scream that they are suffocating for lack of air—go everywhere, fast, often on scenic routes, and are about the cheapest mode of traveling in Italy unless you have loving friends with time and a car. Expensive, but worth it, when one considers the time saved and the mobility, is a hired car, for which arrangements can be made in Italy or the States. The highways, as everyone knows, are the apogees of Roman road building, flying boldly above towns and through steep mountains, and Italian drivers are skillful and generally considerate in spite of their passion for speed.

Remember that no one ever has any change. When you pay a

gas attendant he will ask for *spiccioli* (coins). The girl in the small chain department stores will leave her register and a group of customers to run from one co-worker to another for change from the 1000 lire you have given her for a 750-lire purchase. She returns with 100-lire pieces—no 50's—after a long absence, and one or the other of you has to be sporting about the difference between unimportant sums. A telephone token (*gettone*) costs 100 lire. The telephone center quite near the Main Post Office in Rome, where one can, quite efficiently, be connected with almost any place in the world, rarely has change for the 1,000 you offer. The choices are to make a big-spender gesture and walk off with the *gettone* and no change, or stand staring and be stared at until the coins are found.

Remember that Italians find standing in line an absurdity: learn to push, and an advantageous spot conquered, gyrate in it like an animal marking out its territory.

Remember that the recoil on a salesgirl's face doesn't mean that she dislikes you; she is afraid to cope with your English—or worse still, your Italian.

Remember, when you ask directions, that one of the national characteristics is to point right as one says "left" (*sinistra*) and to point left when speaking of "right" (*destra*). Make sure whether it is gesture or word that counts.

If you are going to be traveling slowly and intensively in a rural area, buy a regional map in a bookshop of whatever big city is your point of departure, or the provincial capital. Should your Italian warrant it and you miss Baedeker, buy the red Italian Touring Club Guides, which treat in separate volumes of the major cities and the provinces; not cheap but encyclopedic. They leave no historic stone unturned, mention every painting, remark on every finial with exhaustive poker-faced seriousness.

Remember that a little learning can be a pleasant thing. Italy gives much, in beauty, gaiety, diversity of arts and landscapes, good humor and energy—willingly, without having to be coaxed or courted. Paradoxically, she requires (as do other countries, probably more so) and deserves some preparation as background to enhance her pleasures. It is almost impossible to read a total history of Italy; there was no united country until a hundred years ago, no single line of power, no concerted developments. It is useful, however, to know something about what made Siena run and stop, to become acquainted with the Estes and the Gonzagas, the Medicis and the Borgias, the names that *were* the local history. It helps to know something about the conflicts of the medieval church with the Holy Roman Empire, of the French, Spanish and early German kings who marked out large chunks of Italy for themselves or were invited to invade by a nervous Italian power. Above all, it helps to turn the pages of a few art and architecture books to become reacquainted with names other than those of the luminous giants.

The informed visitor will not allow himself to be cowed by the deluge of art. See what interests or attracts you; there is no Italian Secret Service that reports on whether you have seen *everything*. If you try to see it all except as a possible professional task, you may come to resist it all. Relax, know what you like and don't like—not the worst of measures—and let the rest go.

Anticobblestone shoes packed, spyglasses and phrase book in flight bag, diet pills back in the medicine cabinet, go. Go slowly and aware, alert to a gesture, a face, a happening, as Italians are alert and aware. Leave time for instructions in living as taught by Italians; for an encounter, perhaps, with a noisy, smiling lady, everyone's pal and yours too. Questioning, "Americano? Inglis?" she repeats, "Goot, goot, fine, fo'pens" ("fourpence," one guesses), "Kent, Soorey, Londra," and having told her rosary of English, gestures broadly to point at her unfettered bosom, *"Sono originale. Non è vero?"* (Isn't that so?) You agree and she beams while you ponder the pride in being eccentric. If there is *one* distinctly European trait, you decide, it is this, as opposed to the American necessity to appear well adjusted and normal, whatever that might be or cost.

By moving ruminatively, all antennae out and receptive you

may learn—in the gesture of an old woman's finger stroking the arm of a baby as if he were the Infant Jesus, in the warmth and pleasure of friends meeting on a street, in the loud rumble of angry café voices when a father boxes his young son's ears, in the infinite bounty of concern among the members of a family, in the working-class coins that drop into the cap of a beggar—more about living, and Italy, than in miles of magniloquent buildings and seas of paint.

Children's spring vacations seem to start with the Easter holidays and continue on and on with hundreds of school groups touring their country for its art treasures. Some are quite young, clinging to one another and their teachers and accompanying mothers; some are noisy and spirited, but not obstreperous, adolescents, their mouths full of shout or ham sandwich, and always crowded around the painting with which you wanted a few moments alone. One wonders about the time for formal school— the three R's quickly proliferating into science these days. But Marconi learned and so did Fermi, and there was a schoolboy named Galileo who must have been shown the art of his time and yet managed to pick up a bit of mathematics and physics. Whatever else the busloads of children crisscrossing Italy today pick up, they will have as permanent enrichment a Palladian roof, a Gothic portico, a Tiepolo ceiling. And some of them may never forget seeing the film *Gandhi* at 9:00 A.M. in rainy Treviso.

Some of the most painstaking and careful travel information still quotes prices—hotel costs, bus tickets, admissions to museums—that have in the course of editing, printing and issuing (and the flights of inflation) gone up. Consequently they are likely to be lower than those you will actually pay. Devise a scheme for estimating the rise, and consider that when the value of the lire vis-a-vis the dollar goes down, prices go up. The fancied advantages of shopping for the dollar are at times quite ephemeral.

Once upon a time the man who helped you get your luggage on a train was hailed as "facchino!" If he still exists at all (in this phrase lies a warning to travel light), he wants the more distinguished name quoted on his cap, "Porta bagaglio."

Where there is a bus system you can use, buy tickets at any tobacconist's; the machines that take coins are increasing their demands from 300 to 400 lire, and more to come, which makes a burdensome weight of big coins in bags and pockets. Tickets weigh infinitely less.

Tipping? Some do, some don't, pointing out the already high prices of meals and service and the fact that Italian wages have considerably improved in recent years. As a general rule, there is no need to leave more than a few coins if a "service" is listed and paid. Otherwise, the usual 12 to 15 percent should be added. Bars usually carry a shiny bowl into which customers drop a coin, about 50 or 100 for coffee alone.

Should you be told that a place you're searching out is only "two hundred meters away" or "a due passi," (suggestions of short distances) arrange for a taxi or prepare to hike, hoping that somewhere in your ancestry is that incredibly sturdy Italian leg that marched in its legions through Europe and into Asia, Africa and is still capable of it. Yours probably is not.

Although the busy networks of Italian trains function efficiently, particularly considering their number and complexity, things happen. If you seem to be getting contradictory information about times and tracks, look for men in dark blue suits that bear the insignia "F. S." They are usually the most responsible and best informed officials. (You don't have to speak Italian; tell them your destination and, by pointing at clocks and tracks, throwing in a few universal finger signals, they will do the rest.)

It is a waste of time and energy, a great despoiler of pleasure, to try to be shrewd, at least as shrewd as you think your hosts are. Drop the distrust—not everyone is trying to squeeze a few extra lire out of you, and those who are usually make a minute profit, nowhere near enough to justify souring your mood.

Never go to a restaurant that serves full meals unless you intend to eat a respectable amount. Some, like at least one in Venice and one in Padua, become angry and obscenely abusive and refuse to serve you a small meal, directing you to a pizzeria or a tavola calda (a type of cafeteria) in roaring tones.

Unless you are a magician planner, it is not always possible to make firm hotel arrangements for short stays in several towns. The Ente Provinciale per Turismo will have a list of hotels for its town but is not necessarily always informed about other places. Your hotel concierge will search out a place for you, not as cheap as one or two the Ente might suggest, if it could, but certainly livable.

It used to be said, and it was almost true, that there was no really bad food in Italy. Not altogether true; poverty-stricken areas served the toughness and acidity of poverty, but in tourist land, the veal was always tender and the pasta heaped gold. Those were the days when pizza was a dish of Naples and sought out as a piece of exotica in the north, a special treat for the kids on Sunday night, as we might take our children to Chinatown. Now pizza blankets Italy as it does our cities and too often substitutes for the fine care with which a salad was concocted and the balance of the ingredients in a pasta carbonara, for instance. Not to despair, however, the good is very good and still available.

There is a line of "name" luggage—a venerable French name that suggests Proustian voyagers—which is available, in remarkable imitation, in several Italian towns. The first imitators were the Japanese, who were sued heavily by the French company. The Japanese desisted and sold their stock to outlets in Italy (which may be making their own copies as well by now). The bags are displayed in and around large market areas, except in Rome, where they are sold, in several sizes and tempting prices, on the corners of the luminous streets they share with the fashion gods.

Most Italian cities and towns have half-day closings, varying from place to place. Check before you launch yourself on a voyage of shopping in silent streets. And, although it is slowly changing, the long, tight-shut lunch and siesta time from one to four is still a sacred Italian right.

You are not driving; local buses will make too long a journey and require too many changes for the two or three places rather close to each other that might logically make one trip. By taxi perhaps? The concierge finds you a taxi driver who estimates the distances will entail a large cost of lire. Fair enough, since gas is very expensive and a taxi is an expensive—even elegant—investment. And here we come to the important matter of the "sosta," the staying, or waiting of a driver, for which he charges you prodigious extra sums, shocking sums—for doing nothing. He will base his mysterious calculations on how many normal trips he might have lost while you wander around foolishly, devotedly, in these odd old places. If you're fool enough for that, if those are your tastes, you deserve to be taken. The shock and anger might be less were you to understand early that it isn't the ride so much as the "sosta" which will figure large, and try to come to an agreement before you take off. Also equate the cost of a "sosta" with the pleasure it bought you in the form of two Palladian villas and the Tiepolos and Veroneses that decorate them. Yours might have been the profit and triumph in the end.

While on the subject of taxis: you should be aware that they ask 25 percent beyond the meter figure as evening and Sunday supplements. This isn't universal, but will probably soon be, as is the request for a supplement for carrying luggage.

In any case, and once again, *buon viaggio* and *auguri*.

Index